$17⁰⁰

TOWARDS A NEW WORLD VIEW

Conversations at the Leading Edge

Russell E. DiCarlo

EPIC PUBLISHING

99 98 97 96 95   5 4 3 2 1

Library of Congress Cataloging-in-Publication Data

DiCarlo, Russell.
        Towards a new world view: conversations at the leading-edge /
    Russell E. DiCarlo

            p. cm.
            Includes index
            Preassigned LCCN: 94-62007
            ISBN 1-886718-00-8

        1. Psychology.   2. Psychology Applied..   3. Social Change.
    4. Paradigm (Theory of Knowledge)   I. Title

    BF636.D53 1996
                                                    QBI94-21262

FIRST EDITION

TO MY FAMILY—
MOM, DAD, LAURIE, JACKIE AND BRIAN,
WITH LOVE AND GRATITUDE.

ACKNOWLEDGEMENTS

It's so often said that a particular book could not have been written were it not for the help of others that it can sometimes seem trite or even gratuitious; yet in the case of this book, it's absolute fact. I am indebted to each of the individuals featured within the pages of this book for being so generous with their time and even moreso with their wisdom and insight.

I'd also like to thank Terry O'Keefe for his expert editing assistance and format suggestions; Mitch Price for his technical assistance; and my mother, Jeanette DiCarlo, for the many hours spent transcribing the interviews.

Contents

PART 1
A NEW VIEW OF THE UNIVERSE

PART 3
APPLYING THE NEW VIEW

PART 4
GETTING THE NEW VIEW

PREFACE

This book is about change and world view—and the realignment of our most basic assumptions and beliefs about the way things are.

Over the past five years, pulled by a childlike sense of curiosity and pushed by an inner impulse too strong to ignore, I chose to make a rather substantial personal investment and learn more about the subtler nuances of both the old world view and the one that is emerging. That journey has taken me through four hundred books, a thousand articles from professional journals, and scores of workshops.

This book distills the work of the best, most seminal thinkers I've been fortunate enough to meet along the way. I offer it those of you whose lives do not permit the path of research I was able to take, so that you too may "stand on the shoulders of giants."

In some cases, the people presented are the thought leaders in their professions; others are lesser known. Their backgrounds vary widely and wildly—they are scientists, doctors, philosophers, historians, priests, management consultants; a few are teachers at some of the most prestigious schools in the world. What brings them together is their shared belief that we live in a period of dramatically shifting world views. Like the facets of a jewel, the perspective of each individual adds a new dimension, a new angle, which culminates in a more expansive panoroma.

As you will see, all of the individuals selected have dared to push beyond the traditional line and to the benefit of all, have opened up new frontiers of knowledge. For many, there has been a downside, a great personal and professional cost. All too often, they have been censured, ostracized, belittled or otherwise harshly (and I should add unfairly) criticized by less visionary peers.

I chose an interview format because it allows information to be presented in a way that is more personable, less scholarly and hopefully more meaningful. We can describe the emerging world view as a shift from seeing the universe as a mechanical device with no mind or will of its own, to seeing it as intelligent, self-organizing, and ever-evolving, but that does little to further our understanding. "Overhearing" the conversation of those who embody the new perspective gives the reader a more intimate glimpse of the author, and a richer insight into how they arrived at their point of view.

A personal observation: I found each person whom I interviewed to be highly intelligent, often "brilliant." Yet their ultimate appeal rested on something less obvious, yet much more compelling than sheer mental prowess. There was a quality to their message that seemed to emerge from the wholeness (or perhaps I should say "soulness") of their being. In other words, it was not just what they said—the information—as the level of being from which they responded which gifted them with extraordinarily clear and penetrating insight. As a result, they were able to touch me in a deep and unusual way.

Towards A New World View is far from comprehensive in that it does not feature interviews with individuals from every possible field or area of interest. Space considerations preclude that breadth. Also, since my premise is that a new world view is clearly breaking through to conscious levels on the planet, I have not included contrary points of view, although that would be an interesting and informative endeavor.

Moreover, I recognize the limitations of trying to define and characterize the emerging world view since to do so is to shamelessly shrink it to the dimensions of our present understanding. The emerging world view is undoubtedly much more than we can imagine. It is, like the human mind which creates it, in a state of dynamic evolution and development.

The individuals represented within these pages offer us much that is new and different. It is my hope that these dialogues will extend your vision as to what is possible for you to be and to achieve in this life.

INTRODUCTION

"What concerns me is not the way things are, but the way people think things are."

Epictetus

How would your life be different if you, and the universe in which you live, were much different than what your parents, teachers and culture had led you to believe?

What would you cherish most in life? How would the quality of your relationships change? What would you do for a living? What risks would you entertain? By what means would you determine what is real, true and meaningful? What would be your criteria for judging a life well lived? How would you define success?

Towards A New World View is an attempt to rough-sketch—through conversations with those on the leading-edge—a new portrait of "the way things are." The book has been written to inform, to stretch, to challenge and perhaps even to inspire. It is not about finding final answers, but about provoking new questions that will nudge you out of your familiar way of looking at things.

No one with both feet planted firmly in contemporary life is likely to debate the assertion that we live in an age of considerable and constant change. Yet as this book will attempt to illustrate, the winds of change are far more brisk and far more penetrating than many realize. The predominant focus has been upon the external, societal changes taking place: the information explosion; shifting demographic trends; technological development and the global economy. Less attention has been placed upon the internal, psycho-spiritual changes echoing 'round the globe: in the beliefs, assumptions, values and capabilities of a growing number of people.

Author Marilyn Ferguson, whose interview sets the stage for those that follow, has been a highly influential commentator on this deeper level of change. Ferguson's early 1980s book, *The Aquarian Conspiracy* has been prophetic in its description of the social and personal transformations currently underway. The book describes a benign conspiracy for a new human agenda that in her words, has "triggered the most rapid cultural realignment in history. The great shuddering, irrevocable shift overtaking us is not a new political agenda, religious or philosophical system. It is a new mind—the ascendance of a startling worldview that gathers into its framework breakthrough science and insights from earliest recorded thought."

What exactly is a world view and how does it different from a "paradigm," a term familiar to more and more people? A paradigm is comprised of our closely held beliefs and assumptions about a particular aspect of human reality. Individuals in the same field of endeavor generally share a paradigm, so there are paradigms in education, science or business.

But each of these paradigms is constructed upon a more general, overarching and cultural paradigm—a world view. A world view (and everyone has one albiet most have not sought to identify it) is our most fundamental picture of "the way things are." As futurist Alvin Toffler explains it, "Every civilization must teach its children to grapple with time and space. It must explain—whether through myth, metaphor or scientific theory—how nature works. And it must offer some clue as to why things happen as they do."

At core, a world view seeks to provide answers to two most important questions, "What is the nature of the Universe in which we live?" and "Who am I?" How we respond ultimately directs all that we do and how we do it. It establishes the overall rhythm, music and melody of our lives.

It's important to note that though world views are necessary and useful, rigid adherence to a *particular* world view can stunt one's growth, especially if it has outlived its usefulness. It should be no surprise then, that most of the leading edge individuals I've spoken with would agree that the traditional, dominant and prevailing world view is hopelessly obsolete, and is the root cause of the prevailing world crisis.

But before going further, I want to make it clear to the reader that phrases such as, "<u>The</u> prevailing world view" or "<u>The</u> Western world view," with an emphasis on "*the*" are largely a fiction. That is, there is really no single world view that everyone in the culture shares. To the contrary, world views vary widely and sharply. Literally, there are as many as there are people, formed through a unique admixture of life experiences, level of psycho-spiritual development, and social and racial imprinting.

Yet, having said this, there is clearly an "official," dominant and prevailing world view that governs and informs our public life and helps the collective Western society decide what's real, meaningful and of value. This world view has been greatly influenced by two—historically at odds—streams of influence: science and religion.

Psychologist Charles Tart has developed a concise credo, which, though hardly ever outwardly stated or inwardly examined, seems to capture the essence of the scientific point of view. When working with a group of people, Tart often asks that together, they read the following aloud, as if reciting the Apostles Creed:

I believe in the material universe as the only and ultimate reality, a universe controlled by fixed, physical laws and blind chance.

I affirm that the universe has no creator, no objective purpose, and no objective meaning or ultimate destiny.

I maintain that all ideas about God or gods, supernatural beings, prophets and saviors, or any other nonphysical beings or forces are superstitions and delusions.

Life and consciousness are totally identical to physical processes, and arise from chance interactions of blind physical forces. Like the rest of life, my life and consciousness have no objective purpose, meaning or destiny.

I believe that all judgements, values and moralities, whether my own or others', are subjective, arising solely from biological determinants, personal history, and chance. Free will is an illusion.

Therefore, the most rational values I can personally live by must be based on the knowledge that for me what pleases me is Good, what pains me is Bad.

Those who please me or help me avoid pain are my friends; those who pain me or keep me from pleasure are my enemies. Rationality requires that friends and enemies be used in ways that maximize my pleasure and minimize my pain.

Virtue for me is getting what I want without being caught and punished by others.

I maintain that the death of the body is the death of the mind. There is no afterlife, and all hope for such is nonsense.

Through the lens of science, the universe is likened to a mechanical clock, slowly winding down to its inevitable demise, a meaningless accident, borne of random events. In this universe, matter is indestructible, objects are solid, time is linear and space is three-dimensional. The physical world (which represents the entirety of created reality) exists independently and objectively, unaffected by the presence of an observer. The purpose of life in such a universe is simple and straightforward: survival and perpetuation of the species.

The other stream of influence shaping the Western world view—the Judeo-Christian religious tradition—offers a different explanation of things. The origin of the universe, we are told, was not at all random. It was the the creation of a sometimes vengeful, jealous, fear-inspiring, and masculine God (if you read the Old Testament) who exists separate and apart from the rest of creation. This God is also given to merciful acts of love, redemption and benevolence (if you read the New Testament.)

Man—born inherently flawed due to the sinful legacy of Adam and Eve—also exists separate and apart. Separate from the universe and separate from the natural and spiritual worlds; indeed, separate from the rest of humanity.

Both the scientific and religious world views may sound pretty bleak and depressing; nevertheless they have steadfastly guided Western culture throughout the modern era.

Finally, it's important to realize that a world view operates as a psychological filter, a lens which determines not only <u>what</u> we see "out there" but <u>how</u> we see it. Any data that doesn't fit our view of the world and runs counter to our foundational beliefs is likely to be deleted or distorted. As a result, two people looking out into the world, but who have radically different world views will see different things or see the same things differently. Many interpersonal and inter-group conflicts are due to this filtering effect. Because of this, we fail to grasp how others can be so "thick" and disagreeable, regardless of how frequently, pursuasively or articulately we plead our case.

There may also be a poor fit between any particular world view and the true nature of things. To operate out of erroneous or limiting beliefs and assumptions can create pain, drama and turmoil as we find ourselves continuously buffetting up against the hard rocks on reality's shore.

For precisely these reasons, there are those who would suggest that it is vital that we bring to the surface and challenge our world view. In the process, we become more tolerant of other points of view and enlarge our window into the Universe.

The book has been divided into four parts. In Part One, we will hear from leading-edge individuals whose work in science, religious studies, history and philosophy calls into question some of the traditional assumptions about the nature of the universe in which we live.

In Part Two, we will explore some of the findings coming out of the fields of psychology, medicine, and human potential research, which are helping us to arrive at a new understanding of our essential nature.

Part Three centers upon the work of a few individuals, who have embraced the new world view, and have begun implementing their vision of what is possible, within the fields of business, education and economics.

Finally, in Part Four, we will get a glimpse of the process by which some individuals claim to have experienced a shift in their perspective, from the traditional world view to that which is emerging.

Prologue: An Interview With Marilyn Ferguson

Marilyn Ferguson is founder and publisher of the "Brain/ Mind Bulletin," a highly respected newsletter which explores cutting-edge issues in human development, education and science. Ferguson is also the author of several books including the classic "Aquarian Conspiracy," (voted by New Options readers as the most influential book of the 1980's) and "Radical Common Sense: Secrets of The Visionary Life." In 1980 Ferguson was invited by then Senator Al Gore to address a group he had co-founded, the Congressional Clearinghouse of the Future. In 1992, she was named "Brain Trainer of the Year" by the American Society for Training and Development.

DiCarlo—"Paradigm" is a term that is being bandied about quite freely these days. Could you please provide us with a good working definition of what a paradigm actually is?

Ferguson—Paradigm is a fashionable term for a working perspective. It's your method of explaining something to yourself. For example, there are paradigms in science, where the term first came into use. It is a mental model which makes it comfortable for people to explain things. But since all our knowledge is incomplete, the paradigm ultimately has to be replaced by another one. Eventually it must yield to new information. In *The Aquarian Conspiracy*, I used paradigms in science as a model for the fate of new ideas in general—paradigms of relationship, education, heath care...

What we know from science is that even people who are supposed to be professionally objective, are very resistant to new information— even if the newly discovered information is more powerful and better explains the data.

DiCarlo—Was there any particular event in your life that caused you to look beyond the traditional explanation of the way things are?

Ferguson—Well, my parents were people who questioned the establishment a lot. My parents used to talk scathingly about the "almighty dollar," and yet they gave me the sense that I could be anything I wanted to be. I suppose I was fortunate in that my parents were the children of immigrants from Italy on my fathers side, and Russia on my mother's. When families have to make it on their own in a new country, they have somewhat of a different perspective.

You see that a lot in the children of immigrants, even today. They are often more ambitious than the natives, even though they're poorer. When I began to question what was going on in this society, perhaps it was because my father had questioned too. Pointing out how ridiculous the commercials on the radio were for example. Challenging the predominant paradigm came with breathing. I was a poet and later a non-fiction writer. I got interested in the cultural paradigm in 1968 when l wrote a book called *Champagne Living on Beer Budget*, a book about how to live well on a modest income. I was kind of looking behind the scenes there, "Who makes brand x?" for example. When you look into institutions, you become increasingly aware of their moral paralysis. There's no point in blaming. We got here through our collective ignorance. I also wrote for trade journals and l was a stringer for *Time*. I got a sense of how creative business people saw things, which was contrary to the conventional wisdom.

When my children were tiny, I became interested in the work of Berkley scientists who found that the brain changes in response to stimulation. l was amazed too, at the early research on Transcendental Meditation. My next book, *The Brain Revolution*, looked at the mysteries of the brain and mind—the interface of the tangible and intangible. The physical brain, which is so complex—the most complex bit of matter on earth and so mysterious—and the mind, which is completely intangible.

"If all of this is true about our potential, if human beings can learn as it appears they can learn, why aren't we doing something," l said, "about it?" One thing led to another. I was writing radio commercials at age 17, so l was already peeking behind the curtain that hides the Wizard of Oz. There was this paradox, of this society in which we let people sell us things all the time, and how intelligent and educated are we going to be that we are going to question what it is that we are being sold?

About the time of *The Brain Revolution* I was also meditating. I also discovered the formal research of parapsychology. This validated psychic experiences I'd had.

After a particularly poignant paranormal incident which had to do with my father's death, it occurred to me that what we in Western society think of as being "real," is a very limited view of the world. From time to time, we all have experiences in everyday life that hint all is not what it seems. Henri Berkson had spoken of the brain as a filter, reducing this whole large body of information to something manageable. Alter the chemistry a little, as William James said, and a whole other kind of experience can happen.

DiCarlo—So even with that book—though you may not have been thinking of it in those terms—you were challenging the predominant paradigm?

Ferguson—Yes I was. Years later, Luis Muchado, who started the first Ministry for the Development of Human Intelligence, a Cabinet position in Venezuela told me *The Brain Revolution* had inspired him to action. I'd said in conclusion, "If this is all true, why doesn't somebody do something about it?" So he did.

We have to believe we can throw ourselves into life and change things. If there is something wrong with the product, if there is something wrong in the community do something. "Drive-by shootings" are only a symptom of a "drive-by culture." We and our leaders really need to stop, take stock of things and ask, "Is this really right or not?" People are doing that more.

DiCarlo—In *The Aquarian Conspiracy,* you discussed at length the paradigm shifts taking place in many sectors of society, from science to education. How would you characterize let's say, the emerging paradigm in business?

Ferguson—The passing paradigm saw business as the 'be-all' and 'end-all' of society rather than one of its tools for functioning. Economic needs had been seen as foremost, superseding considerations of family, quality of life, health and so on. It seems that we have gotten confused about just what the 'American Dream' is all about. We think it was about rags to riches and Horatio Alger, but the original dream was based upon the freedom *to* dream. And to make your dreams come true as long as you did not hurt anyone else. It was not to simply 'get rich'.

Now some people dreamed of amassing considerable financial wealth, but that wasn't the point. Our founders were a diverse group. They were in a sense, the children of dissenters—people who had emigrated for political or religious reasons.

How does this relate to the emerging business paradigm? For a couple of hundred years commercial interests have dominated. As early as the 1800s, people were complaining that their Congressional representatives were bought and sold by special interest groups. So the good of the whole has not always been taken into account.

Quite suddenly, the policy makers, the real movers and shakers, have recognized more the increasingly crucial role of education. It is rather ironic in a way, that because of our entertainment industries—music, videos and television—a couple of generations of people have been raised who are not accustomed to finding pleasure within themselves, thinking for themselves, even imagining for themselves. Education per se could not compete with this extra stimulation, the advertising, the glitzy images. With the declining level of educational standards and performance, these very people who become 'vegged-out' through socialization, are no longer adequate workers for skilled or even semi-skilled positions.

Another example of this kind of 'business karma' occurred in the early 70s when General Motors bought and shut down the main public transportation system in Los Angeles. They had cynically reckoned that Southern California was the biggest potential market for automobiles.

DiCarlo—Just where are we then, in the process of discarding the old paradigm and embracing the new?

Ferguson—At a crisis point, I'd say. If we started doing everything that needs to be done—right this very moment in terms of the environment—it might already be too late. Somebody has said that if it weren't for the last minute nothing would ever get done. Maybe this is the last minute. Suddenly we're saying, "Oh my God, the rain forests!" "The ozone layer."

DiCarlo—Do you find then that these environmental crises are popping up and forcing us to rethink what's really important in life, to rethink our values and priorities?

Ferguson—The Exxon Valdez oil spill could be seen as a metaphor for our whole society. The captain had gone to his cabin to do paperwork. The third mate who was left in charge was not qualified to steer the ship in such a dangerous area. When he was asked if he could handle it he said that he could. There was no watchman on the bow of the ship and the speed of the vessel was increasing rather than decreasing as they headed for the reefs.

It seems to me that collectively we're in that same situation. Things are happening faster. Meanwhile, we are the captains who have gone off to do paperwork.

DiCarlo—As gloomy as things appear, would you not agree that they serve a useful purpose in galvanizing mankind to action, and perhaps also to a higher state of being? This idea of "emergence through emergency?"

Ferguson—Yes. Somebody said the other day, "You have to reach breakdown before you can break through." The chaos we're experiencing now is just a symptom that the forms that we have been operating under have outlived their usefulness. The health care system isn't producing health. The schools aren't producing educated people. Issues of extreme corruption have been coming to light world wide. Our lack of an action is already making a difference.

A challenge shows us what we can do. It's a shame that we have to wait for a life or death crisis before we wake up. But once we are awake, we find that it's actually fun. Too often we think, "Someday I'll have my act together," as if there is some kind of 'never-never' land which awaits us where everything is going to run smoothly and we won't be challenged. As we begin to see that each person has a heroic capacity, we discover that each of us has a destiny to fulfill.

DiCarlo—Are there any signs that people are getting the message?

Ferguson—The polls suggest that the public is way ahead of the leaders on most of these issues. The so-called average person is more likely in a way to hold, and I hesitate to use the word "radical"—but it is a radical position.

An animal rights poll showed that about half of the people in the country embraced the position that the experts would call radically pro-animal. 65% of the people according to this week's *Times* magazine, believe that angels exist. 48% believe that they have a guardian angel. Either the New Age phenomenon went wild while nobody was looking, or people had been keeping their thoughts to themselves.

The animal rights people were startled at this. I'm sure the angel rights people were startled too. The general public, through the polls, have said that they would favor higher taxes if it really helped the homeless and the money wouldn't be wasted. When president Clinton proposed the health care plan, a poll afterwards showed that the majority of people supported it, even though they didn't think they would necessarily benefit. So there's more imagination and grace in the populace than there is generally acknowledged by the people who run the institutions.

DiCarlo—Let's get back to your comments about developing a vision. There's certainly been a lot of talk about vision lately. There is a verse of Proverbs in the bible which reads, "Where there is no vision the people perish." From your perspective, just what is the vision that seems to be emerging?

Ferguson—Well, it's not a vision of just one particular thing. It's really about the use of our "visionary capacity." The formula to achieve this consists of getting you to go deeper into yourself. If we want to get out of the mess that we're in, then we must realize that our old solutions to problems, our old worn ideas of how things ought to work, are not going to get us there.

DiCarlo—We have to rid ourselves of linear, "either/or" thinking?

Ferguson—Yes, thinking which is unimaginative and thinking which lacks common sense. For example, when fire engulfed Yellowstone park in 1988, the foresters adhered to a "Let burn" policy because foresters basically believe that it is better for the ecosystem to let the fires go. But what they did not take into account was the fact that there was a drought. The fires raged out of control as a result. The following year they decided to put out all fires because they were so severely criticized and the tourist industry was so badly hurt. So we seem to lack the ability to make these subtle distinctions. We haven't been educated to think in terms of third choices, or how to create an alternative if you do not like the way things are. I think that is what this talk of vision addresses itself to. Take the example of kids playing. It is the kid who has an idea of something to do on a boring day who becomes the leader. When leaders lack vision then we have to have our own. This is the kind of grassroots leadership that I had originally talked about in *The Aquarian Conspiracy*. You can begin to make "mini-revolutions," people striving to improve things where they are. Out of that might emerge a shift that may eventually cause a change in authority.

DiCarlo—What advice can you offer to those people who want to take a vision and make it a reality?

Ferguson—Let me take some of the key points from some of the chapters of *Radical Common Sense*.... Improve your ability to visualize. Be sensitive to your gut feeling. It isn't just the original vision that is involved. There are steps all along the way. You have to become aware of your intuition and your instincts, these guide in the process of implementing the vision. And you also need to be awake. All of a sudden the world changes and your vision has to change too. The vision needs to be continually defined.

DiCarlo—What's the main difference then, between a vision and a goal?

Ferguson—A vision is a tentative goal. You could even have little goals that you set in order to bring about your vision. For example let's say you're a magazine publisher. Your goal could be that by the end of the year you will have 'x' number of subscribers. But that isn't a vision. A vision is a mode of something working—a kind of dynamic.

So that might mean that you see yourself serving your potential subscribership, envisioning what your publication will do for them;

what they might understand from it; and how that might affect their lives—what they do and how they think. You could even stretch this to include what might happen in society so that you have an even larger purpose.

Tune your vision to the whole. You might say, "I want to publish a glossy magazine," but if there is no market for it—if people don't want it—then the vision isn't grounded in cultural reality.

Things don't generally come out exactly as we envision them—sometimes they're much better. And sometimes they're just different, or even disappointing. The important thing is to not give up on your visionary capacity just because one little vision didn't work out. And realize that no matter the outcome, you are wiser. Most of us fail to cultivate our visionary capacity. Still, most people do have some kind of dream or a vision. But they don't take it seriously. So they resign themselves to humdrum, everyday lives. Therein lies the dis-ease. With a vision, people get better, not older.

DiCarlo—Is there any other advice you could give people about developing a powerful vision?

Ferguson—Well, l would add that we need to work on our communication skills and quality discrimination. Find out, for example, if anybody else is doing the things that you would like to do. And if they failed, why they failed.

Your vision may be to work for a company because you like their vision. Even if your job is not, in itself as challenging as you would wish it to be, you can "fine-tune" yourself so that you become really good at what you do. It may even be that you find your vision in your private life, to find some cause that you really enjoy—saving the dolphins for example. You might pick up litter around the lake because it makes you feel more alive, as though you are doing something worthwhile. "How do l make my children's school better?" or "How do l make my neighborhood better?" So the secret is service.

DiCarlo—In your view, who are some of the "cutting-edge" visionaries of our times?

Ferguson—Gorbachev, Ted Turner, Mandala....We can look to entertainment or sports heroes who have become very much involved in "Save the world" activities. Turn to the local feature section in the newspaper, the stories of people who are making things happen locally. The "cutting-edge" visionaries l would say, include the people who are stepping forth to help their neighborhoods.

DiCarlo—So, a vision would never be founded upon the mundane pursuit of money?

Ferguson— We got into this situation by first thinking of our personal profits. We only win through each other; we don't win over each other. We triumph as a group, not alone. In the past it was the "joy of victory" and "beating" one's adversaries. I recommend a book called *Finite and Infinite Games* by James Carse. The author suggests that we think in terms of winning or losing the game of life. But the real purpose is to keep the ball in play. That's a whole other way of looking at things. For example, what would happen if you were so successful in business that you buy out all your competitors and completely dominate the market?

Now what?

DiCarlo—In 1980, you were decidedly optimistic about the brightness of the future of mankind. Do you still feel that way?

Ferguson—There's a quotation from Virgil that has become a sort of motto for me—*"They can because they think they can."*

We have to act from faith. If we are going to go out, at least let's go out trying our best to save this situation, knowing that we did our best.

Why do the same themes keep getting played over and over again? What are the lessons of history trying to teach us? One of the lessons seems to be that we don't learn the lessons of history very well.

Right now we would be wise to focus our attention on how basic human beings behave in basic selfish ways. What is there in human nature that impels us to act in certain ways? We need to teach people how to parent, how to get along with each other. Common sense tells us that we are going to have to be more visionary and more compassionate if we are going to survive. That is not 'Blue Sky' talk. Nothing short of being imaginative, creative and compassionate is going to save us.

I'm placing my hope in those people who are awake and who have the courage and conviction to see how many other people they can wake up. If that happens, then we will have a Renaissance. Listen to those leaders who encourage us to be better people, not those playing to our fears. As I see it, either we are going to have a very rapid decline into a "worst-case" scenario, or else the dream of a new Renaissance will be made a reality. The choice is ours.

Part 1

A NEW VIEW
of the
UNIVERSE

"I suddenly realized it's all one, that this magnificent universe is a harmonious, directed, purposeful whole. That we humans, both as individuals and as a species are an integral part of the ongoing process of creation."

Edgar Mitchell, Apollo Astronaut

"I'm suggesting to you another realm of reality exists which is other than what you know and experience. There coexists another level of reality that we can enter and play with. They are not illusions. They are absolutely real."

Dr. Wayne Dyer, Author

What is the nature of the Universe in which we live?

To many, the question smacks of philosophical rhetoric—and a world far removed from the day-to-day grind of work and family responsibilities. The gut-level response is, "I don't know, and besides—I don't care!"

And yet, we do care! Consciously or unconsciously, everyone has a world view that provides very definite answers to this question. Our picture of the nature of the Universe gives rise to our individual and collective values. It shapes what we consider important, where we invest our time and energy, what we purchase with our money—in short, it helps us to distinguish between the important and the trivial, the meaningful and the superficial.

It also determines how we react to life's happenings: Do we consider life events that do not work out as we would like as "stuff happening" or "punishment from God," or purposeful avenues to the unfoldment of our human potential? "Is the Universe," Einstein asked, "essentially a friendly place?" If so, the effect on our lives would be extraordinary.

Section 1

NEW VIEWS IN HISTORY

"History is not just the evolution of technology; it is the evolution of thought. By understanding the reality of the people who came before us, we can see why we look at the world the way we do, and what our contribution is toward further progress. We can pinpoint where we come in so to speak, in the longer development of Civilization, and that gives us a sense of where we are going."

Robert Redfield, *Celestine Prophesy*

Richard Tarnas is a historian whose acclaimed book, **The Passion of The Western Mind**, paints a fascinating historical backdrop to better understand the times in which we live.

Tarnas defines a world view as a set of values, concepts, and assumptions about human beings and their relationship to nature, the divine and the cosmos which direct a culture's way of being and acting. World views are far from static, they change with the age. There are many factors which contribute to a shift in world views, some relating to demographic changes, others to religious and psychological orientation. Whatever the forces at play, the shift well underway is historically without precedent.

World views are not to be viewed as right or wrong, but should be approached as works of art, to fully appreciate their role, utility and function. For example, the traditional world view highly values self-determination, individualism and control over the natural world. This has served a beneficial purpose—to allow humanity to forge a sense of identity and self.

Yet, in undergoing this process of differentiation in an unbalanced way, humanity came to see itself as completely apart, or "other than" nature. The result? A feeling of separation and alienation, and a sense that nature is our adversary rather than the very ground of our being. This alienation and separation manifests itself in all of life's arenas—in our relationships with one another, our jobs, even ourselves. Today, the average person in Western society is fragmented, pushed and pulled in various directions by competing externally derived ideologies and conflicting inner impulses. Few people know why they are on the planet; fewer still the intrinsic meaning of life. Most are "numbed-out," unable to feel the pulse of their connection to divinity and the natural world. Public opinion polls tell us that most Westerners feel themselves to be alienated. Cut-off. Alone.

This existential insecurity gives rise to the perceived need to defend oneself and one's being against hostile, potentially annihilating forces— other human beings, the universe—life itself. The perception of living in such a hostile universe leads to fear and the desire to control people, events and circumstances, so as to to buffer oneself against injury or loss. This world view imprisons us in needless pain and suffering, and has set the stage for the present global crisis.

Nevertheless, there exists the possibility of renewal, and the attainment of a new level of connection with others and the Universe. But as Tarnas explains, in order to fulfill that promise, one must die to the old ways of seeing, being and doing. It is a process that can be acted out in one of two ways—either as a psychological and inner experience or more dramatically and painfully in everyday life.

Richard Tarnas

Richard Tarnas, Ph.D. is a historian and professor of philosophy at the California Institute of Integral Studies. A graduate of Harvard University and Saybrook, he is the former Director of Programs at Esalen Institute. He is the author of the bestselling book, "The Passion of The Western Mind," which famed mythologist Joseph Campbell described as "the most lucid and concise presentation of the grand lines of what every student should know about history."

DiCarlo—Why should a person be interested in history? How might a study of the past enable us to deal with the many challenges now before us?

Tarnas—If we are to understand where we are now in our history, if we are to understand our moment in history and where we are potentially going in the future, we need to know what brought us to this point. That means recovering the sources of our world and our world view. I think the two go together. A world view has a tremendous influence in configuring the way the world turns out to be. The way we approach reality will influence the kind of reality we create. It's very important to identify the basic principles and presuppositions supporting our world view because they will go a long way towards revealing how our world has been constellated. A big motive in writing my book, *The Passion of The Western Mind,* was to understand all the different impulses and strands of thought and cultural influences that have gone into creating the way we look at the world and the way our world has come to be in our time.

One of the paradoxes of the Western intellectual tradition is that though it is seen at any given point as "a tradition" and therefore a tradition of conservative elders with an established, authoritarian and therefore potentially oppressive, or stodgy or too traditional character—in fact the major thinkers who have made up that tradition have all been counter-cultural rebels and revolutionaries in their own time, whether we are talking about Socrates, Descartes, Galileo, Nietzsche, or Freud. The rebel in one generation becomes the ruler in a later generation, just as, archetypally speaking, the son becomes the father. We see in the West's whole evolution that we are in many ways deeply informed by this tradition, even when we are rebelling against it. The very principle of critical response to an intellectual tradition is absolutely basic to our Western tradition. Even at the moment we rebel against it, we are fulfilling this grand tradition.

One other general point I might make here: The Western intellectual and spiritual tradition, up until this generation, has been a patrilineal tradition. For the most part it's been constituted by men, who were usually writing for other men. This has had a great influence on the nature of the Western mind and the nature of the Western world view. It has tremendously affected our understanding of the human being, of the relationship of the human being to the world. It's affected our understanding of the divine and the human being's relationship to the divine. It's had a radical influence on our history.

DiCarlo—How would you define a world view? If we are to say that a world view is a paradigm, are there different paradigms for different fields, such as a scientific paradigm let's say, or is there an over-arching, meta-paradigm that is perhaps more basic, and upon which the others are constructed?

Tarnas—I think there are different levels of paradigms. A world view, which is the most general level, is a set of values, of conceptual structures, of implicit assumptions or presuppositions about the nature of reality—about human beings, about the nature of the relationship between human beings and nature, about history, the divine, the cosmos—which constellate an entire culture's way of being and acting. There are many levels to a world view, many inflections to it and many ways it can be differentiated. So for example, there can be a general scientific paradigm which is allied with and in some ways reflective of this larger cultural world view. There is a give-and-take relationship between the two. It's not a one way street. Scientific paradigms can affect the cultural world view, but also, the cultural world view can go through shifts such as it is right now, which will in turn affect scientists and how they go about doing their work and how they go about making sense of reality. So it goes both ways.

Not only is there *"a"* scientific paradigm, there are *many* scientific paradigms. There's a different paradigm, say, operative in evolutionary biology than there is in quantum physics or depth psychology. All of these have claimed to be scientific paradigms, and they may have a more or less conscious relationship with each other, but they are all scientific paradigms. Even within each field, such as depth psychology, or quantum physics, there may be several paradigms within that discipline. For example, there are eight different paradigms of reality in quantum physics that are currently in the arena of discussion. So there can be many different paradigms even within a given field.

I would suggest that at any given time in a culture, in a civilization's history, there is usually one overarching meta-paradigm that underlies all the rest and that affects all the rest and is in a reciprocal relationship to all the "sub-paradigms," let's say, which can be active in science, religion, philosophy and so forth.

DiCarlo—How do world views change?

Tarnas—Many factors are involved in a world-view shift. I believe that you can never say that it's a specific rational or empirical factor that shifts a world view. For example, let's say new data comes in through a new scientific instrument, such as the telescope, which revealed the heavens in a new way through Galileo's interpretations and helped bring about the Copernican revolution. I would say that, generally speaking, it's never an exclusively empirical or rational process. Many factors converge to make possible the world-view shift. There are sociological changes that take place and make it possible, including things like the death of old-paradigm thinkers in a given field. As they die, their authoritative views disappear with them and the younger thinkers in the field bring with them a more flexible perspective that hasn't had a lifelong investment in a given world view. As a result, what is purely a matter of sociology and demographics has an influence on the cultural world view. There can also be shifts in the religious and psychological orientation of a culture which bring about a shift in world view.

For example, in the Copernican revolution, there seems to have been a kind of vast psychological shift that occurred in 15th century Italy, that we now regard as the Humanist Renaissance. This brought with it a certain sense of the world as being numinously alive with divine order and meaning. This helped to create a context within which Copernicus and Kepler's thinking could develop in such a way that the Copernican revolution was made possible. It included the mathematization of the world, the spiritual exaltation of the sun, and the idea that the cosmos could be best understood as the emanation of a divine intelligence whose language was one of supremely beautiful, mathematical order. These are basic presuppositions that were in the air in Renaissance Italy that affected Copernicus, Kepler, and later Galileo, Newton, and Descartes in such a way that the entire Scientific Revolution was deeply influenced by what many scientists would consider nonscientific factors.

So many factors go into a world-view change. Personally, I believe that world views change when the archetypal configuration of the collective psyche—or the collective unconscious, to use Carl Jung's term—goes through some fundamental shift. That shift is only partly responsive to human free will. To a great extent it takes place with a certain autonomous, organic power that we as human beings participate in, and are influenced by. Certainly we are not entirely in charge of this process, although I think we play a crucial role and have a crucial responsibility for its unfolding.

DiCarlo—So there's a shift that takes place at what we would refer to as the unconscious level of the psyche—although unconscious is a misleading term since it is unconscious only in the sense that we are not yet directly aware of these levels—that sort of percolates up to the level of conscious, normal everyday awareness?

Tarnas—That's right.

DiCarlo—Now you've mentioned that a world view would not likely shift simply as a result of the taking in of new scientific data. Expanding on that thought, would you say that a person's world view might change by reading a book, let's say, on quantum physics, which is so novel in its insights and extraordinary in its implications that it might cause them to revise their thoughts about life in general. Or must such a shift in world view be preceded in some way by a personal experience which reveals to them that "things are not the way they seem?"

Tarnas—I don't think it necessarily has to be preceded by an experience like that. Sometimes reading a book on quantum physics or on Eastern mysticism can itself suddenly precipitate a shift. But I believe a shift in the individual person's world view can happen only when there has been a certain development—however hidden it may have been—that has brought that person to a point of preparedness, or readiness, or ripeness. In this sense, the book serves as sort of an activating trigger or impulse.

The book itself can play a major role in precipitating a shift in world view, but that shift is not just a purely intellectual process. In a way, I think it is a moment of grace that uses the book as the efficient cause, but ultimately, it was something that person was ready for. He or she was ready to be drawn forth in that way, ready to be led forth. The original meaning of education was "to be led out from within"—to have one's own truth be led out from within by skillful teaching. In that sense, education, or a change in a world view is never something that can be simply imposed from without or that takes place simply due to instruction by an external person or book. It is something inside that is ready to emerge, ready to be born within the individual's consciousness.

DiCarlo—In his ground-breaking work on paradigm shifts, Thomas Kuhn goes so far as to say that a shift in world view is actually a conversion experience. Why is it so profound, seeming to affect an individual at their very core?

Tarnas—A world-view shift is something that reflects a very profound archetypal dynamic in the psyche whereby one goes through what closely resembles a perinatal process—a birth process. One has been within a "womb," that is, a matrix of thought, a conceptual matrix, a conceptual womb for quite a while. You've developed within it, you've seen the world by means of it, and you have gotten more and more developed, complex, large, differentiated, until that conceptual matrix is no longer large enough to contain your evolving mind. It becomes seen as a problem, or constriction. It is seen as something to be overcome. A crisis is created. In the course of a very critical period of transition, of tension, of deconstruction, of disorientation, a sudden new birth is precipitated into a new conceptual matrix. There is a sudden revelation of a new Universe, which seems to open up. I think that this experience of a shift in a world view is such that one in many ways has reexperienced one's own birth on an intellectual level. It involves this very deep archetypal death and rebirth process. So whether it's a shift in a world view or a religious conversion experience, both participate in this larger perinatal sequence, this archetypal dialectic, which I believe underlies what Kuhn calls "the structure of scientific revolution" and which underlies radical spiritual transformations, such as what St. John of the Cross called "The Dark Night of The Soul" and experiences of spiritual rebirth. A similar death-rebirth process can be recognized in the dissolution of the communist empire in eastern Europe and the sudden euphoric birth after the fall of the Berlin Wall. It can manifest in many different ways.

DiCarlo—Would you say that in terms of human development, we repeat these historical world views as we progress from infant, to child, to adolescent and to adult?

Tarnas—Yes. I think that's another way we can better understand this process. What a whole culture goes through in some way reflects what each individual goes through. For example, Wordsworth's great poem "Intimations of Immortality" is a beautiful rendering of a person's gradual shift in world view. In the beginning, you have the numinous, sacralized, enchanted vision of the child, who is born trailing clouds of glory, still having that kind of archetypal consciousness in early infancy and childhood. Then gradually, as one gets to be more and more of an adult, more and more socialized into the conventional ways of looking at the world, there's the experience of being separate from the world. There's a kind of disenchantment of the world to the point where the adult human being looks out on "the light of common day" to use Wordsworth's terms. So there is a certain way in which this individual process very beautifully describes the trajectory that Western civilization has traveled.

It has gone from the enchanted world view of the pre-Greek indigenous cultures, and even to a great extent the Greeks—the Homeric sensibility—where we can find a certain sense that heaven and earth were not totally separated in the Greek consciousness. In both ancient Judaism and Christianity, and even in the medieval period, there is a certain enchantment of the world. But as the Western mind develops, as in the eighteenth century Enlightenment, with the sovereignty of the rational and scientific—there is a gradual and thorough disenchantment which eventually leads to the crisis in world view in our own century—and, I believe, the potential for a second birth.

DiCarlo—Second birth?

Tarnas—Yes, there are two births to consider. First there is the literal one, the physical one: the birth of the human being out of nature, the birth of Western civilization out of the ancient archaic cultures of the Mediterranean. Then there's a second birth, which comes only through a death. And that second birth is a spiritual birth. It's the initiation of the twice-born. And that requires a sacrifice. It requires a death, which I believe we, as a civilization, are deep in the middle of right now.

DiCarlo—If, as some leading-edge scientists are suggesting, consciousness can affect reality, then is it not true that whatever a person's world view is, he or she would be able to gather evidence to support it?

Tarnas—I do believe that consciousness has a tremendous role. Each individual's consciousness, and also the collective consciousness of a culture and its basic presuppositions and a priori principles, plays a large role in constellating reality.

When you are in a given world view, you discover data and you gather evidence that will be to a great extent configured in accordance with the basic principles with which you are approaching reality. There is a sort of self-reinforcing circularity to the process of human knowledge. This is why it is so important to become conscious of the presuppositions with which you are approaching reality. If anything, this insight increases human responsibility in creating one's world.

The spectator theory of reality, which William James and many 20th-century thinkers have criticized, says that we can see, know, and test reality as someone who is fully, objectively separate from that reality—that we can be spectators outside of it. Yet in fact, we are always in the middle of reality. We are affected by it as we are affecting it. So subject and object are much more mutually implicated than it otherwise might seem to the naive empirical mind. This perspective puts an even greater burden of responsibility for becoming conscious of one's principles of interpretation. It is also tremendously freeing. It shows that reality is not a "given" that we are trying to know from outside, as it were. Rather, we are playing a role in creating it, and therefore we need to bring the values and the aspirations that we believe would create the most life-enhancing world and world view to the epistemological equation.

So things like faith, hope, empathy, and imagination and aesthetic sensibility are critical human faculties and values that play a role in how we know reality, and therefore play a role in what reality becomes for us.

DiCarlo—You're implying that a world view can be selected?

Tarnas—I believe we do play a role in selecting or forging our world view. It's a participatory role, it's not a "Captain of My Ship" role with absolute autonomy. It is participatory.

DiCarlo—What criteria would you use for selecting a world view?

Tarnas— The criteria I would suggest are: does it serve a larger understanding of self so that it's not just the narrow "skin-encapsulated ego," to use Alan Watts's terms? Does it serve a larger sense of self that connects each human being with the rest of the human community, with the rest of the community of living beings and with the rest of the cosmos? So there's a larger and larger sense of identity that can become encompassed and served in our world view.

DiCarlo—I see...It strikes me that a given world view is more or less appropriate given humanity's collective stage of development, which would therefore suggest that all world views are relative—there's no right or wrong world view. Would you agree?

Tarnas—That's a very tricky question. They are all relative, but relative to what? They are relative to each other, they are relative to changing values. I believe that the world view of Dante in the 14th century is a different world view than, say, Thomas Jefferson's in the late 18th century, but that doesn't mean that one is superior to the other, or that one is right and the other is wrong. Each world view needs to be approached, in a sense, as a great work of art, so that we try to understand it with as much empathic appreciation as possible, to understand its human consequences, to let its meaning unfold rather than making some sort of snap judgment or even a judgment after a period of time, but one that somehow puts one world view in a lower position than another. I think reality is much too complex, too ambiguous, too mysterious to be making those kinds of judgments. In fact, my sense is that reality itself is shifting. World views are relative to that evolving reality that is ultimately coming out of some great mystery of the cosmos.

DiCarlo—If, as you point out in your work, the fields of science, philosophy and religion have helped to sculpt the traditional Western world view, what have been the major influences behind the development of the emerging world view? Who have been some of the more prominent personalities in this unfolding drama?

Tarnas—It depends how far back we want to take it. For example, in certain respects you can go back all the way to people like Socrates and Moses. They are still affecting us in terms of the basic Promethean impulse of rebelling against oppressive structures and creating moral and intellectual autonomy for the human being. This is still an operating, underlying impulse in our current world view shift.

More recently, the thinkers of the late 19th century and early 20th century, like Freud, Darwin, Marx, and Nietzsche, set the stage for the postmodern transitional period. I use the word "postmodern" to describe the era that we're in, with the understanding that the term postmodern describes a transitional era. It is an age between world views. Everything is pretty much up for grabs right now. There are many world views in contention. There is much transition. There's a sense of disorientation. There is a deconstruction, or tearing down of many long-established principles, and this is as it should be. This is what marks the period of radical transformation that a cultural world view needs to go through in order to re-constellate itself with a higher level of coherence and greater depth of meaning. And today we now seem to be reaching a new moment, a cyclical acceleration, in this transformation, and perhaps a culmination.

There was a speech that was given by Vaclav Havel, the Czechoslovakian president, a while back that appeared in the New York Times. It's amazing how close his vision of the transformation is to my own. Often, when I read Havel, I feel like he's a brother. He comments upon the ecological crisis, the collapse of communism and the collapse of the conventional scientific assumption that science has—or will have in time—complete, objective, comprehensive answers to the problems of human reality. These great collapses are happening right now. At the same time, new forms of thinking are emerging, such as the Gaia hypothesis and the anthropic principle. There's also the tremendous shift in terms of the masculine/feminine dialectic that I mentioned. In the last 30 and 40 years, humanity has explored space and viewed the earth for the first time from without. These are all signs of really radical, major shifts that are occurring in our self-understanding and in our world view. What's going on right now is virtually unprecedented. There are some partial precedents, such as the end of classical antiquity, or the beginning of the modern era, or even the beginning of Western civilization, but the fact is, the human species is facing its own mortality on the planet as never before. And this suggests that we are at the end of a long trajectory that is coming to some kind of dramatic climax right now.

In science, in philosophy, in religion, the arts—in all of these are major signs of this shift of world view. It's taking place on all these levels.

DiCarlo—What would you say is the essence of the traditional world view—the prevailing and dominant paradigm as it were—and how has it contributed to some of the problems we are now facing?

Tarnas—That world view has been defined by an emphasis on the progressive advance of the human being in history and its relationship to nature, in which the dominant impulse has been to increase knowledge of the world in order to gain *control* of that world and nature for human benefit. It is reflected in a Promethean impulse towards greater and greater human autonomy, freedom, self-determination, an adventurous exploration of new horizons, an impulse towards always overcoming the past. And it has emphasized individualism, promoted the separation of the human being from nature, and elevated reason over emotion, imagination, and communal identity.

Now this impulse has been valuable and essential to much of the best of who we are and what we've accomplished, but it has also caused great problems. The one-sidedness of this development has resulted in a disenchanted world view in which the human being is ultimately alienated, existing in a world that is seen as having no intrinsic spiritual meaning, no intrinsic purpose. We are not at home in this world, we're simply an ephemeral species that lives on a meaningless speck of dust on the edge of one galaxy amongst billions.

This world view has created major psychological and spiritual problems for humanity and an enormous ecological crisis. Clearly, we need to be addressing the aspects of this world view that have created these problems. In many ways, the problems and the crises that are arising are too big for human beings to fix using the old engineering model of, "Well, we'll just figure out the cause of the problem and fix it using our rational intelligence." Clearly, every move that is made to fix one thing, such as antibiotics, creates new problems that we could not have predicted in advance. So these events are in fact making way for a new world view. You have to go through a sacrifice, you have to go through a death, you have to go through some kind of destruction and deconstruction of a whole world view if something new is going to be born. That just seems to be the way of the cosmos. I have deep faith in the ultimate positive character of what this transformation will be; on the other hand, I don't know how much suffering, how much of a global crisis, we will have to go through before this new world view emerges. A lot of this is still in question. It's a race, as someone has said, between education and catastrophe. How aware will we become of the role we are playing in creating the crisis? How much inner work and inner exploration will people do to make possible this great transformation on an interior level so that it doesn't have to be naively and destructively acted out in the world? Some kind of death *has* to happen. There's the death and rebirth of a sacramental initiation, and then there's the death that is acted out on a much more destructive and problematic way in the world.

DiCarlo—You alluded to the fact that we've accrued certain benefits from the dominant and prevailing world view. Tell me, in terms of human development, what has that world view allowed us to achieve?

Tarnas—It has allowed us to achieve autonomy. We have a responsibility, a conscious role to play in our evolution—this is new. We also have a freedom to evolve in a certain way, to choose what kind of a world and world view we will grow within. All of us value that ability to revise our world view, to revise ourselves, to be endlessly self-revising in an attempt to become a better person and create a better world.

Another way of looking at this long development is in terms of the divine marriage, the "hieros gamos" that Jung spoke about. In order to have a marriage, you have to have a differentiation for the two to come together autonomously and join with one another in an act of love. This is also true for the human being in relationship to the divine and in its relationship to the world: that having fully differentiated itself, it is now in a position to embrace the matrix of its being freely and consciously. Rudolf Steiner used two words to sum up what he saw as the evolution of consciousness, and those two words were "freedom" and "love." I think that goes a long way towards describing what we are involved in right now. Having achieved our freedom, we are now in a position to embrace the whole in a kind of loving surrender of self to a larger whole which will preserve autonomy while also transcending the alienation that has been the downside of our forging an autonomous self.

DiCarlo—Would you say that the emerging world view is a regression in some way to that which was held during medieval times?

Tarnas—Of course there is more than one world view in the medieval period, but let's take Dante and Thomas Aquinas as representing the most comprehensive, rich, articulate renderings of the medieval world view. In this view, the human being had a central role in a meaningful, spiritually informed cosmos. It was a fixed and structured and hierarchical cosmos, and there was also a further ambiguity that was present. On the one hand, there was a negation of this world—the world, the flesh, and the devil were seen as something one needs to transcend in order to move towards the good Christian, celestial destiny. On the other hand, there was often a sense of the universe, nature and the human being as constituting an organic whole that the scientific and industrial revolutions destroyed.

I don't see what we are experiencing right now as a regression, although there are elements from the past, from the medieval. But there are also elements from archaic, ancient, traditional, and indigenous world views that are coming up once again to manifest in a new way. It's less a circular regression and more a spiral that takes up certain impulses and insights from these earlier periods and integrates them with all that has been positively achieved in the meantime. In that sense, there is an element of regression, but there is also a sense of moving forward. This is what one would call a dialectic, in which something from the past and something from the present come together and create the future. Two opposites converge to create a third higher synthesis.

DiCarlo—At the outset, you stated that the Western mind has been characterized by the masculine perspective. What would that perspective be?

Tarnas—That perspective is driven by this heroic impulse to differentiate the human being from its primordial unity with nature and with the divine to form an autonomous, rational human self. It reflects an archetypal masculine impulse which, as I mentioned, has brought us to a point of great power, great critical intelligence, great autonomy, and also great crisis. There is something that Jung calls "enantiodromia," which is a term he draws from the ancient Greek Heraclitus, which has to do with the spontaneous shift of opposites. When you get to one extreme, then the opposite emerges, and this recovery and resurgence of the feminine that is happening in our time is an example of that.

DiCarlo—So the emerging world view I take it involves the reclaiming and integration of the feminine aspect of nature?

Tarnas—Yes, and the movement towards overcoming the alienation of the individual human being and human mind from the universe, from the world, from the matrix from which it has arisen. It is characterized by the breakdown of the subject-object dichotomy and the movement towards a more unitive, participatory, world view.

DiCarlo—Could you elaborate on that?

Tarnas—The Western intellectual and spiritual tradition has been influenced by an archetypal masculine impulse that has been informing and impelling the Western mind since its inception with the ancient Greeks and the ancient Hebrews. This in many ways has led us to this very dramatic point of transformation.

The masculine, differentiating approach to the world, to the nature of reality, and to the nature of the relationship between the human being and the world has reached a point of crisis. Yet, we also see now, in many ways, the potential for great transformation and healing, a coming into wholeness by the tremendous resurgence of the feminine archetype. This is visible on many levels, and not just the obvious ones of feminism and the empowerment of women and the new openness on the part of men to feminine values. It is also visible in a whole different approach to life—our scientific theories of the human psyche, the new sensibility of how human beings relate to nature and other forms of life on the planet—all of these reflect the emergence of the feminine archetype on the collective scale of the culture which is manifesting as a new sense of connection with the whole. This ideally could result in the "hieros gamos"—the divine marriage—the coming together of the masculine and feminine on many levels: between the human being and nature, between intellect and soul, between men and women. It's an extremely multi-leveled, complex transformative process we're involved in right now.

DiCarlo—You have stated that the Western mind, as it begins this fundamental shift in world view, must be willing to open itself to a reality, the nature of which could shatter its most established beliefs about itself and about the world. Could you mention some of these beliefs?

Tarnas—One I just mentioned, that nature is completely mechanistic and unconscious and impersonal, and that somehow the human being is utterly unique in being the sole locus of conscious intelligence in the universe. There are a lot of developments challenging this assumption, such as the Gaia hypothesis, which goes a long way towards making sense of evolution and life on earth in ways that refute the presupposition that the only kind of entity that can act with a self-regulating intelligence is the human being or other individual organisms but not the earth itself.

Depth psychology, which in the last 20 or 30 years has evolved into transpersonal psychology and archetypal psychology, coming out of the work or Freud and Jung, has moved to a place where a lot of basic modern presuppositions—the separation of the psyche from the world, of the individual human being from the community of human beings—are all being shattered. We are just starting to see that within each individual human being, his or her psyche is rooted in a much larger psyche, that our consciousness participates in a collective consciousness that is shared by all human beings and is rooted in nature, the world, and the cosmos. This sense of separation of the individual mind is something that is gradually being shattered right now.

DiCarlo—Would you say that the emerging world view tends to reduce the gap between science and religion?

Tarnas—Very much. It's remarkable how traditional scientists, often in their mature years, when they no longer have to prove anything to anybody—when they've already gotten their Nobel Prize—start developing their spiritual side and start connecting it with their scientific interests and insights. Many of the most cutting-edge scientists, like the late David Bohm or Rupert Sheldrake, are clearly informed—as was Einstein—by a spiritual understanding.

To the extent that Western religion is hung up on a fundamentalist, literal interpretation of the Bible, there is always going to be a major problem in reducing the gap between science and religion. Problems also arise from fundamentalist scientists who get hung up with the idea that their particular view of reality, or their particular view that they think mainstream science approves, *is* reality. They take that view as literally and absolutely true, rather than as tentative, partial, and fallible. There will always be a major gap between science and religion as long as science and religion are authoritatively led by fundamentalists of each stripe.

But more and more sophisticated thinkers in both the religious and scientific worlds are way past that. There's a great quote by Robert Bellah in his book *Beyond Belief* which I use in my book: "We may be seeing the beginnings of the reintegration of our culture, a new possibility of a unity of consciousness. If so, it will not be on the basis of any new orthodoxy, either religious or scientific. Such a new integration will be based on the rejection of all univocal understandings of reality, of all identifications of one conception of reality with reality itself. It will recognize the multiplicity of the human spirit," and I would add, "the multiplicity of reality," and the necessity to translate constantly between different scientific and imaginative vocabularies. It will recognize the human proclivity to fall comfortably into some single, literal interpretation of the world and therefore the necessity to be continuously open to rebirth in a new heaven and a new earth. It will recognize that in both scientific and religious culture, all we have finally are symbols. But there is an enormous difference between the dead letter and the living word."

Certainly in psychology, through people like Jung and Grof, there has been a real awakening to the spiritual dimensions of the human psyche. An awareness that as you get deep enough in there, you transcend a purely secular understanding of the human mind and start seeing the reality of religious experience, of spiritual beings, of a spiritual level of human experience that is absolutely basic. To deny that is to live in an artificially constrictive world view.

The religious consciousness of our time is shifting through the influences of Eastern mysticism, of psychedelic experience, of eco-feminist spirituality, of liberation theology—all are coming in and playing a major role in shifting the Western world view. The old secularized, scientific perspective which viewed the world as being mechanistic and purposeless, and basically run by chance and necessity, as being simply material forms moved by mechanistic forces, where God was an unnecessary hypothesis, is in radical decline right now. There is a growing recognition that our whole scientific strategy was propelled by a very idiosyncratic, temporary, local way of viewing the world— one that filtered out all possible spiritual dimensions in the universe, by ruling them out a priori as being not scientifically valid. With that world view breaking down, it becomes possible to look at the universe in new ways. As a result, new ways of understanding spirituality are beginning to emerge.

DiCarlo—How did that gap between religion and science occur in the first place?

Tarnas—The gap between religion and science started taking place in the West in the modern period because the basic conception of the world that had been passed on by our religious tradition was not being confirmed by the advances of empirical science and rational philosophy. This began soon after Thomas Aquinas, who was one of the last great integrators of Greek philosophy and science on the one hand and the Christian world view on the other. After that, with the late medieval Scholastics and with the early modern period, there was increasing sense of tension between science and philosophy on the one hand, and religion on the other. There was no preparation for the Copernican revolution in the Christian Bible. So if Copernicus was right it seemed to call into question some literal interpretations of the Bible. With Darwin, that reached a climax. So the scientific world view seemed to be inhospitable to the Christian perspective, at least as literally understood from the Bible by fundamentalist Christians. As a result, certain forms of Christianity tried to repress the modern scientific impulse, as it did with Galileo and as it attempted to do with Darwin. Similarly, scientists began to see religion generally—and Christianity in particular—as being oppressive, limiting and superstitious, although there are many exceptions to this. There are many scientists and religious thinkers who saw value in the other and saw the necessity to integrate the two. Still, the general drift of modern times has been towards a separation.

DiCarlo—Wasn't a "deal" struck between the church and science in general, where science could have the outer world, and the church would take the inner world of soul and spirit?

Tarnas—Essentially what happened is that there was a kind of division—the church got Sunday and science got the rest of the days of the week. The religious consciousness pays attention to the inner soul and science covers the outer world, the place of human beings in the world, our understanding of nature, and so forth. But that created a dichotomy that eventually became unlivable—a kind of schizophrenia between inner and outer—between the human spirit and the world in which the human spirit finds itself located. Eventually, that created a double bind of consciousness that was impossible to live with.

I think that's why there is such a strong impulse to find a new unity.

Section 2

NEW VIEWS IN SCIENCE

"The universe is not to be narrowed down to the limits of our own understanding, which has been the practice up to now, but our understanding must be stretched and enlarged to take in the image of the universe as it is discovered."

Francis Bacon

It is nearly impossible to separate the Western world view from the scientific world view, for the two are intimately intertwined.

At the heart of the scientific world view is the scientific method—observation; hypothesis; experiments to test theory; results; and conclusions. The method assumes that rational intelligence and logical thought are the highest paths to the truth. Science places an overriding importance on knowledge gained through the five senses. According to the scientific world view, if something cannot be measured, detected, analyzed or studied, then for all intents and purposes it does not exist. It is not considered scientifically "real."

As a result, matter (the brain) is given primary importance, and consciousness (or the mind) is considered an incidental by-product, like foam dancing upon the water of an outdoor hot tub.

This materialistic world view is summed up in a nationally-aired conversation between Dr. Patricia Smith Churchland and the popular journalist and author, Bill Moyers:

> MOYERS: Now the religious idea of the soul...Do you think that's just a metaphor?

> CHURCHLAND: I don't think it can be accurate. Even talking about God breathing life into something...We now know that life isn't like that either, that life also is a function of organiza-

tion of matter. See, there used to be vitalists, and they used to think that there is a life force to explain the difference between living things—like us—and dead things—like rocks and concrete... We now know that that's "not on."

Ever since Watson and Craig discovered DNA and since molecular biology has proceeded, it is very clear that that's not the correct explanation of living things, that life has to do with the organization of very complex molecules, proteins, etc

I think a similar thing is likely to be the case with the mind and the brain. There isn't a special thing—the mind. The mind just is the brain.

As historian Richard Tarnas mentioned, the elimination of spirit, and other realities aside from the physical is attributable to the 17th century impulse of science to break free from the imprisoning dogma of the Medieval church. Though a necessary development, and certainly very beneficial in light of our ever-increasing technological wonders, it has resulted in a world largely devoid of meaning, warmth, intimacy, charm and delight. "Values, purposes and qualities," writes Huston Smith, "slip through science like sea slips through the nets of fisherman."

Some scientists seem confident that science is on the verge of unraveling the innermost secrets of the universe. Others are not so sure. They would question the very assumptions upon which our science is constructed by asserting that consciousness, soul and spirit—not matter—is primary. They ask us to consider that there are other ways of knowing about reality than simply through the agency of the physical senses and rational thought processes. In so doing, they tell us, we open ourselves to the possibility of enlarging the windows of our perceptions, of arriving at a more accurate glimpse of the nature of the Universe.

In some respects, this new glimpse is really an old one—spoken of by our evolutionary forerunners, by saints, mystics, poets and prophets through the ages. "If the doors of perception were cleansed," wrote Blake, "everything would appear as it is, infinite. For man has closed himself up, 'til he sees all things thro' narrow chinks of his cavern." Such a glimpse evokes an unexpected sense of awe and wonder over the intricacy, multi-dimensionality, complexity and mystery of the Universe in which we live. It is a Universe, we are told, that lies beyond complete intellectual understanding or some all-encompassing final concept.

In this section, we will first hear from Willis Harman, who is regarded as being as insightful in business, economics and social change as he is in science. He is convinced that change is taking place at the deepest level, challenging our underlying assumptions about the universe in which we live.

Harman has put forth three different metaphysical assumptions upon which a world view can be constructed. He refers to these assumptions as M-1, M-2 and M-3. M-1 is the prevailing assumption of modern science. It says that the basic stuff of the universe is energy-matter and that we can learn about it through studying the measureable world. According to M-1, whatever consciousness is, it emerges out of matter. M-2 assumes that there are two distinct building blocks: mind-spirit studied by psychology and religion; and energy-matter, studied by science. M-3 proposes that the ultimate stuff of the universe is consciousness, and that matter-energy arises in some sense out of mind. In other words, says Harman, "consciousness is not the end-product of material evolution; rather consciousness was here first!"

Since science clings to the M-1 model, that matter is primary, it is reluctant to explore the subject of consciousness or other areas which challenge the prevailing world view. Dr. Beverly Rubik, a trained biophysicist and director of The Center For Frontier Sciences of Philadelphia's Temple University has proven herself the exception and has helped to extend the territory of scientific inquiry. Through Rubik's efforts, the Center serves as a conduit for the global exchange of cutting-edge scientific, technological and medical information. Annual conferences feature distinguished frontier scientists—some of whom are Nobel Laureates—presenting on topics such as the relationship of mind and matter, fields and living systems, and geobiology (the subtle interrelationship of life and the earth). The goal of the dialogue has been to identify significant questions for future research.

Finally in this section, we will hear from physicist Fred Alan Wolf. The field of quantum physics has dramatically called into question many of our prevailing scientific assumptions about reality and the way things work. For example, quantum mechanics predicts that time is far from constant. It can speed up or slow down depending upon the relationship between two objects. Light can take on the attribute of particle or wave, depending upon the expectations of the observer. We find that there is no such thing as solid "matter." All is energy at the most basic, subatomic level of physical reality. So mind boggling are the implications, one famed physicist said, "if you aren't confused by quantum mechanics, then you don't really understand it." For some, the study of quantum mechanics has so challenged their world view, they've embarked upon a journey of growth and transformation.

Willis Harman

Willis Harman is president of the Institute for Noetic Sciences, founded in 1973 by Apollo astronaut Edgar Mitchell, the 6th astronaut to walk on the moon. The Institute's mission has been to expand knowledge regarding the mind and spirit, and to apply that knowledge to advance health and well-being for humankind and the planet. It funds scientific research; brings top-level scientists and scholars together to share their methods, perspectives and knowledge; and in publications to its 60,000 plus membership, discusses new developments in consciousness research. For 16 years, Harman was on the staff of Stanford Research Institute (now SRI International), involved with futures research and strategic planning. That work is summarized in "An Incomplete Guide to the Future." His other books include "Global Mind Change," "Higher Creativity" and Creative Work."

DiCarlo—You've been president of the Institute of Noetic Sciences since the mid-70s. Could you briefly talk about the origins of this organization and its mission?

Harman—Yes. While Edgar Mitchell, one of the Apollo astronauts was on his way back from walking on the moon, he had a kind of spiritual experience. It struck him that traditional science didn't allow for that kind of non-ordinary experience, nor with what they meant to the people who had them. In general, science didn't handle the topic of consciousness very well. So he set up this nonprofit organization called The Institute of Noetic Sciences to work in this neglected area of science by focusing upon consciousness-related phenomena and experiences.

As the years have gone on, the Institute has chosen two main tasks. One is leading-edge research in consciousness related fields, such as spontaneous remission of cancer, the mind, meditation, healing in general and research on creative altruism. Secondly, and with the aid of a couple dozen scientists and philosophers, the Institute has studied the question, "Why does science have the particular characteristics that it does?" and "What sort of changes would have to take place in order for science to be better suited to handle these areas of consciousness?"

In scientific jargon, we're seeking a different epistemology for science. Put another way, we are wanting to answer the question, "How do we know what we think we know scientifically?"

DiCarlo—Let's begin by talking briefly about healing since that's an area of interest for the Institute. What's the bottom line message that scientific researchers are telling you about the relationship between the body and the mind?

Harman—The evidence suggests that the mind plays a much greater role than has been recognized by the scientific and medical community. This is the heart of the issue regarding complimentary medicine and alternative forms of health care. Most, if not all of them, hinge upon the powers of the mind. This isn't necessarily obvious in an area like homeopathy or acupuncture, but there's a suspicion at least, that the powers of these types of approaches depend upon the body being much different than the mechanistic view that has prevailed in the medical community thus far.

DiCarlo—Energy medicine seems to be an emerging area of Institute interest that seems to offer exciting possibilities in the treatment and prevention of physical and even psychological illness. What is it?

Harman—Energy medicine is a term that is used by some people who believe that there are fields around the human body that are influential in the healing process and in other ways. They propose that through the study of these fields, much knowledge can be obtained to help treat and diagnose people who have the potential of developing an illness. Other people use the same term, but really leave open the question as to whether these fields and influences are really physically measurable or are whether they exist in some other domain, some other dimension so to speak.

I think there is some advantage in leaving the term open-ended at this time. At the very least, the energy field involves the exploration of faint electromagnetic fields around the body and their relationship to health. It may have to do with much more than that.

DiCarlo—In your view, are these energy fields metaphorical or are they real? Who has produced the most compelling scientific evidence to date that these fields exist, that we are more than the physical?

Harman—Well you see, that hinges on the definition of scientific evidence and that's precisely why the epistological question, "How do we know what we think we know scientifically?" is so important. According to the world view of many, many scientists, what is "real" is only what is physically measurable. All their scientific concepts and theories are derived from that assumption. That implies the use of the physical senses in the usual sense. George Solomon, who coined the term, "Psychoneuroimmunology " and who is one of the leading experts in that field, includes among our senses the immune system, because he claims that it's sensitive to things that the other senses are not. Others would go still further and say there are whole realms— levels of consciousness, spirit and what have you—which have not been included in traditional science but which are real in the sense that they produce real effects. Since we apprehend these realms with the deep mind or the deep intuition and not the usual five senses of taste, touch, smell, sight and hearing, they are not physical in the usual sense. So the epistomological question about the "rules of evidence," asks, "Beyond the five senses, how much are you willing to include as being a legitimate organ of perception?"

In fact, what is really at issue is a total world view and the beliefs we hold at unconscious levels. Every one of us resists the change of our own internalized assumptions. We're being called on to answer the deeper questions, like "What is the nature of reality?"

Is it the same as conventional science has been saying? Or is it more like the perennial wisdom found in all the great spiritual traditions, in which the material world is only one end of the spectrum or continuum, with spirit at the other end? Where the human being is potentially capable of exploring the whole.

DiCarlo—What *does* conventional science tell us is the nature of reality?

Harman—Well, according to science, about 15 billion years or so ago, there was a big bang and the universe began to evolve. This involved the evolution of stars and the planets and then elementary life forms on at least one of those planets. This all happened accidentally; that is, things were behaving according to scientific laws and coincidentally, certain chemical elements came together in such a way as to create the first elementary life forms. Then, with other coincidences of random happenings and natural selection, we finally get this evolution up to the present human being with this very complex network of neuronal cells in our crania and out of that, we get something that we call consciousness or mind or spirit. Then, from this basic story, come other conclusions: you are your DNA; you are whatever was given to you genetically. That's the essential "you." And of course, everything that has ever been said about religion and spirituality now has to be reexamined in the light of this dominant story, which we all accept as true, because we were all taught it in school. We know the authority of modern science, especially now with quantum physics and chaos theory, and it looks as though it's on the edge of really explaining everything. This dominant myth infuses our education system, it infuses our health care system, it infuses our legal justice system—every institution in society.

So, what if it were wrong? It would affect everything. Now that's a pretty bold statement—and remember that I was trained as a scientist. I have a lot of respect for science in terms of what it does. But what we've done, in modern society, is to take this scientific world view, which was really aimed at prediction, and control, and creating technologies, and we've given it so much prestige and power that we put it in the position of a world view by which we live our lives by, guide our societies, and shape our powerful institutions. That's where it gets to be misleading. I could quibble and make it sound a little bit better if I just said "incomplete" or a "little bit off," but I don't want to say that. I want us to think seriously about the possibility that within the scientific world view, there is a fundamental error and that's important for ordinary citizens to recognize.

If what I really am is a collection of physical and chemical processes, modulated by some program in the DNA—if that's the essential nature of my being—then it follows that when those processes stop, when I come to the point of physical death, then I am no more. All the meanings and purposes I thought I stood for, are no more. There's little wonder that we then tend to fear death and have all sorts of other fears that link to the fear of death, or the fear of nonexistence. If you really look carefully, you will see that our whole education system teaches us—among other things—the fear of death. So imagine how much of a difference it would make if somehow, culturally, we came to conclude that death is a transition to something else—not to be feared—and that means that most of the other fears in our lives really have no basis either.

Well, there's lots of evidence to suggest that that's a pretty credible point of view. For example, a lot of people have out-of-body experiences. Now, I don't mean a lot in the terms of tens, or dozens, or hundreds—I mean tens of millions of people in this society have had out-of-body experiences. You can take a poll in any group and you will find a pretty good sampling. What that means is that they've had the experience—and it's very real. It's the difference between dreaming and being awake. This one experience has been known to change the lives of many people simply because if you have once experienced yourself as not totally identified with your physical body, then there are lots of implications of that in terms of asking the fundamental question, "Who am I?"

Science for three and a half centuries has been built on the premise that consciousness as a causal factor does not have to be included. Now nobody has every lived their lives on the basis of such a contrary premise. Nobody has ever said, "I'm going to live my life as though my consciousness—my mind—weren't capable of making decisions, weren't capable of making choices, weren't capable of taking action." Science is exquisite for getting a particular kind of knowledge—the kind of knowledge that you need if your main purpose in life is to generate new technologies, or manipulate the physical environment. But the idea that consciousness might be causal in any sense has been left out.

DiCarlo—As you have mentioned, intuition has been regarded by some individuals as an organ of perception that augments our analytical, reasoning mind. Isn't intuition unreliable?

Harman—Everything is unreliable, especially your physical senses. Of course intuition is unreliable—it's as unreliable as your eyesight. You can be fooled by optical illusions and you can be fooled by listening to something you thought was your deep intuition and it turned out to be your internalized mother or something else. And there are ways of checking. We don't believe everything we see, or think we see. We check it in various ways. Similarly, you don't believe everything that is perceived as some sort of inner vision or inner voice. You apply appropriate tests. And in that sense, intuition can be extremely reliable, but it's not necessarily so. Especially if you haven't been using it much, and all of a sudden you hear some inner voice speaking to you that may come from another source.

DiCarlo—Has intuition played a significant role in your work?

Harman—Oh, it's been absolutely central. I think that's probably true of leaders in almost any field although they don't always say so.

DiCarlo— In your writing you mention that the terms "intuition" and "creativity" are code words. Could you explain what you mean by that?

Harman—During a time like this, where emotional and intellectual reactions are part of the picture, you find people using terms that are acceptable in order to talk about things that are really not acceptable. Let me give you an example. The early Christians used the fish symbol as a way of testing the response of another person to see if it was safe to keep on talking. They would draw a little fish symbol in the sand and if the other person responded appropriately they would say, "Alright, here's a brother so we can talk honestly."

I think people are using words like consciousness, creativity and intuition, in very much the same way. Even to a certain extent the term "energy medicine." Some people are deliberately using that to talk about other kinds of energy that the physicist would not recognize as energy at all. So in that sense, it seems to me they are code words. Words that you carefully choose to communicate with those who can hear and still stay out of trouble.

DiCarlo—In your view, what is the essence of the new world view? How does that contrast with the average person's view of "The way things are?"

Harman—Well, in modern society, we've all been pretty well-schooled in a world view in which material goals and the insights of physics, the closest thing to ultimate reality we know, have both been considered to be quite important. It's true that we have had a lot of religious influences, but let's limit ourselves to what is put across in the public schools. Let's say that represents the world view of this society and it's built upon a very mechanistic and materialistic foundation.

Onto that platform we have built an economy with a lot of assumptions which relate to that materialistic world view. We convince ourselves that the economy won't even work unless we are being good consumers and gathering all the goodies we can.

The world view that's emerging—and I think it's sort of foolish trying to describe it since it's still emerging—but at the most fundamental level, it places the cause of things not out in the material world at all, but at non-measurable, spiritual levels. Therefore, the source of meaning and the source of values is out in that spiritual realm, and it's precisely in that realm that our official science doesn't know anything and can't know anything. Nevertheless, it turns out to be the most important area of our experience to know about.

So at one level, the emerging world view is almost upside down, when you compare it to the world view of positivistic science. One of the big shifts—it's obvious to everybody—is the shift from separateness as a way to understand things, to the concept of everything being connected to everything else. We really have to think of things in ecological terms, as whole systems. That's part of what the feminist movement is all about. Certainly a big part of the ecological movement is concerned with that. Even the new spirituality, and so on.

Then another shift is from authority being externally "out there"— whether it's the Pope, or the Encyclopedia Britannica or the white gowned scientist—to much more reliance on inner authority, inner knowing. At a still deeper level, the cause of the things that happen to me is not "out there" somewhere. In some very, very deep sense, the cause is inner and subjective.

That's a very profound shift. It's not obvious to a lot of people who are partly in the new paradigm that it goes as deep as that, but as nearly as I can read the signs of the last 30 years, that seems to be the direction we're headed. That is the direction of the perennial wisdom, so it's been around for awhile. Maybe it's not too surprising that we should be heading there.

DiCarlo—For many years, you were a futurist for Stanford Research International. In your view, what are some of the other major trends impacting us at this time, and what do you suppose the future has in store for us?

Harman—In terms of the new paradigm, *nothing* is impacting us. It's all coming from within. But in the more practical terms in which you meant the question, I think we really have two fundamental problems. One is ecological sustainability. And the other involves the coherence of our society in view of the tremendously powerful alienating forces that are coming about. This sense of alienation is very much related to the increasing rich/poor gap, and the increasing awareness on the part of the poor that this gap is not an accident.

The combination of those two is going to require a total redefinition of society and the social contract. Most people aren't ready to do that.

DiCarlo—All that we have been discussing is revolutionary in its implications. How would you respond to the individual who says that this new paradigm talk is utter nonsense?

Harman—Well, some of it is! Some of the more sensational aspects of the New Age are partly passing fads. The spiritual traditions have been fairly clear on this issue. As you go along the inward path, you are going to find a lot of temptations to explore. There are those who get involved in psychic phenomena, or get totally fascinated with one thing or another that somehow relates to all of this. Those are really digressions from the main task of discovering what Alan Watts called the Supreme identity—your own oneness with the Oneness.

So some of the New Age stuff is probably that. Some of it is becoming commercialized so it's pretty well corrupted. But underlying all of that, is this powerful current of cultural change, and that seems to be, in a historical sense, both new and necessary. It's wholesome. And in a certain sense, it's a wedding of the inward looking of the Middle Ages to the excessive outward looking of the modern era. It's more of a balancing of masculine and feminine, inner and outer. Material and spiritual.

In fact, if there's any one thing that characterizes the emerging paradigm, I think maybe it is this concept of balance; that reality cannot be viewed in terms of black and white or good and evil.

Dr. Beverly Rubik

Dr. Beverly Rubik, a trained biophysicist, is the Director of the Center For Frontier Sciences of Temple University in Philadelphia, Pennsylvania. Established in 1987 by an administrative team which included the university's president, the provost and a few members of the board, the Center boasts a worldwide network of affiliates: medical doctors, psychologists, scholars and scientists. Through their participation, the center has been able to actively explore the frontier sciences, complementary medicine, the relationship of mind and matter and geobiology.

DiCarlo—In starting any kind of enterprise that challenges the status quo, you'd expect to encounter resistance. In your position as Director of Temple University's Center for Frontier Sciences, I'm sure you've had your share. Are you finding that there is more acceptance now towards what you are doing than, say, 5 years ago?

Rubik—I would say there is the usual benign neglect that's typical among academics. You know, scientists are trained specialists in some very narrow aspect of reality and they really do not know much beyond that. What's more, they don't care. The system doesn't encourage them to think in broader terms. In fact, through promotions and tenure, the system rewards focused thinking and only mainstream perspectives.

In the past, I brought very distinguished scientists in to speak. To get people interested and involved, I held faculty lunches. As it turned out, we did get faculty members to attend, but it appeared that their main interest was to simply pick the brains of my visitors with questions that related to their own narrow area of research. I thought that was a reprehensible misuse of our visitors' time, so I stopped having the luncheon meetings.

Keep in mind, this is your average state university. Faculty at other universities would have likely responded in the same way.

DiCarlo—What are the main areas of interest of the Center?

Rubik—There are three. First is the area of consciousness studies, that is, the interactions of the mind—through intention, will and beliefs—and the body and beyond to the larger sphere of the material world. The second area is complementary medicine or alternative medicine—particularly "energy" medicine. The third area is bioelectromagnetics, the interrelationship between living systems and electric and magnetic fields. Those three areas were selected because they are all testable. It's not like the study of UFO's where the evidence takes the form of people's subjective experiences. We wanted to study areas in which we could collect hard physical evidence. There has been a certain amount of scholarly inquiry into these areas, and the anomalies, or events that cannot be explained by our conventional, scientific understanding of the world, keep piling up. Ultimately, these will lead us to a new world vision.

The mechanical vision of the universe has been useful, but I think it's increasingly been one of the sources of our abuse of nature. We don't really assist nature. We try to compete with nature or manipulate it and in so doing, we often create imbalances. Consciousness, field interactions and energy medicine are the softer aspects or the feminine side of nature that have not really been addressed by science.

DiCarlo—Why have these areas been neglected?

Rubik—I think the system selects people who are very much like their prospective mentors—they have similar training backgrounds and look at things in much the same way. My way of looking at things was often in contrast to some of my former teachers.

DiCarlo—As you mentioned, you have been successful in sponsoring some prominent, leading-edge scientists to speak about topics that are not typically considered in mainstream science. Of all the people that have presented over the past few years, who has impressed you the most?

Rubik—That's hard to say. There's certainly been a number of very good talks. I think the presentation by the great physicist David Bohm was very profound. He gave an overview of his idea of information as the bridge between mind and matter. Bohm's idea of information is so very different from the materialistic view of information used in the computer sciences. In Bohm's view, information is something that's really not physical. That's a view I share. Information is something which has meaning and is communicated. My voice is the carrier of the words, and the actual words contain the meaning which is intangible. To state that information is the bridge between the mind and the material realm is a very rich way of thinking because all entities in the universe have information. They have something to tell us. But in order to get that information, we have to ask new questions. When we do, the answers that follow will reveal new insights. So I really thought that Bohm's talk about the notion of "active information"— that's the term he uses—was quite an eye opener. It's a very different way of thinking about information.

DiCarlo—Have there been any other visitors whose work has impressed you?

Rubik—I think the experimental work of Robert Jahn and Brenda Dunn at the Princeton Engineering Anomalies Research Laboratory is certainly important. They have shown that people can skew the numbers on a random number generator towards higher or lower values by simply wishing them to be high or low, respectively. It's one of those exceptions to the traditional scientific world view about "the way things are" that we simply can't explain using the old framework. Their data is a real challenge to the prevailing paradigm. They have shown that mental intention can interact with random physical systems whether they are mechanical, electronic, or radioactive. It's fascinating work, and all of the data pooled together shows high statistical significance. Although their 15 years worth of work is extremely solid—it is so solid that no one can contest it anymore—it has certainly not changed the view of the mainstream. Unfortunately, it has not gained them any respect at Princeton University either.

DiCarlo—15 years! I am surprised they've been able to get research funding for such a long time...

Rubik—I believe they have had funding from the aerospace industry. Robert Jahn is such a distinguished aerospace engineer that he's been an ongoing consultant to NASA. But for most researchers, obtaining adequate funding for frontier type research is an extraordinary problem.

DiCarlo—Why is there such resistance to accepting the results of such studies? Aren't these researchers unveiling aspects of the universe and expanding our understanding of reality?

Rubik—Originally I thought the lack of acceptance was due to the fact that the data was scanty or people didn't know about it. Most of these studies are not published in the mainstream journals, so it's hardly accessible to the traditional scientific community. But I sense that something much deeper is at play here because I have been bringing this data to the attention of the mainstream in meetings at Temple and elsewhere in the world for 6 years now. So it's not simply a matter of being uninformed.

I really think it's about the scientific world view—the conventional, materialistic reductionistic world view. That's really what is being challenged. Keep in mind it is the scientists themselves who form the world view. Any challenge to the world view is actually a direct assault on them—on who they are—so it becomes a highly emotional, irrational thing. I have seen it happen a lot. It's not simply about some lofty ideas. This challenges the essence of who people are in this culture. So the real work involves planting a seed in their minds that there is something more to themselves and reality than they had previously thought. That takes time.

DiCarlo—Do any specific examples come to mind?

Rubik—I remember planting such a seed 10 or 15 years ago when I was in California. I was talking to a scientist about my interests and my work and I could see he was very uncomfortable with the topics. He dismissed what I was saying. Twelve years later I spotted him at a meeting. He came up to me and asked me whether I remembered him. "Yes, I of course I remember you," I said. "I'm surprised to see you here." "I came here, he said, "because I saw your name in the program."

"Well," I responded, "twelve years ago you weren't interested in these things." And he said, "I am now, thanks to you." So, things happen. You plant a seed in people and it settles down into some deep substratum of the mind. Over time, it starts to grow and suddenly it becomes conscious and they're interested in these things many years later as they themselves have changed in response to these new ideas.

The thing about a paradigm shift—and Thomas Kuhn talked about it at length—is that it's not something that's just an intellectual change of mind. It's a deep conversion experience. It's more like a religious shift inside a person. So this work of mediating between paradigms and bringing data to the attention of others and hoping that they will change their minds is very slow work. It doesn't happen overnight.

The younger generation of scientists, who are more open minded, who do not have a vested interest in the dogma, and who are able to appreciate the importance of the new world view will, of course, more easily embrace these ideas. Ultimately, these younger scientists will replace those who are older and that's how world views will shift. Niels Bohr wrote, "Science advances funeral by funeral."

DiCarlo—You've mentioned the difficulty a scientist on the leading-edge may have obtaining research funds. What are some of the other penalties facing scientists who choose to do paradigm-busting work?

Rubik—There are quite a lot of extraordinary things. In essence, nothing is new. Scientists who do this kind of research go the route of Galileo and Copernicus— they are excommunicated from the flock. In his day, Galileo was considered a heretic by the Church. Isn't it strange that it was only a few years ago that the Pope, while sitting in Rome, proclaimed that Galileo was finally "OK." Absolved, 300 years later.

It was on the news. Galileo was regarded as a heretic and excommunicated. Copernicus was excommunicated. These people defied the Church's view of the earth being at the center of the universe. They saw new evidence: Galileo saw moons moving around Jupiter, but his contemporaries refused to look through his telescope.

Even though we don't have the Catholic Church over our heads anymore, we have the "Church of Science," which is almost like the Catholic Church, you know. Those who dare to challenge the dogmas of the Church of Science find themselves essentially excommunicated. They are cutoff from their peers. Isolated. Their funding is removed. In fact, those very words "excommunication" were used to described Jacques Beuveniste, a French scientist who six years ago published a paper in the distinguished journal *Nature,* showing that very dilute solutions—so dilute that there should be no molecules of any effective substance—could produce real biochemical effects on blood cells. Beuveniste has been subtly silenced by the scientific community. Scientists who are treated this way find that they can no longer get grants. This means they will lose their graduate assistants, the "arms of the scientist" who carry out the laboratory research. Furthermore, they are not allowed to publish in the peer-reviewed, mainstream journals that most scientists make the time to read.

There is another example involving a very distinguished American scientist, Linus Pauling. Pauling was a double Nobel laureate with a Nobel prize in chemistry as well as in peace. He proposed that Vitamin C in high doses might help prevent the common cold and might also extend the lives of cancer patients, giving them quality time. Because of this, he was unable to publish in the proceedings of the National Academy of Science—despite the fact that he was a member of the Academy. Those in power made specific rules to keep him from expressing his views, considered dangerous to young minds.

People with points of view that conflict with the paradigm find their research papers have been rejected based upon unreasonable logic such as, "lack of readership interest." But, it's really an unfair way of censoring the work without giving it peer review. There is no real peer review when you're challenging the traditional world view. There are a lot of underhanded ways of dealing with people who have threatening points of view.

DiCarlo—Well, to read Thomas Kuhn's account of paradigm change is one thing, but to see it actually playing itself out, right here and right now, makes me wonder if we've benefitted in any way from his insights. We keep repeating the same mistakes.

Rubik—The sad thing is that most American scientists have not studied the history or philosophy of science. It's not part of the curriculum. You get a Doctorate in the Philosophy of Science and you've never had a single philosophy of science course! That's very peculiar, isn't it, but that's how most universities are. They simply produce trained technicians, able to conduct experiments that they then analyze using statistics. When I enrolled in a philosophy of science graduate course at the University of California at Berkeley over 20 years ago, I was laughed at by my superiors. They said, "Why are you wasting your time taking these classes?" I was dismissed as a kook.

DiCarlo—Given everything you said, do you think that the inevitable changes that will take place in the scientific community will come from the outside rather than the inside?

Rubik—Well, Robert Becker is an example of change coming from the outside-in. Twenty years go Becker was doing research on electromagnetic fields and the regeneration of amputated limbs on animals. As a result of his work, which showed profound biological effects from weak electromagnetic fields, he became concerned about the possible health risks associated with people who live next to high voltage power lines. He found it very difficult to get money from the government to study this and the military had silenced a lot of his reports. So he wrote several popular books on the subject that activated and aroused the general public. People began openly expressing their concerns about the increased risk of cancer to their congressmen, and research monies became available soon thereafter. When consumer groups start clamoring and making noise, then change happens. I think that's a good strategy for making a paradigm shift today, whether it's in medicine or in new energy technology. The scientific community is much more conservative and hard to shake. I didn't use to believe this, by the way, but I do now.

DiCarlo—You have acknowledged that some of the ideas of alternative medicine challenge the very foundations of science. What are some of those ideas?

Rubik—For example, issues of the spirit. A human being may or may not be a spiritual believer or have some spiritual life. That could very much play a part in his or her healing response. Even one's belief about death is not taken into account by conventional medicine. Moreover, the realms of spirit are not addressed by science. That's the 300 year old debate which dates back to Galileo. The rift between science and spirit remains to this day.

Another example is consciousness. The role of the health care provider has been that of the technician administering the techniques for the patient to get well. It would be much more powerful if the consciousness of the practitioner and the patient were aligned in a kind of partnership. In alternative medicines, there is often a much closer relationship between the patient and the practitioner. This may help facilitate the healing response. Conventional science does not pay attention to issues of consciousness because it doesn't believe consciousness can have any active consequences in physical reality, which of course would include physical health and healing.

If we are going to take issues of spirit and consciousness into account in order to study the full efficacy of alternative medicine, then how do we do it using a science in which they have no importance? Furthermore, there is no scientific foundation at all on which to study the nonmaterial realm.

Before we do all of these experiments we need to bring this up front and discuss it. Ethnomedicines that are non-Western have very different assumptions underlying them which do not fit in with Western scientific assumptions. For example, in Chinese medicine, the mind and body are one. There are serious philosophical discrepancies between Western science and these different ethnomedical systems.

Western science is not a universal system of truth testing. It really is bound by its own cultural context, its own system of values and its own hidden assumptions. We need to extend science so that we can accommodate other ethnomedicine systems in their fullness in order to study them. We need to recognize that these are really complete systems on their own, with different assumptions. If we try to test them, we need to give full respect to their depth and their differences.

DiCarlo—I see what you mean. It has always struck me as odd that when Western science studies something like acupuncture, let's say, we try to explain its effects in terms of neurotransmitters and bodily produced chemicals, which fall within the realm of traditional science— chemistry and biology. As you mentioned, in Eastern culture there's a whole different explanation as to why acupuncture might work.

Rubik—That's exactly right. I was asked once to give a lecture to American Academy of Medical Acupuncture on that very topic. In the talk I stated, "Who are we to think that a 300 year old system of thinking is vastly superior to a 4,000 year old way of practicing medicine and thinking about the body? Who are we to have such arrogance?" I don't see one-to-one correspondences between Western science and Chinese philosophy. We find, for example, that when acupuncture needles are inserted to diminish pain, natural painkilling endorphins which have been produced by the body can be found at the site of the needles, in the spinal cord and even in the brain. But that doesn't mean that all of the effects of acupuncture are explainable in terms of ordinary Western scientific concepts. Maybe in the long run they will be, but certainly not now. We have no way of explaining non-local interconnectedness of the body; why for example stimulating the crown of the head is helpful in treating hemorrhoids. Western science has no explanation at all, and we shouldn't fool ourselves into believing that we do.

DiCarlo—These Eastern traditions often times speak in terms of fields of energy. Do you think that's a metaphor or do you think there is an element of truth to that?

Rubik—I think there's an element of reality to that. You can experience that if you do some Qi Gong or T'ai Chi exercises. For example, if you move your hands slowly together, then apart for about 5 minutes, you will feel a ball of energy between them. It's like bringing two North poles of a magnet together and feeling the resistance. Everybody experiences that, yet the Westerner will say, "Am I imagining this, or is it really in my body?" And that's a question only a Westerner would ask because in the East they don't distinguish between your mind and your body. Right away, we slip into our Cartesian duality and try to explain it, "Well, it's just a mental thing. It's not real."

But actually, I think there are some parallels between, let's say, the physical fields that we know in physics and acupuncture. One of the things about acupuncture points is that they conduct electricity more than the surrounding tissues. That's how people who are not good at acupuncture find the points. They have what is called a point finder, an electrical device that they move around until they find a place of low resistance or high electrical conductivity, and that's where they insert the needle. There's no way of simply looking at the body and knowing. Of course, the real master of acupuncture in China can feel the energy and its blocks and knows where to put the needle. They don't have to use a point finder. So it seems that there is some relation between electromagnetic fields and acupuncture but the exact nature of that relationship is not well understood yet.

DiCarlo—Has there been any good scientific work done to demonstrate the existence of the human energy field?

Rubik—I'm intrigued by some work done in Germany. In fact, I've gone over there to work with Dr. Fritz-Albert Popp. This involves extremely low level light that the body and all organisms emit. Some might call it an "aura." However, I don't know if it's the same aura that people who are psychic claim to see since this is a real, physically measurable energy. Though it's visible light, it's not something that you can see easily with the naked eye. Popp uses very sensitive detectors that can count the photons, the particles of light coming out of the body. I think that this may be one of the manifestations of the energy dynamics of life. For example, in the Popp laboratory, they have demonstrated that to a large extent, the light is coherent like a laser. That means that the light probably has a capacity for carrying information, unlike incoherent light. If that's the case, it's probably not some junk radiation, which is the mainstream opinion. I think that the light, if it's coherent, may be involved in both an internal communication system as well as an external one that conveys signals between living things.

It's interesting that in studying the cancer tissues of patients, they have found losses of coherence in the light. Perhaps the light has lost informational value and cannot communicate with the other cells and that's why the tissues grow abnormally.

I did some experiments to explore communication between two cultures of single-celled algae that glow. When I disturbed one of them with a chemical stressor, it emitted a burst of light. Almost simultaneously, the second culture that was in a separate container emitted light too. You could see it with your eyes. It was almost as if it was communicating with the first culture. After doing experiments like that for a month, I am intrigued that there is something significant happening.

I think the idea of this biophoton field is just an indicator of some deeper field in the organism. When an organism dies, it gives up a burst of light. There have also been a lot of interesting findings by German and Japanese researchers that would seem to echo some of the old Hindu ideas about the chakras, or energy centers. Researchers have discovered, for example, that the areas near the forehead, throat and heart have increased photon emission compared to non-chakra regions of the body.

So there's been a number of research laboratories documenting that there are energy dynamics associated with the body which seem to support the wisdom of ancient cultures. To me, this convergence of the new information from frontier science and old perennial wisdom is fascinating.

DiCarlo—You have mentioned that there are some scientists who are arrogant and perhaps closed minded. What do you feel are the essential qualities and characteristics that make for a good scientist?

Rubik—I think it is very important to neither be a believer nor a disbeliever. It's a very narrow line to stand on, but I think the best position to be with respect to old data and new data—the mainstream thinking and the frontier thinking—is to stand on the fine line between them. This is the position of the nonbeliever who is able to maintain an open mind. I want to ask as many questions as possible, questions which challenge all sides—mainstream, frontier and even fringe ideas. Unfortunately, that's not a popular place to be. When I put myself in that place and go into the mainstream, they often accuse me of being too frontier. When I go to the frontier science meetings and challenge them with questions, they accuse me of being too mainstream. But it's really the best place to be because you don't stop asking questions. Science is driven by questions and we must never stop asking them. I feel where there is an open mind, there will always be a frontier. We can never say, "We now have it. This is the truth." This is even a problem with the frontier scientists—many have become true believers in a particular system. I've actually encountered violence while I attended the meetings of some groups. One individual threw a journal in my face in response to my question. He got so upset because he was a true believer. I began to understand he wasn't interested in bridging his work to the mainstream of everyday science. He, and others like him, want to be seen as mavericks bucking the system. That's definitely one type of frontier scientist.

Others would like to see their work merged into the mainstream, but they don't know how to do it. They often take an intense fighting posture in their writing and language. Instead of building bridges they actually cut themselves off. I see various different ways in which people destroy their chances of trying to bring their work into the mainstream, but usually it's because of an, "I'm right and you're wrong" attitude. Anytime we have that, I think we lose the art of being a scientist, which is never to believe in what you have found. Science is about being humble rather than being arrogant, because you know that what you have found is only part of an even bigger picture and that there are many, many more questions that will lead to an even greater unfolding of our knowledge. I believe that our science will never be complete since God's creation is deep and unfathomable.

Over a 100 years ago, one of the deans of Harvard University said our science is nearly complete. He went so far as to discourage students from going into science as he felt there was nothing more to do. That was before quantum and relativity theory! This notion has come up over and over again in history and the present is no different. We think it's almost finished now—we just need a unified field theory and that's it folks—we have everything. I think this is nonsense. We should be encouraging all of our students not to memorize and regurgitate scientific dogma, but to ask new questions. We should ask them to go inside themselves and rely on their own intuition and come up with their own personal questions to ask of nature. I think that nature is so complex and creatively evolving that if all of us were asking questions, we would never unfold all the available knowledge. But of course, that's more of a religious belief on my part. I see that nature is filled with divinity and being filled with divinity, it is infinitely complex. So we will never know it all, but we have to keep asking new questions.

DiCarlo—I'm wondering what role does the inner state of the scientist play in experimentation in scientific inquiry?

Rubik—I think that our inner state and our own beliefs and ideas— the things that make us unique—contribute to the specific questions we pose in science and determine the kinds of things we are going to see in the world. We are all looking for reflections of who we are. Perhaps that is all we can really "see." I'll give you an example. I know an Italian physicist who is also a Marxist. He believes that collective human behavior makes for good societies. When he looks at atoms and molecules he "sees" that they behave cooperatively. As a result, he asks questions relative to the cooperative behaviors of atoms and molecules.

DiCarlo—Is it conceivable that our beliefs could actually affect the outcomes of our scientific experiments?

Rubik—Yes. There are some very famous examples of that historically. I'll mention one for you. It's really one of the most outrageous. One of the most famous microphysicists in the history of science was the 17th Century Dutchman named Van Leeuwenhoek. He and his contemporaries were among the first few people to look through a microscope. When they looked at human sperm, they saw, inside the heads of the sperm, little babies. Now that's a wild idea. Today we no longer see little babies, but everybody saw little babies inside the sperm heads at this time because the world view for 2,000 years up to that time was that men planted little babies inside the bodies of women where they incubated until birth. Of course, they were going to see little babies in the sperm and everybody agreed it was so. They were even comparing the little babies, one from another under the microscope. I mean it's amazing that they all saw this simply because everybody believed it. It just shows you the power of collective expectation and belief, of intersubjective consensus, and how it can influence what a whole society perceives.

I wonder today what collective beliefs we share that force us to see data in a certain configuration because we cannot divorce ourselves from certain beliefs. What questions do we dare not pose about nature because they would so threaten our own beliefs? We should look deeply inside ourselves regarding these things, but it's very had to do. It's very hard to step outside of our own culture, with all its underlying assumptions, beliefs and expectations. That's why I think it's important for scientists to meditate and to enter the void of their own minds to be able to transcend some of their own shortcomings as individuals within their communities.

In the deepest sense, true scientists are really mystics and I don't mean that in the trivial sense, such as in gazing into a crystal ball to foretell the future. I mean that they are on the road to inner, self-awareness and development of their full human potential. Because of this, their questions about nature will change as they themselves change. The real act of being, let's say, a yogi of knowledge—which the scientist is—is to know thyself. I think that's one of the first premises. I think it's human nature that we project what's inside ourselves out into the cosmos. We project it externally and then we think it's objective, but really it's only a means of letting us see more of who we are inside, and working out our interior problems in the external world.

DiCarlo—Beverly, could you sum up what the frontier areas of science seem to be telling us?

Rubik—They tell us that there is a new paradigm emerging. It's not yet finished, and everybody has a slightly different version of what it looks like, but the paradigm is about the new views of life in the whole universe. The whole cosmos is a living, dynamical being. The universe is not just a clockwork mechanism—creativity has been built in. It's always changing, dynamic. It's evolving more complexity and more richness and beauty all of the time.

We're starting to realize that life isn't just something that happened once, on this tiny planet. We shouldn't think we're that special in the universe. The universe was destined to produce conscious life from its very inception. There's a lot of factors that entered into the evolution of the universe from the Big Bang onwards, and the factors were precisely coordinated so that we have an interesting, living universe. It could have expanded into a dust cloud, or collapsed back into a speck of dust, but the dynamics were so well balanced that it initially produced heavy elements, eventually planets and then life forms. At some point conscious life forms developed.

In my view, the universe actually had some rudimentary consciousness from its inception. To ask, "Is mind separate from matter," or "When did consciousness begin?" are moot questions. I really think that consciousness was always there and the evolution toward greater consciousness was purposefully built into the cosmic design. Now that becomes almost a religious issue, but that's my own position on it. In my view, the emerging paradigm is really telling us that life has a lot of subtle characteristics that involve numerous relationships. An organism is dynamic. It has energy properties that have yet to be considered. Life is linked in its many rhythms to the earth, biosphere, the sun, and even the cosmos at large. So the emerging paradigm considers life to be a deep principal of the universe. It's the primary principal. We exist in a nurturing, caring universe that wanted to develop life from its inception and that can sustain us. Nature is not something we should be fighting against and feeling alienated from but it's very much a part of who we are.

If we embrace that point of view—that we exist in a very nurturing place—I think we will experience a new renaissance.

Fred Alan Wolf

Fred Alan Wolf, formerly a professor of physics at San Diego State University, is widely regarded as one of the leading popular interpretors of quantum mechanics. In addition to contributing numerous scientific articles to various journals and magazines, he has lectured extensively around the world. Wolf is the author of several books, including, "Star Wave," "Parallel Universes," "Taking The Quantum Leap," and "The Dreaming Universe."

DiCarlo—Many of the people that I've interviewed have mentioned that the study of quantum physics has triggered what has been for them, a transformative journey. Why do you suppose that's true?

Wolf—Well, I imagine that change would occur at different levels depending on the depth of one's understanding. It's an argumentative issue; it's not clear that because of the knowledge of quantum physics one would necessarily have such a change since transformation really has to do with the belief structure of an individual human being.

The major impact of quantum physics probably began in the early 70's due to a book that my friends and I put out in 1974 called *Space, Time and Beyond*, which contained the statement "You create your own reality." Since then, some people have taken it to mean far more than what we were implying. Some didn't believe it. Those who understood us experienced a shift of consciousness. We were basically saying this: in observing reality, an observer is creating mental reality, and that mental reality is affecting the "out there" physical reality, however, in a very subtle way. That "out there" reality really doesn't exist independently of such an observational act. Many people still don't believe that; they believe that there is an "out there world" which is really independent of any kind of observational power that they may bear upon the world.

They can confirm that by noticing that no matter how they try to make very large objects move by observation, nothing seems to happen. They conclude, therefore, that the act of observation has no effect. But, actually, what we were saying is that it applies everywhere. When it comes to very large objects, the effect is minuscule. But it is pretty important when it comes to very small objects. It's also important to consider what's going on inside the person's brain/mind boundary. At the level of sensory information, there is definitely a perceptive process going on which is largely defined by the expectations one brings to bear upon that world being seen. This could effect everything. This explains why the Buddhists see the world one way and Christians see it another way.

DiCarlo—There seems to be two interpretations regarding what the phrase "creating your own reality" means. One says that our consciousness affects our perception of reality—is the glass half empty or half full? Well, that depends upon the individual. Then there's the interpretation which says that through our consciousness, we actually and literally draw to us events, circumstances and people that together make up the fabric of our life experience.

Wolf—Well, you haven't gone far enough. There is even more. There's a third part and that is that the glass can be totally undefined as neither empty nor full and even if it has wine or water in it is defined by the observer. Let's say I hypnotize an audience of 1,000 people to believe that a glass filled with water is actually filled with wine. If I let everybody have a drink of it some of them will get drunk, some of them will get sick, some of them will get happier and louder. If I later say, by the way, that was a glass of water, nobody's going to believe me. So-called realists would say, "But Fred, you *really* had a glass of water!" And I'm saying, "What do you mean I "really" had a glass of water? Maybe I was wrong in the first place; maybe I really had a glass of wine and I was so confused by what I was doing that the 1,000 people in the audience were correct."

My point: there is no reality without a perception of reality. And there is no perception of reality without an observer of reality. An object is whatever the six senses* tells you it is. If you really get down to just what is "real" in terms of what is perceived, then we open up the door to the ultimate reality. But there is no such thing as an absolute, ultimate reality. There can't be because nobody could ever find it without perceiving it. And that perception will always be affected by what the person brings to bear on the act of perception. That is the observational aspect of quantum physics.

DiCarlo—Please explain.

Wolf—Quantum physics is an observational science. Its major premise is that instead of dealing with observables as objective qualities, it deals with observables as processes affected by operators which are driven by human motivations. Your observational acts drastically af-

---

*seeing, touching, tasting, hearing, smelling, and minding, using the Buddhist notion of sense.

fect the behavior of the objects which are the consequences of those operators. So for example, if in the physics of particles and fields, you decide to look at things wavy, they become wavy; if you look at things particle-ly, they become particle-ly.

DiCarlo—Aren't there different schools of interpretation when it comes to the role of consciousness in quantum physics?

Wolf—Yes. There are many, many schools. Basically, the interpretation espoused is based upon where the scientist/investigator is coming from.

DiCarlo—In other words, their world view?

Wolf—Yes. Absolutely! There are those who say, "God, I don't care what the data tells me. I know there's a real world out there. I just know it!" Those people are going to be very disturbed by subjective quantum physics and will therefore try to dismiss it. Or they'll say, "Well, the reason it looks subjective is because it's incomplete. We don't really understand it."

DiCarlo—Could you briefly discuss the quantum principle of uncertainty?

Wolf—In quantum physics the uncertainty principle says that any object is known by what one measures about it. The attributes of an object that are measured form what are called "conjugate pairs" that cannot be observed with total accuracy simultaneously. For example, energy and time are conjugate pairs. Position and momentum are conjugate pairs; angular momentum and angle are conjugate pairs. Suppose you take a ball and put it on a string and twirl it over your head. At any moment, you could identify where the ball is on the circular trajectory above your head. At the same time, because the ball is twirling with a certain speed and forming a perfect circle, you can determine exactly its angular momentum. In the classically perceived world, you have knowledge of where the object is at any moment and you know it's angular momentum.

But in the case of quantum objects—atoms and subatomic particles— those same measurements cannot be performed simultaneously. For example, the orbital position and the angular momentum of an electron whirling around the nucleus of an atom cannot be measured at the same time. You can identify position or you can identify momentum, but not the two together. There is an uncertainty associated with that. So the more you pin down one of the pairs of the conjugates with greater and greater accuracy, the less you are able to pin down the other of the conjugate variables. You know more about an object's attribute at the expense of knowing less about its conjugate attribute.

DiCarlo—Well, what would the implication of that be for the average person and how they live their life?

Wolf—Let's say you're caught in a particular pattern or fixation and you tend to observe things a certain way. What if you could observe things in a complementary way? In other words, what if you could be taught to look at things so that you elicit the conjugate of the normal operations of observation? You could alter your perceptions in a way which would produce very new and fresh insight. That would stimulate creativity.

In my lectures, I show people how they can look at an ordinary object and by altering their ideas about what they are looking at, they can make the object vanish right before their eyes. They do this with their minds and nothing else. In a sense they become both the magician and the spectator of the magic at the same time. There are many such optical tricks based on this or similar principles. The familiar illusion of the old hag and the young woman comes to mind. In fact, the basis of stage magic is simply that people become fooled because they are led down a path of altered perceptions. For example, an object goes from left to right, vanishes for a moment behind the performer and then is seen again. Therefore it must be the same object. But often it is not.

DiCarlo—OK. Some people have used books like Fritjof Capra's *Tao of Physics* to suggest that quantum physics has proven that reality is as the mystics of all ages have described it. In other words, modern physics leads us to a view of the world which is very similar to that held by mystics of all ages and traditions. Others look dimly upon that. Ken Wilber, for example, thinks that all quantum physicists have done is dug a little bit deeper into understanding the physical level of reality. The information gleaned tells us nothing whatsoever about the higher levels glimpsed by the mystics.

Wolf—Well, Ken Wilber is a brilliant man, but based on what you've just told me, he hasn't gone deep enough with his understanding of quantum physics. From my understanding, the parallels between Buddhist theology and quantum physics are striking. Just striking.

DiCarlo—I think what Wilber keeps coming back to is that quantum physicists are describing one level of reality—the physical—and there are other dimensional levels which cannot be described adequately from a physical frame of reference.

Wolf—Well, that's debatable. There is a certain mystical insight that says, "As above, so below."

It's clear to me that reality is really not as solid and firm as it is and that the reality is fundamentally spiritual. I get this insight from understanding quantum physics and the writings of the spiritual Masters. To say that the path of knowledge and of the mind is not a path to God is foolish.

DiCarlo—So quantum physics and mysticism might be two different approaches to the same underlying reality?

Wolf—Absolutely. If one can get mystical insight and reach God through an understanding of the principles of quantum physics, so be it.

DiCarlo—Why do you suppose that many physicists have not only been scientists but philosophers and mystics as well? David Bohm, for example was drawn to the teachings of Krishnamurti.

Wolf—Well, anybody that studies the mysteries of the Universe at any level of the game is bound to get to a spiritual insight. There's no way to escape it. Physicists particularly want to understand how things are. Now the danger is that some physicists are approaching this from a materialistic point of view, that God is over there and science is over here, and never the twain shall meet.

A good example of that is Stephen Hawking. He understands some aspects of general relativity very well, but his understanding of quantum mechanics is admittedly rather poor. Possibly for this reason, he sees no overlap. I believe however, the fact that he can't see the overlap is indicative of where he's coming from, not his knowledge base. He's limited by his material-based understanding of science. On the other hand, people like David Bohm, Werner Heisenberg or even Albert Einstein could clearly see some overlaps and were disturbed by their discoveries or were exalted by them. It really depends on the ground of being of the person.

DiCarlo—Now, in light of all that you have thought and written about over the years, would you say that quantum physics is essentially in agreement with what some have referred to as perennial philosophy?

Wolf—There is much in common, but perennial philosophy, I am afraid, can be defined in many different ways. Do we include Rudolph Steiner, who some would say is a perennial philosopher? I don't know.

DiCarlo—I'm posing the question from Aldus Huxley's point of view, where there are different strata/levels of being, residing in other non-physical universes.

Wolf—Well, there may very well be, but until I've experienced them, I would have to say, "Should I just believe you because you tell me that's true?" No. I'm not going to do that. I'm too much of a scientist. I want to know from my experience. I don't want to know from what I believe. Belief to me is the great inhibitor. Belief is what blinds people. Belief is what creates a lot of trouble for people and what people want from life is not to believe in things—they want to have an experience of life. To me that is more important than whether there's parallel universes with chocolate cake and parallel universes with God on the throne or parallel universes where you are having sex with every beautiful maiden every nanosecond.

As the Buddha in effect said, "Be here now, man!" This is where it's at.

DiCarlo—In closing, based upon your understanding of quantum physics, what would you say are the implications for the average person, in how they live their lives or how they manage their organizations?

Wolf—Well, there are several implications. In my workshops, I give people what I call, "The quantum rules of the Universe," or how to commit magic. One rule is: "Expect the unexpected." Be open for surprise.

The major implication is that I label as Rule 1) is that one cannot look at the world as being "out there," objective, separate and independent of you. The Universe is nothing more than the mind looking at itself. Consciousness is in everything. The division between "I" and "not I"— the separation—is not as clearly defined as one would think by our normal perceptions of ourselves as being bodies. So, therefore, if an observation occurs, it's really the Self, the big Self, or the soul, looking at itself. It makes little difference if I observe a tree, a rock or my image in a mirror. They're all me, in some instances recognizable and some not. At the present moment, I have little perception of myself as a tree or a rock, but have great perception of myself as a human being.

Rule 2: "Alter the way you look at events." For example, suppose you meet somebody and find yourself being fixated on a certain way of looking at that person. You may become aroused. You may become angered. Whatever your response, try to alter your perception of that person so that you see something that you weren't looking for before— something that may give you a different perspective on what it is you're seeing or what it is you're experiencing.

Then there are also certain rules about how to maintain things constant. With some people you want to just maintain the status quo and with others have things change. For example, you would probably treat your fellow workers the same way each day, but it would be stupid to treat your closest friends the same way, and even worse, to treat your spouse or lover that way. There are rules of novelty and rules of consistency.

There was one great speaker who used to be nervous about giving a public address and he couldn't figure out how to change that nervousness. One of the things that he finally did was imagine that everybody in the audience was naked except him. That got rid of his nervousness.

Another rule would be called "the rule of outcomes." Once you set in motion an initial event, which has not been done before, transitions may occur. Things may travel in unexpected directions. The implication: if you're going to incite an action, you've got to let it go. Don't try to force things into a predetermined direction. If you do, you're going to stifle the action. You can't control the position and the direction of motion of any thing you set in motion.

Finally, you have to recognize that what you think not only affects the world—it is the world. There is no world outside of your thought perceptions of that world. There is no way that you will ever, ever know that there is a world outside of your thought perceptions of the world. Therefore, accept that you create the world. There's no way to avoid that power. And whatever YOU are, is exactly the same "You" as there is in every other form of life that you see around you. When you say that you create the world, you're speaking for every living sentient thing.

Section 4

NEW VIEWS IN RELIGION

Perhaps in no other area is the friction between old and new world views as intense as in that of religion. Individual and group *beliefs* about human nature, God and the relationship between humanity and God, have historically been hotly contested issues which have led to war, persecution and incomprehensible brutality directed towards those with differing points of view.

As various polls suggest, public interest in spirituality is rising, while the numbers of people enrolled in traditional organized religions are dramatically declining. This paradox is due in part to the following:

- The recognized distinction between spirituality (the personal experience of a higher power) and religion characterized by theology, dogma, narrow interpretations of the scriptures (influenced by period, tradition and background) and material and political ambitions.

- The awareness that Western religions have focused exclusively upon God transcendent, residing outside of his creation, an Observer. Yet, God is also immanent—always noted by Eastern traditions—residing deep within the human heart. This is causing a synthesis of the two views, and the perception that God, greater than the created whole, is also present in every part.

In this section, ex-Dominican priest Matthew Fox shares his views on the Catholic tradition. Through his work, Fox has questioned the theological teachings of the church, the tendency towards non-inclusivity, and imposed ecclesiastical authority. He calls his new view "Creation Spirituality" and those in power have seen it as threatening heresy—a turning away from God—versus an example of boldly creative spiritual thinking, a liberating step forward in our relationship with the Divine. Fox's experience illustrates what can and does happen to individuals who dare to challenge the prevailing world view.

Matthew Fox

Matthew Fox is a religious scholar, popular speaker, innovative educator and former Dominican priest. He holds a doctorate in history and theology of spiritualities from the Institut Catholique de Paris, and is the director of the Institute in Culture and Creation Spirituality at Holy Names College in Oakland, California. He is the author of several books, including, "Creation Spirituality," and "The Coming of The Cosmic Christ." Through his work, he has introduced the teachings and insights of several of the mystics and saints of the Catholic church to thousands.

DiCarlo—So to begin, could you please elaborate upon the nature of "creation spirituality?"

Fox—Creation spirituality is the oldest tradition in the bible. It's the tradition of Jesus and of the medieval mystics: Orion mystics, Hildegard of Bingen, Thomas Aquinas, Francis of Assisi, Meister Eckhart, Julian of Norwich and Nicholas Cusa. It's a tradition that honors original blessing because it's non-anthropocentric. It encourages people to relate to all beings and to all of the Universe as a blessing—as something good. To celebrate that. Original sin ideology, on the other hand, is totally anthropocentric. It's about the human problem. But that's very late in the history of the Universe.

Creation spirituality also relates to science. It has always honored scientists as people who can tell us more about nature and, therefore, about the Creator. So Hildegarde of Bingen in the 12th Century said "all science comes from God," and Thomas Aquinas worked with Aristotle—the best scientist he could find in the 13th Century—bringing Aristotle forward into Christian theology and spirituality (even though he was a pagan). Nicholas Cusa was very much a scientist in the 15th Century. In fact, David Bohm, the contemporary physicist, said he owes more to Cousa than to Albert Einstein.

Creation spirituality is also the feminist tradition of the West; that is to say, it honors women's wisdom. The wisdom tradition of Israel in the Hebrew Bible is profoundly creation centered. It's about cosmology and about playing in the Universe and relating to all things. It's the tradition of the Song of Songs and the Psalms and other books of wisdom. For that reason, it's also very Christian because the first name given Jesus in the New Testament is "Lady Wisdom" or "Sophia."

So this tradition cares passionately about ecology and cosmology and about the mystical life in all of us—that we're all mystics because we are all born with the sense of wonder and awe. It is recovering this sense of praise for being here. By doing this, we can deal with human frailty and foibles and sin which, of course, are a reality. But you can't deal with it just by reiterating lists that decree more guilt. You have to show people a way out. And you show them the way out by demonstrating our divine capacities for creativity and compassion. So this tradition also celebrates the divine element in all things; that we are images of God; we are cosmic Christs. It's a classic Christian tradition—an idea that parallels the Buddhist notion that the Buddha nature is in all things.

DiCarlo—So creation spirituality presents us with a much more expansive playing field than traditional religion has offered?

Fox—Exactly. Yet it's really not about religion—it's about spirituality; it's about spiritual practice and it's about experiencing the joy of life and the grief of life; the creativity of life and the compassion of life.

DiCarlo—Now, many of the people that I have spoken with would make a distinction between religion and spirituality. I take it that you do the same.

Fox—Definitely. Bede Griffith, the Western monk who ran an ashram in India for over 50 years said that "if Christianity cannot recover its mystical tradition and teach it, it should just fold up and go out of business. Without that, it has nothing to offer." If religion cannot teach spirituality, it's a hollow business. I think that is becoming more and more evident. The irony is that Jesus himself was a mystic and many people in the Christian Church have declined to follow his lead. Some of the churches mystics have been canonized as Saints; others have been considered heretics.

It's too bad that we have to point out the distinction between religion and spirituality, but unfortunately, that's the reality.

DiCarlo—You've quoted Carl Jung as saying that the mystics represent a cross to the Church. Why do you suppose that has historically been true?

Fox—Yes, he says a cross to the Church, but he also adds that they represent the best that humanity has to offer.

Mystics celebrate experience—our experience of the divine. Religion often begins to institutionalize itself, bureaucratize itself. Then, the people who occupy the bureaucratic pigeonholes do not get rewarded for their mysticism, they get rewarded for keeping things in order and keeping things straight—orthodox supposedly. It's a pity because then the people running the organization are the least mystical of all. So in many ways it's an institutional problem—an organizational problem. It's also an ego problem. Not just the personal egos of the bureaucrats, but also a kind of ego of the institution—insofar as institutions take on their own shadow and their own egos and the quest for immortality. A refusal to let things go and let things die when it's time that they die, sets in. In one of the Gospels, Jesus taught that the seed has to die for something to be born. Often, people who latch on to institutions—especially religious ones—think that these things have to remain forever in the same familiar form.

So the real issue is the lack of faith (I should say a lack of trust) to allow things to be reborn. To let old forms die and allow new expressions to come forth. And to trust the spirit who touches all people and speaks to all people and makes mystics of all of us if we only allow the spirit to do so.

DiCarlo—If you look at the origins of certain words such as "Pope" for example, which is derived from the phrase "pontificus maximus" or supreme bridgemaker, you find clues to the main purpose and thrust of the Catholic religion, do you not?

Fox—Well, "pontificus maximus" comes from the Roman empire. That's a very telling phrase in itself. The Church took over the empire in the 4th Century and it took a lot of its trappings out of them. "Pope" actually means "Pappa" and that's a dangerous word because that feeds on any unresolved addiction of child to parent. I know there are analysts who claim that the number one addiction behind all addictions is the addiction of child to parent. This is why Catholicism so often, I'm sorry to say, falls into honoring fascism. It's feeding this addiction of child to parent instead of allowing people to leave the parental mode of relating and grow up.

DiCarlo—Well, do you think that the Catholic Church has really gone far astray from its mystical heritage?

Fox—It's a pity, but yes, of course it has. The kind of people that are today being expelled from the priesthood and the theologians who are being silenced are people who are standing up for justice. There's Leonardo Boff in Brazil, Eugene Drewermann in Germany and Bill Callahan here in the United States, who raised over 20 million dollars for the people of Central America. I myself have stood up for women, for gays and lesbians, for the ecology and for mysticism. The present Papacy has a very different agenda from that of Jesus Christ. This papacy, remember, was the only government in the world to recognize the military junta of Haiti when it was overthrew president Aristide.

Jesus did not spend all of his days talking about birth control, sex and homosexuals. In fact, he never talked about homosexuals. Since he went out of his way to befriend the unbefriended of society, we know that today, his position would similarly be to go out of his way to defend the unbefriended.

The fact that the Church is ignoring its own mystical tradition has already been discussed, but I was the first to get Hildegarde translated into English. As a result, we in effect rediscovered Hildegarde. We rediscovered Meister Eckhart. I did a major work on Aquinas as a mystic and I got booted from the Dominican Order in spite of this. So obviously, the Church is very threatened by its shadow side which is indeed the way it has treated the mystics, the way it has treated women, the way it has treated artists and scientists and gay and lesbian people. It's a pity. But, of course, as people would say in Latin America, there are two Churches—the Peoples' Church and the Pope's Church. Unfortunately—for not all the Church is retrograde—the Pope's church just happens to include those with ecclesial power. The present Papacy has taken a giant step backwards since Pope John the 23rd opened the windows in the 1960's.

DiCarlo—Can you tell me, what is the purpose of the Peoples' Church versus the Pope's Church?

Fox—Well, I think that the Pope's Church is trying to make order. Cardinal Ratzinger, the current inquisitor general who is the Vatican's number one spokesperson says, "I want a smaller Church." In a sense, that's exactly what they are getting. They are more interested in control than in spiritual experience.

I think that the Peoples' Church is interested in justice and celebration and that includes equal justice to women. It is also interested in spiritual experience. The Peoples' Church is not a corporation, it is the people themselves. They have to facilitate their experience for themselves and for their community. It's a community-based church; it's not about Vatican bureaucracies.

DiCarlo—What would you say are some of the more common beliefs and assumptions that are put forth—in this instance by the Catholic Church—that are counterproductive, if not erroneous in your view?

Fox—Well, certainly the position on birth control flies in the face of all morality. The human population is out of control. We are bringing down many, many species with us and in the same act, we are destroying our own nest. So I think that the issue of birth control is a very serious moral issue today because the human species is over populating the world. The Dali Lama spoke here a year ago at Berkley and he said, "You know, our tradition has been against birth control because we feel all life is precious. But now you look around," he said, "and you realize that human life, which is precious, is overwhelming all of the other life forms which are also precious." "So, he said, "we have to change our position on birth control." Well, that's just common sense. It's a moral position to take and it took courage to do it — all morality takes courage—but for this Pope and his "men" around him to just keep repeating the shibbeloths that birth control is a sin is itself sinful. It shows a paucity of trust. They don't have the ability to let go and change their rigid dogmas. So I say the Dali Lama gets my "Pope" vote.

DiCarlo—Are there any other beliefs and assumptions contained in creation spirituality that fly in the face of traditional wisdom, as it were?

Fox—Well, of course, putting original blessing ahead of original sin shakes up those people who are anthropocentric and want to begin religion with guilt or sin. That disturbs them. I have proven that original blessing is the tradition; original sin was not used until the Fourth Century A.D. It's not in the Bible. The Jewish people don't have it; Jesus never heard about it.

I think we have to honor the dignity and beauty of gay and lesbian people; they were made by God and we now know enough about evolution to know that a certain percentage, whatever it is—7 to 10% of the human species everywhere is gay or lesbian. So it obviously pleases God to accept and celebrate diversity, and it's not up to the Church to interfere with that diversity and make moral pronouncements about it. I think, of course, that the issues of women's rights in the Church, including women's ordination, are issues that this present Papacy would not agree with me on. Then there's the ecological issue, which is the number one moral issue of our time. It's far more basic than any other issue and has received very, very short shrift from the present Vatican. They are so preoccupied with sex that they don't get around to ecology, and, of course, they continue to ignore the possibilities of creative worship in liturgy because they are afraid of all creativity. So we are ignoring the possibilities of art for really awakening the people and telling the new creation stories from science. So there's a lot that this present Papacy ignores.

DiCarlo—Why do you suppose that organized religion has become so fixated on struggle, redemption and original sin as opposed to creation, love and joy?

Fox—Well, it's become seduced by the modern world which was anti-mystical. The anti-mysticism is not just in the Church, it's everywhere.

It's in our educational system, it's in our physics of the modern world (not today's, post-modern world) so the church was sucked into the world view, really, of the modern era. It's anthropocentrism and anti-mystical bias. Also, Saint Augustine, the fourth century theologian, has been given far, far too much attention in the Western Church. He's been given far more attention that Jesus in terms of teaching. He, who had invented the word "original sin," also split nature from grace. If you split nature from grace, then you have a shortage of grace. You also set nature up for ecological destruction. So I think that this cutting off of nature and grace is a great calamity in Western religion.

The creation mystics fought this. Meister Eckhart said, "nature is grace." Aquinas insisted that nature is the source of revelation, along with the Bible. But this has certainly not been the attitude of the current Papacy and I think John 23rd's thoughts are of a different ilk.

DiCarlo—Now, does the phrase found in the Bible "The Kingdom of God is within," hold any significance for you?

Fox—Well, I don't think that's a good translation. The Greek words mean that the "Kingdom of God is among you." I think that's a better translation. "Among" means both within and around us. It also means it is in the community. Surely it's the whole heart of Jesus' teaching and I think the most operative word in the whole sentence might be the word "is." Not that the kingdom "will be" at some future time or some future life or future place—it's already here. But we have to wake up to experience the kingdom and queendom of God in our midst and that's what Jesus' whole teaching is about. That's what all spiritual practice is about: waking up and realizing what's already here—the grace in which we are swimming on a daily basis.

DiCarlo—Some authors have suggested that the word "sin" means to be off the mark as opposed to an aggrievance or a breaking of the rules against God? What's your view on that?

Fox—I like Rabbi Hescel's definition of sin, that sin is a refusal of humanity to become who it is. This begs the question, "Who are we?" Well, we are the images of God. We have to stand up and be counted, so to speak. We have to take responsibility and rediscover our great dignity as human beings and as sons and daughters of God and as co-creators and as those responsible for compassion in the world. So it's a great challenge to be called images of God and when we fall short, that's a sin. So you might say that when we miss the mark of being the images that we are and that we can be, then we sin.

DiCarlo—A common criticism of Eastern Religious traditions, such as

Buddhism, is that there is no belief in a personal God. Does that concern you?

Fox—Well, I feel that too many Westerners have turned the idea of a personal God into a projection—into "theism." I think that's very dangerous. Theism is again part of the modern world view—God's out there some place with an oil can behind the machine Universe, ready to pop in to fix it. Then we project all over God and we reduce God to our size. I, myself, am not a theist—I am a "pan-entheist." Not a pantheist, but a pan-entheist which means "everything is in God and God is in everything." This is a mystical way of experiencing the divine and I think this is far more appropriate for our time. After all the word "environment," (and we are hopefully moving into an environmental consciousness) comes from the French word "environ." That means "around." So God is around us and through us and we have to wake up to experience that.

DiCarlo—Let's talk briefly about the soul. It seems that there is a paucity of information regarding the soul when you look towards traditional religion. "Yes, you have one," we are told, but there is no meaningful elaboration. It seems we're learning more about the soul from psychologists and doctors than ministers and priests. Why the gap?

Fox—Descartes, the founding philosopher and father of the modern world, reduces soul to our pineal gland. That's the one inch gland in our forehead. He took the soul away from our passions, away from our feelings of anger and love, away from our sexuality, of passion towards injustice—even our hearts. He pushed it to the top of our heads. But that's not the medieval teaching of soul. In fact, the medieval mystics taught that "soul is not in the body but the body is in the soul." So the soul is very large—it's as large as our thoughts and our passions and our desires and our hopes and our fears and our dreams. All this is soul. So it's not true, frankly, that our religious tradition has a paucity of soul. This happened with the modern era, but our medieval mystics have a tremendous imagery around soul and profound understanding of it.

Aquinas was a great elaborator on soul as have been all the mystics. I did a study once on 52 images of soul in Meister Eckhart and in Teresa of Avila. They have wonderful images of soul because they were exploring it. An example would be Teresa of Avila's image of the seven rooms in the castle—which she calls the parts of the soul. She explores in considerable depth each of these seven rooms in your soul and then she says, at the end of her book, "well, there are millions of such rooms in our souls, but most of our doors never get opened." So she had a lot to say about soul—much more than any psychologist today. So I don't agree that psychologists are that far ahead. They are doing something, but I think they also need a good dose of our mystical heritage to really explore the deep meaning of soul.

DiCarlo—Would you say, then, that one of the objectives of human development and human evolution is to get into contact with who we are on a soul level and to actually begin to live from that center?

Fox—Definitely. That is the mystical work and it should be the work of ritual and worship—the soul of the community—the microcosm in the macrocosm which awakens those connections. Soul is the sensitivity of our relationships and our passions and our powers and our ability to connect them to the greater powers of the Universe. This is all soul work. In that context, I certainly want to honor the practice of psychology as a way of helping people keep their souls together, but it was in this century that psychologist Otto Rank said that when religion lost the cosmos and society became neurotic, we had to invent psychology to deal with the neurosis. Psychology really deals with the mass neurosis which was born from the fact that we do not have a cosmology. The cosmos and the psyche ought to go together. They do in any healthy religion; they do in any healthy indigenous culture. Because we had no cosmology except a machine, we had to invent psychiatry to deal with the neurosis that was spreading.

However, now that science is becoming cosmological again, finding the mystery of the Universe—and scientists are becoming mystic as a result—now that this is happening, I think that frankly we will have fewer psychologists and more spiritual directors. And frankly, that's the case. A lot of psychologists are definitely taking up mystical practice and mystical teachings today. They are discovering our mystical tradition, as well they should. We all have to, but they're kind of on the front-lines because they are listening to peoples' dreams.

Meister Eckhart says that "the soul is where God works compassion." This means that if we are not yet instruments for compassion we do not yet have soul.

DiCarlo—Now, you have addressed the issue of spirituality in work and I am wondering what the connection might be?

Fox—Well, I distinguish between job and work. A job is something we do to make a living and to pay our bills, but work is the reason why we are here. It has to do with our heart and joy and all the mystics, East and West, write about this. The Tao Te Ching, the Chinese Scriptures say, "in work, do what you enjoy." The idea that there is a connection between joy and work is new to a lot of people because in the machine world and the machine universe of the Industrial Age, joy was not one of the great values to be esteemed. Obedience and efficiency, yes, but not joy. We need to bring the sense of spirituality and work together again which is something that I have learned from reading the mystics, East and West. It is a requisite for good living and it's also one reason I think that we have so much unemployment. We have been defining work in such a narrow fashion during the Industrial Age of factory work that we have missed the other aspects at work like heart work and art and healing and celebration and ritual; all of which are works in healthy communities. Native people spend at least half of their time celebrating and doing rituals. We don't and there is widespread violence in our culture. I'm very involved today in working with young people who are developing new forms for celebrating, even celebrating ancient liturgies using rap music, house music, techno music and dance—some of the forms that we have available today at the edge of our youth culture and our urban culture to rediscover celebration. That's very good, very needed work. Celebration is one way that people heal—it's the most fun way—and the cheapest too.

DiCarlo—Do you have any other advice on how a person might find this sense of vocation that allows for the blending of work and spirit?

Fox—Well, the practical test I give people is this: "What joy do you derive from your work" and "what joy do others derive as a result of your work?" I think those two questions take you into the heart of one's vocation. And if you can't come up with much, then that means that you have a job and not work. That's OK, but you should be looking for work as well. We need jobs, but I think the key is, how can others derive blessings from our work? Because that's what work really is; for human beings—it's a return of blessing from blessing. It's our thank you to the community for being here and that's why unemployment is so disastrous to the human soul. Unemployment creates despair and when there is despair, you have crime because you have self-hatred and you have violence. You have all the things that we're building prison after prison for in this country. I think a much cheaper and simpler solution would be to have a big debate on what work Gaia or the earth is really asking of us today. There's all kinds of work—new kinds of work—that we need to do on the human heart to bring about ecological and social justice in our time.

DiCarlo—Concluding question: Are you optimistic about the future?

Fox—I don't use the word "optimism" but I do use the word *hope*, and my biggest hope today comes from this community of young people who are working in Sheffield, England. They're coming here to the Bay Area to reinvent—to deconstruct and reconstruct—our liturgical tradition of the West, using multi-media rap and rave, etc. In other words, people who are discovering the importance of celebration. If humans could learn to celebrate "being" once again then perhaps we can learn to be reverential and grateful too. With that as our spiritual basis, we could reinvent our culture and, yes, that gives me hope. The new cosmology and the rediscovering of spirituality can be brought into all of our professions—all of our work worlds. When it does, that will bring the value issues to the forefront and all that gives me a lot of hope. Yes, I have hope.

Lester Brown of the World Watch Institute says that we have 16 years left to bring about the environmental revolution. If we don' t get it done in 16 years, we are on a dead end path. So I think these 16 years are really significant. They should be filled with both seriousness and fun. Joy, because that's how you change human beings. We transform each other that way. So given the fact that we've got a common deadline, there's really no sane reason for all of us not being involved in changing our ways on the planet. All that gives me hope.

Section 5

NEW VIEWS IN PHILOSOPHY

Philosophy—literally, the "love of wisdom"—owes its existence to the human power of self-reflection, a capability that distinguishes man from animal.

Philosophy relies on the ability to mentally distance oneself; to step back, to question. We employ reason to lay bare the most basic assumptions of our world views. Through our philosophies, we weave a story about the universe that helps us to make sense out of a chaotic world and satisfies the ever-questioning intellect.

Still, for many, to invest time asking the big philosophical questions, "Who am I," "What is the nature of reality?" or "What is the relationship of man to the Universe?" seems like a largely irrelevant pasttime. Yet, the maps that are derived from these questions unerringly guide us in all of life's arenas, from how we govern, to how we educate and raise our children, to how we act towards one another in the most casual and intimate of relationships.

Why do we ask? Certainly not to arrive at some final answers, as much as to stimulate and enlarge our concepts of the Universe in which we live. This can, in turn, open up new and exciting possibilities for exploration, enrich the mind, and reduce, as Bertrand Russell observed, "the dogmatic assurance which closes the mind against speculation." It keeps us intellectually fresh and "on our toes." Philosophy provides us with a useful map that helps move us towards what's ultimately "real."

Since the turn of the century, the map informing Western society as to what is "real" has been, for good or for bad, predominantly materialistic in flavor; that ultimately, reality is the world of material things. This philosophical map has deeply influenced how we keep score in economics and business, and is revealed in the humorous, though at the same time sadly to-the-heart-of-the-matter bumper sticker, "He who dies with the most toys wins." The accumulation of possessions distinguishes those who are successful and those who are not. It is a point of view that has spawned a vast consumer-driven—and hopelessly unsustainable— economy, deeply influenced by powerful, Madison Avenue advertising agencies.

Yet for an increasing number of people, the materialistic perspective has been played out to its logical conclusion and has failed to satisfy, sparking a search for insight into what are largely philosophical issues of meaning and value.

For some philosophers, such as Mark Woodhouse, the emerging world view is a variation of what has been called the perennial philosophy, "the dominant official philosophy of the larger part of civilized humankind throughout most of history," according to Alexander Lovejoy. The perennial philosophy can be thought of as that common core of wisdom found at the center of all the great religious traditions throughout the ages and across cultures. According to Aldous Huxley—who popularized the concept—it is characterized by the following: (1) The physical world of people, animals, trees, things and matter is an expression of a Divine reality, the source of all things. (2) Human beings can come to an apprehension of this Divine Ground of all being—not intellectually through reason and the mind—but experientially, by a direct intuition which joins object and subject, perceiver and that which is perceived. (3) Man possess a dual nature, an outer personality that is born in time and dies in time, and an inner spark of divinity, that is immortal, eternal and exists beyond the limitations of time and space. It is possible for a man to identify himself with the spirit, if he so desires which is of the same nature as the Divine Ground of all being. (4) Man's life on earth has only one purpose, to wake up from the slumbering sleep of the lower nature, of the outer personality and to recognize itself as being one with the source of all things, the Divine Ground.

Ken Wilber, who has been referred to as the Einstein of consciousness studies has remarked, "So overwhelmingly widespread is the perennial philosophy that it is either the single greatest intellectual error ever to appear in humankind's history or it is the single most accurate reflection of reality yet to appear."

Implicit in the perennial philosophy is the notion that the universe and its evolution is purposeful, and directed by divine intelligence which permeates all levels of existence. This world view clashes with the scientific world view, which sees life as more mechanical, happening via chance events and without intrinsic meaning or purpose.

Woodhouse calls his version of the perennial philosophy "energy monism." In it, he suggests there are many different but continuous levels or dimensions of reality which range from the most dense, most limiting and least conscious to the least dense, least limiting and most conscious—that the physical world we know so well is not the totality of existence.

Furthermore, there is no absolute barrier between dimensions. The great divide between spiritual and material worlds, and between science and religion, is more apparent than real.

Mark Woodhouse

Mark Woodhouse, PhD. is associate professor of philosophy at Georgia State University. Author of "World Views in Transition" and the widely used textbook, "A Preface to Philosophy," Woodhouse also serves on the editorial board of the journal of Near Death Studies.

DiCarlo—The study of philosophy conjures images of lofty, theoretical discussions regarding the nature of good and evil, man and God. That's the public perception perhaps. What's really going on with philosophers these days?

Woodhouse—Well, philosophy is something that you do as well as something that you study. There are some philosophers who are putting forth new arguments and revising old arguments. A colleague of mine is putting together a book on the ethics of physician-assisted suicide, and that has him embroiled. There are probably only two or three people in my department who do serious history of philosophy in the sense that they read and study Descarte, Hume and Hegel.

The study of philosophy provides an individual with the best critical training you can get anywhere. If you don't know what you want to major in, major in philosophy because not only will it open up a whole new domain to you, it will also give you the tools to analyze things. There's a lot of mindless opinion in the world, and philosophy gives a person the tools to uncover it, to deal with it, and dispose of it.

DiCarlo—Do any contemporary philosophers touch on issues of the soul and human spirit?

Woodhouse—Most philosophers—perhaps 80%—don't believe there is a soul. Some of them are sophisticated dualists who view brain states as being not exactly material and not exactly beyond material. To these people, theology is the province for such matters.

DiCarlo—But I thought Plato and Socrates talked at length about the soul?

Woodhouse—Plato more than Aristotle, but philosophy has a long history, and it has progressively become more and more materialistic.

DiCarlo—Well, throughout history there has emerged across cultures and ages what some have called the perennial philosophy? What exactly is it?

Woodhouse—Well, it's a broadly-based perspective that has a four or five thousand year tradition in the East and perhaps as long in the West. The perennial philosophy suggests that when you consider all the spiritual traditions throughout the ages which have been articulated in different languages, there is a core tendency, a common truth, that is evident. It has never died, it's always been kept alive in some way or another. It is making a comeback on the current scene. The perennial philosophy is associated with dimensional interpenetration, and seeing God in all things but not reducing God to being all things. The perennial philosophy contains the idea of levels of reality which differ by degree, rather than by absolute principle. The perennial philosophy is associated with the notion of reincarnation. It also takes paranormal abilities seriously. It sees personal spiritual growth as ultimately the reason why we're here. It gives us a big picture to assist with that.

If it turns out that there are extraterrestrials seeking to make contact with us, this would not surprise the perennialist. The perennialist already has an open view of the universe and of all the paradoxical possibilities in it. If there is anything that God loves to do, it's to create for the joy of creating. So to suppose that we're the only thing that could bring God pleasure to create is pretty shortsighted.

It doesn't say—and this is a widespread misconception—that all religions provide different paths to the same truth or that all religions are pretty much the same. All religions may compliment one another in different ways, but it's not as if they are all straight roads up the mountain of consciousness.

Those are some of the main ideas that come to mind about perennialism.

DiCarlo—If these ideas are central to most religions, why haven't more people heard about them?

Woodhouse—They have, but there's always been a special hitch. Christians have heard about heaven and they've heard about realms of outer darkness too, but there's a speck of untruth put on it in that you can't get there except with the addition of something else. A lot of what's come out in popular religions is a subverted and limited form of perennial teachings.

DiCarlo—Now you have developed a theory you call "Energy Monism" which I take it is a further refinement of the perennial philosophy?

Woodhouse—Yes, I teach half a dozen classes from graduate level to sophomore introduction and I discuss Energy Monism in a couple of those. I don't indoctrinate. I simply present the model as information.

We look at a variety of scientific studies, and we look at the pro's and con's—something every philosopher is trained to do. Skepticism is always encouraged. I have students who don't believe a bit of it and they make "A's" handily.

I do find that there is a thirst for this kind of material. Students are yearning to talk, and there are probably no more than 3 faculty members out of 1,000 who are conversant in these areas. Needless to say, my courses always fill up.

Incidentally, academics like to get wrapped-up in their own specialized worlds. I think there are some surprises coming fast and the academic world is poorly prepared, aside from the little snippets they may pick up in *Omni* magazine. One of my concerns has been how to introduce these ideas in an intellectually respectable fashion.

DiCarlo—Could you explain some of the features of the Energy Monism model?

Woodhouse—First of all, I should make it clear that I coined the term "Energy Monism" as something convenient. I'm basically a perennialist so I subscribe to the idea that there are levels of reality. Some people will object to that because the word "energy" will pop right out, and they'll say, "Oh, God, there's somebody saying 'Everything is energy.'"

Well, I'm not saying everything is energy.

DiCarlo—What do you make of scientists who are trying to measure energies that go beyond those discussed by traditional physicists?

Woodhouse—The core of my position is that energy is everywhere, in all different levels and frequencies, but energy is the outside manifestation of consciousness. Consciousness is the interior side of energy and grids all the way up and down the ladder, too. So, not only do you have levels of being, you also have this interior/exterior everywhere in the Universe. I think some scientists concerned with proving the existence of subtle energies get too caught up with the "energy" part of reality and overlook the consciousness aspect.

If I see a red aura around you, a scientist might say: "Oh, let's take a measurement from this new machine that we've developed." Fine, take a picture of it, measure it, show me all the little things that it can do electrostatically, and so on. But you haven't taken a picture of anger—you've taken a picture of the energetic representation of anger. Only *you* feel the anger. The person who simply looks at the picture is not going to experience anger for a second. What you've captured in the picture is the outside—the energetic manifestation of it. The interior aspect is never going to be captured on film.

Even if we were all in a spirit world walking around and communicating telepathically with each other, we might see visual representations but that's not the same thing as the experience of the thought itself. I know it's a huge debate with people like Ken Wilber who vigorously asserts, "Everything is consciousness." I'm sympathetic to that. You find others who just as vigorously proclaim, "Everything is energy." But energy and consciousness are correlates of each other, and the way you get them together is, I think, via this "inner-outer" metaphor.

DiCarlo—Physicists say energy is adequate but that the term information is better.

Woodhouse—Yes, it's better in that it's more functional. It gives you something to latch on to, but information has to be carried on something—that's the bottom line. It just doesn't appear. Normally, whether you want to call information consciousness or energy, you have to have something, some sort of carrier for the information. I have no problem with supposing that there may be dimensions of energy that we have yet to discover.

DiCarlo—Some might say that every state of consciousness is actually an energy state—that it's all accompanied by energetic phenomena.

Woodhouse—Right. I would agree 100%. There is a 100% correlation, so every state of consciousness has an energetic manifestation. That doesn't mean that consciousness *is* energy. It just means that consciousness always goes along with it. Energy always goes with consciousness. That's an impasse of paradigms that is so prevalent today among leading-edge thinkers. I've been going to national conferences every year since 1978. Speakers will present their view, but they often times don't really argue it by comparing it with other viewpoints. They simply say, "Here are reasons for my view." They just tell you the way it is, and that's fine, but I wanted to move a step beyond. Through this idea of Energy Monism, we can put Wilber, Richard Gerber, Elmer Green and Larry Dossey in different positions in the *same* ballpark. We can make sense of what they are saying.

DiCarlo—What are the benefits of the Energy Monism model?

Woodhouse—First of all, it allows us to put together these domains which had been formerly been apart from one another. The standard analogy is that we've split off science and spirit and it now appears that there may be a way to put them back together again.

DiCarlo—How has this been done?

Woodhouse—The way that I do this is by introducing the notion of divisions of degree. There are differences between dimensions, but they are not insurmountable differences. The analogy that I use for this is the spectrum of electromagnetic energy. On one end, we have x-rays and gamma rays, and who knows whatever else. At the lower end we have, let's say, radio waves. Now if I ask you, can x-rays do something that radio waves can't, or would they be measurable by certain devices that radio waves are not measured by, you would have to respond, "yes." They're quite different things, occupying different levels of reality, but yet they are all parts of the spectrum of electromagnetic energy. The frequencies for x-rays are different than those for radio waves. So the difference is one of degree, not one of principle.

All are part of an interconnected series so this not only allows us to have two dimensions—namely, consciousness and the body—but a whole series of progressions. For example, one level up from matter, you would have the bio-etheric body because it connects your biology and spirit. This is what you would see actually leaving the body or coming back into it. This is the template and organizer of physical matter. Without it, biological functioning would collapse and deteriorate. We may have taken pictures of it in kirlian photography, where we have the phantom leaf effect.

DiCarlo—So there would be another level above the bio-etheric I take it?

Woodhouse—Yes, we simply keep going up the ladder—there's the bio-etheric body, then the emotional body; then we go to the mental body and from there, to more progressively subtle bodies.

DiCarlo—What would you say are some of the implications of this model?

Woodhouse—For one, Energy Monism makes sense of a lot of what we see going on with psychoneuroimmunology, or PNI. We hear continued talk about the "mind/body connection." Now we know that attitudes can influence the physical body, for example, that depression is implicated in certain kinds of cancer. But how? Where's the depression? It's still just as hidden and mysterious. You can trace it back up through these neurotransmitters, all the way back up to the brain. But now that we have done that, where's the depression?

According to Energy Monism and perennialism, each of these dimensions interpenetrates the others, so our emotional bodies are literally penetrating our entire physical body. I don't know whether to laugh or cry when I read in a newspaper pieces such as, "Scientists discover the love hormone." This is the hormone that is in your body when you feel romantically in love with somebody. What they found is no doubt in some way correlated with that, but being correlated with something is not the same thing as being identical with it. So using this analogy of seeing the emotional body permeating the entire physical body, it's not so hard to understand why, if you're depressed long enough, or stressed out long enough, or guilty long enough, that it begins to take its toll on various parts of your physical body.

DiCarlo—How does something that takes place initially on a mental level find its way down to the physical?

Woodhouse—Well, I don't have the exact scientific answer for that—I don't think anybody does. But the broad scale mechanism is pretty clear. It's a matter of transduction of frequencies. Let me give you an example...If we are speaking with one another on the telephone, our words are translated into electrical impulses that are then carried through telephone lines. What goes through telephone lines are not words, they are just "beeps" which are retranslated on the other end. There is transduction of energies from one level to another. I think that happens in the case of mind/body interaction. It's a matter of different frequencies.

DiCarlo—As I listen to you talk, I once again thought of Ken Wilber, who suggests that higher states of reality can be defined as representing all the lower plus some additional qualities or characteristics. It's an inclusive way of looking at all these realities—wheels within wheels as Dr. Elmer Green would say. Is that in keeping with your Energy Monism model?

Woodhouse—Yes, it's straight Ken Wilber in that each level in the "Great Chain of Being" as it has been called, encompasses the level below it. It suffuses it, but yet is not reducible to it. This goes all the way up to the Source of all, God, and so this leads me to what I call a "panentheistic cosmology." That's a real important distinction. God is in all things—right down to the atoms—but not all things are equal in their awareness. That's what makes for differences. We suffer from limitations of perspective. That's part of what a spiritual pathway is all about—it's about expanding perspectives and as you move up that chain, you see that God was always there all the way up and all the way down.

Energy Monism and the true perennialist paradigm have interesting suggestions for empowerment. We are hearing more that, "We can find love within ourselves"; "We can overcome"; "We can know"; "We can heal ourselves." That's all wonderful. But give me a model in which all this banter makes sense. That's the philosopher in me coming out. If all of these other dimensions are already superimposed in me, that really helps me understand how I can do that. It becomes understandable how I can access information on the other side of the planet, or how I can heal myself, or heal somebody else, or radiate unconditional love. It doesn't make a whole lot of sense if we think of ourselves as fragmented individuals walking around in physical bodies.

DiCarlo—What are some of the other key distinctions about Energy Monism that you think are important to mention?

Woodhouse—Energy Monism is consistent with materialism in so far as it incorporates whatever the materialistic paradigm would say, but then it moves beyond it. It keeps moving beyond it in degrees. It doesn't just lump everything on the other side and say "Over on this side is matter and over there, all the rest is spirit." Energy monism is not dualism because dualism says that there are basically only two levels in the Great Chain of Being and I want to say there are multiple levels—some of them are more physical and some of them are less physical. Some of them are more mental and some of them are less mental. So I want to introduce variations of degree rather than differences of principle. That's the kind of thinking which will help us begin to make the kind of scientific breakthroughs that many are working towards.

DiCarlo—You have used the word dualism. What do you mean by that?

Woodhouse—The idea that humans are two things, spirit and physical body.

There is a debate in parapsychology as to whether or not the out-of-body experience is really about travelling anywhere as opposed to "remote viewing" it. But for the sake of the argument, suppose we had good evidence for supposing that people could actually do this. The scientist is likely to say "Well, that is impossible because that violates my paradigm. I say that humans are just complex biological organisms and whatever is inside your head is going to stay inside your head. The most magnetic energy we have ever measured is about 3 inches outside the physical body and that's when somebody is having a 'grand mal seizure.'"

In my view, on the other hand, it ought to be possible through advances in technology to someday take a picture of whatever it is that leaves the body.

Notice what has happened here. As soon as you are able to measure it, take a picture of it and localize it somewhere, it becomes fair game to science. Interestingly enough, as soon as you have the technology to do that, all of a sudden you have a whole new branch of science and everybody says, "Gee, why didn't we incorporate this before?"

But that's what happened to germs and atoms and everything else. In 1888, the American Chemical Society suspended further talk about atoms at its national meeting, on the grounds that they were metaphysical. Well, that gives you an idea how today's speculations can be tomorrow's science. So I see it as a matter of steady progression. Now, is science going to be able to go all the way back to the ground force of all being? I don't think so. However, science can certainly go a lot further than it has now in terms of opening up to these other dimensions. That's the meeting of "science with spirit."

DiCarlo—Aren't there mathematicians who have come out with proofs for possible alternative reality levels?

Woodhouse—Well, that is the point that physicist David Bohm made. He said that there is more condensed energy than can be accounted for by the entire known physical universe. If that is so, then you've obviously got to account for it in terms of other levels of reality. If you can't account for it by summing up all the mass-energy available in our current physical universe, then it has to come from somewhere else. That's one way the theory is sometimes framed. But I'm cautious here, because I don't want to make it seem like everything is coming down to some form of primeval unified field theory. The string theory supports the unified field theory. String theory supports a unification of the four forces—they are (1) strong nuclear, (1) weak nuclear, (3) electromagnetic and (4) gravitational. If we do get a unified field—and that's something physicists are still debating—it's still the unification of the four known *physical* forces. But it doesn't really account for all these other subtle bodies that we talked about.

One feature of the new world view is that it incorporates a sophisticated knowledge of subtle body anatomy that is correlated—but not reducible—to electromagnetism and things of that sort. There's a gentleman at Maharishi International University named John Haeglin, a brilliant physicist, who has produced an incredible deduction. It's one of the most dramatic things that you could ever ask to look at. You've got complex equations on the right side and on the left side various qualities of expanded consciousness.

DiCarlo—He's given it mathematical proof?

Woodhouse—Yes. He thinks that there is a kind of convergence between infinite consciousness and infinite fields in physics and it's mathematically described as well as phenomenally described. I'm attracted to that, but I would have to ask some more questions, such as,

"Are we really saying that consciousness begets field energy or that field energy of which this universe is made is simply one of the expressions of an infinite consciousness that goes far beyond it?" It's hard to get a grip on that.

DiCarlo—Barbara Brennan talks about the fact that these higher dimensions appear every bit as real as the chair I am sitting on, but because they have a different vibrational frequency, they appear insubstantial within our physical frame of reference.

Woodhouse—And that's very harmonious with Energy Monism. Differences of dimensions are ultimately created by differences of perspective. The more limited your perspective, the more fragmented your dimensional reality will be. The more expanded your perspective, the more dimensions you have access to.

DiCarlo—You've said that your daughter can actually see into these other dimensional levels?

Woodhouse—There are all kinds of things out there that for better or for worse can influence a person's work and behavior. For example, she can see the spirit of a person who has died but has not yet moved beyond the earth plane. She can see thought forms as they come out of a person's chest. She can see form and color. She can see demonic and extraterrestrial energies just by scanning around. The proof of the pudding is in the effectiveness of the work. We've had tumors shrink through our work. We've seen other cancers disappear the next day. That's an unusual situation of course. Normally healing takes a little longer than that.

I serve as a consultant to some psychologists. Recently, a woman called who is an expert in dissociative phenomena. It seems that her bright, very articulate seven year old daughter had picked an imaginary friend, a guy named Joseph. Joseph was getting to be a little bit intrusive. He was coming to visit her, keeping her up at night. Her mother was concerned that Joseph might just be a projected altered personality. This whole situation was complicated because the little girl had other imaginary friends too, and so the task for me, and the task for my daughter, was to discover which of the beings were imaginary and which were actually little spirit kids running around.

It turns out that Joseph was a little spirit kid who was scared to death about something, so he continued to stay around the little girl. It seems he had found a friend. Well, the girl couldn't see Joseph but she could hear him. She started using terms like "dimensional portals," and others equally unfamiliar. So we worked with her for about two hours, and finally convinced Joseph that he had to go with these angels and take a little walk to another place. It worked out beautifully. Joseph now occasionally comes back for some visits and just says "Hi, how are you doing?" and keeps on going. I don't know if that's proof or not but according to her mother there was a 90% change in three days.

DiCarlo—Would you say that most mental illness could be ascribed to influences from other dimensions?

Woodhouse—I think it always takes two to tango. I think that there is something about the individual, either in terms of their brain chemistry, their past upbringing, abuse, what have you, that sets them up for this. Past conditioning and experience sometimes combine to invite these kinds of influences to come around, and that compounds the whole problem. I run into debates with therapists about this all the time. They tell me that even if there are negative energies out there, removing them from my client is no substitute for doing the personal work the client needs to do. I agree that it's no substitute at all, but it will help accelerate your client's growth profile if we can remove these influences.

DiCarlo—Why should a person open up to these other dimensions?

Woodhouse—By opening up to these other dimensional realities, they'll find themselves happier and more content and fulfilled, assuming they do it correctly. There are all the standard qualifications there. Don't just look at it as a psychic exercise. You can become clairvoyant and still grapple with emotional issues that will render you almost dysfunctional, in which case your clairvoyance may come to naught.

DiCarlo—Would you say the emerging world view has any basis characteristics which it shares with the Energy Monism model and the perennial philosophy ?

Woodhouse—The emerging world view *is* the perennial philosophy modified to take into account recent historical and scientific developments. My guess is that it's going to be more perennialist than anything else.

Take the idea of reincarnation. That in and of itself is a complete paradigm buster. Talk about changing your world view! The way I approach this with some of my beginning students is not to enter into a big debate as to whether or not reincarnation is true, but to simply point out that as of 1987 or '88, about 21% of the American population leaned towards some version of reincarnation. And it's been going up every year since. At this rate, I think that around the turn of the century you are going to have half the population being reincarnationists. Even if you don't buy reincarnation, you at least need to know how reincarnationists think, because what they think is going to start having an impact on your life

There are questions very relevant to society now, such as "How do we know when to pull the plug on somebody?" "When are they dead?" "How long should we keep them artificially alive, and at what expense and for whom?" "Who is going to pay for it?" If that's not a real life issue today I don't know what is. If you begin to think like a perennialist, you start to ask other questions such as, "Well, has their mind/soul departed yet or not?" If they are still there, then they have something to learn about being in that vegetative state. If they are gone, they are gone and it's a waste of taxpayer money to keep a frog leg twitching. So then the task is to find someone who is discerning enough to say, "Yes, the soul has gone. Nothing is left. The vehicle (body) is no longer needed."

That's applied metaphysics.

DiCarlo—How might a perennialist view something like the abortion issue?

Woodhouse—I think perennialists are pretty much pro-choice. They are more inclined to take the whole question of fetus rights more seriously than pro-choice people do, because it is a very momentous decision. I have talked to women who had an abortion who specifically offered up prayers to this soul who was waiting to be born, and have said, "Look, this just isn't the right time. Maybe in a few years." Some years later they conceived.

There is free will. You can agree to birth a certain soul, then change your mind. Then you are potentially in trouble karmically. "Oh, oh. I can't give birth now because my husband just lost his job and we can't support this baby. I'll have an abortion and I am in my 4th month." If you have made a prior agreement with that soul coming in, then presumably you are going to have to get that worked out at some point.

DiCarlo—Could you talk about how the perennial philosophy might speak to areas of interest such as, say, personal relationships?

Woodhouse—It's useful to divide the topic of relationships into what I call old paradigm models and new paradigm models. There are two aspects to the old paradigm model of relationships, one I call "controlling" and the other I call "caretaking." A lot of us have had experience with that. If we start from the assumption that we are separate and alone in the Universe, and we have to compete with each other to get our needs met, then controlling others or being controlled by others or viewing ourselves as care-receivers and care-givers is the most we can hope for.

Under a new paradigm scenerio, which is where I think the perennial philosophy comes in, we begin to think in terms of intimate relationships, we begin to think in terms of vulnerability, of mutual empowerment and growth—all built into the relationship itself. There are two categories in the emerging paradigm: intimate and being spiritually integrated. What they have in common us that neither begins from a position of lack. Neither needs to find in another person what's going to help me address that lack or fill me up, whether it be sexually, emotionally or what have you. Rather, there's a high level of self-esteem possessed by both partners. There's the ability to access energy from the Universe, as it were, and the ability to create meaningful paths, both for oneself and for the relationship, which is almost a kind of a third entity.

So the emphasis in the new paradigm perennialist relationship is on growth. It's on creating. It's not based upon need. It's focused more upon integration and vulnerability and expansion.

DiCarlo—Would the perennial philosophy view relationships as mirrors to your own self?

Woodhouse—Absolutely. Each partner in a perennially based, new paradigm relationship will consciously pay attention to how the other partner is mirroring certain issues within themselves that they need to look at. That's one of the big differences between the old and emerging paradigm, there is conscious co-creation with the partners rather than an unconscious falling-in to various roles.

DiCarlo—Finally, what might the perennial philosophy have to say regarding environmental issues?

Woodhouse—Let me begin by making a three-part distinction of the ways in which we go about thinking about the environment. There's an old view which has us pretty much dominating the environment. God put the earth and the animals there for us to do with as we best see fit. We can pretty much do to the earth what we want and the earth can receive this abuse more or less indefinitely. That attitude is beginning to change, perhaps not fast enough for some people. What we see replacing it is an attitude of stewardship, of less emphasis on development, of not killing so many animals, of trying to live in greater peace and harmony, and also a concern about toxicity in the air and the ground—things of that sort. But in this second attitude about he environment, you still find a kind of enlightened egoism. We are going to kill ourselves if we don't quit pumping all of these chemicals into the air, and eating so much meat, and destroying the rainforests in Brazil, etc. That's an enlightened point of view relative to where we were twenty years ago, and all thinking people need to support it, but it's still coming from a standpoint of separateness. It's in effect saying, "Well, let's redefine our relationships with one another. Since we're all in this together we need to stop polluting the environment the way we've been doing. If we don't, we're all going to suffer."

There's a third point of view, which is where the perennial philosophy comes in, and that is that ultimately, not only is everything interrelated, but at a fundamental level, they are all one. We are all expressions of the Divine, and spirit runs all the way down the scale to simple bacteria. So honoring the trees, and microorganisms, and the water, and everything else, because we see them as a reflection of ourselves, and of a Divine Source is ultimately going to be the answer to this. To put it into stark contrast, "Are we going to quit poisoning the environment to save our own asses, so to speak, or simply because we love trees?" My hope is that ultimately, the latter more perennially-based attitude will prevail.

Part 2

A NEW VIEW
of
OURSELVES

The problem in middle life, when the body has reached its climax of power and begins to decline, is to identify yourself not with the body, which is falling away, but with the consciousness of which it is a vehicle. This is something I learned from myths. What am I? Am I the bulb that carries the light, or am I the light of which the bulb is a vehicle.

Joseph Campbell, *The Power of Myth*

Obviously, when I say I doubt there are any paranormal phenomenon, I don't think there is any life after death, people don't like it. They want to believe in such things. I think one can live better by living in the moment, accepting death for what it is, and getting on with it. The argument is really about what we are as human beings. I think that we are just lumps of flesh, evolved for no reasons at all.

Susan Blackmore, scientist

Are we all victims of our own mistaken identity?

If you ask the question: "Who are you?" people are likely to respond, "I am an accountant"; or "I am a mother." We tend to identify so much with our social roles that we come to believe we are those roles.

According to those on the leading-edge, our mistaken identity does not stop there. Because we identify so much with our physical bodies, we think that is all that we are, that when our bodies die, we are no more. Yet research emerging from the frontiers of psychology and medicine suggests that our true identity does not stop at our skin. According to the new world view, we are much greater than we know. We are, at core, inherently loving, creative, multi-dimensional and boundless, with an existence beyond time and beyond space.

The idea of living from this deeper identity stretches us to the limits of our imagination regarding what may be possible. At the same time, it cultivates a deeper sense of responsibility since our effect upon others is not limited to our physical actions, but also extends to less tangible attititudes, emotions and thoughts.

Section 6

NEW VIEWS IN PSYCHOLOGY

"Western psychology has traditionally viewed as normal the rational linear view of reality which perceives the world as a multiplicity of separate objects and organsims, and experiences life as a sequence of events in time. This view of reality posits a duality of subject and object, and a split between spirit and matter. It is based on a mechanistic Newtonian model of physics which is now outdated."

Frances Vaughn, psychologist
Awakening Intuition

Humanity's inquiry into the workings of the human psyche dates back to the Greek poets and sages of sixth century B.C., to the Buddha in India and Confucius in China.

In the beginning, psychology was the province of Greek philosophers who sought to understand more about the nature of man and the universe. Within a few centuries, Plato, Socrates, Hippocrates, and Democritus would develop many of the ideas and principles that have served as the conceptual underpinnings of Western psychology. It was the Greeks who discovered that human beings are capable of examining, understanding, altering, guiding and even controlling their thoughts, emotions and behavior.

The story of modern Western psychology is told in the emergence of four major schools, referred to as the "Four Forces of Psychology": psychoanalysis, behaviorism, humanistic psychology and transpersonal psychology. Each school has its own theories on the nature and cause of psychological illness, and on how illness should be treated. Each pivots upon a different world view.

The First Force, psychoanalysis, was introduced by Sigmund Freud. It is essentially a medical model of the mind which looks to early childhood experiences as the root of any psychological difficulties.

Behaviorism, the Second Force, dominated Western psychological thought from the 1920s through the 1960s. It concerns itself primarily with the measurement, prediction and control of behavior. Up through the 19th century, psychology had been based upon philosophical speculation, not scientifically-derived knowledge. Behaviorism was the attempt to make psychology a respectable science.

Humanistic psychology, the Third Force in Psychology, arose in the 1950s and 60s as a means of studying the whole person. Its principal contributors include Fritz Perls, Abraham Maslow, Carl Rogers and Virginia Satir. The primary focus of humanistic psychology is upon growth and human potential rather than psychological illness. It considers the role of feelings—something the behaviorists were happy to exclude altogether since an individual's inner mental processes or consciousness could not easily be understood and studied. Behaviorists believed that any talk of mind or consciousness smacked of mentalism, the belief that there is such a thing as "mind" that exists apart from the physiological and chemical processes of the brain. This belief was considered to be outdated, subjective and mystical—and definitely unscientific.

In the 1970s, the Fourth Force of psychology—the transpersonal—grew out of the humanistic school. Transpersonal psychology seeks to understand the individual human being not as an isolated unit, but in the spiritual context of a larger whole which expresses itself through the individual. It expanded upon the humanistic school, focusing not only upon healthy psychological development, but also upon the spiritual dimensions of experience.

According to the transpersonal school, human development does not stop at adulthood, but continues throughout life. Vaughan and others explain human development in terms of an "outward arc," which involves the formation of the personality, and an "inward arc" of more advanced levels of development. As individuals reach these advanced levels, intellectual capability is augmented by intuition. We all possess intuitive capacity just as we all possess the ability to think, although fear, our inner mental chattering, and emotional predispositions can distort or even block our intuitive messages.

The term "transpersonal" was initially suggested by Dr. Stanislav Grof, whom we will hear from first in this section. Grof has been a pioneer in the area of non-ordinary states of consciousness and along with Abraham Maslow, is considered to be one of the principle founders of

| *Page 96*

the field. Grof's research has enabled him to sketch out a map of the human psyche that is multi-dimensional, and in basic agreement with quantum physics and the perennial philosophy.

Transpersonal psychologists believe that to reach advanced levels of development, it becomes necessary to open up to these non-physical, transpersonal, more spiritual dimensions. Human beings possess a strong need—some say stronger than the drive for sex—for the spiritual peak experiences that are inherent in the more advanced levels of human development.

Grof's work calls into question the world view which states that consciousness is the by-product of matter, and that the mind is the brain and nothing more.

Dr. Joan Borysenko is a pioneer in the field of mind-body medicine. Co-founder of the Mind/Body Clinic at Harvard University, her interests overlap both medicine and psychology, fields which are rapidly converging as new linkages between thoughts, feelings and physical illness are discovered. Borysenko feels that the field of psychology has limited itself by focusing on what's wrong with people, rather than on the development of higher potential. Like Grof, she touches upon the multiplicity of the human psyche, composed she says of an inner cast of characters called subpersonalities, which push and pull us in conflicting and oftentimes contradictory directions. Attaining the more advanced stages of human development also requires that an individual recognize and embrace these various subpersonalities. By doing so we avail ourselves of all of our creative energies.

The new view that is emerging in psychology allows for less limiting and more expansive insights into human nature and our place in the Universe.

Dr. Stan Grof

Dr. Stanislav Grof, M.D., Ph.D. is a psychiatrist with over thirty-seven years of research experience in non-ordinary states of consciousness. Born in Prague, Czechoslovakia. Dr. Grof, along with Abraham Maslow is considered a primary founder and theoretician of transpersonal psychology. He's the author of "Realms of the Human Unconscious," "Beyond the Brain," "Human Survival and Consciousness Evolution" and co-author, with his wife Christina, of "The Stormy Search for The Self."

DiCarlo—Through your pioneering work, you have developed a means of triggering non-ordinary states of awareness in individuals. For what purpose?

Grof—Non-ordinary states of consciousness are certainly a unique source of profound insights into the deepest recesses of the human psyche. In my opinion their potential significance for psychiatry is comparable to the importance of the microscope for medicine or the telescope for astronomy. It is hard to believe that this area has been largely ignored by traditional psychiatrists and psychologists. I myself have been particularly interested in two aspects of non-ordinary states. First, it has been their extraordinary therapeutic or healing potential, naturally, if they are used properly and under supervision of an experienced guide. Since I am a clinical psychiatrist, this was my primary area of interest. Second, it has been their heuristic potential, that is, what we can learn in or through these states about the psyche, the unconscious, human nature, and the universe.

DiCarlo—While browsing through a variety of psychological journals, I noticed that increasingly, many of the prevailing assumptions of traditional psychology are being called into question. Some examples: "Psychological development largely ceases once biological adulthood is reached;" "Psychological health is nothing more than not being sick;" and "Transpersonal or mystical experiences are at best insignificant and at worst, signs of mental illness." As one of the principle architects of the emerging paradigm of psychology, what does your work suggest about the validity of these assumptions?

Grof— To your first point: Transpersonal psychology has amassed ample evidence suggesting that human psychological development can proceed far beyond a good interpersonal and social adjustment and adequate sexual functioning of a mature adult. The author who has written about this in the most articulate way is Ken Wilber. In his books, he offers an impressive and comprehensive synthesis of various schools of Western psychology and Eastern spiritual systems. He describes in great detail additional stages of psychological development—the subtle, causal, and absolute. Since all these levels involve the spiritual dimension as a critical element, they require that spirituality be understood as a healthy and evolutionary manifestation, rather than an indication of lack of education or mental illness.

As far as your second assumption is concerned: The attitude of Western psychiatry that sees mental health as simply the absence of symptoms certainly has to be radically revised. In the new understanding, emotional and psychosomatic symptoms are seen as expressions of the healing process of the organism, not as manifestations of disease. Obviously this applies only to "functional" or psychologically determined disorders and not to clearly organic conditions, such as tumors, infections, or hardening of the arteries of the brain. Nor would it apply in certain states which are clearly manifestations of mental disease, such as severe paranoid conditions. This new understanding can be described as "homeopathic." In the alternative system of medicine known as homeopathy, the symptoms are seen as expressions of healing, not the disease. Therapy in homeopathy consists of a temporary intensification of the symptoms to achieve wholeness. This approach results in profound healing and positive personality transformation rather than the impoverishment of vitality and functioning that accompanies the suppression of symptoms through the use of prescribed drugs. The emphasis on constructive working with symptoms instead of their routine suppression is the first major difference between the strategies based on modern consciousness research and those used in mainstream psychiatry.

With the new strategies, we can do much more than remove the symptoms or reach the goal of psychoanalysis—as defined by Freud in his famous statement : "to change the extreme suffering of the neurotic to the ordinary misery of everyday life." That certainly is not a very ambitious plan, particularly if you consider the amount of time, money, and energy that it takes to undergo psychoanalysis. However, to achieve positive mental health—increase of zest, joi de vivre, vitality, creativity—requires that an individual open up to the spiritual dimension of existence. Abraham Maslow conducted extensive research in many hundreds of people who had had spontaneous mystical experiences, or "peak experiences" as he called them. He showed that they were conducive to self-actualization and self-realization and much higher levels of development and functioning than those that conventional psychology talks about.

This brings us to your third point, the problem of spirituality and mystical experiences. This is an issue, which represents the core difference between traditional psychiatry and transpersonal psychology. Mainstream psychiatry is based upon the Cartesian-Newtonian materialistic world view which maintains that the history of the universe is basically the history of developing matter. The only thing that really exists is matter and life; consciousness, and intelligence are its accidental and insignificant side-products. In this kind of a world view, there is no place for spirituality. To be spiritual means to be uneducated, unacquainted with modern scientific discoveries about the nature of the Universe. It means to be involved in superstition, in primitive, or magical thinking. Traditional psychoanalysis explains spirituality as a regression, as a fixation on the infantile stage—a step backwards in development rather than a step forward. In this context, the concept of God is interpreted as the projection of your infantile image of your father to the sky. Interest in religious ritual is seen as analogous to obsessive-compulsive behavior of a neurotic and explained as a regression to the anal stage of libidinal development.

DiCarlo—So it is a sort of reductionism, taking what lies beyond our current conceptual models of how things work and reducing them to what we already know to make them comprehensible?

Grof—Yes. And here lies the fundamental difference between traditional psychiatry and transpersonal psychology which considers spirituality to be an intrinsic dimension of the human psyche and a critical factor in the universal scheme of things. This conclusion is not some kind of irrational belief or a speculative metaphysical assumption. It is based on systematic study of non-ordinary states of consciousness in which we can have direct experiences of the spiritual dimensions. These experiences fall into two distinct categories. In the first one are experiences of the Immanent Divine; they involve direct perception of unity underlying the world of separation and a realization that what we experience as material reality is actually the manifestation of creative cosmic energy. The second category includes experiences of the Transcendental Divine; here we perceive dimensions of reality that are normally hidden to our senses, such as visions of deities, or archetypal figures as C.G. Jung would call them, and of various mythological domains.

DiCarlo—Could you give me some other examples of the categories of transpersonal experiences described by the thousands of people you have studied over the years that would tend to shatter the assumptions of materialistic science and the traditional world view?

Grof—Traditional psychology and psychiatry have a model of the psyche that is limited to the body and more specifically the brain, which is seen as the source of consciousness. It also confines itself to postnatal biography, which means to the history of the individual after he or she was born. It tries to explain all psychological processes in terms of the events which took place in infancy and in childhood. In addition, we also have the Freudian individual unconscious, which is basically a derivative of our life experiences. It is a kind of "psychological junkyard" that harbors various unacceptable tendencies that have been repressed.

The model of the psyche that has emerged from modern consciousness research and from transpersonal psychology is incomparably larger and more encompassing. It has additional domains that are extremely important from the theoretical, as well as practical, point of view. For example, the cartography of the unconscious that I have suggested on the basis of my studies of non-ordinary states has, beside the biographical level, two vast additional domains, which I call perinatal and transpersonal. The perinatal level has as its core the record of traumatic experiences associated with biological birth. The memories of the emotions and physical feelings that we experienced during our delivery are often represented here in photographic detail. However, the perinatal level also functions as a kind of gateway into the next domain of the psyche, the transpersonal.

For example, people who relive different stages of birth, often experience simultaneously elements of what C.G. Jung called the "collective unconscious"; this can be either its historical or mythological aspects. Thus people who reexperience the stage of birth where they were stuck in the womb before the cervix opened, might identify with different people throughout history who were in a prison, or who were abused and tortured, such as the victims of the Inquisition and people who were in Nazi concentration camps. Similarly, the reliving of the desperate struggle to free oneself from the clutches of the birth canal after the cervix dilated can be associated with images of revolutions and with experiential identification with freedom fighters of all ages.

These experiences of one's birth can also open into archetypal visions of the collective unconscious. People who feel stuck in the womb can experience themselves as being in hell, with actual experiences of the demonic figures or of infernal landscapes as we know them from mythology and from religious art. Similarly, individuals who re-experience the difficult propulsion through the birth canal at the stage of birth when the cervix is open often describe archetypal visions of various deities who represent death and re-birth such as Osiris, Adonis, Attis, Persephone, and Dionysus. They might also have the visions of crucifixion or actually experience death and resurrection in full identification with Jesus Christ.

Beside the perinatal level, we have another vast transbiographical domain, the transpersonal level. As I have described earlier, some people can first get in touch with the transpersonal realm in connection with the death-rebirth process; however, others experience it independently in a pure form. The spectrum of transpersonal experiences is extremely rich. Beside the already mentioned elements of the historical and mythological collective unconscious, it is possible to experience convinced identification with various animals, plants, and other aspects of nature and of the cosmos. A particularly important type of transpersonal experiences are karmic or "past-life" memories. These experiences can suddenly catapult us into another century, another country, and another culture. They are extremely vivid, intense, and convincing and are typically accompanied with a sense of personal remembering ("What I am experiencing now is not happening to me for the first time. I once actually was this person living in that historical period"). In many instances people are able to bring from these experiences astonishing and accurate new information about the times and cultures which they had visited. We have also observed that past life experiences have an amazing therapeutic potential.

DiCarlo—Why should a person consider that the types of experiences you have just described are more than simple fantasies or hallucinations?

Grof—This is the attitude that is usually taken by those people who have traditional scientific training. But if you really study these experiences, as I have done for the last thirty-six years, you find out that the situation is much more complex. The information that these experiences tend to provide is often incredibly rich and specific and of such a kind that it could not have possibly been acquired through ordinary channels. It is not something that one can get from teachers, books, movies, or television. Identification with animals typically involves dimensions that cannot be conveyed by traditional means. Take for example, specific nonhuman instinctual feelings, body sensations, and emotions. In experiences involving other cultures and historical periods, it can be very detailed information about architecture, costumes, weapons, and social organizations of various societies. In some instances, the information concerns specific historical events and can be verified by independent research in historical archives.

Also, people frequently discover that their past life experiences are in some way connected to their present life situation. For example, certain emotional and psychosomatic problems which could not be explained or alleviated by various forms of traditional therapy, disappear after a profound experience of this kind. In addition, karmic experiences are often associated with meaningful synchronicities. For example, a person has a difficult relationship with another person and has a past life experience that shows the two of them engaged in some sort of violent conflict. One of them is the victim and the other the aggressor. If this person completes reliving that incident and reaches a sense of forgiveness, his or her attitude towards the other protagonist changes in the positive direction. That is in itself impressive and interesting. However, what is quite extraordinary is that at exactly the same time a significant change in the same direction often occurs in the other person, whose attitude is also radically changed. This can happen even if there was not a conventional communication or connection of any kind between these two persons.

These observations suggest that the belief in reincarnation is not a product of wishful thinking or some superficial metaphysical speculation; it is clearly a pragmatic concept, reflecting an effort to understand the complexity of these experiences that spontaneously emerge in non-ordinary states. Psychiatrists who deny that the phenomenon of reincarnation is a fascinating and legitimate field of study are obviously not very familiar with non-ordinary states of consciousness and, more specifically, with the complex and fascinating nature of karmic experiences.

DiCarlo—Would you say your cartography of the psyche tracks the perennial philosophy—the inner teachings which all religions throughout the ages seem to share? Does it correlate with the experiences of saints and mystics who have purportedly peered into these other domains?

Grof—Very much so. I have written a book called *The Cosmic Game* that specifically explores the insights from non-ordinary states of consciousness regarding the "Big Picture" of life. The book shows the deep similarities between the experiences that many people have reported to us in our research and those described by different systems of perennial philosophy. The book also shows how the insights into the nature of reality—matter, time, space, consciousness—strikingly converge with the concepts that characterize what has been called the new or emerging paradigm in Western science. In other words, the insights that people get into the nature of the cosmos in non-ordinary states are in fundamental conflict with the old, Cartesian-Newtonian world view, but are very similar in nature to descriptions that we find in quantum-relativistic physics and other avenues of the new paradigm.

DiCarlo—Could you share with us what some of these insights have been?

Grof—For example, the Newtonian understanding of the world is that matter is indestructible, objects are solid, time is linear, and space is three-dimensional. The universe is a totally deterministic mechanical system, where everything is connected through chains of causes and effects. In the worldview of traditional science, the material world exists objectively in an unambiguous way. The observer reflects more or less accurately this "objective reality," but his or her presence does not change anything—the world is uninfluenced through the act of observation.

In non-ordinary states, the material world is experienced as a dynamic process where there are no solid structures and everything is a flow of energy. Everything is perceived as patterns of energy and behind patterns of energy there are patterns of experience. Reality appears to be the result of an incredibly precise orchestration of experiences and the observer plays a very important role in the creation of the universe. This is exactly the picture that is now emerging from various areas of new paradigm science. It has become apparent that consciousness has a very fundamental role in the cosmos. It is not a side-product of inert, dead, and inactive matter that somehow appeared in the universe more or less accidentally after billions of years of evolution. Consciousness and creative intelligence permeate all of nature and the entire universe has an underlying master blueprint. This is also an image that comes very close to the mystical worldview and to the understanding that one finds in the Eastern spiritual philosophies.

DiCarlo—So you would, I take it, be in agreement with Willis Harman's M-3 metaphysical assumption, that consciousness is primary, that it existed before matter?

Grof—Very much so. In view of my own findings, it is the only perspective that makes any sense. As I briefly mentioned earlier, in transpersonal states of mind, one can subjectively experience identification with other people, with animals, with plants, and even with inorganic materials and processes. Everything that one can experience in the everyday state of consciousness as an object, has in the non-ordinary state of consciousness a subjective correlate. This shows that the psyche and consciousness of each of us is, in the last analysis, commensurate with "All-That-Is," because there are no absolute boundaries between the bodyego and the totality of existence. In this sense, we can experience ourselves as anything between the bodyego and the totality of cosmic consciousness, or the creative principle itself. That is very reminiscent of the message of the Upanishads, "Thou Art That" (You are Godhead, identical with the creative principle of the universe).

There exists substantial evidence that consciousness is not a by-product of matter, an epiphenomenon of the neurophysiological processes in our brain, but a primary attribute of existence. The material reality is a creation of cosmic consciousness. To use modern terminology, the world we live in is "virtual reality," created by the technology of consciousness. In the course of this century, quantum-relativistic physics has seriously undermined the belief in the tangible and unambiguous nature of our material reality. It has thrown a new light on the ancient Buddhist idea that form is emptiness and emptiness is form. In the subatomic analysis, matter in the usual sense of the word, disappears and what remains is pattern, relation, mathematical order—elements which we would certainly associate with consciousness rather than matter.

DiCarlo—Would you suggest that the transpersonal domains of the psyche which you describe, are other-than-physical *realities*, with a life and vitality of their own? That independent of the person who may be perceiving them, these domains of experience exist with their own inhabitants, their own natural laws and their own phenomenon?

Grof—Traditional science claims in a very authoritarian way that the material universe which we experience through our five senses, is the only existing reality. And if we experience other realities, such as historical or archetypal elements of the collective unconscious, these are seen as illusory experiences derived from the perceptions and memories of this world. In other words, transpersonal experiences are fantasies or hallucinations. This position is presented as an evident scientific fact that has been proven beyond any reasonable doubt, but a closer examination clearly shows that it is an unfounded metaphysical assumption. Modern consciousness research actually has brought ample evidence that there are other experiential dimensions of reality with specific and demonstrable characteristics. To borrow an analogy from electronics, material reality is just one "holographic cosmic channel." There are other "channels" that are equally real or unreal as this one.

DiCarlo—Would you also be in agreement with people such as Robert Monroe who has reportedly explored different dimensional levels of reality in his "out-of-body" experiences?

Grof—Robert Monroe has developed some very effective means of inducing non-ordinary states of consciousness, with special emphasis on those that are conducive to out-of-body experiences. In non-ordinary states, the sharp difference between what is "real" and what is "unreal" tends to disappear. Our ordinary material world appears less real and the world of the archetypal beings and other aspects of the transpersonal world become very convincing and believable. Careful study reveals that they are more than fantasies or hallucinations. Once we realize that in both instances we are dealing with "virtual realities," the distinction between what is "real" and what is derived becomes rather arbitrary. In view of all that we have discussed earlier, at least some of the experiences that Robert Monroe describes represent legitimate and relevant dimensions of existence.

DiCarlo—What would you say is the new image of the human being that is emerging from your research and also from the new sciences?

Grof—The traditional point of view of Western materialistic science is that we are Newtonian objects, made up of atoms, molecules, cells, tissues and organs, that we are highly developed animals and biological thinking machines. If we seriously consider all the data amassed in the last few decades by modern consciousness research, we discover that this point of view is incorrect, or at least incomplete. It is just one partial aspect of a much more complex picture. It can be maintained only when we suppress all the evidence from parapsychology and the study of non-ordinary states of consciousness, such as mystical, psychedelic, and near-death experiences, or trance phenomena and meditation. In all these situation, we can also function as fields of consciousness which can transcend space, time, and linear causality.

Quantum-relativistic physicists have a definition of subatomic matter and also of light that combines in a paradoxical fashion two seemingly incompatible aspects of these phenomena. This is the wave-particle paradox described by Niels-Bohr's principle of complementarity. To understand the nature of subatomic matter or light, you have to accept that they are phenomena which can have characteristics of both particles and waves. These are two complementary aspects of the same phenomena and each of them manifests under different circumstances. We are now discovering that something similar applies to human beings. We are Newtonian objects, highly developed biological thinking machines, but we are also infinite fields of consciousness that transcend time, space, and linear causality. These are two complementary aspects of who we are and each of them manifest under different circumstances, the first in the ordinary state of consciousness, the other when we enter a non-ordinary state of consciousness.

DiCarlo—In your work, you discuss "spiritual emergencies." What are they, and how are these episodes dealt with in the old paradigm of psychiatry?

Grof—The most important thing is to realize that traditional psychology and psychiatry do not make a distinction between a mystical experience and a psychotic experience. From a traditional point of view, all forms of non-ordinary states of consciousness—with the exception of dreams where there is a certain tolerance—would be interpreted as pathological phenomena. Strictly speaking, Western psychiatry has pathologized the entire history of spirituality.

Transpersonal psychology, on the other hand, is interested in spirituality, which is something that you find in the mystical branches or in the monastic branches of the great religions. Spirituality is based on direct experience of the transpersonal realms or "numinous" dimensions of reality, either in terms of the Immanent Divine or the Transcendental Divine, as we discussed earlier. "Numinosity" is a word that C.G. Jung used in lieu of such expressions as religious, sacred, or mystical that might be confusing and have often been misunderstood.

At the cradle of each major religion are direct spiritual or transpersonal experiences of the founders, saints, and prophets. Buddha meditating under the Bo tree experienced the onslaught of Kama Mara, the master of the world illusion, and his terrifying army. The Koran and the Moslem religion were inspired by the "miraculous journey of Mohammed," a visionary experience during which he was guided by archangel Gabriel through the seven heavens, the paradise, and the infernal regions of Gehenna. Similarly Jesus, according to the Bible, had a powerful visionary encounter with the devil during which he was exposed to his temptations. Both the Old Testament and the New Testament abound in descriptions of transpersonal experiences reflecting connection and communication with God and with angels. We have seen many similar experiences in the holotropic breathwork sessions, in psychedelic therapy, as well as during spontaneous psychospiritual crises ("spiritual emergencies"). We could add to the list St. Theresa of Avila, St. John of the Cross, St. Anthony, and many other Christian saints and Desert Fathers, as well as Ramakrishna and Shri Ramana Maharshi—they all had powerful visionary experiences of one kind or another.

According to traditional psychiatry, all these people would be seen as psychotics or people suffering from some other serious psychiatric condition. We actually have many psychiatric articles and books that discuss which psychiatric diagnosis would be most appropriate for the founders of various religions, their prophets, and saints. Franz Alexander, a famous psychoanalyst and founder of psychosomatic medicine, even wrote a paper entitled Buddhist Meditation as an Artificial Catatonia, putting spiritual practice into a pathological context.

Similarly, anthropologists argue whether shamans should be viewed as hysterics, epileptics, schizophrenics, or maybe ambulant psychotics. Many people who have transpersonal experiences are automatically treated as psychotics, people suffering from a mental disease, because psychiatrists do not make a distinction between a mystical experience and a psychotic experience.

The concept of spiritual emergency suggests that many episodes of non-ordinary states of consciousness that are currently diagnosed as psychoses and treated by suppressive medication are actually crises of transformation and spiritual opening. Instead of routine suppression through drugs, we should give these people support and guidance to help them through these experiences. When properly understood and properly guided, these states can result in emotional and psychosomatic healing and positive personality transformation.

DiCarlo—So, far from being a sign of illness, such episodes presage unfoldment of our true spiritual nature, allowing for the full expression of that aspect of who we are?

Grof—Yes, my wife Christina and I wrote a book *The Stormy Search for the Self,* in which we expressed our belief that the possibility of spiritual emergence—spiritual opening, growth, and development—is something inherent to human nature. And that the need for spiritual experiences represents a very strong force in human personality. Andrew Weil expressed a similar opinion in his book the *Natural Mind*; he suggested that our need for the transcendental experience is a force that is more powerful than sex. If you look back at human history, you will find that many people have invested enormous amounts of energy in the spiritual quest. They have also made tremendous sacrifices for this purpose—the sacrifice of material possessions, professional careers, as well as of personal and sexual life. In transpersonal psychology, the impulse toward spirituality is viewed as a very natural and very powerful drive in human beings. In Western culture, we have lost all socially sanctioned contexts in which people can experience non-ordinary states of consciousness and have spiritual experiences. Our attitude toward spirituality is certainly peculiar. There is a bible in every motel room and even leading politicians pay lipservice to God; but if a person would have a powerful spiritual experience in the church, an average minister would send them to a psychiatrist.

DiCarlo—Would you say that someone has to have this contact with the transpersonal to shift their world view? Can a person change their world view simply by reading a book that causes them to change their beliefs about the way things are?

Grof—You generally will not convince people, particularly Westerners, about the significance of the spiritual dimension just by giving them books to read. The critical factor in a genuine spiritual opening will probably always be a direct personal experience, since it is very difficult to describe the spiritual dimensions in a way that is meaningful. The obvious parallel that comes to mind is sexuality. It would be very difficult to explain to a preadolescent what sexual orgasm is like, convey how important sexuality is in adult human life and why, or to discuss the difficulties that might be associated with sex. They would not be able to understand, since they do not have an experiential frame of reference. But once the person has a sexual experience, there comes an instant understanding of that entire domain.

However, there are many people who go through spiritual emergence in a much more subtle way than the one we describe in our book, *The Stormy Search for The Self.* William James calls such a gradual opening "the educational variety." It can begin by reading some books and hearing some lectures, attending spiritual groups, and undergoing some subtle forms of transformation in meditation and other spiritual practices.

DiCarlo—Abductions by extraterrestrials, encounters with angels, Near-Death Experiences, past life memories...is there any underlying significance to these phenomena that ties them all together in your view?

Grof—From my point of view, all of these experiences represent different forms of contact with the transpersonal dimension of reality, with the historical and archetypal domains of the collective unconscious. Under favorable circumstances, they can have very positive consequences, but they are also associated with definite risks and pitfalls. Experiential contact with the archetypal domain in and of itself is not necessarily beneficial. It is possible to get inflated by identifying with an archetype, and it can leave you in a state of grandiosity. For example, some people who experience identification with Jesus Christ, which is a very common experience in non-ordinary states, can end up believing that they are actually the historical Jesus. Another common pitfall is to experience one's own divinity (in the sense of the Tat tvam asi of the Upanishads) and attaching this insight to one's body ego (I am God and that makes me special). Many difficulties result from indiscriminate talking about the experiences with friends, family, or business associates who are unable to understand them. Unfortunately, in view of the present ignorance concerning non-ordinary states, this group also includes traditional psychiatrists.

In general, if we have transpersonal experiences, have the right context for understanding them, and are able to integrate them well, we are learning about important dimensions of reality and that has to be beneficial and enhancing. Fortunately, as the sophistication in regard to non-ordinary states is gradually increasing in the general population and among professionals, more and more people will be able to experience the transpersonal realm with adequate support and under favorable conditions.

Joan Borysenko

Dr. Joan Borysenko is president of Mind/Body Health Sciences in Boulder Colorado, and the author of several books including the New York Times best-seller "Minding the Body, Mending the Mind," "Guilt is the Teacher, Love is the Lesson" and "Fire In the Soul." Borysenko is generally regarded as being on the cutting-edge in her knowledge of mind-body research, a principle ambassador who brings the latest scientific findings to mainstream doctors and the general public. She is one of the principle architects of the field of psychoneuroimmunology.

DiCarlo—Dr. Larry Dossey has come up with a model to help explain the evolution of the field of modern medicine which he terms Era-1, Era-2, and Era-3 medicine. Could you briefly trace the evolution of psychology, where the field has been, where it is now and where it appears to be heading?

Borysenko—Sure. The evolution of psychology began with Freud, who was a neurologist. He certainly began to look into what can be regarded as an Era-1 and Era-2 psychology. Era-1 psychology would be an understanding of things like neurotransmitters and areas of the brain that have been associated with certain emotions. It's very, very important. In my own life, I spent a long time exploring psychopharmacology, looking at the different structures of the brain and what kind of structures were localized there. We need that knowledge.

The 2nd era of psychology, to borrow from Dossey's Era-2 medicine, recognizes the connection between the mind and the body. Oftentimes, psychologists think of the mind as divorced from the body, and what we have begun to realize in psychology is that if you give someone a massage, as a massage therapist will tell you, and touch certain parts of the body, specific memories will suddenly be triggered. We understand now that memories are stored in certain parts of the body and that the emotions are the bridge between the body and the mind.

Era-3 psychology is truly a transpersonal psychology, where we recognize that in addition to one's own thoughts and one's own personal history effecting one's mind and body, that in a certain sense we all effect each other through our thoughts. This has been substantiated in prayer studies. Most of us have no trouble recognizing that our own thoughts effect our body. That's common knowledge now. What we don't know, or tend to forget, is that our mind can effect someone else's body and that their thoughts can effect our body. I think that when a psychologist has the capability of being what we call "naturally thera-peutic," it's partly because they look at their client, whoever they may be, with a mindset of great respect and love. Through that sense of respect, they bring forth healing. Eric Fromme said that a parent ide-ally looks at their child with an attitude of hopefulness. He defined hopefulness as a passion for the possible. When a therapist looks at a client with a passion for the possible and knows that there is indeed a Godseed within them that is going to grow, and knows that no person is flawed beyond their capacity to heal, and understands that every wound is a sacred wound in terms of being able to lead the person to a state of greater compassion and wisdom— that attitude alone crosses space and time and leads to healing.

DiCarlo— What have been the triumphs and shortcomings of Western psychology?

Borysenko—I think there have been a lot of triumphs in behavior therapy. I spent years of my life as a behaviorist, looking at operant conditioning ala Skinner. I think it's very important to understand how people learn and to take notice of how this understanding effects people. For example, take a very simple behaviorist concept, like continuous reinforcement. You give a child a reward every time something hap-pens and they always expect that reward. If you do it only once in a while, then they will always expect it. You will never easily extinguish the behavior of looking or waiting for whatever it is they want. So operant conditioning is useful in understanding the reasons why you have to be consistent with a child if you are a parent. If you are not consistent, if every once in a while you give them something that is forbidden, they simply will not learn that they cannot have that thing and it will bug you forever. These are useful concepts and methods which have been the gifts of behavior therapy.

I also think our knowledge of brain structure and behavior is very im-portant. It's very important to understand where the reward centers of the brain are located, and what neuropeptides are produced in re-sponse to emotion. Psychopharmocology is also very important. Pre-scribed drugs can oftentimes help people to regularize their brain func-tion and emotional response. Many of the psychoactive drugs have been extremely helpful. The whole aspect of psychology that deals with self-awareness has been enormously important. Without self-aware-ness, how can we ever make a choice? How can we ever have free will? We could go into much more detail, but globally, there is much to be said for psychology as we know it.

On the downside, I think the limitations of psychology has been its reductionist theory. That is, just because we can find brain areas that have to do with emotions, or just because a certain drug can alleviate a certain affliction, to reduce the human being to a stimulus-response system or to certain chemicals in the brain that produce certain responses is inadequate. We are clearly more than that. Some people try to reduce and explain away near-death-experiences as the trick of dying brain cells starving for oxygen. There is some truth here since research shows that if the right temporal lobe is stimulated, it will give rise to religious thinking. It will also give rise to light experiences—as of course it should. We live in a physical body. Why shouldn't there be circuitry? But to say that just because there is circuitry there is nothing beyond that—that there is no soul or spirit—is extraordinarily limiting.

The other limiting tendency of psychology is to look at people more in terms of what's wrong with them—their pathology—rather than in terms of their potential. Psychologists seem quick to categorize and say, "What is wrong with a person's character?" or "What is wrong with this person's behavior?" rather than saying, "Oh, is there a difficulty or a wound here, that for this person, has particular relevance to the way that they become whole, and the way that they become creative, and the way the way that they awaken their inner intuition and capacity to love."

DiCarlo—Certainly the transpersonal movement proposes that in addition to physical body, mind and emotions, there is an aspect of being some would refer to as the soul or spirit, which plays a vital role in human existence. How would you define the term "transpersonal?"

Borysenko—I would define the term transpersonal as actually that which is most deeply personal on one aspect, and also what binds us together with everybody else. It goes beyond the limit of the individual. In one sense, I would say that what is beyond the person or "transpersonal," is that one mind that all people are part of. When the great quantum physicist Erwin Shroedinger was asked how many minds he thought existed in the universe, he laughed and said, "If the sum total of the number of minds could be counted, there would be just one." If you look into the esoteric core—the spiritual core of all religious traditions—then you also find there is the discussion of one divine mind, of which we are all a part. Part of that divine mind dwells within each human being as some sort of essence or core.

If for example, you were a mystical Jew, you might call that core the "shekhinah" the indwelling feminine presence of God. If you were a Buddhist, you would call it the Rigpa, or your own true nature. If you were a mystical Christian, like Miester Eckhart, you would call it the Godseed that dwells within. There has been a name for it in every tradition. In the Hindu tradition it might be called the Atman, which becomes one with the Brahman or the larger mind. It's certainly been talked about in psychological circles as well. Jung had a concept of the Self with the big "S" and that's the same thing. So did Roberto Assagioli, the founder of psychosynthesis who was a contemporary of Freud and Jung. We find in modern-day psychopathology, that in the most abused members of our society, this creative, immortal aspect of self, the part of the one mind that dwells within you has also been described by people with Multiple Personality Disorder (MPD) when they are hypnotically regressed to see when each of their alter personalities was formed in response to trauma. Regardless of their religious orientation or their lack thereof, a certain personality can be found within each multiple which says, "I have been with this person from before the time when they were in the body and I will remain with them when their body dies." It makes statements that sound like lines from the Upanishads, the hindu holy scriptures. It frequently describes itself as a conduit for a greater wisdom or divine love. That part was originally described by a psychiatrist Ralph Allison, who called it the inner self helper, because when he could connect with that part of a person, it would tell him exactly what was needed for the therapy to proceed and for healing to occur. It's like an inner physician, or inner wisdom that many people simply think of as their intuition or their creativity.

DiCarlo—Could you describe the experience of being connected to your core self?

Borysenko—Well, for me, when I am in that core or essential self, I feel spacious. I am not prone at that point to judge anybody or anything. My heart and mind are both open, which makes me a lot more perceptive as a scientist and psychologist. It makes me happy. My whole body feels relaxed, at ease, at peace. I feel a sense of unity with something greater than myself. A feeling of connectedness. For me, that experience always brings forth a tremendous sense of gratitude. The recognition that life is a tremendous mystery and a tremendous gift and that we are most fortunate to be living it.

I think everybody probably has that experience several times a day, but it might pass by very, very quickly and we just don't notice it. It happens every time you become present in the moment. Maybe it happens when you are looking out your window at the rising sun and for a moment you forget your fears and concerns and obligations, and are fully present to the experience. Perhaps it happens when you are around small children. There are so many moments when a child will just erupt with such laughter or such joy that you will just find yourself pulled into the moment. That's when you are in touch with that essential core.

The rest of the time we are in touch with the persona or the ego. That's when we feel closed down in some way. That's when we are judging. That's when we don't feel spacious. That's when we feel worried by something or are fearful.

DiCarlo—Do you feel that at this time in our collective history, it's important that we come into a recognition of this aspect of ourselves?

Borysenko—Not only is it important, it is inevitable. This part of ourselves is being spoken of in so many different ways. Take for example, the people who have near-death-experiences and who talk about experiencing some purity within themselves, some wisdom within themselves. They come back and others are interested in their story. What is this all about? What is this light experience within us?

Also, if people are connected to that part of themselves, then that is one way that healing will occur within our community and within our world. Our individual communities are going to have violence to the extent that we fear one another, to the extent that we judge one another and to the extent that we are unforgiving. There are going to be difficulties of every sort, from schools that are not nurturing our children, to corporations which take advantage of the public, to the war machine which is ever active. I think the hope of the world is truly in recognizing this oldest, oldest spiritual principle that exists within each of us. Then, you end up with a whole different paradigm and way of viewing the world. This world view is exemplified by the Dali Lama and how he felt about the holocaust in Tibet. He wasn't in the old paradigm of "an eye for an eye, and a tooth for a tooth." Instead, he practiced a form of loving kindness and compassion towards the Chinese. Every time he thinks of them, he tries to think of their pain and what he returns to them is his peace and blessing. We could stop war instantly—instantly—if people could do that.

DiCarlo—In your work you talk about the three stages of courage: willful, psychological, and spiritual. Could you explain their significance?

Borysenko—Sure. First of all, it's very important to have some sense of courage if we are to effectively deal with life. Without courage, when faced with difficulty we would just fold. But there are three stages, three types of courage. In *Fire in The Soul* I talked about my mom who had quite a bit of willful courage. That is, she could rise to any occasion, and do whatever needed to be done next. She could just "keep on truck'n" and go through it without looking forward, and without looking back, and without necessarily enquiring into the meaning of anything. She just said, "This is where I am right now, this is what I am supposed to do, and I'll do it no matter what." That will take you pretty far in life, but you can get a little bit further if you enlarge the idea of courage beyond the plain old will to keep on going.

Psychological courage, the second type of courage, comes from self-awareness. For example, there is a book out there that essentially says, "feel the fear but do it anyway." Oftentimes, that's what we have to do in this life. You can do that through either through "willful courage"—feel the fear and do it anyway—or through "psychological courage," where you enquire into the origins of that fear. You look and see what the fear has to teach you. Through that, you become a lot wiser and your heart tends to open. You develop compassion. And so that's a broader form of courage.

The third type of courage, spiritual courage, comes from having a higher perspective on the whole situation. From a psychological point of view, we can look at who copes well when under duress and we say they are stress hardy. They are optimistic. They look at change as a challenge. But when we look at it from an even a broader view of spirituality, that's when we reach a whole new level of transformation. I want to borrow a line from Ram Dass, who once said, "We have a choice in either viewing ourselves as human beings who might have an occasional spiritual experience or viewing ourselves as spiritual beings who happen to be having a human experience." That is the viewpoint of spiritual courage. It reveals itself when you have contemplated the meaning of life, and have come to the point where you recognize that no matter how difficult, no matter how painful, no matter how nonsensical something may seem to be, that there is a higher form of meaning involved. It is the faith that though our perceptions may be clouded, on another level of experience, things make sense and that the universe is a friendly place.

DiCarlo—Abraham Maslow was an explorer of humanity's higher possibilities and potential who shunned the prevailing fixation of mainstream psychology upon emotional and mental illness that you mentioned earlier. Those he studied were able to bring out and express, to varying degrees, their latent potential and wholeness. He referred to these individuals as being "self-actualizing." Many understand a self-actualizer as being a better performing human being, displaying a multitude of talents and abilities. Would you agree with that definition?

Borysenko—It's interesting...I think we have to be very, very careful when we talk about self-actualization because everybody has a slightly different idea about what a truly creative human being is. For me, a truly creative human being is one who has gotten some sense of what their unique gift is and is using that gift. The gifts vary. The gift of one self-actualizing person may be that they are extremely nurturing and their gift is to mother. Sometimes in this particular society we look at someone who has made the choice to mother and we say, "Oh my, poor thing. She hasn't actualized her potential—she's just being a mother." So I think one of the first things we have to do is take the blinders off our eyes and let people be who they are and to recognize that self-actualization has to do with being who you are. It's not about being a perfect person in some way. One self-actualized person may in fact be highly creative in one area, and yet still have blindspots in another. They are not "perfect." What they are able to do is say, "I see I have this blindspot or that blindspot. I'll try to deal with it as well as I can, but it is part of who I am at this time." So I would say that a self-actualized person has a degree of self-awareness and has become spacious enough that they can accept the pairs of opposites that they are. They can accept that they are great in some areas, but maybe not so great in others, and that's OK.

DiCarlo—So they would to some degree be in touch with their inner core?

Borysenko—Oh, yes. Without being in touch with your inner core at some level, you don't have enough of a feeling of spaciousness to become who you are.

DiCarlo—I suppose that the opposite of being whole and self-actualizing is to be fragmented...When we say someone is fragmented, what do we mean?

Borysenko—When somebody is fragmented it means that they have become identified with one aspect of themselves and have closed off other aspects. Much like an individual with multiple personality disorder has different alters or personalities, we all have different subpersonalities. This is the theory called Psychosynthesis, created by the Italian psychiatrist Roberto Assagioli. For example, many people have the subpersonality called the victim. They grew up in an abusive home or an alcoholic home and they might have a variety of subpersonalities. There might be the hero, or the mother or the teacher. All are different aspects of themselves, and they go from subpersonality to subpersonality rather unthinkingly. Somebody who is used to being in a victim subpersonality most of the time and doesn't have much conscious awareness of it, will tend to associate—because it is behaviorally familiar—with other victims who then support one another in their sorrows. Or a person might associate with the subpersonality of being an aggressor, because they are used to that. Or if they are used to being victimized, they may associate with or marry people whom they can rescue because that is their best way to get out of that victim sense of self.

When this happens, other aspects of a person are blocked from aware-ness because the person has become so identified with one aspect, one fragment of themselves. So this is what we would call being fragmented. A person who is aware of their different subpersonalities, aware that "Yes, I have all of this within me" is more spacious. So when this comes up, instead of necessarily feeling like a victim, they can see the old feelings and that part of themselves might rise to the occasion but they can also make the choice to respond from a larger aspect of self and not fall back into the same holes. So a person who is integrated has far more choice. They are more flexible and they are more creative. To the extent that they have become more whole, they will tend to respond to people and situations with more kindness and love.

DiCarlo—Would this integrated person, this whole person, be balanced in mind, body and spirit?

Borysenko—Well, in balance generally, but I think we can also go over-board with this because there's a sense that once you are "on the road to self-actualizing" you are going to be an idealized human being who is not going to fall into periods of depression, jealousy, anger or any-thing else. I think people need to give up these limiting ideas and realize that these so-called negative states are all part and parcel of being human. But as you begin to recognize these negative emotional states sooner, you begin to realize that you have some choice. All emo-tions that come up in some way serve the realization of our wholeness. But you must be willing to pay attention, accept the message and not get stuck there. So wholeness, once again, is not about perfection. It's about awareness and choice.

DiCarlo—You have stated that the number one affliction of Americans is a sense of unworthiness, which perhaps causes us to disconnect with this inner core that you speak of. Why is low self-esteem so prevalent?

Borysenko—To discover the reason for this prevailing sense of unwor-thiness, you need look no further than the media. From the time we are children, we are sold a bill of goods about what it is to be a worthy person in our society and it has everything to do with money and looks. Most people don't have that much money and they don't look like mod-els. You can see this preoccupation begin to take root as little children, when for example, little girls, five and six years old, begin to look in the mirror and say, "I'm too fat" or "My nose is too big." What a sad thing to measure our value and worth as human beings by. We have a very injurious society that sets people up for a good deal of self-judgement. We have a very injurious society in terms of defining the value of a life well lived. If we could define the value of a life well lived in terms of a person who develops some compassion, caring and a strong community—a community of people who help one another—and if we determined that a truly fine human being is one who has let go of judgements, and helps others, self-esteem would be a lot higher because these are qualities that a person can choose to cultivate.

Our sense of low self-esteem and unworthiness can also be traced to some old, European ideas about how children were supposed to be raised. Most of us in this country are still heir to the old type of child-rearing that says, "A child should be seen and not heard" or "Adults know best." Every time a parent with an authoritarian point of view raises a child, self-esteem will be low because the child never quite measures up. In some way you are being told what's wrong instead of what's right. There has been a great deal written about changing modes of child-rearing. That has everything to do with self-esteem. The more authoritarian the parent, the lower the self-esteem of the child.

DiCarlo—Do the roots of our unworthiness also trace back to traumas that may have been suffered during this lifetime or others?

Borysenko—Sure, it has to do with lots of different things. In *Guilt is The Teacher, Love is the Lesson* which was my second book, I discussed child development, self-esteem and experiences of shame—whether we were shamed by a parent or shamed by a teacher or shamed by peers. It turns out that shame is the master emotion, and that as soon as you feel shame, which is the feeling that you are so unworthy that you wish a hole would open up in the ground and swallow you, it brings with it other negative emotions. Shame is the master emotion.

Kids who have had very shameful experiences carry these wounds for the rest of their lives. Oftentimes they are the consequence of school experiences, where an unthinking teacher shamed a kid in front of their peers. Some people who have had parochial school education may have had many positive experiences, but many people are beginning to step forward and say, "Gee, I was beaten by the nuns." One little girl I know peed on the floor in front of the other students when she was shamed by a nun. She never got over the experience. Throughout our lives we have these kind of experiences and we've got to know how to integrate them.

And I don't think the wholeness of who we are is limited to just this lifetime. Who knows? Every parent will tell you that their child has a personality that they noticed from the time their child was just a few months old. Beyond the nature-nurture controversy—"is it in our genetics or is it in the way we were brought up?"—there are personal differences that go beyond that explanation and which are most likely soul experiences, soul residue; old patterns that we bring in. Whether these are from past lifetimes or parallel realities, who knows? That's all within what I would call the purview of the sacred mystery.

DiCarlo—It seems that many of the people that I have interviewed have alluded to the existence of interpenetrating, interdimensional fields of energy which serve as the true link between mind and body. In your view, are these energy fields metaphorical or are they real?

Borysenko—I think they are real. They clearly correspond to levels that people, such as the Eastern yogis, have noticed in meditation. They have noticed that when they learn to control their energies fields to certain degrees, they develop different abilities, such as the yogic ability to leave the body, or to bi-locate and be present at two different places at once. Elmer Green has studied yogis who can stop their heart, or control blood flow to certain aspects of the body. These yogis are true mind-body researchers in terms of understanding those different aspects of their subtle energy field.

Modern medicine cannot begin to explore that yet because there are no widely accepted measuring instruments that measure subtle energy fields. There have been many attempts to do that, but presently the technology simply doesn't exist. From the point of view of medical science, all we can say is, "there is something to acupuncture which has to do with a system of subtle energy which runs through some tributary-like system that those in the east call "meridians." When this energy is effected by acupuncture needles, then certain things happen that we *can* measure."

But we can only say that something is going on without saying what. Perhaps in the next decade or two we'll find out more, but right now we simply don't have the ability.

DiCarlo—I am very struck by your boldness in articulating a world view that conflicts with that of many people in our society. You touch upon seemingly taboo subjects—the soul, reincarnation, the human energy system, spirit guides and angels. What has been the reaction from those in the mainstream?

Borysenko—It's a fascinating thing for me to think about. On the one hand, perhaps I don't meet the mainstream that much. I have the sense that the physicians and psychologists who come to my workshops and speaking engagements are the ones who are more curious. So I don't know if I can truthfully answer that question other than to say that what we think of as the mainstream is certainly interested in much of these same topics these days. If you look at the best-seller list, you see books which delve into these subjects at the very top. And they stay there for a long period of time.

There is certainly a tremendous interest in angels. What a resurgence. There was a cover story on angels in both *Time* and *Newsweek* recently.

Even though what I am talking about may not be "mainstream" in terms of traditional psychology or traditional medicine, I think that it strikes a chord that most human beings wish to become more aware of.

DiCarlo—How would you react to those skeptical about the multidimensional aspects of reality that you describe?

Borysenko—I have very little response to the skeptics. Someone once told me this story that stuck in my mind when I was a medical scientist, and that was, that a battery of scientists can get together and tell you about all the scientific proof for the fact that bananas are bitter. But all you have to do is taste one once to realize that there is this whole other aspect to bananas. I think it's the same with skeptics. They are not reached by intellectual arguments, but by being touched in some way by the sacred.

Section 6

NEW VIEWS IN MEDICINE

"If there is a physical body, there is a spiritual body."
Paul 1 Corinthians 15:44

"I think we have way overrated the brain as the active ingredient in the relationship of the human to the world. It's just a real good computer. But the aspects of the mind that have to do with creativity, imagination, spirituality, and all those things, I don't see them in the brain at all. The mind's not in the brain. It's in that darn field."

Valerie Hunt, UCLA professor

In one of the major paradoxes of our time, Western medicine may at the same time be science's biggest beneficiary and its greatest victim.

Driven by advancements in science and technology, Western medicine has produced miraculous results. Human suffering has been reduced, the average lifespan has increased significantly and once dreaded diseases such as polio and rheumatic fever have been virtually eliminated within the span of a generation.

Yet, in the process of achieving this remarkable success, Western medicine has reduced the human being to little more than a bag of bones, muscles, and chemicals—a biological "machine." If a part is defective, then one simply needs to replace the part. In such a world view, there is little room for soul since physical illness is attributed to strictly physical causes. Mind, emotions, and soul are rendered irrelevent concepts. As a reflective physician commented, "I was a body mechanic, trained to look at the sea and the land as completely separate. Suddenly, I realized that the water, land, and air were all related—something medical school had never addressed."

It wasn't always that way. Wise physicians throughout the ages have known that body, mind and soul are connected. "Soul and body, I suggest," said Aristotle in 350 BC, "react sympathetically upon each other. A change in the state of the soul produces a change in the state of the body, and conversely, a change in the shape of the body produces a change in the state of the soul." It seems that in this modern era, we are beginning to understand the mechanisms of that relationship.

In our first interview of this section, Dr. Larry Dossey discusses the three eras of modern medicine, each possessing its own beliefs about the nature of the human being, the cause of illness and its proper treatment. According to Dr. Dossey, Era-1 medicine began in the 1860s when medicine first became scientific. It is the era of the body mechanic just mentioned. Era-2 medicine, which began in the 1940s, centers upon the impact thought, feeling and belief can have on one's physical health. In the 1990s this world view became widely accepted by the mainstream of society, as evidenced by the explosion of newspaper, magazine and television stories exploring the mind-body connection.

In the Era-1 and Era-2 model, thoughts and feelings are seen as affecting the body through anatomical, neurological and chemical pathways. Dr. Dossey has proposed that we are entering a 3rd era of medicine in which mind, consciousness, spirit and soul cannot be merely equated to the physical brain. In Era-3 medicine, one's thoughts, feelings and intentions not only can affect one's own health and well being, they can extend out through time and space to affect the health and well being of other people.

Rigorous scientific studies have linked the intention, prayer, or visualization of one person to the healing effects it can have on distant individuals (in some cases separated by thousands of miles). In one study 200 cardiac patients were randomly selected to receive prayer; the other 200 were not. After a year, those who didn't get prayed for were: more likely to be dead; five times more likely to require antibiotics; and three times more likely to develop complications. Twelve patients required ventilators. This study and hundreds of others, says Dossey, seriously call into question our assumptions about the way things are.

It is within this Era-3 framework that the work of Caroline Myss and Barbara Brennan becomes comprehensible. Myss is a medical intuitive. In partnership with Dr. C. Norman Shealy, M.D., she has achieved a 93% accuracy rate in diagnosing physical illness through intuitive means. Myss suggests that before the actual onset of a disease, there is a feeling of loss of power and vitality, which, if recognized and acted upon in time, could possibly avert the development of an illness.

According to Myss, those who are suffering from depression and chronic illness can, by using their intuition to deal with the unfinished business of their past, accelerate and enhance the healing process. She advises that unless we directly face our fears, we lose energy to the past and future. By living in different times zones, we speed up the aging process, develop illness and disease, and diminish our creative ability.

While Myss can diagnose illness, Barbara Brennan is a healer who is able to both diagnose and treat a variety of dysfunctions through unconventional methods of treatment. Like Myss, Brennan agrees that the root cause of disease is oftentimes not found strictly on the physical level. In her view, the physical body is organized and contained within a field of non-physical energy that has its own "subtle" anatomy. When the field is balanced and charged, an individual is likely to experience good health. When it is unbalanced, microorganisms are better able to invade the physical body and illness results. The field, which can be sensed by everyone in some manner, has been described across many cultures and throughout many historical periods. Brennan simply calls it the human energy field; some Russian and American scientists have referred to it as the bioenergy field; others have called it the aura.

Through the work of Dossey, Myss, Brennan and others, the Western model of medicine has been expanded to accomodate complementary forms of health care, some of which take into account the non-physical dimensions of our identity.

Dr. Larry Dossey

Dr. Dossey is the author of "Space, Time and Medicine," "Recovering The Soul," and "Healing Words," which explores remissions of illness that are unexplained by the traditional paradigm of medicine. A physician of internal medicine, he served as battalion surgeon in Vietnam and was former Chief of Staff of Humana Medical City Dallas Hospital. He lectures internationally and in 1988 was invited to deliver the annual Mahatma Ghandi Memorial Lecture in New Dehli, the only physician ever invited to do so. Dr. Dossey is cochair of the Panel on Mind/Body Interventions of the National Institutes of Health in Washington, DC.

DiCarlo—In your work you describe three eras of medicine: Era-1, Era-2, and Era-3. Using that as a framework, could you explain the emerging paradigm of medicine as you see it?

Dossey—I formulated this three-era approach to medicine basically to make sense of all the therapies that are out there and to characterize the way that we define ourselves as human beings. If you start at the time when medicine first became scientific, which began in the decade of the 1860s and move forward from there, at least three different eras "shake-out" in terms of the nature of health-care and how we think about the nature of who we are.

Era-1, which began in the 1860s, is plain old mechanical medicine. It looks at the body and the mind as purely physical, as purely pursuing the blind laws of nature. The predominant therapies that arise out of that approach are medications, surgery, radiation and so on. The body is not functioning properly, so the "doctor-mechanic" uses whatever tools of treatment are available to fix the problem.

In the 1940s, a different way of thinking about who we are emerged as people started talking about psychosomatic diseases. This was the second era, Era-2, or what is today called "mind-body medicine." Originally, it suggested that negative thoughts can do bad things to the body, thus the term psychosomatic disease. Now, this has been sort of turned on its head and we recognize that thoughts, emotions, attitudes and feelings can really be used to make people healthy. You can even make dreadful diseases go away by activating these positive emotions. An example of this is the scientific work of Dr. Dean Ornish, who's developed a program proven successful in reversing coronary artery disease. So basically Era-2 is the impact of thought, feeling and belief within an individual.

DiCarlo—Would you say then, that television programs, with titles like "Healing and the Mind" and "The Heart of Healing" are basically rooted in Era-2 medicine?

Dossey—Almost totally Era-2. One of my frustrations with these types of TV programs is that they neglect a tremendous body of evidence which supports putting a third era on the table, Era-3, which I want to call "Transpersonal Medicine" or "Non-Local" medicine. This emerging era of medicine—although it has probably been around as long as human beings have been here—is contingent upon the ability of the mind to function non-locally. That is to say, the ability of the mind to function beyond the person, beyond the individual.

In Era-2, you are concerned about what your thoughts, feelings and attitudes can do to *your* body. Period. That's what most of these television programs have centered upon and that's great. But there is compelling evidence, such as the evidence for the effectiveness of distant intercessory prayer, that the mind has some quality which allows it to reach out across space and time to affect the physical course of a distant living organism—whether that's a human being or something else. So many people in the alternative health care movement think that mind-body medicine is just about as far out and exotic as the new model is going to get. But I think that's just the tip of the iceberg. We need to begin to focus upon and acknowledge this emerging Era-3 type data which shows the ability of the mind to function at a distance—irrespective of the spatial separation from the object of its concern. We need to begin to ask questions about what this may mean.

Prayer is not the only body of available evidence which supports the ability of the mind to function at a distance. In the book *Healing Words,* I look at several categories, among which is transpersonal imagery. Most people think this is just the use of positive images to do something nice for your body. That's one definition and one use. But Dr. William Braud has shown that people who hold positive images of a distant person in a way that is caring, compassionate and prayer-like can actually bring about physical changes in that distant person.

So you see, we can differentiate three different categories or eras to define consciousness, and its relationship to the body which exists in space and time. Although my personal interest in the 1970s and 80s centered on Era-2, "Mind-Body" medicine, today, my interest has been captured by the emerging Era-3 medicine. There is a lot of neglected data that I want to make public. And secondly, I think there is more philosophical, spiritual, and practical "bang-for-your-buck" in this Era-3 medicine. Era-2 can still be explained based upon the chemistry and the anatomy of the brain and body. And you can still say, "So what?

That's great while you are alive, but take away the brain, and you've got nothing." So there's nothing more following death when the mind is confined to the brain. But in Era-3, the stakes are completely different. You can't hold on to the idea that it's all brain and body. If you honor this Era-3 type data, it is patently obvious that consciousness is capable of things that brains are incapable of. In other words, you cannot completely account for the workings of consciousness by studying the brain. This means there must be something about the psyche over and above the brain and the body. Working out the implications of all this has been my task.

DiCarlo—How did you first become interested in researching the effects of prayer?

Dossey—As a child I was naturally curious. I grew up in a Protestant religious community in Central Texas where a lot of praying went on all the time. At one time or another I think that most people who pray wonder if their efforts are working, and ask themselves, "Is it doing anything?" I was curious about that.

After I became a physician, I began to notice that some people got well even though no medical treatment had been rendered, except prayer. Sometimes these people had fairly dreadful diseases. So again, one wonders, "Is the prayer operative? Did it do anything or is this one of those funny coincidences?"

I think many physicians have this sense of curiosity. I was propelled forward again when I discovered a 1988 controlled study out of San Francisco General Hospital which involved nearly 400 patients in the coronary care unit. The group that was prayed for appeared to do much, much better than the group which received no prayer. I went to the medical literature to see if there had been any previous studies involving prayer to support this. I was astonished to discover over 130 studies in this general area. All demonstrated that prayer really does something remarkable—not just in human beings but in a great many other living things—from bacteria and germinating seeds, to rats and mice and so on.

So it was a curiosity which propelled me to the discovery of scientific data in the area of the prayer and its observable effects.

DiCarlo—I have to say that I was struck by the comprehensive number of studies you have reported on.

Dossey—That's one of the things I have taken pains to do. Every book I have ever written has at least 20 pages at the end which list references—mostly from scientific journals—to exemplify the fact that we're not just talking anecdotes here. This stuff flows out of science. If you want ammunition, there it is.

DiCarlo—What would you say has been the essential finding of your research?

Dossey—The essential message is that belief in prayer is no longer just a matter of faith. We've always said, "You can believe in this stuff if you want to, but you are on thin ice and shaky ground." Now, there is overwhelming evidence that if you take prayer into the laboratory and subject it to testing, you can show that it works. So, that's the big news. This information has been marginalized and it is practically unknown, even to physicians. It is not taught in medical schools. But it's out there. Through my work I hope to bring this information forward, so that it can be placed out on the table for discussion and dialogue.

My primary interest is not the practical applications of prayer to make diseases go away. It's really the larger message about who we are, and what our origins and destiny may be. How consciousness manifests in the world. Those are the real issues that go far beyond whether you can use prayer to bail yourself out of a difficult situation or illness.

DiCarlo—How do you define prayer?

Dossey— The prevailing notion that prayer is asking for something— basically talking out loud to a cosmic male parent figure who prefers English—either for yourself or somebody else is woefully incomplete. I want to get away from that common way of looking at prayer. Prayer for me is any psychological act which brings us closer to the transcendent. It's not the territory of any specific religion. Belief in a personal God is not even necessary. For example, Buddhists pray all the time, but Buddhism is not a theistic religion. They don't even believe in a personal God.

Prayer may involve words. We don't want to disenfranchise people who like to talk when they pray. That's fine. It's just that it goes deeper than that. It can involve silence, non-activity. It can even be done in the subconscious or when we sleep at night. So I prefer to use the term "prayerfulness" to capture those activities we have traditionally called prayer. One of the common features of prayerfulness that really makes a difference in the world is empathy, caring, compassion, love and so on. This has been demonstrated in the laboratory. It is clear that the experiments don't work very well if a person does not have empathy, love, compassion and caring for the object or subject they are trying to influence. The experiments work so much better if there is an empathic connection, a unity, a caring bond.

DiCarlo—So in the case of these experiments that you have uncovered, love was found to be more than a nice sentiment or feeling—a real force critical to the healing process itself?

Dossey—Let's say this. Love is a felt quality that can change the state of the physical world. We are beyond metaphor and poetry here. We are talking about something that literally can make a difference in outcomes in the world.

DiCarlo— How would you respond to the materialists who explain away the concept of realms of existence that go beyond the physical? That the mind is the brain and nothing more?

Dossey—I think the best response is to play science. You see, the theories and hypotheses of the materialists work fine as long as you restrict yourself to a certain class of data and ignore other data. The materialists cannot account for non-local events. There is currently nothing within the field of biological science that can explain distant, non-local, consciousness-related events. Period. To discover an explanation, you have to revise the materialist manifesto, which states that there is nothing beyond matter, there is nothing beyond what is perceivable through the five senses.

The problem is, the skeptics and the materialists won't look at non-local data at the level of biology and psychology. They will grant you that non-local phenomena occur at the quantum level—the level of the very small, such as atoms and subatomic particles. That has been proven beyond a reasonable doubt. But the notion that these things can happen at the level of the psyche and at the level of biology is just not being entertained. They have some classical ways of dismissing the kind of data that I have been focusing on. They paint it with the term, "parapsychology." They will say, "Oh, that's just parapsychology." But it doesn't matter what it's called. The real question is, "Is the data good?" And if the data is good, then the materialists are in a world of trouble, and the materialist way of looking at things by saying that "It's just all matter and energy" falls flat on its face.

Let me tell you why. These non-local manifestations of consciousness— among which prayer is one type—display characteristics that are not displayed by any known form of energy. For example, prayer, transpersonal imagery effects, and so on, are not a function of the amount of distance a person is from their target. These activities are just as effective when done on the other side of the earth as when they are done close up. All known forms of energy display something called "The Law of the Inverse Squared" which means that the farther away from the source of the energy you get, the weaker the energy becomes. Prayer doesn't do that. Transpersonal imagery effects don't demonstrate that principle of physics either. Robert Jahn's data at Princeton doesn't display dissipation with distance. Furthermore, you can put the object of the prayer in a shielded Faraday cage lined with lead, which for all practical purposes shields out electromagnetic energy of all types. Even so, the prayer gets through. The transpersonal imagery still works.

What I am saying is that the psyche has ways of manifesting far beyond anything known to materialistic science. You need to get a feel for what's at stake here. The reason that many of the dedicated materialistic scientists are so infuriated over the mere discussion of prayer and distant healing, is that it really begins to call into question their world view. It calls into question the adequacy of materialistic science, upon which these people have staked their careers, self-identity and self-esteem. And when you begin to question somebody's world view, that's more inflammatory than making derogatory comments about their mother. It generates tremendous animosity and really draws a line in the sand. If the data is right, then the materialist's model of the universe is inadequate. It's down to that. That's why you see people libeling and slandering other people over these issues in the scientific journals. These are really fighting words, and that's why people get angry about them.

DiCarlo—In a lot of respects, I would guess that many researchers in this area have been forced into a "Catch-22" situation. Prestigious scientific journals will not publish the research results, for the reasons you just mentioned. A researcher who is unable to publish is essentially put out of business, since research funds go to those who are well known to the mainstream.

Dossey—It's slowly changing. If it were all as intractable as it seems at times, things would never change. But historically, science and medicine have been dynamic. World views do change. Thomas Kuhn's work at Harvard regarding paradigms demonstrates this. Up to a point, everything seems secure and people are locked-in to a particular world view, but gradually, the exceptions that just don't fit the prevailing world view tip the scale. And when the scale gets tipped, the paradigm switches rather rapidly. I personally get the feeling that the data is mounting up inexorably on the other side of the scale. The tip is visible in the not-too-distant future. I just think you can never put this genie back into the bottle. According to Kuhn's model of scientific revolution, it's predictable that the critics and the skeptics are never more vocal and hostile than right before the switch in world views.

Right after I began to attract the attention of cynics, materialists and skeptics in medicine, I pulled a book off my shelf called *Garrison's*

History of Medicine, written in 1929. It's one of my favorite books. I went back and I looked at the way the great medical authorities of the day treated Oliver Wendell Holmes, who was among the first to suggest hand-washing. He was vilified for proposing the silly idea that washing your hands could cut down on the incidence of infections and death following childbirth, in spite of the fact that there was supportive scientific data which had been collected from the hospital. It showed that the practice of physician hand-washing tremendously lowered the death rate following childbirth. The data was in, yet in spite of that, this man was unbelievably hounded by other leading orthodox obstetricians.

This kind of response never changes. It has been played out time and again in the history of medicine. You are seeing it again here, and I will tell you, it will probably make the objections to hand-washing look very tame in comparison. You have world class researchers and a great many other philosophers saying all this stuff is silly. And they will claim that they have carefully looked at the data and it's all baloney. What we have is a basic disagreement. Although this may not be perfect science, I believe that a great many of these experiments are so clean and tight, with such great controls that you can take them to the bank. Look at it this way, if just one of these 130 experiments is right, the materialists viewpoint is bankrupt.

DiCarlo—Marcel Truzzi, a self-acknowledged skeptic, suggests that the focus needs to be on the preponderance of the evidence, not simply isolated studies. Would you say that the preponderance of the evidence in the studies that you have researched indicate that prayer works and that the prevailing materialistic paradigm is inadequate?

Dossey—Yes. I would emphasize the word inadequate. I don't want to say invalid. We haven't thrown away Newtonian physics just because quantum physics came on to the scene, but it certainly did show Newton's view was incomplete. I love Truzzi's phrase, "preponderance of evidence." There is variation in all areas of scientific work. I don't care what area it is. All the studies in any given field never show exactly the same results and this is true in the 130 experiments I have identified. Over half of them showed statistical significance that something phenomenal was going on. But the skeptic will say, "Ok, well look. Half of them show significance, but half don't. Trash the whole thing." That's not fair. That's not the way science is played. One must look at the preponderance of evidence.

In any given field, one looks at the most precise and accurate experimental protocols. You don't look at the experiments that are not as well designed. You look at what the best-designed studies show. And

I would be willing to say that the best studies in this field offer the best evidence. They show the most powerful effects.

Actually, there are about three or four areas of parapsychological research which have been subjected to "meta-analysis," a powerful form of statistical analysis developed by people with world-class reputations, like Robert Rosenthal at Harvard. Rosenthal has made a career in figuring out how to do this kind of analysis in tough subject areas. He was invited to analyze parapsychological studies by the National Research Council (NRC), a materialistically-oriented organization. They were putting together a report on human performance. After looking at several areas in the parapsychological literature, Rosenthal concluded that the quality of the research was extraordinarily high. This so angered the NRC that they asked him to withdraw his statement in their report. He refused. Turns out, they eliminated it anyway. This is an example of the ends to which people will go to keep the prevailing paradigm propped up. Physicist Max Planck, commenting about the controversy surrounding quantum physics around the turn of the century said that, science changes funeral by funeral. That's a clever way of stating that some people are never going to change their mind.

DiCarlo—What evidence exists to support the assertion that a new paradigm is emerging within the field of medicine?

Dossey—You can get a feeling for the profound changes taking place within medicine by looking at Dr. David Eisenburg's 1992 Harvard survey which found that over 60 million Americans went to alternative therapists that year—one-third of the adult population. That sounds like a huge shift to me.

DiCarlo—It's interesting that much of the change that is taking place in medicine is occurring through forces outside of the medical profession.

Dossey—One of the great examples of that is the way the Office of Alternative Medicine became established within the NIH. It came about as a result of outside political pressure. Senator Tom Harkin from Iowa was the prime advocate. And I think it's still true that most doctors within the National Institute of Health wish that this office didn't exist and would go away. But it has been established by order of law. It really is a landmark development and it does illustrate your point.

DiCarlo—What is the purpose of the Office of Alternative Medicine?

Dossey—First of all, it is not an advocacy group. It's not advocating anything. It's purpose is to dispassionately evaluate alternative forms of medicine in this country to see if further exploration is warranted.

It's intended to apply science to areas of therapy other than drugs and surgery, which typically get evaluated within the rest of the NIH. It really is a window of opportunity to take a look at therapies that otherwise would not be evaluated.

We want to see what will shake out. There are basically three questions that we must ask of any alternative therapy: 1) Does it work? 2) What's the downside or side-effects? 3) Is it cost-effective? And that's the role of this office. It's not to advocate anything.

DiCarlo—Are there certain assumptions that we have about ourselves as human beings that your research would tend to reject?

Dossey—Yes, I think we have been laboring under some fairly dismal and erroneous assumptions about ourselves. The most erroneous assumption is that we are separate individuals. By definition, if something about minds is non-local and there aren't any boundaries around them, at some level there cannot be some five and one-half billion individual minds walking around on the earth all safely separated from one another. At some point, they are one. This was the point that was put forth by Erwin Shroedinger back in the 30s—a Noble Prize-winning physicist.

Now, I would propose to you that if people could really "get it"—that at some point we really are not separated but instead we share identity at a certain psychological dimension—this would constitute a radically different ethical and moral imperative. It could have the effect of reducing a lot of international anger and war. Why would you want to go and make war on another individual if at some level you and they were the same? I think this raises brotherhood and sisterhood to a new level. It takes it out of the dimension of just being nice towards another person. It really does take it out of the level of metaphor to the level of fact. It makes it very, very real. This makes literal for instance, the Golden Rule imperative, "Do unto others as you would have them do unto you." Why? Because at some level they are you. And so I think you can see how non-local implications of mind reverberate through virtually every human activity we can think of.

I think that this could have a transformative effect on business. For instance, as a natural urge, why wouldn't you, if at some level you and another human being were the same, want to make the very best possible product for them? You are not doing this for somebody who is totally different and isolated from you. You are doing it for yourself, to yourself.

DiCarlo—Are there any other limiting assumptions many of us tend to have?

Dossey—I think that a lot of people in this culture have been deeply brutalized by the false assumption that there are only two ways you can live a life and you have to choose one or the other. You can choose to be intellectual, rational and scientific on the one hand, or on the other, you can live your life intuitively, spiritually. It's being either the scientist or the artist or mystic and there is no way to get those two abilities together in your life. This schizophrenic assumption has caused immense suffering for people in this culture and I think that's a false divide. If you look at the implications of these prayer studies for example, where you can show under laboratory controlled conditions that things like empathy, compassion, love, and caring can make a difference, and that there is some aspect of the psyche that is eternal, non-local, immortal—spiritual if you will—the fact that we can show that scientifically suggests that this great divide between science, religion and spirituality is false.

I would hope that this dialogue over Era-3, non-local aspects of consciousness, can help heal this gap between science and spirituality. But to do this, you have to have the courage and integrity to honor this data and go through it, instead of around it, as we traditionally have done.

DiCarlo—Some people make a distinction between being a healer and being a doctor. Is there a difference in your view?

Dossey—There certainly seems to be in this culture. Healing is a word that is practically forbidden in medical schools and hospitals. You don't talk about healing. You talk about the mechanics of medicine. It's really that simple. If you were to actually use the word "healing" the way you just used the word, people in these places would look at you with very strange facial expressions.

The very possibility that some doctors might have healing capacities unshared by others is a foreign idea. My wife, who is a cardiovascular nurse and an author who is widely known in her profession, got a fax today from a nursing chairman at a major US hospital. It said, "Dear Barbara Dossey, although we do not currently plan to invite you to our next annual nursing conference at our hospital, I can assure you that we will do so in the future when we get into healing." My wife came and showed me that and said, "What do you suppose they are into now?" So, figure it out for yourself. It's all mechanical. That there may be other qualities that could be called healing potentials, healing powers or healing skills is an idea that has not yet come for hospitals. It's changing though.

DiCarlo—Many of the people I have interviewed have admitted the vital role intuition has played in their lives. Has intuition played a significant role in your work?

Dossey—Well, I think intuition has played a major role. One of the ways that surgeons have of describing internists, of which I am one, is to call them crystal ball gazers. This is not intended as a compliment. This is one of the labels that is always levied by surgeons to the internists because "They think too damn much."

But I think there may be an element of truth to it. I believe that doctors frequently make intuitive diagnoses that have nothing to do with the known facts, physical examinations, and assessment of lab data. I had a long section on this subject in my previous book, *Meaning and Medicine.* There was a phenomenon called "snap diagnosis" that was the rage on this continent back in the late-1700s up to the mid-1800s. The great teachers in the medical schools would vie with each other to see who could make the most accurate diagnoses with the least amount of information. Napoleon's physician was one of the best. These individuals would have diagnostic information just come to them from within. They would walk past a room and say, "The patient in that bed has this disease." Or they would look at a portrait and say, "This is what the diagnosis is."

Well, few people will talk about snap diagnosis because that's been laid to rest. You have to dig that out of history books. But here's a connection you can consider. If there's some aspect of consciousness that is non-local, that cannot be confined to space and to time, if the mind can reach into the future (which a non-local mind by definition can do) and if there is no separation between minds at some level, then intuition takes on a whole new luster.

For example, if a diagnosis will one day be known, why can you not intuit it right now if there are no temporal barriers? If someone in the world knows the diagnosis, why couldn't you know it too if consciousness is omnipresent and there aren't any divisions at some level? So intuition takes on a whole new flavor through the lens of non-locality. Where this becomes practical is illustrated in a series of experiments by Dr. Norman Shealy with Carolyn Myss who is an intuitive. Carolyn is 93% correct at a distance in her diagnosis of 100 patients. I know of no internists, relying upon the data and physical exams, who are that accurate in the early stages of diagnosis. So if you can make intuitive diagnosis with that degree of accuracy, this is no longer a laboratory fluke. It is no longer an irrelevant play-thing or a stage trick. This has stunning medical implications.

DiCarlo— "Who are we?" and "What is the nature of the Universe in which we live?" are questions that cut right to the heart of the shift in perspective of the emerging paradigm. In light of your research, what is your response?

Dossey—For at least the last 200 years, our culture has embraced an idea, born of science, that the universe is a pretty dismal place. When we die, that's it. There's nothing that survives. Life is all a matter of chemistry, anatomy, and the physiology of the brain. When the brain and body die and rot—that's it. That's a very dismal outlook, and that doesn't sound like a very friendly universe to me.

On the other hand, if you take seriously the implications of these prayer studies, and other categories of experiments that have been done in addition to prayer, the research seems to suggest that consciousness can violate time and space. It seems to be non-local. It seems to be infinite in space and time in the way that it behaves. If you take those experiments and data seriously, then you can arrive at a completely different conclusion regarding the nature of the universe. You are able to say, for instance, that there is some aspect of the psyche, of consciousness, that is not confined to time and space or to brains and bodies. It is apparently infinite in space and time. And if it is, then by definition it must be omnipresent, eternal, immortal. This turns the tables on the dismal, traditional view of science. It says that something about us survives. It has no beginning. It has no ending. It is eternal and immortal. Now I will grant you that we don't have any "soul meters" to give you a direct readout on whether or not anything like the soul exists, but we've got the next best thing. We have reasonable empirical evidence that is indirect, that something about us is non-local in space and time. That to me sounds like an extraordinarily friendly universe.

DiCarlo—What beliefs do you hold about "the way things are" that you feel are especially empowering in the turbulent times we live in?

Dossey—The most important is a felt sense that no matter what happens, at some level it's OK. I basically give a "yes" answer to what Einstein once said is the most important question in the world, "is the universe friendly?" I think there is a pattern, a process and design in the universe. I think there is place in the universe for enduring human consciousness. I think that the most essential aspect of who we are is immortal. In view of that, what happens on this scale is relatively less important. This belief has contributed immeasurably to my peace of mind and my serenity. For me, the notion that whatever happens is OK, drives me to even greater activity, not less.

CAROLINE MYSS

Caroline Myss is an international lecturer in the field of human consciousness, and is widely recognized for her pioneering work with Dr. C. Norman Shealy, former president of the American Holistic Medicine Association, in the area of the intuitive diagnosis of illness. Together they have written the book, "The Creation of Health." According to Myss, the root cause of disease is not to be found at the level of the physical body, but rather at emotional, mental and spiritual levels.

DiCarlo—One aspect of the emerging paradigm of medicine seems to be the cooperation between healers and doctors or in your particular case, between intuitive diagnosticians and doctors. In that regard you and Dr. C. Norman Shealy have been pioneers. Is that a trend you feel is likely to continue?

Myss—We're already seeing that. I was recently on a panel for the American Holistic Medical Association with another medical intuitive by the name of Mona Lisa Schulz, who is both a Ph.D. and a medical doctor. She's a very well-lettered scholar who happens to be a superb medical intuitive. It is unimaginable how many physicians want access to an intuitive—a good one. And there are very few of us. The skill of medical intuition is just now emerging, and it is my hope that it is going to become a profession. Just because an individual may be able to tell when someone is ill does not qualify them as an intuitive. It requires highly sophisticated skills.

Over the past twelve years, I have observed that more and more physicians are coming to my workshops. I am also being invited to teach at their meetings. They know the value of an intuitive. Not so much to tell a physician what's wrong with a patient—medical tests do that effectively. An intuitive is most valuable when a doctor and a patient both know something is wrong, but it's not physically observable yet. I am developing a language to help physicians and patients speak in this zone, where the patient can say, "I'm losing power." No disease has developed yet, but it will if the condition persists. And a physician worth his or her stripes will say, "You're absolutely right. This is a signal, 'May-day, May-day, you're going down.'" The questions become, "Where are you losing power?" "What is it?" "What's the source?" And if you can reverse the power loss at that level, believe me, you will never see the illness in your body because the law is, "Your biography becomes your biology."

DiCarlo—Can these "power losses," as you call them, be perceived in the human energy field?

Myss—Well, first of all, the human energy field has to be understood differently. Words don't do justice to the structure. The human energy field shouldn't be called that at all, but since we do call it that, let's define it very clearly. It's better understood as an information center because that's what it is. And that's where you store all your messages. That's where you store all your faxes. That's where you warehouse everything. Your responses to everything and everyone, all your fear—everything—is stored in your energy field. Your responses form patterns that influence your electromagnetic circuitry. This dictates a quality control signal that influences the creation and quality of cell tissue.

It's important to understand that this is an energy system, and if I were queen as they say, I would schedule this subject into our school curriculum. In addition to your basic five sensory subjects—math, history, science—you would learn energy anatomy. You would learn the fundamentals of energy reality and that, "thought comes before form." Period. End of it. This is not negotiable. And because that is so, guess where we start defining responsibility? Here, in the energy field. This means you would be taught to take responsibility for your attitudes and for the thoughts that you generate because you would be taught that from that moment on, every thought you have has a consequence in the physical world. It is irrelevant to me that you can't see it. You're going to live your life by that fact.

DiCarlo—Let's take a moment to clarify something. Many other people seem bothered by the term energy. They prefer the word information to describe the human energy system. On the other hand, Dr. Elmer Green of the Menninger Institute doesn't seem to take issue with it. He has talked to various healers who told him that when they do what they do it is similar to working with energy, it has similar characteristics and properties.

Myss—Well, it is energy, but we have never credited energy with having intelligence. That's the gap. Energy *is* intelligent. It is alive. It is information—energy is information. It is one and the same thing.

We use the word energy, but we're one degree beyond understanding it as electricity. But until you recognize that we are transmitting information, it's invisible so we call it energy. But that's what it is, it's information.

DiCarlo—What is the most compelling evidence that these fields exist?

Myss—My own work. First, is my background as a Christian theologian. Everything I ever studied in theology validates this. Everything. My area of study was mysticism and schizophrenia. I was fascinated why everyone goes mad on their way to God. It's absolutely true. Nobody ever goes to heaven sane. You have to go quite insane before you get enlightened. But the journey into divine insanity is really the journey into realigning your power authority from external to internal. So everything I have ever read, whether in sacred texts or in my own work in medical intuition supports the existence of these energy fields.

I also know from personal experience. The reason I knew about the chakras, or energy centers, is because I saw them. Actually, the word "see" is not quite right. I don't see them and I don't hear them. I've never seen anything. The most magical things I have seen have been on television. As an intuitive, I'm the most undramatic one you'll every find. I don't shake, rattle or roll. To watch me in action is actually very boring—it looks like I am daydreaming and that's it. I don't see anything. All I do is start reporting information. I get impressions. How do you describe an impression? If someone was incapable of having an impression or a dream, how would you tell them? What would you say? And that's the challenge I have. But what I "saw" is that information organizes itself in the body. When I encountered the language of chakras, I said, "of course," because I had already organized information that way, in certain zones of the body.

Also, look at the language we use. We have already recognized the existence of these energy centers in our social language. If you gave people biological slang and then asked, "In which circumstances would you say, 'I've been stabbed in the back?'" And you gave them the following choices: a) When someone doesn't show up for dinner; b) When someone doesn't call you on time; c) When someone does something financial that harms you—they'll circle the last statement about the lower back. That's because biologically speaking, the lower back is where you store your finances.

If someone said, "You're a pain in the neck," under what circumstances would they use that phrase? Again, if I gave you the checklist and asked you to select, "A", "B", or "C" you'd circle exactly the one where they are a pain in the neck, such as when they talk too much. If I asked, "In which circumstance is this, 'just sickening?'" Or, "when such and such happens, 'this makes me___'" you could fill in any of the anatomical words we use all the time to say exactly what I am saying, although we do it very crudely. We already know everything I am talking about, the only difference is, I've made it a very sophisticated science. Everybody else is using street slang.

DiCarlo—Could you describe each level of the human energy field?

Myss—I break it down into three levels, which is tribal, individual and symbolic. I cluster the 1st, 2nd and 3rd chakras under what I would call the tribal or the group mind. But instead of looking at each of the chakras individually, I cluster them. So the 1st, 2nd and 3rd are one unit. 4th, 5th, 6th and 7th are another. Then there's the 8th, which is the symbolic.

Let's say I was doing a reading of someone's chakras. 1st, 2nd and 3rd chakras represent all the material and information that corresponds to your physical life. That's one of the reasons I call it tribal, because all your tribal data is in there. For example, "What country are you from?" or "What nationality?" "What kind of influence has it had on you?" In other words, "How have you been tribally programmed?"

Now in addition to your biological tribe, your social tribe is in there. So you may come from an Italian background, and I presume therefore Catholic, but you are also going to have a social tribe, meaning you are going to be an American. That's a larger tribal group. Then, because you're an American, you are going to have a democratic zone in your biology. So you have your patriotism there. Know what else is in your 1st chakra? Your coordinates for time and space. I can tell how fast you are aging in that one chakra.

Said another way: these three chakras tell me how linked you are to letting the tribal mind—meaning your biological, social and global tribal mind—control you. Because the stronger you are linked into the tribal mind, the weaker will be your personal willpower. It's directly proportional. So, to say to somebody, "You create your own reality," is a relative truth. It is truth, but you have to water it down, because people who are tribal do not create their own reality. Their tribe does it with them and for them. So they are in the evolutionary stage of the group mind.

At some point, every one of us, somewhere along the line—this life, next life—is destined to break free of the tribal mind and develop the upper 4th, 5th, 6th and 7th chakras. It is inevitable. This is the stage of individuation. The 4th thru the 7th chakras have nothing to do with time and space. Only your bottom three do. So, your 1st, 2nd and 3rd tell me: 1) Your biology; 2) Your sexuality; 3) Your finances; 4) All your control issues with other people; 5) How you interact with others; 6) All your physical contacts. All of this is contained in that stage of your biology and I promise you, that information is in your cell tissue.

Your 3rd chakra has to do with your definition and working relationship with external power. Repeat: external. "Do you give your power away?" "Do you look for approval from others?" "Do you take power from others?" "Are you afraid of criticism?" "Have you been criticized?" This information is in your cell tissue. Now we draw the line at these lower three—which we can group together and call your personality. Your personality and ego is contained in these lower chakras.

Now, if you were someone who is extremely tribal, for example someone who is in a gang, or someone who can't get out of religion (religion is 1st chakra, spirituality is 7th. There's a difference, yes?) If you are completely tribal, then your 4th, 5th, 6th and 7th chakras take their commands from the bottom three. The bottom three completely control the upper three. So now watch: I am sitting in front of an individual who has cancer of the colon, and I say to him, "Now, here are your options. In addition to surgery you have to deal with other issues, such as your absolute fear of change. And then there's the issue of losing control because things are moving too fast for you to order." People who get cancer of the colon deal with these kinds of issues. They can't stand losing control. They absolutely can't tolerate it. Why do you think Reagan suffered from it when Gorbechev ascended into power? He was losing global control. Perfect timing I must say.

So then I might say to this person, "In dealing with these issues of control, you can do a couple of things. You can go to a therapist and work this out, and then you can try_____" and I would list all these alternatives. And what I always see—always—if this person is an incredibly entrenched tribal being, I'll watch them while they absorb the information I am giving them and they will transfer it to their tribal data base. They will run it past their family so to speak, even though their body has not left my room. After doing this they will say to me, "No, no, no, I can't do that." What they are really saying is—and they don't even realize it—"I can't do it because no one in my family has done it before."

Now do you think those people create their own reality? Absolutely not. That's preposterous. Their reality is created by the weatherman on TV for god's sake more than it is by themselves: "Oh, it's going to be sunny? Ok, I'll be happy."

When I watch television, I hear, "Are you going to give us good weather today Willard Scott?" or, "Willard, what's wrong with you today?" What a trite, ridiculous comment—as if he's responsible for these things. But you see, that's very tribal.

DiCarlo—So what you are saying is that this marks the difference between someone who is outer-directed versus being inner-directed and therefore aligned with their soul?

Myss—You could reduce it to that kind of thing, but you know what? That doesn't explain the technology of how this works. And that's what's so rich about my work. I have got the technology down to a science. Literally. I can tell you what thought is associated to a particular chakra, and at what speed, such as, "This thought will cause a particular physical condition in four months."

So, in looking at the top level, when you start the journey of individuation—being an individual by pulling away from the tribal mind—you begin the journey of becoming congruent, of getting all seven chakras lined up with a more mature will. That's when you have to go into conflict with the tribal mind, because you are now purging yourself of what you want to believe versus what you have been programmed to believe.

And then the 8th chakra is where your contract is. The agreements that you make with the universe before you are born. So that's how I divide it.

DiCarlo—What are some of the possible consequences of being fully aligned with our soul—the essence, core or totality of who we are?

Myss—Well, for one thing, I don't think you age. I think you mature, but I don't think you age. Let's go through the door of mystics, shall we? All mystics, east, west, up, or down—and this fascinated me in my theological years—share certain abilities. Now from the ordinary mortal's point of view, they would seem to be gifts, but when you actually get into it, they have earned these abilities every step of the way. And by becoming congruent with your soul, you alter your relationship with time and space. I teach it this way: "Imagine that you have got 100 circuits going through your head. Every day, you get to distribute these circuits whenever you want. Any place you want—within yourself or outside of yourself. Now here's what you need to understand: for every circuit you distribute outside of yourself, you increase the amount of time required for anything to manifest in your life. For every circuit you contain within yourself, you increase your experience of what you would call synchronicity and at a master level, instantaneous creation. It's as simple as that."

DiCarlo—How do you do that?

Myss—That's where discipline comes in. You must have a spiritual discipline. You must be strong enough to begin the process of taking your will out of illusion and into yourself. So you face yourself. You face every fear you have got and how much authority it has over you and you begin to challenge it. If you don't do this, that means you are losing your circuits to that fear. That fear has more authority and every day you are giving that fear more of your circuits. You are keeping it alive. Example: I have no fear of my stereo system. None. Zero. I don't give away any circuits at all. Now, how about the fear of being mugged? That has got two of my circuits. I feel it every time I am in New York City. So until I can eliminate that fear, as in the case with my stereo, I am giving it fuel. Now I don't have a fear of rocks dropping on my head. I don't have a fear of slipping into a sewer. There are a lot of fears I don't have. I don't have a fear of heights. Being on top of a tall building doesn't phase me in the least. But wherever it is that I do have fear, I have work to do. I have to face my fear directly. I have to honestly say to myself, "Do I have a fear of being alone? Or do I have a fear of being in a crowd?" If I do, I have to walk into it, deal with it, until it is nothing to me. That's what inner discipline is all about.

DiCarlo—All Eastern psychologies talk about the importance of being fully present in the moment. Energetically speaking, what is the significance of the present moment?

Myss—Everything. That's the only thing that is significant. For the *vast* majority of people I do a reading on, illness is the consequence of living in two time zones. If the majority of your energies are in the past, you get cancer. Let me talk to you as if I were your guardian angel. This is what I do in my workshops. Now, if I were your angel, and you had a prayer, "Help. I need an opportunity to come to me." I, as your guardian angel would say, "I know you do. But sweetheart, the kind of opportunity you want is going to require 65% of your circuits in present time—you've only got 20%. So the way I've got to answer your prayer is to make whatever it is that you have attached 40% of your circuits to, to come into your life. In this way, you can deal with it. It's going to look like you are going to have one crisis after another. But it's the only way I can get you into present time.

DiCarlo—So it's kind of like a slap in the face to wake you up and get you out of the past and into the present. Why must a person have to physically have that experience in order for them to be fully in the present? Can't they simply will themselves to be more in the hear-and-now?

Myss—I think that most people aren't strong enough to call their spirits back by themselves. How many people do you know who live in the past in some way, shape or form?

DiCarlo—More than a couple.

Myss—If you said to them, "Ok, let's call it back—1,2,3, up, up, up..."

Do you think that would work for most people? Look, you don't know how much power people have invested in holding on to their past. You have no idea.

Here's what we've done. I am convinced that our culture never, ever had a language of intimacy until this massive movement started toward psychology in the 1960s. A language of intimacy didn't exist. I know people who have been married to one another for over 40 years and they never had a talk about sexual needs. None whatsoever. They only had a talk about stuff like "What time are you getting home?" Or, "What do you want for dinner?" Or, "How much money are you making?" Or, "Are you cheating on me?" But personal needs? Nothing. So what was intimacy? How was it defined? Intimacy was defined by what was in the 1st, 2nd and 3rd chakra. "How much money do you make?" "Where do you work?" This was intimate.

Then we took the language of psychology out of academia and out of the clinics and mass marketed it, and wove it into everybody's mind, so that *now*, how do we define intimacy? By the exchange of wounds, not wallets. So, now two people meet. One asks the other, "Where are you from?" The 2nd says, "Ohio." "Really? I'm from Chicago." That's not going to bond two people. That's 1st chakra information. 2nd chakra: you will exchange something at the 2nd chakra level, and you say: "I am an attorney" or whatever since that's where occupations are. That's not going to bond you either. Now let's go to the 3rd chakra. You say, "I really like the color blue and the color green." Nope, no bond there. Now watch this: go to the 4th chakra. Let's pull out a wound, but it can't be too big in the bonding ritual. We have to share something tribal, something small and bite-sized. After all, you don't want the other person to run away. So you say, "You know days like this remind me of my childhood." I'd send part of me back to my 1st chakra saying, "Hurry up, produce an equal bit-sized doughnut childhood memory." And we have a bonding ritual going on. "You never got doughnuts? I never got twinkies." Bingo—friends for life. And, every time you call me up and say, "Doughnut, doughnut, doughnut," I drop everything because that's how we have defined support.

Now why would you heal that? I ask you, "What's in it for you?" Especially if you have me dancing on the end of a rope every time you yell doughnut. You're going to give that up? I don't think so. I have seen people go to their grave rather than give up that power.

DiCarlo—Some people have spoken about a process called "Soul retrieval." When a person experiences a trauma in life which they are unable to come to terms with, part of their soul departs and must be brought back. Would you like to comment on that?

Myss—That's just another word for what I would call having your energy in your past. There's no difference. "Soul retrieval" is shamanic language for the very same thing. I would say your circuits are going backwards. That's my language for it. I prefer non-superstitious language. I like a language that is much more technical, because I think the Western mind adjusts to it better.

Shamanism is a 1st chakra skill, so it tends to use very earthy or occult language, which by no means invalidates it. That's simply the level of that language. The 1st chakra is the language the church would use and they would say exorcism, wouldn't they? Getting the spirit back from a demon. So it's the same thing.

The interesting thing to notice is that these things are surfacing en masse simultaneously. Why is this? I think it's time to recognize that our energy gets stuck in different zones, and there is a consequence to that. One, our cells age differently. Two, it causes disease. Three, it makes you function in as many as 17, 18, or 30 time zones simultaneously. You lose creative ability. And you wonder why people are nuts? How's that for an explanation?

DiCarlo—One of the by-products of living in the modern era seems to be stress, which can precipitate poor health and physical illness. Could you describe what happens to an individual's energy field when they experience stress or anxiety?

Myss—Imagine that you have 100 circuits coming into the top of your head. Now, something triggers anxiety. What would trigger anxiety in you?

DiCarlo—Feeling that I said something to somebody that I shouldn't have said.

Myss—Ok that's your 3rd chakra. So you have the perception that you shouldn't have said something and somebody just stormed out of the office. If you have anxiety over that, what's really going on is you have given a cluster of your circuits to that person, and that person is walking out of the building with part of your energy. It's not unlike having someone take a knife and rip your gut open, only it's at the level of your energy field. You are energetically bleeding. You are hemorrhaging.

Whereas, when you experience something like love or safety, there is no hemorrhage. So when you are not losing any energy at all, you get high. You feel vibrant. You are in ecstasy.

DiCarlo—So would that be referred to as a flow state or peak experience?

Myss—Yes, absolutely. Which is why there is such an unbelievable high when you find out good news after you've been anticipating something horrible. You were losing your energy. Have you ever really wondered if someone you love is safe? Seriously wondered? You feel yourself losing your energy, moment by moment by moment. And then you get the phone call and all is well. They've made it and they are home.

In finding out that everything is OK, you feel this sense of overwhelming expansion as your spirit comes back to you, it's like life coming back to your cell tissues. It's just like that. You return to being in present time, and in present time you are always going to feel energetic. You cannot "not" feel energetic if you are in present time.

So my advice to people is, "Keep your attention in present time only." Try never to project into tomorrow or back into the past. It costs too much. No one can afford to live in 30 time zones simultaneously. Nobody. If people could stay in present time for two days, their whole life would change, because the consequence of having that much energy would activate synchronicities—coincidences in their lives of being in the right place at the right time and that would change everything.

Barbara Brennan

 *Barbara Brennan is a teacher, healer, therapist, author and scientist who has devoted the last 20 years to research and exploration of the human energy field. She holds a Master's degree in Atmospheric Physics from the University of Wisconsin and worked as a research scientist at NASA's Goddard Space Flight Center. In 1982, Barbara founded the Barbara Brennan School of Healing, which offers a 4-Year Professional Healing Science Training Certification Program. She is regarded as one of the most adept spiritual healers in the Western Hemisphere.*

DiCarlo—You are generally regarded as one of the pioneers of the human energy field. What exactly is this energy field that you've devoted so much of your life to understanding?

Brennan—I have a scientific background, and from a scientific perspective, there aren't any adequate experiments to tell you what the field really is. So I am going to have to speak solely from my experience as a healer who is able to perceive the field and work with it. From this perspective, the human energy field—which can be perceived by anyone with practice—is the matrix structure upon which the cells of the physical body grow. It is the template of the physical body.

It is also the vehicle for psychosomatic reactions, or the "mind-body" connection. It's of vital importance since it is a foundation for the physical body. It is directly connected with health and illness. Based upon my experience as a healer conducting private sessions with clients spanning a fifteen year period, and as a teacher for as many, I can tell you that anything that happens in the physical body will happen in the pattern of the energy fields *first*.

So the energy field precedes the physical body. It sets the foundation for the physical body, and anything that goes wrong in the energy field will eventually make its way into the physical body.

DiCarlo—Is the human energy field fairly stable or does it tend to be fairly volatile?

Brennan— Actually, your field changes with each thought. Once you open your high sense perception as I call it, and can see the field (the major two senses I use are seeing and feeling but any of the inner correspondences to the outer five senses can be used) you will be amazed at how it changes from moment-to-moment. It moves very, very fast.

The field has several different components and can be broken up into at least seven different layers. These seven layers are commonly reported in the esoteric literature and by people from different cultures around the world who have the ability to directly perceive it.

From my perspective, every other level of the energy field is structured, with organized lines of scintillating light which form a specific pattern. The structured layers can be perceived as a frequency band, with each layer having its own frequency. Little sparks of light can be observed moving along these lines.

In between the structured layers of the field is a bioplasma-like energy that simply flows along the lines of the structured field pattern. It's the energy that flows along the lines of the structured field pattern that changes very fast with thoughts and emotions, not the structured pattern itself. For example, if you stop yourself from feeling something, it will stop the flow of energy in the field. And if you experience the feeling, the energy will be released. There is a direct correlation. There are even correlations between the energy field and the part of the brain you are thinking with. As you change your thought patterns, the patterning of the field changes.

DiCarlo—So if you switched from being very analytical and left brained, to being very intuitive and right brained, there would a perceivable change in the field?

Brennan—Yes, there would be definite flow patterns that change. For example, we are trained from very early in our childhood to be rational. And traditionally, we go to school and we learn to think logically and we memorize information. And that shows in a particular field pattern or a generalized flow. And intuitive thinking is very different than that. Different parts of the brain are used and the flow and pattern of the field is different.

What's really interesting is that it corresponds more or less to what a PET scan shows.

DiCarlo—Let's try to make this rather abstract concept of an energy field permeating the physical body a bit more concrete. What are some of the common experiences people have that directly relate to activities which take place in the field?

Brennan—Knowing something before it happens, because it's happening in the energy field first. Feeling that someone is staring at you when your back is turned to them. You turn around, look, and yes, someone is looking at you. You may not even know that's why you turned to look. There are streams of energy that come out of the eye and you can feel it on your body. Another example: the phone rings and before you answer it you already know who the person is and that they have good news. Also, feeling good when you wear specific clothes, even specific colors, because they are the colors that your energy field needs that day. Interactions with animals. People can communicate with their pets and know what the animals are feeling. These are all energy field interactions.

DiCarlo—Now let's say I have an affinity to someone I have never met before, or on the other hand there is someone I immediately dislike, is that phenomena related to activities taking place at the level of the human energy field?

Brennan—That's directly related to the interactions of the field. Everybody's field pulsates within a range of frequencies. If the range is about the same for two people, then they will usually have a lot of affinity with each other. If it's not, it will make them nervous. If you have a higher general frequency tone to your field than someone else, you might feel drugged out. On the other hand, if somebody has a higher frequency than yours and that frequency is chaotic, it will make you nervous. There are many of these examples.

DiCarlo—Another example you have mentioned in your work—one I especially find interesting—is the dynamic that occurs in the human energy field when a man and woman meet for the first time, let's say at a social function. By all outward appearances, they may pretend not to notice each other, yet at the level of their fields there is a great deal of activity, cascades of energy moving back and forth between them. This suggests a genuine interest, a testing of each other's field for compatibility.

Brennan—Right. That happens a lot. All of the beginning stages of courtship can be seen quite clearly in the field.

DiCarlo—If you read all the self-help literature that is available, it would seem that we could all benefit from learning to forgive ourselves and others. That certainly seems like the right thing to do in life but I'm wondering, from a more practical perspective, what happens in our energy field when we do this?

Brennan—When you forgive yourself, wonderful things happen. There is a certain tension and stagnated energy that is held in the field whenever there is anything that you won't accept within yourself. It's kind of like a mucous that you get when you have a cold. So you actually create distortions in your own energy pattern that have to do with unforgiveness towards yourself. These distortions will eventually lead to illness. When you forgive yourself, you are actually unblocking the flow of energy in your field so that it can flush itself out. It allows for the resumption of the normal life flow.

Life is associated with constant movement in the personal energy field, so any attitude of non-forgiveness within the self will create blockage. When you have a non-forgiving attitude towards an individual, there will be a definite pattern in your field. The outer edge of your field will become rigid and brittle when interacting with that person. There will be additional ways that you will not let your life energy flow out towards that person.

There are great bands of energy or bio-plasmic streamers that normally flow between people when they interact. There's an exchange of life energy that normally goes on between all living things. It's not just human beings: there's a flow between humans and animals, humans and plants. But if there is a sense of unforgiveness, all that will be stopped. There will be the same type of stoppage in the other individual also. It's usually a two-way street.

DiCarlo—Would that be the same phenomena you would observe if someone, let's say, were judging another person?

Brennan—That would be a little bit different. All of these different attitudes and mental states would result in a little bit different flow. Usually judgement has to do with an energy flow running up the back of the body and sometimes hooking over and a rigid withdrawing back. Also, energy running up the front of the body and kind of "hooking over" towards the other person.

If you look at the energy field, there are three major aspects: reason, will and emotion. All are associated with psychological phenomena. When you judge another, you stop the flow of your emotions towards that person which would be on the front of the body, and you would be pushing your energy to the back of the body, into the will, and then running it up into the mind. So you "will not" accept this person, and then the energy moves up your body to the head region and you rationalize it in the mental sensors.

DiCarlo—What if someone is experiencing love?

Brennan—With love, especially when both people are feeling love towards each other, there is a tremendous flow of energy between the two. But you don't even have to have two people. When a person allows love into their field, the field becomes very soft, very flowing, resilient. The whole field blows up sort of like a balloon. It becomes very energized and the energy flows out of the field in a very healthy way.

All fields have different kinds of boundaries, so the boundary of someone who has a lot of love or is feeling love toward a particular person,
will be soft and more resilient. As a result they can interact with another human being in a much easier way.

DiCarlo—Well, how would that compare with a person who was experiencing gratitude in their life?

Brennan—To feel grateful is one of the most important experiences we
need as humans. When we feel it, there is an acceptance of everything
in our life and a surrender to basic values in life. We can see the positive in everything and also feel thankful for it. That's essential, because it allows a connection to take place between the personality self
and the deeper regions of the human being, the core essence or the
divinity within. The intense energy from the core essence then radi-
ates out. It's as if a corridor opens from the core essence of an individual, and the energy is able to flow out and into the entire world.
Also, the connection from the personality to the spiritual or divinity
within, is open and made more solid.

Gratitude also puts the individual in synchronicity with the universal
energy field that connects all of life, the flow of the life force, or the
morphonogenic fields of the whole planet and the solar system. That is
also very important because it puts you in sync with your life. When
you can flow in that way and find that place in life then the entire
universe becomes very supportive. The feeling of gratitude is an essential experience we all need.

DiCarlo—In such a state, do more positive events, circumstances and
people come into one's life experience?

Brennan—Yes, because you will allow them. You won't be stopping
them. This is the opposite of judgement, which stops the flow of energy. You don't let anything in and you don't let anything out—or
what you do let out isn't so nice.

DiCarlo—Have you found that the environment effects the human energy field? For example, someone works in an office where there's fluorescent lighting.

Brennan—Yes. The environment effects the field very much and there
are several chapters in *Light Emerging* about that. I can't work under
fluorescent lights. I have spoken with Dr. Brainard, a professor at
Thomas Jefferson Medical Center in Philadelphia who's been studying
the effectiveness of fluorescent lights in reducing "Seasonal Affective
Disorder" (SAD). He has helped develop a very high frequency (40
kilowatt) pulsing fluorescent light with x-ray shield. It as well as halo-

gen work well for SAD without disturbing the field as much as normal fluorescent lighting. Full spectrum fluorescent lights also need to be converted to a higher frequency and have x-ray shields.

There are several things that happen with fluorescent lights. The pulse of the fluorescent beats against the human energy field. It's like two fields beating against each other, which I realize sounds terrible. Fluorescent lights also emit x-rays. So it really disrupts the human energy field. In my book there is a case study about a female client who came in for a healing session. The woman had been working on a computer under fluorescent lighting for about six months for 12 hours a day. She got very, very ill. She was in her twenties, and she was able to take the skin under her arm and stretch it out four inches. The first layer of her energy field was breaking down. After she quit her job she got well right away.

DiCarlo—Are there any misconceptions about the human energy field that you commonly encounter?

Brennan—Yes. People think it's layered like an onion and it's not. It has levels that extend all the way through, or frequency bands. That's the best analogy I can use.

Anybody looking at it with high sense perception will see the same thing if they are looking at the same structure. Many people seem to think they will see different things in the field, that what is perceived is determined by who does the perceiving. I don't think that is true.

The field changes very fast and some people don't understand that. Also, it's much more complicated than what people think. A lot of people will come up to me and say, "What color is my aura?" Well, the human energy field is comprised of all the colors there are, so some people might think they have, let's say, a "blue aura" and that means something. A person might have a lot of blue in the aura and that could mean a lot of different things. So it's not really simple.

The study of the human energy field is as complicated as the study of the anatomy and physiology of the physical body. There is a subtle anatomy and physiology in the human energy field.

DiCarlo—I have gotten into discussions with scientific researchers and doctors about the very term "energy" and as you know, that is the subject of a big debate. These fields are comprised of an energy, the properties of which seem to violate some of the accepted laws of physics.

Brennan—Yes. I am using it rather sloppily here... I think that as we learn more about basic physics, all of these issues will be resolved. I am using the word "energy field" because it is more meaningful to most people than talking about holograms or something more difficult. From my perspective, there are energy fields. An energy field is the matrix or mold for the physical body. But it's that and much more than that. Take the phenomena of prayer for example. I can relate prayer to what happens in an individual's energy field and it's clearly something beyond that. Certainly life goes beyond the limited definitions of an energy field.

I know this from my own work with the deeper levels of the human energy field, where the healing methods are totally different. It is not like running energy or projecting energy into the field of another individual. It is more like healing with intentionality and there are very specific steps to that.

So in one sense we do in fact heal with bioplasmic streamers and certainly bioplasma has been measured. There are fields and there are field structures. And the deeper nature of the human being is much more than that. It goes much beyond that. I find the idea of a structured energy field to be very, very useful. When people learn to see it and we teach people how to do that all the time, it becomes extremely useful. And yet there are many things that happen that are beyond that concept.

I don't tend to argue with people. I tend to find the bridges between somebody else's interpretation of reality and my own. They are all limited ideas actually.

DiCarlo—You have said that the major cause of illness stems from how we habitually imbalance our fields, thereby making it weak and ourselves susceptible to physical illness. Why do we do this?

Brennan—Our fields become imbalanced because we all have certain belief systems that we grew up with and a whole string of childhood traumas. When you put both the traumas and belief systems (which most of the time are unconscious and actually based on traumas inflicted during childhood) together you create a picture of the world—a world view— which is not in keeping with what the world really is. In childhood, you try not to feel any traumas experienced in order to survive and the way that you succeed in not feeling these traumas is to block the flow of energy. They then become stuck in your field. So we create a way to hold these "blobs" shall we say, of consciousness and energy, so that we might never have to experience them. This is strictly an automatic system that happens in everybody and in order to do that we have to distort the healthy field pattern. Once we've done that several times, once we've found an effective way not to feel terror let's say, as a child, we will adapt that as a coping strategy. Eventually, that will become a habitual pattern in the human energy field. The field will become imbalanced in order not to feel terror, fear or anger.

Then we act as if the world *is* terrorizing and a belief is formed. We approach the world from the perspective of terror. Because we see it that way, we eventually draw to us more experiences that make us believe in terror even more. But fortunately, what happens is at some point things get so bad the individual cannot tolerate living that way anymore; they set out upon a path of personal change and healing.

That's actually what's happening to many, many people in this country now. Especially people in mid-life crises. The school that I have is filled with people in their late 30s and 40s. These people are saying in effect, "This isn't what I wanted in my life."

DiCarlo—So they are searching for the deeper causes of their unfulfilled life experience?

Brennan—Right. And it's about finding out what they really want. Usually it's the situation where you want something in your life and you just can't get it. No matter what you do you can't seem to create it and you know something is wrong. Actually, that is the negative carrot that turns us around. It's really a "fail-safe" system. If you are not getting what you really wanted to create, then what you are going to do is to create pain. That pain then will motivate you to change.

DiCarlo—When a person consciously decides that they want to psychologically and spiritually grow in life, what happens to their energy field?

Brennan—There are many, many steps along the way. The field of anyone who hasn't done a lot of personal development work and transformed themselves will be quite brittle. It will be laden with blocks, stagnated energies, and probably tears, disruptions and imbalances.

When I first began seeing fields, I was very surprised and discouraged to realize just how imbalanced most human beings are. But the more I could perceive the field, the more I could understand how easy it was to work with and change.

When you begin working with your field, the frequency levels and the power running through your field increase and blocks of stagnant energy are cleared. When these blocks are cleared, you usually experience the consciousness and energy in it.

One major thing about the human energy field: energy and consciousness cannot be divided. So whenever energy moves, you also experience it. You become consciously aware of it. Transformation is about becoming consciously aware of everything. In other words, awakening.

In the process these blocks are cleared. As they are moved out, you experience the energy as it is being released and you end up experiencing the feelings and thoughts connected to that traumatic energy. Afterwards, there are stages of confusion. This is because the framework upon which you have based your life and reality starts to change. It's not an easy process, but it's certainly well worth the effort. Your field becomes more sensitive. It flows more and you become much more healthy. Your whole life begins to change as very basic things that were left unfulfilled become fulfilled. The deeper longings that you have within you become naturally fulfilled. Many of the things that you thought you could never do in your life become natural to you. Life completely changes for the better.

DiCarlo—Would you say that the ultimate goal of human development is to connect with the deep aspect of self—our divine core as you call it—so as to bring its energies into the physical world in an unobstructed way?

Brennan—That's one of the steps along the way. I would say that an ultimate purpose of human development is to become completely awake and aware. And there are three stages along the way: transformation, transcendence and transfiguration. When you move into the stage of bringing the spiritual light into the "lower" aspects, dualism—the sense of a separation between you and anything else in life—begins to dissolve. When you get further on the path, what we call "negative" is experienced differently. This won't make sense to anybody unless they've gone there, because it can be turned around to say, "You mean wars are good?" And of course that's not what I mean.

But in my view, the ultimate goal is to expand your conscious awareness to include everything so that you experience divinity directly. You expand from the center of your being to the far reaches of All-That-There-Is, manifest and unmanifest, so that the universe becomes absorbed within you.

DiCarlo—So that the inner life and the outer observable world become one?

Brennan—Yes, and duality—good/bad—dissolve. The inner and the outer become one, and the outer includes All-That-There-Is, manifest and unmanifest. And the inner is still centered within your individuality.

DiCarlo—In speaking about creation, it seems that the battle cry of the New Age is, "You create your own reality." Would you agree or disagree?

Brennan—The statement is a limited one and I've said it many times. From the broader spiritual perspective we are all connected in concentric spheres. Those who are closer around us are more involved in the creation of our personal reality than those who are outside of that sphere. You can expand that out concentrically. We not only create as individuals, we create as groups, as communities, as nations, and as the whole of humanity. I think it's really important to understand how this works in illness. Let's say someone creates AIDS or cancer. It isn't an individual doing that. It is the whole of humanity. As a group we are creating the three major health problems of heart disease, cancer and AIDS. From that perspective, yes we create our own reality. But it's not because we are bad; others are involved in this creation process because we are all connected.

From that perspective, you can then go to an individual level and see how each individual is distorting their energy field, which again, is the basic matrix structure for the physical body. This would thus make the physical body weak, allowing a microorganism to invade and cause illness. Any of those major illness, like heart disease will have certain and specific configurations or patterns of energy in the human energy field that are not healthy.

DiCarlo—What happens on an energetic level when an individual holds a creative intention?

Brennan—That's a really good question because the intentionality emerges from a deeper level of the human energy field. By aligning with a positive intention, you can shift your auric field immediately— the whole field can shift. The more you work to clarify that intentionality, for whatever it may be, for health, etc., and hold that, the stronger your field will become. It is a more advanced healing technique. The beginning techniques of centering, grounding and opening the energy centers are usually necessary for the person to go through so they can actually learn to hold intent. One can be an expert at holding intent, or one can sort of fantasize and think they are holding a particular intent.

So intentionality is actually a learned process that directly affects the human energy field and therefore effects health very strongly. I have seen people turn around in one healing session. For example, there was a woman who was going blind in both eyes from detached retinas. An operation was advised, which may have worked, but which might also have left her blind. Rather than take this chance, she chose to have me work with her. During one session I did a lot of restructuring of her energy field. Then, I worked with her intentionality. In the one eye she immediately went back to 20/20 vision after just one healing.

That's kind of amazing. The other eye was much worse. She had 20/70 vision in it and was almost blind. After a series of healings over a one year period that eye improved to 20/30.

In another case, a young girl had curvature of the spine. In one, 3 minute healing the curvature was corrected by 15 degrees. So things can happen quite rapidly although those are unusual examples. I am telling you the best cases.

DiCarlo—Can the type of energetic healing you do result in "Miracle cures?" for those considered terminally ill?

Brennan—Yes, though it's actually quite unusual. A miracle cure isn't really a miracle—it's simply speeding up what the body can naturally do. The body is a self-healing organism, so it's really about clearing things out of the way so the body can heal itself.

I have never seen a healer do anything the body can't do. But the body needs a lot of support. For an individual to heal a terminally ill condition, a lot of work is involved—work on the energy field itself, psychological work, better diet, etc...

When I had a practice, I would always work in conjunction with physicians, therapists and nutritionists. All of this is very important. So I don't see any separation between conventional medicine and healing. Everything is a miracle.

Section 7

NEW VIEWS IN HUMAN POTENTIAL

"We are evolving towards those attributes that the ancients have traditionally ascribed to Diety. But it's a matter of choice, choosing."

Edgar Mitchell

"Up to the 20th century, "reality" was everything humans could touch, smell, see and hear. Since the initial publication of the chart of the electromagnetic spectrum in 1930, humans have learned that what they can touch, smell, see, and hear is less than one-millionth of reality. 99% of all that is going to effect our tomorrows is being developed by humans using instruments and working in the ranges of reality that are non-humanly sensible."

Buckminster Fuller

In the preceding section on the emerging view in medicine, we heard from Caroline Myss and Barbara Brennan, two individuals who possess amazing abilities to perceive the human energy field and other dimensions of non-physical reality which surround the physical body.

Are these exceptional capabilities the province of a chosen few? Or do all of us possess similar potential, which is waiting to be recognized, embraced and developed and used for the betterment of the world?

Michael Murphy has written an encyclopedic 800-page book called *The Future of The Body*, which draws on 16 years of research in medical science, anthroplogy, sports, the arts, psychical research and comparative religious studies. According to Murphy, individuals from a varietry have demonstrated abilities which he terms "metanormal," g they are not typical of most living people.

These metanormal abilities include the ability to sense the location of lost objects before physically looking for them; communication abilities, such as saying something in unison with someone else; the ability to alter the environment, e.g., an athlete who can change the flight of a ball through mental intention; and movement abilities, such as in those who report out-of-body experiences. These capabilities are not limited to a select few, but can be developed in others.

In this section, we will first hear from George Leonard, who, together with Murphy, is credited as being the co-founder of the human potential movement. In the mid-60s Leonard was a senior editor at *Look* Magazine. In 1964, he did an article entitled "Revolution in Education" in which he used the term "human potential." Due to the favorable response he received, Leonard decided to do a feature article on the topic. In his research, Leonard zig-zagged across the country to interview 37 psychiatrists, psychologists, philosophers, theologians and brain researchers on the topic of human potential. Though none of the individuals Leonard spoke with felt we used more than 10% of our inherent potential, Leonard has come to believe that the real figure may be closer to 1%.

In the course of his travels, Leonard eventually made a stop at the Esalen Institute in Big Sur, California, where programs were being offered under the banner, "Human Potentialities." It is here that he met Esalen co-founder Michael Murphy.

Few are as qualified as Leonard to put the human potential movement into its proper historical perspective. Leonard believes that the explorations into human potential of the 1960s—though at times imprudent, excessive and tinged with youthful idealism—placed the agenda for change and transformation on the table. To unfold our potentials, we must recognize and eliminate the social barriers that inhibit their development and free expression. To do so involves the transformation of the Western world view.

Another individual whose work contributes to a greater understanding of human potential is Dr. Elmer Green. Green, with his wife and colleague Alyce, has been one of the principle pioneers of mind-body research, especially in the area of biofeedback. Biofeedback training enables an individual to regulate normally uncontrollable bodily functions, such as heart rate, circulation, digestion and blood pressure.

This ability has enabled stroke victims to regain movement in paralyzed muscles, migraine headache sufferers to alleviate their pain, and tense and stressed out individuals to relax. Some experts estimate that 80% of all illness is stress related. Therefore, the health benefits of invoking the relaxation response—the opposite of the stress-producing fight-or-flight response—are obvious.

According to Green, learning to direct normally uncontrollable bodily functions is but the first step in learning to sense and direct the human energy field, which is the interface between mind and body. Green suggests that our intentions activate what he calls the "subtle energies" of our body.

"Subtle" refers to the fact that instrumentation does not yet exist which is capable of measuring or detecting these energies (though Green and others believe the development of such instrumentation is close at hand). Despite this, the flow of subtle energy can be experienced as warmth, weight, or a sense of feeling very grounded, tingling and expansiveness (as though your head reaches up into the sky and your legs reach far into the ground).

In his "Copper Wall" experiments with healers, Green has measured shifts in electrical voltages that occur when an individual expresses an intention to heal another. He believes these electrostatic bursts are related to activity which initially takes place in the subtle energy domain. Green's work is important in that lends scientific support (not proof) to claims that there is a non-physical energetic anatomy that plays a role in physical illness and health. This makes complementary medical approaches more understandable and potentially, more useful.

Perhaps our greatest creative potential lies in the power of our conscious intentions to sculpt our very lives. David Gershon and Gail Straub teach people how to enhance their ability to visualize, hold intent and surrender to the creative process. By doing so they tell us, we can become a co-creative force with nature and influence our life experience. *Influence,* they stress, *not* control.

While it's hardly news that we have undeveloped resources, that there is a power within, the focused, multidisciplinary and scientific investigation of the farthest reaches of our human potential is without precedent. The insights derived from this exploration are sure to radically change the world in which we live.

George Leonard

George Leonard is the former senior editor of "Look" magazine, where he wrote groundbreaking articles on education and human potential. His books include, "The Transformation," "The Silent Pulse," "Mastery," and with Murphy, "The Life We Are Given." Leonard has also developed Leonard Energy Training, a self-empowerment program which he has taught to over 40,000 people worldwide.

DiCarlo—In light of the many years you have been at the leading-edge of the human potential movement, I'm wondering if you can help put things into their proper perspective. More specifically, how have the 60s, 70s, 80s and 90s set the stage for the emerging world view?

Leonard—First of all, I must say that a lot of people don't want to take a look back at the 60s. All the big 60s books really haven't sold well. We still haven't come to terms with that decade. I think that many people are still afraid of the 60s and the ideas that were presented. Some people think the 60s were a period in parenthesis—a decade that really didn't count—when our whole culture suddenly got out of step. But I don't think that's true. I think the activity of the 60s was a very much needed and long overdue reaction and at certain times over-re-action, to years, decades, and centuries of repressiveness and injustice. In think what the 60s basically did was set the agenda for necessary change that we still haven't gotten around to. And I'm hoping the 90s can be a time when we get to work on that agenda.

Look at all the things that came up in the 60s—the whole idea of ethnicity, race, of gender. The women's movement. The gay movement. The environmental movement. All of those things began in the 1960s. There was a sudden sunburst before the powers-that-be reacted by clamping down on much of it. There was a counter-60s movement. To use a body metaphor, it is true that many of us during those years were kind of short-sighted, but we were literally ahead of ourselves. And a lot of things were done without too much wisdom. But it was a very euphoric and crazy time that clearly and powerfully set the agenda for change.

The 1970s, on the other hand, was a period of what I would call "cultural diffusion." The ideas that had been circulating around college campuses—mostly in certain enclaves on both coasts but also scattered throughout various pockets in the country—began to diffuse throughout the whole culture. Some of the ideas were better absorbed than others. The sexual revolution, according to Yankalovich surveys in the late 70s, was the most pervasive. Certain sexual practices that were only being promulgated by hippies and the like on the West Coast began to show up wildly throughout the culture— in Des Moines and in Texarcana—wherever you wanted to look. Many have said, "Well, these ideas were co-opted. They have lost some of their fine purity." Well, that's OK. Compromise is part of change. But there was a tremendous cultural diffusion.

Also, the 70s was a period of rationalization and commercialization of a lot of good practices. Organizations like "est" took ideas from gestalt therapy, Zen, and so forth, and packaged it very neatly and put it out in hotel ballrooms. I think those organizations probably did more good than harm. But here again, it was a little too pro-forma, it was a little too pat. Of course some people who wouldn't go to Esalen might go to a hotel ballroom where they could still wear their coat and tie and see there was another world and that other possibilities could exist. And we really are a bizarre culture in not recognizing these other spiritual possibilities that have been our birthright since the human race became human. Humankind emerged on this planet with vision, with tremendous vision of an unseen world, of a spiritual realm that held meaning and guidance for us all. The consequences of lack of vision are quite clear— "Where there is no vision the people perish"—as the bible says. So all these things were part of the cultural diffusion. Some of these new, "old" learnings, which go way back yet seemed new in the 60s, spread. Ideas found in Eastern philosophies were introduced in the 1960s and spread widely in the 1970s.

Then in the 1980s, it continued spreading quietly, but at the same time, there was a tremendous backlash against it. The twelve years of Reagan and Bush presented much opposition. They were very, very opposed to many of the ideas. Of course, a lot of democrats were also opposed to the ideas of the 60s. It's interesting, Reagan was elected to be governor of California on the basis of his promise to clobber the University of California. That was his primary platform. And he did it. He held back the free-speech movement. The Reagan administration sent helicopters to drop tear gas not only on the university but all over Berkley. I was there during the People's Park uprising and I was gassed—we were all gassed. All the *Look* people were trapped right in the middle of the campus. We were the only ones there on The Terrace who were watching this battle unfold beneath us. It was very bizarre. But there was that kind of backlash. So the movement entered into national politics in the 80s.

Now, during the 90s I think we are kind of teetering on the brink. We can go forwards or backwards, but I feel necessity will force us to realize that the old ways are simply not working. Repressiveness is not the answer. On the other hand, total license is not the answer either. Total freedom to do anything, the freedom to buy assault weapons or do anything one wants, doesn't work. There has to be some kind of long-term, disciplined practice. There has to be this understanding that this is the way things work. I think there are quite a few hints that's now happening.

DiCarlo—Do you think the 60s represented a kind of a "dress rehearsal" for the real transformational work taking place in the 90s?

Leonard—The 60s certainly put the agenda for transformation up there. Now we've got to do it. There is so much more transformative activity going on now than in the 60s. Everybody thinks the 60s was radical. What was considered radical back then is kindergarten stuff compared to what's going on now.

DiCarlo—What are some of the more hopeful signs which indicate that things are moving forward?

Leonard—There are many. For example, never before in human history has so much of the great wisdom teaching of all ages and all cultures been so available throughout the world. It really is a global village. You can go to the corner drugstore and buy the *Tibetan Book of The Dead*. The easy availability is something new. Even a thinker as wise as Hagel did not have as much access to Oriental thought as an average college student does today. And of course a lot of information is being spread throughout the world via the satellites and through the communications network—the bad as well as the good. And that is something new. Very revolutionary. It contributed towards the downfall of communism. Havel, president of Czechoslovakia, said, "rock-and-roll caused the Berlin Wall to go down." That was his quote.

Another significant development is all the understanding we're getting now on human evolution. You constantly see new headlines about the new male Lucy, the early ancestor of our species, for example, and the understanding of the power of the evolutionary process. One of the hallmarks of the project that Mike and I are working on, is the idea that evolution has not ended. *The Future of The Body* is about the next step. We are still evolving and I think things are really moving.

We have such a rich legacy of positive accomplishments. Just consider the Eskimo, Aruba tribesman, East Indian, Japanese Samurai, Christian Desert Fathers, the shaman, the Penitenti, Victorian Novelists, 20th century scientists. Consider all the different kinds of governments, governance and philosophies that we have had. Embedded in this flamboyant richness, we've always had hints of further evolution. But now, all this diversity is becoming accessible everywhere on the earth. No one living before the mid-20th century—even the privileged king or monarch or greatest scientist of the time—has had as much access as we do today to the descriptions of metanormal capacities in people. Never before was there a medical science that could precisely measure the physiological changes produced by transformative practice. At no other time have so many people practiced so many different disciplines for growth and transcendence.

In public meeting places you find people practicing Sufi exercises that were once reserved for initiates. This stuff is really happening. Shamanic practices of Stone Age people are offered at workshops. It's really spreading, more now than ever before. There's a magazine called *Common Ground* published in the San Francisco area that has advertisements for literally hundreds of these activities. It is incredible. In the 60s this was simply not available. We have much, much more of this paradigm-busting lore now than we had back then. It's not even close—it's a thousand times more than what we had in the 60s.

Psychoneuroimmunology has had a powerful influence in the medical profession and is showing that emotions and feelings influence every aspect of bodily functioning. Ideas of the mind-body connection grace the covers of the news magazines now. The Bill Moyers Special, "Healing and the Mind" has had a very powerful influence on a relatively large audience. Not like Roseanne of course, but it doesn't take *all* the people to make changes. It takes some of the people who are controlling the instruments of power, like those in the media.

A lot of experiments are going on, even though mainstream science is very loathe to admit it, which demonstrate that the minds of individuals can influence living tissue at a distance. They can influence bacteria, plants and other human beings. And these have been demonstrated in good, rigorous experiments, where the protocols and the procedures are much more closely monitored than they would be in a normal scientific experiment, where people are not so suspicious.

The anthropologists and sociologists have made so much progress too, in showing how our facial expressions, the way we walk, the way we move, how these things are influenced by culture. And how we can break out of these cultural traps.

Martial arts such as aikido are now spreading throughout the world. Aikido is a very transformative martial art that is based upon love and harmony—that's a very radical idea.

Very quietly the shift is occurring.

Also, the attitude of the media towards things such as Esalen has greatly shifted since the 1960s. In the very beginning before they knew what was happening, there were some wonderful articles about Esalen. Then by the 70s everybody who wrote about Esalen would talk about "touchy-feely" things while sticking their tongues in their cheeks. There was so much sticking of tongues in the cheeks that on Madison Avenue they had to develop a special operation to plug up the holes. But now, I have a whole press kit of articles that were written in 1987 about Esalen and every one of them is favorable. Part of the favorable response was simply a celebration of survival. Esalen endured and that's pretty good. Nobody expected that. And when it hit its 30th birthday in 1992, there were even more favorable articles. It's almost as if it's now in the main-stream, an edge of the establishment. Recently *Vogue* and the *New York Times* all had very nice articles about Esalen. Today, Esalen is packed—you can't even get in. So very, very quietly these "new/old" ideas are integrating into the very fabric of our society. It's about some-thing that appears to be almost essential to humanity. Without vision, without the understanding that there is the realm of the spirit that can give us guidance, that can give us meaning to life, I don't think we can do anything. Life that is just consuming is totally an empty life. You can never get enough of what you really don't want.

DiCarlo—Speaking of this realm of the spirit, do you think there are beings that exist on different levels of reality who somehow guide the unfoldment of human potential?

Leonard—Well, I don't think there is any question. What an impover-ished universe it would be if what we see with our senses, and what we can pick up with our instruments of science represented all that there is in existence. Before the understanding of radio waves anybody who said you could hear a message from someone far away would have been labeled a kook. Are we arrogant enough to say that our instruments have now picked up all the emanations of life that exist? Of course there are more! Wherever you go, there is always more. And I don't know what they are. I am not one of those who follows the idea of aliens and angels, but I would by very surprised, in fact, *it's unthink-able* to me that our science and our senses have now picked up all the forms of life or energy that exist. There's no question about it.

In my own L.E.T. work, Leonard Energy Training, we do exercises that are absolutely reliable, where average, untrained folks can wander around the room with eyes covered with cloth so they cannot see. When I clap my hands, the great majority of these people can point to the location of their partner who might be anywhere in the room or even outside the room. It takes a little induction to get people ready for this. One half hour—that's all. But this is now routine. This is not special and it's not extraordinary. We call this, "The Synchronization Process." I describe it briefly in the back of my book, *The Silent Pulse.*

So obviously, there is some kind of energy there that is not in the electromagnetic spectrum. We don't want to be electromagnetic chauvinists you know. There's got to be more to the world than the electromagnetic spectrum.

But there's no question, there are other beings. There have got to be.

DiCarlo—Do you think scientists who are attempting to map and measure these other dimensions of "subtle" energies are heading in the right direction?

Leonard—Yes. Many years ago, myself and my ex-wife went to the University of California at Davis and were measured as we attempted to move our life energy from the right to the left hand. I still have the graphs. They were picking up electrical potentials off the back of each hand, and we would say, "Move energy right" and you would see the pulsations going up, up, up, above the mid-line on the graph—just by intention alone. Then we would say, "Now bring the energy to the left" and you would see the line on the graph go down and over to the other side. Now, how is that done? I don't know.

So I think, yes, let's try to measure these things. You have to keep trying or else you're not a real scientist. You're not a scientist on the edge of discovery. I think it's a wonderful idea.

DiCarlo—Could you elaborate on the integral practice for the development of human potential you have developed with Michael Murphy?

Leonard—Mike and I have written a book called *The Life We Are Given.* In a sense it is the follow up to Michael's, *The Future of The Body* but it can stand totally alone. You might say that it is a book of instruction for the average person, which tells them what they can do to begin an integral transformative practice. Integral means, to integrate "mind, body, soul and heart." Transformative mean that it's based on positive change. Practice is a wonderful word, meaning something you do on a regular, disciplined basis. Not primarily for the goodies you get out of it, but primarily for the sake of doing it. A practice is the path you walk. You do it for its own sake. Paradoxically, the people who follow a practice for its own sake are the ones who get the most extraordinary results.

In part three of *The Future of The Body* Michael posits that the best way to achieve metanormal capacities, of perception, communication abilities, vitality, volition, etc... is through integral transformative practices. So for two years we ran an experimental class. There were 33 people in the first group and 30 in the second group. We met for just two hours every Saturday but everybody had a number of commitments, things that they had to do every week. We kept very close statistics. We also had affirmations as to positive changes in their life and especially in their bodies. That's something a lot of human potential workshops and experiments don't do. They don't keep close statistics which helps make things more understandable. We are offering a way for the average person to embark on this practice, just through reading this book and getting together with other folks.

DiCarlo—So this is a step-by-step methodology for individual transformation?

Leonard—Well, we have developed a step-by-step methodology for integral transformative practice. By doing that—and you can't be sure—the odds are very good that you will get some positive transformation, because almost everybody, especially in the second cycle, got some very, very significant, positive changes. The amount of change is really quite spectacular. All sorts of wonderful changes in their body, some of which would have to be called metanormal and extraordinary.

DiCarlo—What would be some of the key elements of this practice?

Leonard—First of all, before we started these classes, I developed a less-than 40-minute "kata." Kata is just a convenient term in the martial arts which simply mean "form." It's a specific form where you go through a certain series of moves, always in the same sequence.

We asked that everyone in the course perform this kata at least five days a week. Some people did this seven days a week. It takes only 40 minutes because from the very beginning we wanted to make this a "householders path." That is, a practice that can be engaged in by people who have jobs and a family. Not just people who live in a monastery or go on a retreat. So we wanted to do something that was feasible, and that was an important part of the experiment. These people all had jobs and families of sorts—they had a life other than this practice. But by doing the practice they got really remarkable results.

We asked all the participants to attend the class punctually and regularly. Also, we asked that everyone do at least three hours of aerobic exercise every week, in no increment less than 30 minutes. Everyone was also asked to be conscious of everything they ate, and a very low fat diet was recommended. We also recommended strength training but that was not absolutely required. We asked that everybody stay current in their emotional relations—not letting things build up—with all the people in the class and in their lives. In other words, keeping the emotional information flowing to the appropriate people. We also did some emotional group work in the class, but we allowed people to do whatever they needed to do to handle that and report on it.

We also had affirmations. Everyone made four affirmations near the beginning of the class. These affirmations were written in the present tense, and went something like this, "I George Leonard, intend to see that the following circumstances have occurred by November 21, 1992." Then, the rest is written in present tense. For affirmation number one, we asked people to do things that are normal—not metanormal by any means. In other words, something that if you just did what you were supposed to do, you would achieve it and nobody would be surprised. It would be quite understandable through all the canons and concepts of present day science and medicine. For example, a person might affirm in writing, "My waist measures 32 inches" whereas it might measure 34 inches in the beginning.

All participants fill out a record of their affirmations, which is kept in a file. At the end, on November the 21st using this example, they would make note of their progress. If they have really watched their diet, and if they have done the aerobic exercises and perhaps the strength exercises, no one should be surprised that they have achieved this intended outcome.

The second affirmation for the first year was what we call, "exceptional." Something that could still be explained by modern, mainstream science, but which would be an exception. Such as, "I measure 5 foot 6 inches" and your measurement right now is 5 foot 5 inches. Well, to grow an inch at age 40 is kind of unusual isn't it? I think most people can grow about a third of an inch or a half of an inch just by improving their posture. But to actually grow measurably a whole inch would be kind of exceptional.

We rated people on a scale of 0 to 10 to see how well they achieved their affirmations. We tried to make it as objective as possible with measurements. We didn't restrict it to the objective because that would be too limiting, but we had people make it objective as much as possible. In other words, if a person were affirming an improvement in eyesight, we asked them to go to an eye doctor and have the eyes measured. That way, they had a record of it in the beginning and again, eleven months later. Incidentally, in that particular case we got remarkable results.

The third affirmation was the metanormal, something that could not be explained by traditional science and something that rarely happens to people. For example, a metanormal affirmation might be to grow two inches. And we got fascinating results. In fact, during the second test group, the success rate in achieving affirmation number three was 6.67 on a scale from zero to ten.

The fourth affirmation was the same for everybody, "My entire body is balanced, vital and healthy." We wanted to cover this base because we didn't want someone to achieve an unusual metanormal state at the expense of their health and balance. And that was one that we really excelled at with an 8.2 overall improvement in health on a zero to ten scale.

Taking a look at all this gave us some ideas for some very practical applications. We cannot solve our health care crisis in a financially viable way. It is impossible to do it no matter what method we use as long as we continue to use our present method of medical technology, which is sickness based and relies upon expensive drugs and expensive technology. The only way we can make it work is through a radical change in life-style. And if we can change the life-style of a group of ordinary Americans, improving their health by 8.2 on a scale of zero to ten, we can save hundreds of billions of dollars in this country. So it's very practical.

So we asked that everyone fulfill their affirmations. In other words, they continued to speak their affirmations in various ways. In practice we used focused surrender, which was one of our best methods and inductions for achieving these meta-normalities.

DiCarlo—Focused surrender? What do you mean by that?

Leonard—While writing **The Silent Pulse**, I noticed there seem to be certain magical moments in life, which I call periods of perfect rhythm, where everything seems perfect. If you go one way that's exactly the right way and you'll find something marvelous there; if you go the other way that's the right way, and so forth and so on. These moments of perfect rhythm generally come in a period where you have concentrated very hard on something. You are really focused. After this period of intense concentration, you surrender. You let go of that which you were focusing upon. Focused surrender is a combination of these two actions.

There's a big debate going on right now: Is the petitioned form of prayer, where an individual requests something specific, like a cure from an illness, more effective than accepting prayer, thanksgiving prayer, like "Thy Will Be Done?" There has been research studying the effectiveness of various kinds of prayer on various kinds of organisms. The debate is still open. Some people come down on the side, "Thy Will Be

Done" as the best way to go about it. In other words, surrender.

Now what I have done—and I did this way back in the 70s—is to devise a way where you really get both. A combination of the two. And it's really at the point where you surrender that magical things might begin to happen. Extraordinary things. I call this the "mental-material interface." In Integral Transformation Practice training we have an activity where we sound a gong. As long as the participant can hear the gong, they are to focus with all their power on making whatever state they want to achieve absolutely real in their consciousness. This is *real* in the present moment in this universe, because your consciousness is a part of this universe. If you want to experience yourself as being an inch taller, you see yourself as an inch taller. That exists in your consciousness. Take the example of the wiring diagram of a little radio. The radio itself is real. No one would dispute that since it is concrete and exists in three dimensions. Of course, if you drop it and step on it, it won't work anymore. It's broken. There's also a wiring diagram. That's real too, though it's primarily on two dimensions. Now, how about the diagram as it exists in the mind of the inventor, of the person who works on that radio. Is that real or not? My argument is that these represent three different forms of reality, but they are all equally real.

So next, the person is instructed to follow the tone of the gong down into the void itself, into the nothingness. When it reaches that void and nothingness from which all things arise—the creative void—they completely let go of whatever they are envisioning. The way we do it, you are lying on your back and you hold your left hand up over your abdomen as long as you can hear the sound. If you can no longer hear the sound, drop it. Say, "I give up." What we have found—and we can't prove this—is that at the moment of surrender, the mental-material interface somehow clicks in. In other words, what was real in the mental realm, to some small extent becomes real in the material realm. Of all the methods we have tried, focused-surrender has turned out to be our most effective induction.

The great warrior works to achieve control, then acts with abandon. In aikido, I have worked and worked and worked on certain techniques, but when I'm being attacked, if I think about the techniques, I've had it. You have got to let go totally. Just let it happen. Achieve control, then act with abandon. Many great sports achievements, and many great achievements in the world, I think, result from the combination of the two.

DiCarlo—I like that because then you get a blend between personal will and perhaps Higher Will.

Leonard—Boy, you've got it exactly. It's not one or the other. The idea of focused surrender in which the mental and material can touch, individual will finally letting go to grace. As Mike said in his book, "The winds of grace are always blowing; you just have to raise your sails."

DiCarlo—What sort of metanormal capabilities have manifested for some of the people?

Leonard—There's one woman in her mid-40s whose grandfather on her mother's side went practically blind from cataracts. This was before the condition could be treated through surgery, and this man could barely see. Her mother had the cataract operation in her 40s. This woman has three older sisters, and each of them had the cataract operation while they were in their 40s. It was an absolutely genetic condition. When this woman in the class had achieved the age of 42, she developed cataracts, which was noted in her yearly examination and she assumed she too would have the operation since one of the cataracts was near the middle of the cornea.

So she made an affirmation that her eyes were free of cataracts. Unfortunately, when she went in for the first examination, she told the eye doctor. He scoffed at the idea. He said, "Well, you can change some things, but cataracts you can never change." Still, she was a good student and every time she did the kata she would take the palms of her hand and place them three or four inches from each eye, kind of stroking the eyes with the energy in the palms of each hand, saying, "My vision is clear. My eyes are free of cataracts."

At the end of the training period, this woman just couldn't face going in for her eye exam because the doctor had been so certain the condition could not be healed without surgery. If you've ever wondered why people don't achieve their potential, this is one example. The cultural pressure of the current world view is extremely powerful and is enunciated in so many different ways by the experts and the acknowledged authorities in each field.

Although the woman had given up on it, she continued doing the affirmation every time she did the kata, which was five times a week. Near the end of the second year of the program, she needed some prescription sunglasses and her old prescription was out of date. She went to the same hospital as before and after she had the exam she waited for the usual cataract lecture. The doctor said, "Do you have any inherited eye problems?" She responded, "Don't you know? How about my cataracts?" "What cataracts?" said the doctor. They were gone.

DiCarlo—That's an incredible example of realized human potential. I'm wondering, how does this potential, which is inherently in us all, get blocked? You've already mentioned cultural pressures.

Leonard— Let me give you some examples... You know how as school-children, we all worried that we didn't have enough ability. We weren't sure that we were going to do well enough on the achievement tests. Well, I really believe that the biggest threat to the establishment is not underachieving, but rather it's the threat of overachieving.

When I was covering education back in the 1960s, I was going around the country doing an article on programmed education. In fact, it was that same story, "Revolution in Education" that gave me the idea for the human potential story. It was in Roanoke, Virginia, where I had heard about this student at a local junior high school who had taken a simple programmed course on solid geometry home for a long, Friday until Monday weekend. He finished one semester's worth of work over that period. Now do you think the school system would cheer about that?

DiCarlo—You'd think they'd have been in awe.

Leonard—No, they thought, "What the hell do we do with this guy?" What do you do with the kids who come into first grade reading very fluently? The system is set up to keep everybody in lock-step. Those who are not in lock-step are a threat to the system.

I think that the natural tendency of humans is to learn. We are learning animals. We are put here on this planet to learn. We are genetically endowed to learn a great deal over a lifetime rather than having to wait through the mechanisms of evolution, of mutation and selection and so forth. Because of this, changes can be made during one lifetime. But unfortunately, there is actually very little positive reinforcement, and much aversive conditioning which is opposed to people achieving their full potential.

DiCarlo—Would you say that it's a control issue?

Leonard—Control?

DiCarlo—Insofar as a certain segment of society wanting to control the masses, so to speak.

Leonard—I don't think it's any conscious control. In my book, *The Transformation,* I offer the whole idea of the human individual as being a component of society as an example of one of the inventions of civilization. The first pyramid building gangs you might say. We specialize and standardize components so they are reliable and predictable. A true learner is none of those things. A learner is eternally surprising. Unpredictable. Not necessarily reliable to do the same job the same way every time. So the entire system works against the full development of human potential. The system works against learning. Our present school system is actually set up to stop the human organism from learning in a really radical and deep way.

To learn is to change. Education is a process which changes the learner. How willing are we to have our school students change? You know, they see, "2 plus 2," and before they have learned elementary addition they will just look at it with a blank expression on their face. After being taught, they can say "4." And that is a change. So that's definitely a learning. Our children are learning certain amounts of symbolic manipulation and the memorization of a bit of the common cultural material, but in learning to be a learner, and learning to create, in learning to love, in learning to feel deeply, there is a tremendous constraint against learning, if learning is any kind of significant change. And if learning is not any kind of significant change, then what the hell is it? In other words, if you don't change after a learning experience, if you are not different from when the learning experience started, you have not learned much. Education as it is now constituted really works against learning in the deepest sense. You don't want people to change deeply because it would be very worrisome to the system.

I have often thought about this: Let's say that learning is done in segments. I am not sure that's even the right way to do it, but if learning is done in segments in school, at the end of each segment, the teacher should not be necessary. In other words, the teacher should fade from prominence. Maybe one of the jobs of a teacher is to set the learners on a course of learning, and then gradually fade away so that the last day, the students wouldn't even notice whether or not the teacher was there.

We need to cultivate a real respect for learning. You know, people's thought of the human potential movement does not normally include calculus. I think it does include calculus. Mike and I both feel that way. Another requirement we had in our Integral Transformative Practice Club (ITP), was that everybody would agree to read assignments and write essays. That doesn't sound very New Age does it?

DiCarlo—Nope...

Leonard—But that's integral transformative practice—it's across the board. We feel that to neglect any of those four aspects of being human—mind, body, heart or soul—is a big mistake. People will do things if they know why they are doing them. If they have some kind of vision as to why they are doing them. We need vision. Every viable culture and every successful individual needs at least two guardian angels— vision and practice. Both of those have been totally lost. They have become endangered species in the culture of the freeway and shopping mall.

Vision is given away to obsession with short term goals; practice is given away to the quick fix—*The One Minute Manager*; *Total Fitness in One Week*; almost all 'how-to' books. New Age books are mostly quick-fix books. And you don't learn anything by the quick fix. It takes long-term, regular practice.

There's an old Eastern idea that "where there is no practice, nations fall into ruin." I think we have to get the idea of long-term, regular practice for everybody, rather than "10 Easy Lessons" or "Fast, Temporary Relief"—all the slogans you hear in this culture.

Just take a look at the areas in which we have our biggest problems— the economy, health care, politics, pharmacology, crime, and environment—the most important one of all. The factor that is common to each problem involves long term versus short-term. In all of those, we tend to do what seems best in the short term, but what we are really doing is losing the long term. Almost always, the short term is inimical to the long term. Sometimes you have to do both, but we've almost totally neglected the long term. So I think that factor, long term versus short term is something people need to take a look at.

When you adopt a practice, you're in it for the long haul. You work, and work and work on a thing. You diligently keep practicing the same thing over and over again. You are not getting anywhere—or so you think. But you are getting somewhere. It just doesn't show itself. Then finally when it clicks in, you have this little spurt of apparent progress. But where did the learning take place? *It took place on the plateau.*

Just think about all those years people worked against the whole communist system. Then in a period of a few weeks, the Berlin wall goes down. Then a few months afterwards most of the eastern satellites had given up communism. Some said, "My God, change occurred very fast." But in reality, that change was occurring over the last 20 or 30 years. The change occurred because of long time learning. And the learning occurs on the plateau. So if I have any message, I want to preach the plateau—you have to preach the plateau to young people.

Just hang in there.

Dr. Elmer Green

Dr. Elmer Green, Ph.D. is the founder of the Voluntary Controls Program at the Menninger Foundation in Topeka, Kansas. Along with his wife Alyce, he authored the pioneering book, "Beyond Biofeedback." Green has also founded the International Society for the Study of Subtle Energy and Energy Medicine, (ISSSEEM) an organization that is helping to extend our understandings of human capabilities.

DiCarlo—Over the past several years you have spent your time on a project you have named "The Copper Wall Experiment." I have to admit, that sounds pretty intriguing. Please explain.

Green—When I was a student in the department of physics at the University of Minnesota, I had read a book called "The Mahatma Letters to A. P. Sinnet," which discussed the use of a copper wall, placed in front of meditators who were sitting on a glass platform to induce deeper meditative states. It occurred to me, if people were meditating in a really potent way, they may very well be generating electrical voltages in their body; otherwise, why insulate them from the ground? Over many years, the idea stuck in my mind. About ten years ago we finally had the chance to test it. We set up a copper wall which people sit in front of, with their body facing true north, isolated from ground by glass blocks. A bar magnet is placed over their heads. After doing all this set-up work, we began to measure the voltages that developed on the walls as a way of finding out whether or not their <u>body</u> changed voltage. I didn't want to put wires directly on the body at first, for a number of technical reasons. If you change the voltage of an electrical object in a room, it has an effect on others things too. So I just wired up the wall to see what was happening to the human body. Later, we also studied voltage pulses directly from healer's bodies.

DiCarlo—How do you know that these voltages being measured were not attributable to normal electrical fluctuations of the body that have been commonly observed?

Green—In the first place, the person is sitting alone in the room, isolated from ground. The normal body voltages that are generated in a situation like that are usually in the milli-volt range, which is very small. Also, you would expect a person's body voltage to drift by as much as two volts from a buildup of static electricity. So you might expect some fluctuation.

But the voltages that we were getting during a healing session were shooting up and then returning to baseline by as much as 200 volts on occasion. These are not normal body voltages. They are at least 1,000 times bigger. So that's the problem. We asked ourselves, "In the first place, where did all the voltage come from? In the second place, where did the charge go when it disappeared?" Generally, the pulses of electricity in the body of the healers lasted only 4 or 5 seconds. So a huge voltage would appear, then disappear. That was quite fascinating.

DiCarlo—Were these surges in electrostatic charges accompanied by an intention to heal?

Green—Generally speaking, yes, the healers were trying to heal, although over a period of years, they had generated so much of this kind of phenomenon with their bodies, that even when they weren't trying to heal people—if for example they were just meditating in the room— we got electrical pulses from their bodies.

During 6, 45-minute meditations sessions, one of our 9 nationally-known healers produced only one pulse of voltage. But in the first healing session, there were 15 to 20 large electrical pulses generated, and that was definitely connected with the intention to heal. And that was generally true, although one of the healers was bursting with energy to such a degree that this pulsing phenomenon occurred many times during meditation sessions.

DiCarlo—Fascinating! Well, what sort of preliminary conclusions have you drawn from these experiments?

Green—Well, in the first place, I have accepted that healing at a distance is a fact. I think that the religions of all times which have talked about this are not wrong. Of course, these anecdotal types of accounts do not constitute scientific evidence. But I think that there has been enough double blind research now regarding the effects of prayer at a distance to indicate that it really is happening. So I accept that. That's the first point.

Second point is, whatever the energy may be that does the healing, one of its correlates is electrical phenomena. I am not saying that electricity is the cause of healing. If it were that simple you could do it with a battery.

DiCarlo—So would you say your work has focused upon understanding the mechanisms involved in healing?

Green—Yes, that's right. But it's taken for granted that something is happening. We were not studying patients. We were not trying to find out if healings took place. We were merely trying to find out what was going on in the healer's body, not in the patient's body.

DiCarlo—Well, if something is happening, I am wondering if the medium involved might prove to be what you and other researchers would regard as "subtle energy," which you would define as...

Green—...something that hasn't been detected in any scientific way except by its effects. For example, if you look at the careful, clean studies on intercessory prayer on heart patients in a cardiac unit, in which the people being prayed for were a block away, you find that sure enough, prayers produced healing effects. So, we assumed that something was happening, but not in the normal, scientific sense of electromagnetic energies. It was something else. Since it can't be defined or directly detected except by its effects, it was called "subtle." Chi is a good example of subtle energy. Subtle energy is that which must exist in order to produce the effects. I can't imagine healing taking place without any energies at all being involved. That's the first point.

The second point is, if you talk to healers, or to Qi Gong people, or to people who are talented in their ability to affect physical objects using their minds, they always speak as if they are handling some kind of energy. If you question them about it, they say, "Well, it's sort of like electricity." I have assumed—and this is part of the metaphysical tradition—that this energy exists at four different levels, the crudest of which is the one we call electrons. I expect that instrumentation will be developed before long for directly detecting and photographing this stuff. It's very similar to the development of electricity. In the early days, researchers noticed frog legs twitching on a wire rack when lightening struck nearby. They didn't know anything about electricity or electrical induction or magnetic induction. They simply assumed there was a connection of some kind.

So in those days, you could say that electricity was "subtle energy," since it could not be measured.

DiCarlo—So you feel that we'll someday be able to measure this energy directly?

Green—I believe that it's inevitable that we will be able to develop instrumentation to measure it, analogous to the way we now measure electricity.

DiCarlo—What would be the implications of your work to the average individual, if these subtle energies associated with the body, are scientifically validated?

Green—The importance is—and I believe it will happen in the next century—that most physicians will have healers as part of their medical team. On occasion, medical people can't keep a patient alive long enough during surgery to complete their work. Also, healers can help a patient maintain health.

Not only that, I am assuming that future medical teams will include what we would call an intuitive diagnosticians, people like Caroline Myss, who presently works with physician Norman Shealy. Medical people, however, as is the case nowadays, will still be in charge.

DiCarlo—There would be a partnership?

Green—There would be a partnership, yes. At the present time, many people who are sick don't go to a medical doctor, they go to a healer, an alternative therapist. There are thousands of people out there who call themselves "Healing practitioners." But they are not accepted scientifically. Nevertheless, a time will come when healers will get medical recognition and their services made use of.

DiCarlo—Are you personally able to sense subtle energy?

Green—To tell the truth, I have never attempted to document that. But my feeling is that everybody on the whole planet who has a physical body, has a body of subtle energy also. I accept the yogic theory that the physical body is the representation of an energy structure. If we knew enough about it, we would call it a subtle energy structure.

DiCarlo—Do you think this energy field represents the ultimate link between mind and body?

Green—Well, yes. Sure. In fact, I believe that is actually how biofeedback works. Subtle energy, I believe, is the mind-body link. I think that's how every action of the physical body works. Say you want to move your hand. First you think of it. But the question is, "How does your intention move your hand?" After you have the thought, how does that thought make your hand move?" The nerve network started in the cerebral cortex of the brain. But it is intentionality that causes those nerves to fire. The way the yogis would explain it, the mind and the body are different forms of energy and the interface between mind and body is the subtle energy domain." Anytime you think of anything, subtle energies are activated, and according to yogic theory, *that* activates the neurology.

It's like this: Say you have somebody working at a computer. They have an idea and they want to write something, so they tap on some keys and words appear on the monitor. But the mechanism in between involves what they intend to do. There are quite a few intermediary steps before words can be seen. In an analogous way, our intentionality activates the subtle energies of our body, which some of the Russian experimenters, by the way, are calling the bio-plasma body. The subtle energy body then influences the neurology and makes your fingers hit appropriate letters on the keyboard.

Actually, even though becoming an Olympic athlete consists of training the neurology, it is always trained through intention. All the athletes I have talked with train themselves through intention. Now yogis would understand that perfectly. They would say that it's the training of the energies that manipulate the physical body.

DiCarlo—One of the great characteristics of the emerging world view is that the domain of the spirit and soul is now being considered, acknowledged and embraced. In many fields, people are discussing the "reality" of this aspect of our being. According to yogic tradition, what is the nature of the soul?

Green—From the yogic perspective, the soul is a structure in another level of energy. Aurobindo, the great Indian philosopher who died around 1950, put it very clearly when he said, "The highest spiritual levels that we know of are energy states also." The physical body is manipulated, generally speaking, by the emotions. Emotions have an effect on the physical body. But he said emotions themselves are an energy state in a subtle energy domain, and they are focused on the body. Ideas and mind are also an energy state in yogic theory. And above that, there are various spiritual levels. In the Tibetan system, the most subtle levels are called "the void," and according to the Tibetan Teacher of W.Y. Evans West, there are 28 different levels of substance and energy in the void. And each one of those levels, according to Aurobindo, is an energy state—wheels within wheels within wheels.

DiCarlo—Through your work, you are exploring the frontiers of human potential. Have you discovered any boundaries to that potential?

Green—We haven't found any boundaries. It's sort of like crossing the ocean and coming to the edge of a new continent—we don't know where the boundaries are. We're just beginning to explore the continent.

I don't think that scientists as a whole have done more than landed and planted their flag. As yet, not much has been discovered.

The ultimate human potential has been nicely described by the Tibetan Teachers: to become conscious of all the different levels of who you are and to be able to work on all these different levels at the same time instead of having a "conscious self" and an "unconscious self." If you talk to psychologists and psychiatrists they will agree that there is an

<u>unconscious</u> self. That's what Tibetans, Hindus, Chinese, mystics and shamans have always said. But in the unconscious self are all the spiritual energies as well as the subconscious energies which Freud talked about. Our ultimate human potential is to become aware of <u>all</u> these things, and when we do, it is said, we are able to answer the question, "Who are we?" and "What is our own nature as a human being?" As a corollary, we find our relationship to the larger whole, to Divine Being. That's the idea of the ultimate of human potential, to find your relationship to the whole.

The Christians might say, "To find your relationship to God." Modern scientists might talk about finding your relationship to Nature.

DiCarlo—So would you say that we are in a watershed period now, where collectively and on a wholesale level we are actually redefining our understanding of that relationship?

Green—Well, yes, I think so. Don't you?

DiCarlo—From my research I'd have to agree, yes.

In his book, *The Future of the Body*, Michael Murphy draws upon decades of research into extraordinary human capabilities. Do you believe mankind is evolving into what some have called a "multi-sensory species?"

Green—Well, yes. Yogis have said all along that as you develop in this way, you finally become aware of your connection with Gaia, and with all other human beings. What are presently known as parapsychological abilities, are only indicators of what will, I think, be common human faculties. At the present moment, these talents are called non-sensory, but that's wrong. It's not non-sensory. All it is, is nonphysical.

As people move towards these stages of human development, they gradually becoming more secure, and less fearful. Most every person at some time in life has a psychic experience. For example, they might know what some distant relative was thinking, without getting a letter or phone call. Because of modern interest, we can expect these phenomena to happen more often. It isn't all of a sudden though, like, "One day everything is red, and the next day it is green." It's a gradual development, the same thing as when we grow up from being a baby. We gradually become more and more aware of our world and what we can do in it.

The baby starts out being conscious only of itself. In terms of awareness, the baby is the center of the universe. But gradually it develops and finds its relationship to family members, to the clan, to society, and to the world. It's a gradual development which parallels what happens to humans in the larger sense. As we expand into awareness of the "collective unconscious," parapsychological events happen more often.

DiCarlo—As we've seen, in the Copper Wall experiment you've developed a means to demonstrate the power of intention to produce measureable results in the physical world. In this case, a change occurs in the voltage of the walls of a room. In my own life, I have been intrigued by the ability to use intention to actually dissipate clouds, to make them disappear. Sounds very strange, but anyone can test this for themselves.

Green—Physician Rolf Alexander discusses that in his interesting book, *Creative Realism*. It has to do with how you develop these abilities to focus your attention in such a way that you can become part of the "collective mind," which includes Gaia, the planet. When you can change a specific idea in the mind of Gaia, the cloud upon which you are focusing your attention disappears. That can be done because we are all part of the world. Every individual is part of the planet, every individual is part of Gaia. All the clouds, all the rivers and lakes, and all the animals are part of Gaia. When you generalize yourself, generalize your consciousness so that you become aware of Gaia, then you can start thinking in the mind of Gaia and when you do, things like clouds begin to come under your control. Alexander, by the way, is the one who invented the phrase, "The Field of Mind." He said, "Everything you see on the planet is in Mind." If he had been a minister instead of a physician, he might have said, "Everything is in God's mind."

To summarize: if you can learn to think in God's mind (since you are part of the Divine Being itself) and you change an environmental idea, then things happen in the environment. That's the explanation of psychokinesis, of healing, and that's Alexander's explanation of cloud dissipation.

DiCarlo—If you think of the earth as being your extended body, it's almost like learning how to control certain processes within the body.

Green—Well, sure. What is the body of the planet? The body of the planet is Gaia's body. You are part of Gaia. The way you learn the ABC's is by practicing inside your own skin. The rest of the alphabet is outside your skin. But after you learn how to think in your own mind, and control your own physiological self, that ability is gradually extended. You become aware of your relationship to the greater whole. You start thinking in terms of the greater whole. This causes something to happen in the greater whole.

DiCarlo—Is it because you shift your "identity" to the greater whole that you have the ability to influence the greater whole?

Green—Sure. Theoretically, if you could change a single idea in the mind of God, then something would change in "reality," right? From the metaphysical point of view and from the yogic point of view, every chair, every door knob, every plate, everything on the planet exists in the mind of God. If you move, or erase, that idea in the mind of God (and the dense level of this physical world that we know so well is called the Maya) if you can change that idea in the Maya, then that thing will move, or disappear. That incidentally, is how Sai Baba explains his "miracles." Some people think of Maya as an illusion—but that's incorrect. Rather: Maya is like the clouds, which appear and disappear. The "solid" things on the planet, like chairs and tables, appear and disappear more slowly, so we tend to think of them as fixed. But they aren't. They are just part of the constantly changing energy structure of the planet, part of the Maya.

Sai Baba says, "You don't perform miracles. There is no such thing. All you do is manipulate the Maya." Well, how do you manipulate the Maya? You find your connection to the Divine Being, begin thinking in Divine Mind. And the Cosmos reflects the thought. This parallels, as you may know, the basic ideas of "A Course in Miracles." So all those pieces fit together.

DiCarlo—How significant is the work of frontier scientists, such as Bill Tiller, a professor at Stanford University, who has developed a model for understanding these subtle energies? The Universe, he says, is multidimensional—and he is working on a mathematical proof for this—with the physical, three-dimensional universe embedded in a larger four-dimensional universe, which is embedded in an even larger five-dimensional universe.

Green—Bill Tiller is a scientist who is aware of the fact that these internal domains or other energies exist and he's helping build a science of it. Scientists are the "Priests of Acceptance," and it's important for the "graduation of humanity"—to use Buckminster Fuller's expression—that scientists learn enough so that they can break through, expand the frontiers, and lead the way. People depend upon scientists. Specifically, Bill Tiller and others who are working in this area are interested in developing knowledge of how the Maya functions.

Rolf Alexander said, "Everything happens according to natural law." And scientists like Bill Tiller are trying to make it objective so people can understand it. That will help them go through the transformation in consciousness which the next century will bring.

These explanations are important because they help people in general, shape their world view. If a correct world view <u>includes</u> these subtle energies, then when the energies become commonplace, we won't be so "shook up," so to speak. It makes it possible to move through the transformation process with less pain.

DiCarlo—Some people might argue that science doesn't have any business sticking its nose into the domain of religion, spirituality and the nonphysical?

Green—Well if that's true, then science doesn't have any business of any kind. The business of science is everything. There isn't anything that science isn't connected with. What does science mean anyway? It means to become conscious. To understand. Science doesn't have a single domain to work in. That's an unfortunate idea that some scientists have. That's like wearing blinders that you have manufactured for yourself.

DiCarlo—Well, certainly pioneers like yourself and Bill Tiller are exceptional in that you have open-mindedly pursued a particular area of interest that most other scientists would recoil from...

Green—A scientist that I worked with—when he understood what was implied—said, "I won't accept any of this, or any of these energies." I said, "Well, why not?" And he said, "If this turns out to be true, then everything that I am would go down the drain. Everything I learned in graduate school, and ever since, would be worthless."

I said, "No, it's not that way at all. Everything that you are and everything that you learned is still there. It is still factual. All of this is just an addition to what you know. It's not 'Instead of.' That's the problem with most people's world view. As their world view changes, they think that it means that everything is now done away with. But it isn't done away with, it's merely expanded. It's like the baby's view. As the baby grows up its world view keeps changing. But that doesn't mean that the world view as a baby was wrong.

DiCarlo—What is the real reason behind the resistance to new ideas and to the new models of the way the world is?

Green—It's simply fear. If you have a fixed idea of how the world functions, and somebody comes along and shows it isn't that way, then you start trembling inside. Perhaps everything that you believe has been called into question. The platform of your world has been shaken. Unfortunately, many scientists make the mistake of linking their identity to their world view. Isn't that amazing? People's identities are linked to their views of the world, so when the world changes they feel that their identity is threatened.

Scientists are like everyone else in that way. They are not superior to religious fundamentalists in that regard. They are just as nervous about having their world view shaken as anyone else.

DiCarlo—But I thought scientists were supposed to follow the truth wherever it may lead? Isn't that what distinguishes the true scientist from the technician?

Green—It does, but who is going to say what a true scientist is? After an Einstein does his thing and his work turns out to be important, then he's called a true scientist. Before that, he's called a "nut."

An interesting article was published in the journal *Science*, of all places, having to do with why scientists resist progress. The most fascinating part of this, to me, was that the writer found that scientists were a lot like priests. They are like leaders of a religion. And they hate progress in the same way that priests as a whole, fight tooth and nail against any change in religious belief. (Barber, *Science* 134, 596-602, 1961)

DiCarlo—How would you respond to the scientists who explain away the concept of realms of existence that go beyond the physical?

Green—That's no different than any other kind of religious belief is it? That's just lack of experience. If somebody is color blind and you start talking about red and green, they don't know what you are talking about. It's lack of experience.

It's interesting that when students go through the processes of "mind-fulness" meditation, Vispassana, they have experiences that convince them that "reality" isn't the way they thought it was. But most people, when they start to find out about that, get frightened because they start to realize their world view may have to change. But it's interesting, isn't it, that the people who really want to meditate are often dissatisfied with their world view? They think there is something more and they want to find out what it is.

DiCarlo—As a scientist, what do you suspect happens during meditation?

Green—According to the Oriental traditions—and it's beginning to be talked about even in the West—as you turn your attention inwards, you first become aware of the energy structure of your own body, emotions and mind. Normally, you know, our sensory systems are turned outward. We are aware mainly of what is going on from our skin out. When we turn our attention inwards, however, we become aware of an "energy structure," of what in yoga is called the "etheric" body, or we might call it the "subtle" body. In other words, the physical body is the representation to our physical senses of the energy structure which we really are, which is a subtle energy structure.

But according to the yogic theory, what we are really becoming aware of, are different *levels* of energy of our own nature. Roughly speaking, these different levels are called chakras. Chakras, theoretically, are energy centers located in the etheric body. They are not to be found in the physical body. And each chakra's location is associated with a different level of consciousness. For example, meditators often speak of the "heart" chakra. As we become aware of this energy center in our nature, we become aware of the interconnectedness of ourselves with other people. If we become aware of other people through the solar plexus chakra, which lies below the heart chakra, just above the navel, then we tend to become aware of people's emotions. When people meditate, they usually become aware of the fact that they have a variety of inner domains that they didn't know they had. Normally, people are stuck, looking at the outside world. They don't look at the inside world. They generally don't even know that it is there. When they meditate, however, they become aware of the fact that there is a lot of internal terrain.

DiCarlo—So would you say that most of the people in the world are operating out of this third chakra that deals with our emotional nature?

Green—That's it exactly. In fact, the yogis say that this is a third chakra planet.

DiCarlo—So if development goes from one level to the next higher, I would assume that the next stage in our collective development involves learning to become more focused in the heart?

Green—Yes. And that's called the "transformation." Identity moves from the emotional, self-centered domain, to the next domain, which is called the heart chakra. The heart chakra deals with collective consciousness and with ecology. It's like this: "Instead of just taking care of myself, I am going to take care of Gaia." That's a movement, or change of orientation, from the third chakra to the fourth chakra. That's the movement from disposing of your rubbish by throwing it out the window, to being a recycler. That's the movement from being destructive in the environment to being re-creative in the environment. That's why environmentalists are important. They may not think of it that way, but they are part of the paradigm shift because they are essentially helping the planet move from third to fourth chakra.

And that's the movement from the emotional planet to the heart planet.

Page 184

DiCarlo—Fascinating. Tell me, I've found that people on the cutting-edge have strongly relied upon their intuition. Has intuition played a significant role in your work as a scientist?

Green—I would guess that it has. But paradoxically, it was planned. When I was first in college, I became a student of a meditation teacher in Minneapolis. I learned an approach that nowadays has become popular as Vispassana, or mindfulness. It means to be totally aware and conscious of everything that you are doing, and to become the <u>observer of yourself</u>—to be objective and to see everything that is going on, everything that you think, everything that you feel, everything that you do. You become the <u>witness</u> of yourself at all levels. That was the goal.

For example, as you become aware of yourself as a <u>physical</u> entity, you become increasingly aware of yourself as an <u>emotional</u> being. And eventually, you begin to think of emotions as objective <u>things</u>. So if you think of anger, "Oh, there's <u>that</u> thing again." Most people think of anger as, "I am angry," instead of "There, is anger." If you have a thought about something, people don't normally say, "Oh, there is that thought again." They normally say, "I am thinking." But in mindfulness meditation you become objective about your own subjectivity. That's a great step forward. That's how you escape from subjectivity. That was something I learned to do.

When you get into that state of mindfulness, you can ask your unconscious questions, and it will start giving answers. The answers that the unconscious provides are connected with what Carl Jung called the, "collective unconscious." And according to theory, all of the knowledge contained in the collective unconscious is available to everyone. Normally, people call that "intuition." Intuition is actually becoming aware of the collective unconscious and some fraction of the knowledge and wisdom therein.

After I learned how to do this, when I needed to solve problems I went into this state of mindfulness, turned attention towards those problems, and answers would come—spontaneous answers that I "never would have thought of." Now people might say, "That's creativity," or they might say, "That's intuition." But I would say, that's simply tapping into the knowledge that exists.

Fortunately, it can be done intentionally. You don't have to wait for intuition to strike, like a bolt of lightening. You can learn how to turn it on, the same as you turn on any other skill.

DiCarlo—You've mentioned the idea of the collective unconscious. In his work, Jung describes phenomenon related to the unconscious which he refers to as "archetypes." What is an archetype, and how might they influence us in our lives?

Green—An archetype is one of the characteristics, or entities, or objects which reside in the collective unconscious. In other words, the things that humans think about in general start taking on a form of some kind. Tibetans call it a "thought form." Let's say that collectively, people develop some particular religious idea about the nature of God, such as "God is the great judge." Those ideas of God become a powerful thought form in the collective unconscious. That thought form then exists and begins to control people unconsciously. It's like a piece of furniture in the collective unconscious, only it's alive. But it has been created to a certain extent by humans. I am not saying that God was created by humans, but the religious *idea* of God was created by humans.

Gods in some religions are vengeful, sometimes playful. All those characteristics are archetypal ideas that have been constructed by humans and embedded in the collective unconscious. When Carl Jung started studying the collective unconscious, he found there were a lot of things in it that were like permanent fixtures—there all of the time—which had been reported by many people in many different cultures. Those things he called the archetypes.

In his book *Dreams, Memories and Reflections*, Carl Jung explains how he discovered this. It's one of the most important books that I know of. Jung was not only a scholar, but he was aware of these archetypes from personal experience. In his presence, many kinds of archetypal psychic phenomenon occurred. He didn't talk a lot about that, but that's what caused the split between himself and Freud, who was Jung's mentor. Freud was frightened of the archetypal "powers" which couldn't be accounted for intellectually. Jung merely took it as a manifestation of the way nature is. That caused the split.

DiCarlo—Didn't Freud talked about psychic energy?

Green—Yes. But he wanted to perceive it intellectually, not <u>experientially</u>. In fact, Freud said, "We have to prevent the black mud of occultism from sweeping over us." Jung's attitude was entirely the opposite— "We have to find out what's going on in the cosmos."

DiCarlo—Jung was influenced by the *Tibetan Book of the Dead*, which you discuss in your work. According to this text, what happens after we die?

Green—Well, we go through various energy levels until we rise to a certain place—and this may seem odd—according to the density of our nonphysical nature, which is still an energy structure. When people die, they move completely into a more subtle field of energy and continue on with experience. The place where they exist after separating from the physical body is called the Bardo, which is a realm so different that it's like going to another planet. I am not saying they go to another planet. But it's like going away from the earth. This doesn't necessarily mean, however, that they have totally vanished.

DiCarlo—If you had to boil things down, what would be the essence of the emerging paradigm?

Green—From my point of view, the essence of the emerging paradigm is the development of Human Potential, finding the place of humans in the earthly collective unconscious that we call Gaia, and finding the place of humanity in the spiritual collective unconscious that is called the Planetary Being. Humans like to think of themselves as individual entities, but I think it was John Dunne who said, "No man is an island." I think that's what human potential is moving towards. We are finding our relationships.

If people pray, and effects are felt, what that really means is that no person is an island. They may not be conscious of it, because much of it can be experienced only in a kind of superconscious state. The Tibetan Buddhists, the advanced Hindu Yogis, the advanced Christian mystics, the Sufis, the American Indian medicine people, and shamans all over the planet, agree that we're all connected, part of one Mind. Scientists as a whole, have paid little attention to that. They think it's nonsense. Turns out not to be.

I would say that most people are just like children. They are aware of themselves, and gradually they become aware of the fact that they have bodies. Humans are the same way, even when they are grown up. They are not aware of their connections. That's what I think people are moving towards.

That's why the quality movement in business is so important. Literally, that's what it is about—finding the right relations of all the parts of an organization so that they can function properly. If you have a human body and you don't feed it properly, then the organs don't function as they should. And if the organs don't function, then the whole body doesn't function. We're beginning to understand that, large or small, a company is an organism. It has "organic" parts that must be cared for properly if they are to perform properly. Then the whole benefits. The individual entrepreneur who thinks of himself as an individualistic, non-connected being, is finding out that he is a connected. And there's nothing he does that doesn't affect the collective, and vice versa.

DiCarlo—You have already stated that subtle energy may well be the link between mind and body. Would you say that this would also be the medium of that connection between the individual and the collective?

Green—Absolutely. That's what the yogis say. That's what the Tibetans say. That's what the Qi Gong Masters in China say. Employees are all submerged in an energy we call a corporation, in the same way we are all part of the earth, and in the same way we breath air. At the same time, these energies are not just local. They are planet-wide. As we handle these energies, handle our corporations, we effect everyone else on the planet.

David Gershon and Gail Straub

David Gershon and Gail Straub are cofounders of the Empowerment Training Program, which was first offered in 1981. Organizers of the 1986 "Earth Run"—a world event for peace that involved 25 million people, 45 heads of state and 62 countries in 1986—they've coauthored the book, "The Art of Empowerment," a guide to help individuals uncover and make real their most deeply held dreams through the actualization of latent human capacities.

DiCarlo—It seems like everyone is talking about empowerment these days. Why do you suppose this is the case?

Gershon—I think that the reason empowerment has become so popular is because it addresses one of the most fundamental challenges of our times: the willingness for an individual, an organization, a community, a country, ultimately the entire human species, to take responsibility for what it has created and not blame anyone. To forego the temptation of seeing oneself as the victim of something external and recognize that we are accountable for our experience. We have to be very clear that this is not what we want. Then we have to be clear what we do want and to be willing to go for it. To put ourselves on the line—with passion, with conviction, with gusto and with boldness of imagination.

DiCarlo—So how you would define the term "empowerment?"

Straub—The way that we defined empowerment when we began this work in 1981 and the way we still define it is that empowerment is the art—and we underline art—of creating your life as you want it. Obviously there is a lot that goes into your life but as a one-liner, that's our definition.

DiCarlo—What are the qualities and characteristics of an empowered person?

Straub—I think an empowered person is one who has given balanced attention to the many dimensions of their life. In other words, they are spending as much time on their spirituality, emotions, relationships, family and sexuality as they are on their work and pursuit of material things. Our premise is that all seven of these areas of life need equal nourishment and attention. As a result, the individual's life is much more holistic and balanced.

An empowered person has the maturity to realize that empowerment consciousness is an ongoing process. It's not something they ever finish. It's not a product, it's a process, and they need to have the proper support systems that will allow them to continue that journey. We're such a product-oriented society that we expect to attend a 3-day workshop and "get empowered." Certainly people do get a lot of empowerment when they work with us but it's really an ongoing process of awareness. It's a path or a discipline. We are so conditioned in Western Society to have things come to a point of completion and empowerment is a process that never ends.

DiCarlo—Some would say that empowerment is the clear expression of the totality—unseen and seen—of who you are. The process if empowerment would thus involve the clearing away of whatever gets in the way of that full expression. Any thoughts on that?

Straub—I very much like what you said. I feel that is a richer definition. In our work, we have placed a tremendous amount of emphasis on those five core beliefs: responsibility, self-esteem/self-love, trust in a Higher Power (the Universe, God, faith—whatever words are appropriate), positive attitude (which is the lens that we bring to any life experience) and finally, the ability to flow with change. I agree with you, the whole process involves the clearing away of the beliefs, attitudes or mind-sets that get in the way of our being the full beauty and power that we are.

DiCarlo—Generally speaking, why is it that someone becomes disempowered?

Straub—Oh, there are so many reasons...There are so many societal beliefs that we buy into that disempower us. Much of the work that we do in our workshops is to look very carefully and very compassionately at these collective-societal belief systems that disempower us. By doing this, we realize that we can extricate ourselves from them. For example, when we work in the area of relationships, and to some degree in emotions and sexuality, a lot of gender issues come up. Men and women have been enormously disempowered by the stereotypes of their respective gender roles. Some of that comes through media advertising. Some of it comes from our culture. It's interesting that the work of the women's movement and the men's movement has been to dismantle our "limiting beliefs" about these things so that we're all able to function from a much deeper, subtler and more individualistic truth. So a lot of what disempowers us are the large, mass societal beliefs that we buy into before really looking deeply at our own truths.

Another thing that often disempowers us is our childhood. Many of us were not given all the love we necessarily needed to really live fully, so we grew up feeling a lack of belief and love for ourselves. As a result, we need to go back to our childhood and see if that's a source of disempowerment.

As almost any psychological point of view or any spiritual tradition will say—and I am oversimplifying—all of us have had an imprint at childhood and the blessed few of us who received a lot of love from very clear parents have had much smoother lives. Many more people have not been as fortunate—I know this from working with thousands of people over the years. People become disempowered if they do not work with the false belief systems they took on as children. The most common I have already alluded to: lack of self-esteem; lack of self-responsibility; lack of ability to see life through a positive lens. There are lots of different battle scars that happen during childhood. But a major cause of disempowerment is when one goes through life without re-examining those beliefs and acts as though they were absolute truths. Of course they are not. We were programmed with these beliefs by our parents, peers and society while growing up.

We need to go to battle—each of us to varying degrees—with those limiting beliefs. To do so involves taking a courageous journey. Unfortunately, many people don't have the opportunity or the support to deal with their childhood wounds.

Also, and this is changing somewhat, but our schools have not given us the needed tools to be empowered. If we were really lucky, maybe we were. It's exciting to teach young people the empowerment tools: how to change limiting beliefs; how to create vision; what to do when we fall short of the vision or the dream that we want. These are very pragmatic, everyday skills.

Clearly, our workplace can potentially empower us, where we gain a sense of mission and passion and we can feel like we are connected with the very reason for our being. On the other hand, a workplace can potentially be a place for disempowerment if one does not have the skills and the openness and courage to confront a boss, a manager or a colleague who is disempowering. The workplace is a powerful influence. With the proper skills and abilities, it can be a place of empowerment as opposed to a place of disempowerment.

I think that our religious traditions can sometimes disempower us. I would be the first one to say that we need our spiritual traditions to give quality and meaning to life. On the other hand, we have to be rather astute in these times to be sure that we have carefully filtered out the beliefs that may have been true for our parents but which are not relevant in the day and age we live in. So we have to look at all these powerful facets of life with a sensitive awareness and an appropriate lens for the time that we live in.

Unless a person is quite awake, conscious and committed to their journey in life, disempowerment can take place.

DiCarlo—Would either of you say that the process of empowerment involves gaining more control over one's life circumstances?

Straub—It's a very interesting paradox actually. The image of the sacred archer with bow and arrow is used in many spiritual traditions to help people hold that paradox. We need to use our will and our sense of control as we draw back the arrow—the arrow could be the dream, or the intention or the vision or whatever it is we most skillfully want to put our life energy behind. This drawing back involves a certain kind of control. And then, there's the moment in which we release that arrow, that intention, into the universe. This involves a kind of surrender to something larger than our personal will, our ego, and our capacity to control things. So there is the need to work skillfully with the ego which is the place within the human personality where we do have a certain amount of control. But we also need to be aware of the certain paradoxical moment when we need to surrender and realize the outcome is out of our hands.

DiCarlo—So it's kind of a creative dance with the universe.

Straub—That's exactly what it is, and that's not oftentimes understood by people as they are trying to learn about the process of creation. Creation comes from that inner action with the universe. First, we very skillfully put forth our intent, our vision, our affirmation—there are lots of different words for it. Then we begin to recognize the moment when we must surrender all of that. The third step would be to skillfully listen and interpret the feedback from the universe. Many people will say to us, "Well, gosh, this vision of mine didn't come true." We're very quick to say, "Well, you realize a vision is an ever-evolving impulse that interacts with the universe, so you have to skillfully listen to the feedback that you get from the universe."

DiCarlo—Are there any guidelines you can give people to help them recognize this feedback?

Straub—I'll tell you what I've done. I've prayed and affirmed. I call this "Big Ears." It is the kind of listening that is skillful and compassionate enough to hear and receive—especially the difficult lessons of life—as feedback steering us to the places we need to go. Of course this takes time and patience.

It's part of spiritual maturity. You talk to someone who has lived their life richly and deeply and you are immediately aware that this person has learned to listen to what life is saying. It's quite striking.

So I think the process of becoming more masterful in interpreting the feedback from the universe *is* the dance of life. That's one of the reasons why we are here. It is the gift that we get through becoming more awake and more conscious.

DiCarlo—What would you say are the necessary conditions that must be present in order for a person to become empowered?

Straub—A philosophical concept that enables empowerment to take place—sort of the container upon which our work rests—is what we call a shift from pathology to vision. This simply means that what we place our attention on, we nourish. So if I am constantly putting my precious energy and attention on what doesn't work in life—in other words, my pathology—that's what grows stronger. For example, if I am constantly focusing attention by thinking about and analyzing what doesn't work in my relationship, that which I don't want gets stronger. The reverse of that is equally true: if I focus my attention, my mental energy, on the vision of what I *want* from my relationship, then that tends to get stronger. Through our work with thousands of people, we've come to realize that most of us spend an excessive amount of time focused on what doesn't work. If we have the courage and the skill to shift our primary attention to what we call "vision" or possibility, there is a pronounced difference in the quality of our lives.

The same holds true for organizations by the way. And it doesn't mean that once we make that shift everything will be easy. Lots of resistance will come up. But it's extremely important that you take note of your world view. Is it a visionary world view or is it a pathological world view? Do you see possibilities or do you see problems?

Now the second part of the model is the shift from what we call "static" to "organic" growth. The "static" model is sort of the old world view that my life should fit into solidified and unchanging boxes or pictures. First I'll go to college, then I'll get a job, then I'll fall in love, then I'll get married. And the job should look like this and my relationship should look like that. This way of viewing life is so very black and white and so very, very oversimplified. Life and growth isn't like that. It's organic and fluid. Life is chaotic and exciting—very, very rich and multidimensional.

This comes up a lot with jobs these days. If an individual feels, "My life should fit into this box and my work should look like this" and then they lose their job, they can be rather devastated if they see growth as static. We try to get people to understand that the shift in jobs is an organic, ever-changing part of life, an opportunity to grow and change.

I'm not saying they still don't suffer or experience plenty of challenges. I think that the static model is the model of the great judge that says, "I am never good enough," that, "I should be better than I am." People need to develop more compassion for themselves. Life is fluid and wherever you find yourself is the place where you can learn from. This point of view seems to welcome more realness and vulnerability. It liberates people. On the other hand, the static model tends to keep people in very strict and limiting roles and masks.

DiCarlo—And the third piece of your model?

Straub—The third part of the philosophical container is what we call "The integration of self-awareness with skills to manifest." In the very simplest sense, this is the marriage of inner work with action. Over the years, we found that certain people had done lots of interior work or self-awareness work to uncover their limiting beliefs, but nothing was changing in their outer lives. They were spinning around in self-awareness yet they didn't have the skills to implement their vision in the concrete world of everyday experience. So our model teaches that, yes, we need to make the journey within, but if the journey within is not partnered and balanced with very pragmatic skills which help us manifest those changes, it tends to become rather self-indulgent. A very simple way of saying this is that the inner is balanced with the outer, or the feminine balanced with the masculine.

DiCarlo—You both have talked about "higher purpose" in your work. What do you mean by that?

Straub—Like so many of these words we have talked about, each person must discover their own meaning. Yet, it's an important word and different people call it different things. Some people refer to higher purpose as mission, other people refer to it as their task or role in life. A friend of mine once said higher purpose—and I love this phrase—"is our unique engagement with life." That is, the engagement that we are here to take part in. For one person, it may involve being the CEO of a company, running things in a way that is both powerful to the bottom-line and humane for the employees. For another, it is to be a poet or an artist, and to bring meaning to life through words, painting or sculpture. For someone else, it may be through instilling values in their children that enable them to carry on in a very complex world. For yet another, it might be selfless service. It's so multifaceted. Ghandi referred to this as the life force, the fire that gives passion and a sense of purpose to life.

When we work with people, we find that if they are in touch with that, it's like a spiritual thread that motivates them and carries them through some very tough life experiences. Our purpose or our engagement is like a place we keep coming back to. With some people we work with, they knew very early on as kids, "this is what I am here for," and that point of focus remains steady until the end of their lives. Other people we have worked with find their purpose is like an onion they keep peeling. There may be a purpose or a mission in the early part of life and then a rather new one will evolve later. So it can be one steady, sustained point of focus and for others it is something that unfolds and evolves. Either way, it's almost like a spiritual focus. Often, it's described as a work or a mission but I don't think it has to be that. We've worked with people who have said, "My purpose is to learn to forgive. To learn to be loving and compassionate towards those I find it hard to love." So it's very multifaceted I think. But it's something we return to that gives us a spiritual kind of heartbeat.

DiCarlo—By what means can a person discover their higher purpose?

Straub—We advise people to meditate, to affirm and to pray for clarity on their purpose. Affirmation or visualization is just the lay person's term for prayer. Prayer is the highest form of visualization. It's a talk between me and my God. Some people are inclined towards prayer, others are not. They might be more comfortable putting forth a clear intention to the Universe. But our primary emphasis in our work is that there is a Universe—or a God if one wishes to refer to it in those words—who responds. Our responsibility is to put forward a clear intent. If we do that in a heartfelt, sustained way, amazing things happen.

DiCarlo—Are there any principles that you have identified regarding making one's vision a reality?

Gershon—Yes. The basic concept of manifestation is simple: "Thought is creative." We cannot avoid manifesting since it comes with the territory of thought. So we teach people how to consciously manifest what they want by creating affirming thoughts and beliefs which best represent how they wish to live their lives and how they wish to be. First the person articulates what they want. Next, they focus their mental attention on it through the tools of affirmation and visualization, which is really directed thought.

Once someone has begun to focus on what they want, what inevitably comes up are all the reasons why they think this is not possible—their limiting beliefs. So we teach a variety of techniques on how to transform those limiting beliefs so that they are no longer an undermining influence. It's not so much about avoiding the limiting belief, or pretending the limiting belief is not there, or getting caught up in trying to fix a limiting belief system. The emphasis is on learning from our fears and limiting belief systems. Once we do this, we can adjust our vision accordingly.

So in a nutshell, the creative process involves the principal of vision, the principle of mental clearing and the principle of creative thought.

DiCarlo—What's the difference between a vision and a goal?

Gershon—Well, this is a subtle question. A goal is usually a bit more concrete and a vision can be a bit more abstract or a bit more general. A vision is clearly a direction—"I want to live a more prosperous life." A goal would be, "I want to have 'X' amount of dollars to do that." A vision might be, "I want to have fulfilling relationships" and a goal might be, "I want to find my life partner by such and such a date." So, there is a certain sense of coherence and refinement to goals, but a goal doesn't touch the spirit per se. It's the vision that excites.

DiCarlo—Does an individual's vision evolve over time?

Gershon—I think that if a vision is truly alive then it's always evolving. It's always getting more refined. It first comes as an impulse. Then, as you begin to work with it, it becomes more and more concrete. You start with a simple vision of wanting to live in the country, and then you begin to see the house, then the lawn and a garden. Without realizing it, you then begin to raise the money to buy the house.

DiCarlo—Could you describe in more detail the stages in the manifestation process?

Gershon—Our empowerment methodology has four components. The first is self-discovery: "What is it that you really want?" To find out, you gather knowledge. You touch deeply into your values, your dreams, your desires. You find out what it is that's really important to you. Hopefully, the knowledge is not superficially gathered. If it is, it will direct you in a way that will be unfulfilling.

Then, you craft a vision of how you wish things to be based on the knowledge that you have gathered. This involves the process of mental clearing in which all the reasons why you can't have what you want will come visit you. You don't need to seek them out. After the mental clearing, an affirmation and visualization is created, which is like the seed that you begin to nourish. Once you get the seed, the affirmation and the visualization, you then have to be aware of whether or not it's manifesting. If it's not, begin to find the reasons why. This is where a lot of people get off track. They think that if it's not manifesting, then they are obviously not doing it right. Or they may doubt that thought is creative. In fact, what they really need to learn how to do is to work with feedback. In the natural world, when something is being born or is germinating, it may hit a rock and have to adjust its course. The process of manifestation is very much like the process of natural growth. It's always adapting, adjusting, or changing course as one receives feedback from the world.

DiCarlo—Could you give some examples of the kind of feedback people sometimes get?

Gershon—The feedback may be, "This idea is too early." Or the feedback may be, "I don't have the skills to develop this." Or, "No one believes in what I am saying." For others it is, "I don't have enough knowledge to really move forward." It may be my own resistance to believing it—I don't feel confident enough because I haven't owned it at a deep enough level. All of that is part of how things manifest. We have to be attentive to this feedback and learn from it while we maintain our focus on what we're wanting to create. Affirming the vision is just the beginning. The skillful interpretation of feedback is the real act of mastery and manifestation.

DiCarlo—So in your world view, would you say that we in fact have an influence in what happens to us, that we can shape the events, and the circumstances that weave the very fabric of our lives?

Gershon—Definitely. I would say that this is one of the fundamental premises of our empowerment model. We can't avoid responsibility, though we may try. If someone doesn't believe they are responsible for the circumstances of their life, they just need to look at what they are believing and what they are thinking about all day and see if in fact that it hasn't already manifested as their life. So if one does not want to believe that you create all of your reality, that's fine. You can decide how much you want to accept that you create. But the point is that you need to take responsibility for your thought as a major influence, if not the primary influence.

DiCarlo—Have you ever speculated upon how thought and emotion might produce real consequences in the world?

Straub—Indeed we have. Whenever we hold a strong intention (an affirmation, visualization, or prayer if we were to use more spiritual language) a "thoughtform" is created which goes out into the Universe. As I say that affirmation, it does not yet have physical form. It is "etheric" if you wish. Through repeated intent and clear focus, the etheric thoughtform takes concrete form. It becomes substantial. You can feel it and touch it in the physical world. For example, if I want more courage in life to be able to work with a difficult boss, to stand up for myself and say what I want, I need to affirm that on a repeated basis. Each time I do, it's as if I clothe, or give more substance to that original etheric thought, until slowly but surely, I feel the courage. I have manifested the courage in this plane, in the plane of everyday reality where I am standing face to face with my boss. But several very important things are required. One is faith. That is, when I affirm that I have courage, even though I know that I don't feel that courage in that moment as I face my boss, I need to make a literal leap of faith that that courage exists in the invisible plane, even though it doesn't yet exist in this concrete world that I live in. And it is my repeated intent, and my full-hearted desire and passion which gives that thought more and more substance until it becomes real.

I also have to clear away the natural resistance or the limiting beliefs that get in the way, that prevent me from truly believing that I can be courageous in confronting my boss. So, unless I honor, face and clear beliefs like, "I don't have what it takes" or "My boss is much stronger than I am," how could I ever affirm what I really want? It will be these beliefs and not my intention which I will manifest. This is a very important point. To have a full-hearted intent to manifest courage, I must do battle with the dragons that get in the way of the courage. We call this mental clearing.

DiCarlo—But can these dragons be cleared by an individual on their own behalf, or is it sometimes necessary to go to others for assistance?

Straub—I think it's both. In my own journey, there have been simple situations where I have done my own mental clearing. Let's say I was grumpy with David yesterday, and I don't want to be in the future. That's something I can handle myself. But when it comes to the major dragons, I think we do need help, whether that be a mentor, a spiritual counselor, a support group, a 12-step program, someone I love, or someone I trust. The support can come in many different forms.

DiCarlo—Do you have any success stories relating to how you've used this process to manifest things in your life?

Gershon—Well, there have been many, but the story about the "Earth Run," a seemingly impossible world event for peace that involved 25 million people and 45 heads of state in 62 countries, is probably the most notable story about manifestation. That came out of a clear vision and a real attentiveness to my interior process. It involved a continual holding of the intention.

What I want to suggest more than anything else is that this is not a magical process. It is a natural process, although there are certainly some aspects that may have some quality of magic. But it's the same magic as planting a seed in the earth and watering it and nurturing it and seeing it grow. Some people who become students of manifestation have the misconception that, "I'll create an affirmation and then I will get everything that I want." That's very naive. It's more like, "I'll plant a carefully chosen seed. I'll nourish it. I'll water it. I'll learn how to garden well and become a student of gardening and then I will see the fruits of my effort."

DiCarlo—What are some of the most common mistakes people make in their attempt to manifest things in their lives?

Gershon—Well, as I have mentioned, people often do not know how to interpret the feedback they are getting. Also, people don't seem to understand the factor of time and the nature of the seeds they are planting: "Is this a seed that will take 10 years or 5 years or 2 days?" People need to recognize that in the physical world, things take time before they manifest.

DiCarlo—Can groups of aligned people use these same skills to manifest events on a much larger scale?

Straub—Yes. In our work, we point out, "Now we've learned a lot about manifestation. Everything we've learned can be applied to change our families, our society and our world," and then we tell our story of the Earth Run, which was one of the ways we applied the manifestation tools to allow for large scale change.

DiCarlo—So, if you could create an environment which would allow for a group of empowered people to work together in a synergistic way, they would be able to significantly increase their creative capabilities?

Gershon—Yes, to an extraordinary degree. If you could have six, eight, ten people, all focused and aligned around that vision, working through all the stuff that gets in the way, remarkable things could happen. And it's not just in the organizational dimension, as Gail mentioned. It could be within a community, or any sphere of endeavor. Our creative potential is vast. We need to be people of great imagination and great social ingenuity. We need to really open up our vision to what's possible, to be absolutely clear about the world we want to create. If we are not, the old, unconscious fears that have now manifested as our reality will overwhelm us.

Part 3

APPLYING
the
NEW VIEW

For those whose perceptions allow them to apprehend the vision embodied in the new world view, it can be a highly frustrating endeavor to measure the gap between what can be and what is. An overwhelming system change is what is needed, the breadth and depth of which can cause frustration and a tragic sense of futility.

Though we are somehow aspects of one sacred life and one humanity, our families are held hostage through horrific acts of violence. Though we have come to recognize our special role as stewards and caretakers of planet Earth, environmental degradation continues. The pieces all seem to be there and the agenda for change has been set, yet much work remains. It's a slow, frustrating process, described by some to be the equivalent of trying to turn a briskly moving cruise liner in the opposite direction it's traveling. There is much inertia and resistance to overcome.

Business, economics and education are areas of enterprise that affect us all, key determinants of the quality of our lives. The individuals in the following section are steadfastly working towards creating structures and forms that can better accommodate a different order of vision and values. In so doing, inch-by-inch and row-by-row, they are helping to create a better world for all to enjoy.

Section 8

NEW VIEWS IN BUSINESS

"The dominant principle of organization has shifted, from management in order to control an enterprise to leadership in order to bring out the best in people and to respond quickly to change.

John Naisbitt & Pat Aburdene
"Megatrends 2000"

Is there a higher purpose for business, one that goes beyond the traditional goals of survival, profit and growth?

Those on the cutting-edge of business thought believe that there is. They hold that business, as the dominant institution in the world, must become the global steward, overseeing the welfare of the planet and all its passengers. In this new view, organizational objectives center around the development, learning and expansion of everyone in the organization coupled with service to the surrounding community.

The most courageous and farsighted of business executives have begun to ask some heady questions: "What is our mission and purpose? What is the basis for our decision-making? What role if any does spirituality play in business? What is the level of our responsibility to the local community, nation and environment? What is true leadership and how is it cultivated? What assumptions do we hold about our employees and about human nature and human potential? What is the most effective way to structure and organize a business?"

In their book, "The Fourth Wave," futurists Herman Maynard, who spent 22 years with DuPont corporation and Susan Mehrtens, present four historical eras that have shaped human civilization. Each represents a different world view as it applies to business. Borrowing from Alvin Toffler's ("Future Shock") imagery of waves of social change, they suggest that the First Wave entails the development and spread of agricultural methods. The Second Wave is characterized by Industrialization, a trend which in some lesser developed countries, is just now beginning to play itself out. The Third Wave of Post-industrialization is followed by a Fourth Wave, which exists for the most part as a compelling new vision of the future of business. Each wave has its corresponding worldview, summarized as follows:

	2nd WAVE	3rd WAVE	4th WAVE
Relationships	See ourselves as separate and needing to compete	See ourselves as connected and needing to cooperate	See ourselves as one and choose to co-create.
Authority	Externalized; power seen as outside oneself	Begin to question authority and retain personal locus of authority, take back power	Manifest collaborative systems where authority is fully internalized; power seen as within the person
Values	Rooted in materialism and the supremecy of man	Manifest growing concern for balance and sustainability	Focused on the integration of life and responsibility for the whole
Mode of Inquiry	Stresses linear thinking	Incorporates intuition & nonrational	Moves beyond intuition to tap full range of human abilities processes
Motivation	Make money	Make money & help solve societal problems	Leave valuable legacy for the future

Third Wave societies increasingly value balance and sustainability, with a deeper appreciation for all of life, natural resources and limits of growth. Profit is but one motivating factor, since there is a growing impulse to serve the needs of all stakeholders, contribute to the general well being of the community, minimize damage to the environment, and create a work environment that facilitates personal growth and fulfillment. The definition of success cannot be strictly limited to material possessions, because without peace of mind, integrity and balance, one's quality of life is severely diminished.

The Fourth Wave seeks to integrate all the dimensions of human life, and to assume responsibility for the whole. Fourth Wave motivation is derived not from profit but from service. Profit is placed in its proper perspective as a means and not an end in itself. Business leadership broadens and deepens so as to include a sense of community, national and planetary stewardship.

In this section, we will hear from three Fourth Wave thinkers who have been influential in shaping the emerging world view in business. Peter Senge, will discuss the characteristics of the emerging business, which he calls a "learning organization." A learning organization strives for continuous learning and growth, in order to constantly renew and tranform itself in a changing environment.. Towards that end, it engages in five major 'disciplines' or 'practices': personal mastery; evolving our mental models (paradigms) to a get a clearer approximation of reality; systems thinking; group learning; and building a shared vision.

Next, Stephen Covey will share his ideas on empowerment. To many in business, empowerment means granting decision-making authority and a greater level of responsibility to all individuals in an organization. It is something you give to someone else. Others, such as Gershon and Straub whom we met in our last section, see empowerment as the liberation of an individual, the improved capability to fully express latent abilities and potentials. According to Covey, an organization empowers no one since the power—the potential capability—is already present within the individual. All the organization can do is create a supportive environment in which self-awareness, imagination, will power, an abundance mentality, courage and consideration, creativity and self-renewal, can unfold.

Michael Ray is a graduate business professor at Stanford University. He has co-developed a course called "Creativity In Business," which enables business students to get in touch with their own creative process. There is the tendency to think of creativity as simply the generation of ideas to solve problems, but in Ray's view, the issue runs much deeper—creativity he suggests, is a state of being.

Finally in this section, Marsha Sinetar will discuss the characteristics of the emerging employee. As employees grow and mature into the self-actualizing mode of human development, motivational drivers such as money, title and position become secondary in importance to the growing impulse to discover one's central life task, a sense of vocation. An increasing number of people are asking themselves, "What is my higher purpose in this life and how can it be expressed in what I do for a living?" Through the focused clarity of mission and purpose, one is able to experience extraordinary levels of personal fulfillment and actualize higher capabilities while making a meaningful contribution to the whole of life.

Peter Senge

Peter Senge is Director of the Systems Thinking and Organizational Learning Program at MIT's Sloan School of Management, and a founding partner of Innovation Associates in Framingham, Massachusetts. He has introduced thousand of managers at Ford, Digital, Apple and other major corporations to the disciplines of the learning organization through seminars. He is the author of the book, "The Fifth Discipline: The Art and Practice of the Learning Organization."

DiCarlo—In your influential book, "The Fifth Discipline," you successfully layed the groundwork for what you've referred to as "the learning organization." Could you describe what one is?

Senge—Well, for starters, it's not a "thing." There is no learning organization; there are no learning organizations. I don't know if there ever will be. It's not so much to describe a reality, as to make a certain distinction that can be the basis of a vision. People really don't understand visions very well. The learning organization is a vision in the most genuine sense. What's really important about a vision is what it does, not what it is. Does it lead to changes? Does it lead to a burst of creativity and inspiration and new movement?

Alan Kay tells a story that helps to explain how visions really work. In the early 1970s, Alan was the Director of Research at Xerox PARC, the research center that produced all the critical, technical breakthroughs that led to the personal computer, especially the user interface which enabled the PC to be easily utilized by everyone, even by those with no prior experience. They had a very clear vision that they were aspiring towards when they worked together. They described that vision with one word—they called it "dynabook." They were trying to build a dynabook. Now, keep in mind, at that time, there was nothing like today's personal computer, only big, mainframe computers operated by trained technicians. The personal computer industry didn't start until nearly 10 years later and it was based very much on the pioneering work at Xerox. So they had this vision of a dynabook; it would be like a book, in that you could carry it with you anyplace.

Despite their many breakthroughs, Alan said that their research had failed. "We never produced a dynabook," he said. "The machines that we produced were much too big to carry around and the interface that we developed was completely 'readable,' meaning almost anybody could use it, but it was not 'write-able,' meaning that you still needed an expert to create new programs."

That's a wonderful story about what vision is all about. It's not what the vision is—it's what the vision does. Sure, they failed in creating the dynabook, but what they accomplished was extraordinary. It spawned a whole industry, and interestingly, today, we're getting closer and closer to the original vision. Computers are getting more portable so that a person can carry one around like a book, although you can't drop it, so it's not quite like a book, and it's still not write-able, although Alan and a lot of other people are working on just that.

To me, that's the principle people need to understand. When you talk about learning organizations, you are talking about a compelling vision. The purpose of thinking about and articulating the vision is to generate energy for change—to create a focus, enthusiasm, a sense of what might be possible. Now, who knows <u>what</u> will actually develop? Who knows the <u>ways</u> in which it will develop? It may be as we imagine it, or it might also be in a way that is completely unimaginable today. The important thing is that it produces change in a desired direction. The research at Xerox PARC produced change in a direction. It was very much in the direction of that vision, even though it never fully achieved it.

So, today, you can look all around, in businesses in particular, which is where I have most of my experience, and you can find a lot of examples of change in this direction, yet you will find no "learning organizations." The further any organization progresses in this direction, the further out we'll push the vision. We're not interested in being a learning organization, we're interested in the kind of changes that can be brought about in that pursuit.

DiCarlo—Well, then what is your present vision of a learning organization? What sort of characteristics, attitudes or capabilities might be present?

Senge— I would say that there are three core qualities or perhaps "capabilities" might be a better word. One capability has to do with aspiration. Most organizational change occurs because of desperation, not aspiration. People change when they need to; organizations change in times of crisis, not because they want to. So, learning how to tap collective aspiration would be a core capability of any learning organization. In other words, you learn because you want to learn, not because you need to learn. The difference between a child at the age of one, two, or three, learning to walk, learning to read, learning all the incredible stuff that kids learn, and that same person at the age of ten or twelve learning grammar because they have to, is the basic difference between aspiration and fear.

DiCarlo—What are the origins of this?

Senge—For most of us, it started off in school because school ironically enough, violates a lot of the basic principles of how human beings learn. The first principle of real learning is that learners learn what the learner wants to learn. That's the principle of aspiration, and that holds true in an individual's working life. People are "forced to learn" on the job because they need to keep their job or they need to advance or they need to improve their salary. Maybe they need to because if they don't, the company is going to go out of business. But, by and large, the amount of learning that people are doing in their work is very small. You take that same person on a weekend and they're off learning to ski, or they're learning stuff with their kids. This is not the case, however, on the job where people are usually pretty discouraged, disgruntled, cynical and have some kind of a love/hate— but mostly hate—relationship with their employer.

This whole idea of tapping the capacity of human beings in an organization to learn because they really want to, not because they have to, is key for two reasons. Reason one: if people were really learning what they wanted to learn, they would be enthused and excited about what they were doing. The other reason it's key is from an organizational standpoint. Learning based on desperation or fear is always going to be episodic in nature. In other words, people will learn as long as they have to, as long as there is a threat that they have to respond to. As soon as that threat goes away, the learning will stop. So you will get episodes of learning and change.

I think one of the obvious differences in the world today is that there are some parts of the world where management systems are producing continuous learning and others that are producing episodic learning. You don't need to build a fancy computer model to know that over the long haul, one is going to overtake the other. The Japanese are very, very good at continual learning. It's part of their culture; part of the way they manage. For most Westerners, learning is what happened to us in school and when we grow up, we work. We're not learning anymore. So with that kind of a mind-set, we tend to only learn when there is a crisis that compels us to learn. That's a very important, practical difference between learning that's based on aspiration versus desperation.

The second core capability of a learning organization would be the ability to have reflective conversation in organizations.

DiCarlo—What do you mean by "reflective conversation?"

Senge—Much important work gets done through conversation. Decisions are made through conversations; decisions are implemented through conversations—people talking to one another. Most conversations are marginally productive; often they are counterproductive. People come in with different views and they end up polarizing and having a debate rather than a conversation. It's usually not even a very good debate. What people really have in mind remains unsaid. They're afraid that if they expressed their true thoughts, things would get worse, not better. Or they would get punished, or they would just end up in an argument, or it's not what the boss believes—or a whole host of reasons. So people don't even bring out into the light of day what they have on their mind, let alone have conversations where two people can actually influence one another's thinking.

In productive conversations people become more aware of the assumptions they hold, the very basis of why one sees things the way they do. It's important to realize how relative these assumptions are. Nobody carries God's truth in their head. We carry views, opinions, interpretations—things that are a product of our life experience. They're very idiosyncratic to us; they're not absolute. Yet we treat them as if they are absolute. Let me give you an example: in sales, the V.P. might say a product won't sell unless the price is cut. So then the manufacturing V.P. says, "the product won't sell unless the quality of the sales force is improved." Those people can argue until the cows come home, but you can't resolve that difference at the level at which it is presented. We usually don't have the capability to have a conversation in which people are probing their own assumptions, their own "mental models."

These two core capabilities are closely related. One of the reasons that shared visions don't exist and why we can't tap collective aspiration is because we don't know how to manage the communication process whereby individual visions can be articulated and can interact so that, over time, people can truly start to feel a part of something larger than their own individual vision, a part of a really shared vision. That's really a complex and sophisticated communication process. Literally, a conversation that might involve hundreds or thousands of people. We have very little capability for doing that.

By the time many managers rise to any kind of a position of authority, they are usually extremely good at advocating their views and getting others to "buy in." In fact, what's really needed is not just the advocacy of my views but an inquiry into my views and the views of other people. There needs to be a balance of advocacy and inquiry. It's almost completely absent in most large organizations. Everybody is busy trying to convince everybody else that they're "right" when in fact, on some other level, we know nobody is "right." The real questions are (1) Do we have a good set of assumptions to guide our action?; and (2) Can we act in a coordinated fashion together? If we can't, we're not going to get anything done. So, that's the second key area that really has to do with the disciplines of mental models and what I call "team learning." Or you might say the discipline of dialogue, a deeper type of conversation.

DiCarlo—And the final core capability?

Senge—The third core capability has to do with the ability to deal with complexity. We've all been trained to look at the world as fragments, as bits of snapshots. We see something a certain way and we say, "We've got to change that; it should be this way." We have no idea of the process of going from A to B. We tend to see problems as isolated from one another. If I'm in manufacturing, I see a manufacturing problem. If I'm in research, I see a research problem. If I'm in product development, I see a product development problem. I treat these separately when, in fact, often they are highly interdependent. And the same can be said within any of those functions. If you're building an automobile, you have 12 or 13 major engineering subspecialties. Each of those specialists is off solving their own isolated problems, but in fact they have to produce one car. The success of the car actually doesn't depend on having the best transmission system and the best drive train and the best steering. You can put all the best parts together and you won't necessarily get the best car. What makes the best car is the way all the parts fit together.

So, life is integrative. Whenever we're trying to produce something, we're producing something that has to work as a whole, but our patterns of thought and our ways of identifying and solving problems are highly fragmented. In our culture, being an "expert" literally means knowing a lot about a little. So the whole notion of expertise is very counterproductive to being effective in organizations because organizations have to produce something that is integrated.

Customers have real needs and real problems—they don't care about 13 different features that you have, each of which is world class. They really care about how it all comes together into an integrated product or integrated service. This is just as true in a service business as in a manufacturing business. So you can talk about building a car where the quality of what makes the car effective is its integrated capabilities, or you can talk about the telecommunication industry where what customers really are looking for are integrated solutions from a very fragmented industry. Computing is on one side, video technology on another. You've got a telephone service over here. You've got all this new multimedia technology and you've got data you're trying to transmit. Probably no organization today is very good at offering anything that looks like an integrated service. That's really what customers want because the customers have problems that are highly systemic. So the third capability has to do with the ability to deal with complexity, to deal with high degrees of interrelatedness and processes which are far from static. They are dynamic, changing over time. It involves systems thinking.

DiCarlo—When you talk about learning, do you mean simply the assimilation of new information?

Senge—This is, again, a particular cultural problem we have. In the West, we tend to think of knowledge as something that we have in our heads. We actually don't make any rigorous distinction between knowledge and information. We treat knowledge as a little more important than information.

In our work, we tend to define knowledge as the capacity for effective action. In effect this means you really know how to ride a bicycle when you know how to ride a bicycle. You know something about human relationships when you have some capacity to produce meaningful relationships. It's not something you've read about in a book. You have some capacity to work with other people, particularly those whose ideas, emotions, backgrounds and previous experiences might be very different than yours. To say, "I know a lot about human relations because I've read 32 books" is pretty irrelevant if you actually can't work or live together. If you think of knowledge as the capacity for effective action, then the essence of learning centers upon the enhancement of knowledge, the enhancement of capacity for effective action.

In that sense, there is a profound difference between the East and the West. In the West, we tend to think of learning as an intellectual process, something we learn from a book in a schoolroom. If you ask a person, "What do you first think of when you think of the word "learning?" they'll say "schoolroom." And what does schoolroom suggest? "Sit down and be quiet," they'll say, or "be passive and follow the rules."

DiCarlo—It would seem to me that this demand for conformity and obedience would make learning more difficult. It's a wonder we learn at all!

Senge—Yes, it's very ironic because passivity and relying upon authority is, in many ways, the antithesis of real learning. Real learning is learner directed; it involves self-assessment. In school, we learn that what's most important is what the teacher says, not what we say about how well we are doing. It's ironic: for the rest of our lives, we're not going to have a teacher around to tell us how we're doing. Yet most kids do not develop any capability for objective self-assessment, which is absolutely critical for lifelong learning. And so we have a lot of very strange and I would say, counterproductive, notions about learning in the West.

DiCarlo—How is learning viewed in Eastern cultures?

Senge—In Eastern cultures, it's typical for people to think of learning as something that's actually in the body, not just in the head. When you say, "I know," in most of the Eastern languages such as Chinese or Japanese, you literally are saying it from the center of the body—"I know it; it's in me." In the West, we tend to think of it as in our heads. This is a part of the dualistic Western philosophy that makes its presence felt in so many different areas. There is a real disconnect in our thinking about learning between the head and the hand, between our intellectual knowledge and our capacity for action. It actually is deeply rooted culturally.

In many traditional European cultures, there was a very rigorous, rigid cultural distinction between the people who worked with their hands and the people who did not have to work with their hands. It's always sobering to remember that Michaelangelo could not have dinner with his patrons because the artisans occupied a different social class because they worked with their hands. That fragmentation is very deeply imbedded in Western culture and it's very relevant to these questions of learning and what we mean by knowledge.

We have a lot of executives sitting around in American corporate suites who really think that, "We come up with the big ideas here, right?" "We create the strategy." Think about the parallel to this: "We create the strategy—you guys have to implement it!" And, of course, what's one of the biggest problems facing domestic organizations? They can't implement strategy. The reason they can't implement strategy is because their entire way of thinking about it is so deeply fragmented. Our notion is that the top of the organization thinks and that the people at the local level, in the guts of the organization so to speak, take action.

DiCarlo—The Japanese, generally speaking, don't look at things that way.

Senge—That's right. The Japanese think of strategy as something that emerges throughout the whole organization. A lot of the best strategic ideas come from the front lines, and conversely, the people at the top should be spending their life involved at all levels of the organization. If you go to Honda's corporate headquarters, you will never find any executives there.

Somebody who was visiting Honda's new corporate headquarters told me the following story a couple of years ago. It seems this individual got off the elevator at the top floor, looking for the "corporate suite." He said, "We thought we were on the wrong floor. First off, there were no offices anywhere, only a big, open room, with a bunch of desks around. A "Bullpen" they called it." And the visitor said he was very surprised to find that there wasn't anybody there except for one employee sitting at a desk who invited the group in. The employee put his stuff away, bowed and slipped out the door. He was embarrassed to be caught at his desk because the executives are supposed to be out in the organization. They're not isolated, sitting up at the top, thinking these grand thoughts. They're out there in the middle of the organization, trying to understand the issues and concerns the people are actually wrestling with.

So, you see, this whole separation of head and hand, of intellect and action, of corporate management and local actors, is really a Western product. It's very much a product of our culture and our heritage, and it represents a huge problem when it comes to learning because real learning, is by its nature, integrative. Real learning integrates new ideas, new insights and new actions. If there is no change in behavior, there's no learning. But also, if there's no change in understanding, there's no learning either. There has to be both.

DiCarlo—You've made the following comment: "Learning organizations require basic shifts in how we think and interact. The change goes beyond individual corporate culture or even the culture of Western management; they penetrate to the bedrock assumptions and habits of our culture as a whole."

What might some of these bedrock assumptions be?

Senge—Well, we've just been talking about one of the key ones. This concerns the basic notion there really is a difference between thinking and action, and this difference is embedded in how our organizations and institutions are set up.

Another bedrock assumption really has to do with the theory of knowledge, which in the West is, again, a fragmented theory. I made the comment a little bit earlier that to be an expert in our culture is to know a lot about a little. They used to say Ph.D. stands for "Piled Higher and Deeper." Anyone who has ever gone through the formal education process to the point of getting a Ph.D. knows how true that is. You become more and more knowledgeable about less and less. That's a very deeply embedded notion which underlies our theory of knowledge in the West.

There's a famous library in Oxford, England that has an ancient, circular courtyard with 12 or 13 different doorways leading in. Over each doorway is printed "Geology," "Physics," "Biology," "Literature," etc. It is a wonderful symbol of our theory of knowledge in the West. You enter through each of those doors and you leave the knowledge contained behind the other doors. So, the whole notion that knowledge could be a more integrative activity is really lost in the West. It's a profound problem and so is this deep, cultural tendency towards fragmentation—the breaking up of wholes into pieces. Of course, if you really wanted to push the image a little bit further, if you entered a door called "Biology," you would find yourself in a new courtyard where you would find additional doors labeled "Molecular Biology," "Experimental Biology," and so on because the further you go in any of these fields, the more you find yourself going out along a smaller, narrower branch.

DiCarlo—I like the image—it really gets to the heart of the issue.

Senge—Yes. There is a profound need to develop integrative disciplines in the sciences. What we have today is an enormous tendency towards educating people in very narrow ways. Occasionally, someone comes along who, just by the sake of their own brilliance, is integrative—they cut across different disciplines and we consider those people real geniuses. Well, I don't know if they're real geniuses or they're just real contrarians. They somehow manage to resist the temptation to fragment knowledge.

We have expressed this in terms of a fundamental shift we think is necessary culturally—a shift from seeing the primacy of parts to the primacy of the whole. A lot of people today advocate systems thinking. They say, "We really ought to have a more systemic viewpoint." How are we going to fix our health care system if we just look at all the fragmented self-interests? In the world of politics, fragmentation takes the form of self-interest groups or PACS and in Washington, that leads to grid-lock. The self-interest groups just bang heads against each other and nobody can move forward collectively.

Now we all know that it's necessary to break gridlock. It's important to develop a systems perspective. So we say, "We need to learn how to put the pieces together to see the Big Picture." But seeing the "Big Picture" won't change anything because the deeper fundamental assumption is that it is the pieces which are primary. A profound shift takes place when you start to think that what's actually primary is the whole and that the pieces—the parts, the isolated fragments—are actually a product of our consciousness. They are a product of our way of looking at the world. They are not in the world itself. There is that wonderful phrase of John Muir's, where he says, "If you tug on any piece of the Universe, you find everything else is attached to it." It may really be that reality is more of a seamless whole and that we create the pieces by the way we look at it. The pieces are a reflection of our interpretations, not the "way it is."

We tend to see individuals, for example, as isolated pieces. We've reified this with the notion of "ego." What is an individual? Well, an individual is ultimately an ego. It's this ego thing. We tend to think of ourselves as things isolated from one another. If you take seriously the notion of the primacy of wholes, then you arrive at an entirely different view. You see an individual as the reflection of a community; a strand in a web of interrelationships.

There is an interesting experiment we sometimes do in the courses we lead. We let people pair up and talk to one another. The directions are real simple: tell the person you are partnered with something about yourself. So the people just start talking and you can imagine the things they talk about. They talk about the work they do. They talk about their kids. They talk about what they enjoy doing for fun, skiing, sailing, etc. Then, after about 5 or 10 minutes I'll ask, "Well, what are you actually talking about?" And people respond, "Oh, we're talking about our families." Or, "We're talking about the projects we're working on," and so on. I'll say, "Oh, no, you missed the direction. The direction is, talk about *yourself*. Don't talk about the people you know. Don't talk about the things you do. Talk about yourself."

You find out pretty quickly that you can't talk about yourself. Our "self" is a notion that we have sort of "bought into." That somehow we're this isolated thing called a "self" or an "ego." There is a well known sociologist named Clifford Gertz who says there is no notion of the self independent of community. That's a very non-Western notion. We've used the phrase "the community nature of the self" to highlight that. In many ways, it's a special case of this higher principle, which is, "the primacy of wholes, as opposed to the primacy of parts."

DiCarlo—Would you say that this shift in being able to see fragments to being able to see wholes requires a personal transformation?

Senge—Well, it requires fundamental changes in us as individuals and it's probably pretty hard to do by yourself. That's why the term "personal transformation" is a little bit tricky. First off, I don't like the word a lot and I try to avoid it as much as possible. It tends to be a pretty static image in a way. The better way to say it would be "continually transforming." The term "transformation" tends to suggest a movement from point A to point B— "I was that way; now I'm this way." It's a big problem we have in a lot of our religions. There's the washed and the unwashed. Right? There are those who are the true believers and then there is everybody else. There are those who have been transformed and those who have not been transformed. It tends, once again, to evoke a simple dualism, a simple category, the good and the bad. So in many ways, transformation is a funny term. Although it points in the right direction, it actually evokes all of the things that we are trying to get away from, which is a simple, static, and fragmented image of the world—there's "A" and there's "B."

There's no question that these changes are: (1) Personal. In other words, nothing will change unless we as individuals change; (2) Quite profound—we're talking about very bedrock assumptions and ways of looking at the world; but (3) I would also add that they are never over. You don't get there; there is no one who is a "systems thinker" or a "dialogue expert" or a "transformed" person. There is no "there." It's a lifelong process.

That's the reason we've come to use this term of "discipline" in our work. What's actually needed in organizations is the practice of disciplines. No musician ever gets "there." There is no "there." The whole essence of music or pottery or writing, as an artistic discipline, is that it's a lifelong journey.

In that same spirit, you can see where the word transformation is problematic. No one who practices Zen will talk about themselves as being personally transformed. It's a very Western concept. Someone who practices Zen, a "Zen Master," would still see themself as a learner.

DiCarlo—What would you say Peter, is the primary job of a leader in a learning organization?

Senge—Well, I think you have to be careful on definitions here. Does leader mean senior manager? Or does it mean "leader" in the sense that anyone can be a leader. We tend to use the words now as a senior manager, the person who sits at the top of a hierarchy of some sort. But many parents are great leaders and many people who are leaders do not occupy any position of authority whatsoever. So it's always hard for me to answer questions like that because of the ambiguity. If you ask me what's the most important leadership job of a top manager, that's one thing. If you ask me, "What's the essence of leadership?" in a fashion that every single person really can be a leader, that's another.

DiCarlo—OK, what would the *essence* of leadership be?

Senge—For me, the most powerful image of leadership is that of the person who walks ahead. The person who has the courage to move forward in a particular area. Now obviously, these people don't walk ahead alone. So the essence of leadership has to do with vision, a real deep conviction and commitment. Would you ever follow somebody voluntarily who wasn't doing something that you and they really thought was important? So leadership involves vision, conviction and courage—to put your heart into a task, stick your neck out, and walk ahead. For thousands of years people have said the same thing so I don't think there is anything very original about that.

But there's one another facet to the issue of leadership that's a little subtler. Particularly in this day and age, the real leadership that matters is actually the leadership of groups. I believe this very strongly. The day of the "individual" hero-leader is past, an artifact of a certain time and place. We don't need better heros now. We need groups of people who can lead, groups of people who can walk ahead.

That being the case, there is another aspect of leadership and that's the ability to tap and harness collective intelligence, where it's not just my insight, and my vision that matters—it's *our* insight and *our* vision. It's not just my conviction that matters, it's our conviction.

To be the sort of person around whom other people will grow and flourish is something that Robert Greenleaf pointed to in a very particular way when he used the term, "servant-leadership." He said that for him, the ultimate defining quality of a leader is the sort of person around whom other people naturally grow. They become more mature, more self-confident, more able to serve.

DiCarlo—Let's shift gears for a moment. I am intrigued by your discussions of the symbolism found on the dollar bill. For example, you stated that the Great Pyramid of Giza represents the integration of the highest in consciousness in the material world, the Great Work. You also mentioned that in the original design, the phoenix—symbol for spiritual transformation—took the place of the eagle.

Senge—These are ideas that have been around for a long time although they are not really of much currency anymore. If you look at the Great Seal, you see an incomplete pyramid. There are actually two sides of the seal, both of which are on the backside of the dollar bill. On the left backside, you'll see this picture of the pyramid, but it's incomplete. Above the pyramid is a second triangle, which is often called the cap stone, floating separately. It has the same proportions that the pyramid would have if it were complete. That is, if it were put onto the top of the pyramid, it would complete the pyramid. The solid pyramid base—that incomplete solid pyramid—represents the material world and material accomplishments of humankind which are fundamentally incomplete. It can only be completed with the integration of that cap stone on the top. What's in the middle of the cap stone? The all-seeing eye, the symbol for a higher consciousness, for God. So, it's been said for many years that this is a symbolic representation of the spiritual vision of the United States. The spiritual vision in the United States is the completion of the pyramid—the integration of the highest in consciousness into the material world.

You also see several Latin phrases around the pyramid. The very well known one, "E Pluribus Unum," means, "Out of the Many, One." Then there is the other phrase "Novus Ordo Seclorem," or "New Order of the Ages." It's pretty clear that the architects of this Great Seal were, by and large, the "Founding Fathers," people such as Madison, Jefferson and Ben Franklin. They met for many, many years in study-group-like-settings as they were trying to develop their basic philosophic ideas about this new government. They were articulating a very unusual vision of the United States. I don't know if this is factually true or not, but certainly it's interesting to consider that the United States may have been the first—certainly one of the first—nations founded on the basis of an explicit, articulated spiritual vision.

On the other side of the dollar bill is the eagle. Some people claim that it was originally the phoenix. I first came across the idea in a book of Willis Harman's called *Higher Creativity*. According to Harman, all the founding fathers were members of the Masonic Lodge, which at that time was quite different than it is today. It was a place where people gathered to talk about philosophical matters. Harman states: "Dominating the obverse side is the bird that is now the eagle, but in earlier versions was the phoenix, ancient symbol of human aspiration towards universal good, and being reborn toward enlightenment and higher awareness."

It's interesting to consider what the process that led to the Great Seal must have been like. It involved many, many years of intense inquiry and study. The very fact that they could come together in extraordinarily difficult times and agree to the words contained within the Declaration of Independence, which starts, "We hold these truths to be self-evident," is amazing. Think about the process that they must have gone through, with people who were so different. Some were farmers. Some were merchants. Some came from the south, while others came from the north. It was an extraordinarily highly charged time, yet all signed on at the end of the document and committed, as they said, "their lives and sacred honor." There must have been something pretty interesting going on with that group of people to be able to author something with that level of clarity, conviction and agreement. That's a great example of the learning process that a group must have gone through. And the Great Seal is just one more window into that.

DiCarlo—You've mentioned the word, "spiritual" as it relates to the vision that our founding fathers had for this country...In your view, do issues of the unseen dimensions of soul and spirit have any place in business?

Senge—Oh, absolutely. Absolutely. I think that this is something that people are going to feel more and more comfortable talking about as time goes on. It's very interesting. I've noticed for many years that the word "spiritual" is very problematic with business audiences. It's a word that people avoid. I think the reasons are pretty obvious. It immediately seems to suggest religion and there are so many differences in people's religious convictions and in people's religious histories that people understandably avoid the word spiritual.

By contrast, people have no trouble talking about the word "spirit." They use the word spirit all the time. Good managers will often talk about the spirit of a team. If you ask people, "How many of you have ever been around a team that had real spirit?" people have no trouble whatsoever responding to that question. So I think it's very interesting. When you think about it, one of the things that really makes management interesting is that it is about people. Ultimately, what marks or demarks the craft and the art of management, is the question of how you get diverse groups of people—people who are diverse in their ways of thinking and their background—to somehow align with one another, to somehow come together and act in an effective, coordinated manner with spirit, imagination, excitement, enthusiasm and passion. That's the domain where management and leadership come together. So I don't think you can avoid this. I think that managers who really love their work, love what they do for precisely these reasons. You are always dealing with the unseen, the subtlest qualities which can energize and make the difference between a mundane group of people simply carrying out their tasks and a truly creative, generative group of people who can do things that others might call impossible.

My experience is that typically two-thirds to 90% of any group of people who have had any significant experience in business have at one time or another been part of an extraordinary team. When you ask them about that, they will really talk about the same things: they'll talk about spirit; they'll talk about vision; they'll talk about caring; they'll talk about love. They'll talk about all the "unseen stuff." The "soft stuff."

Dr. Stephen Covey

Stephen R. Covey is founder and chairman of the Covey Leadership Center, an 800-plus-member international firm. He has taught leadership principles and management skills for over 25 years to business, government and educational organizations, including many Fortune 500 companies. Covey is the author of several books, including, "First Things First, and "The Seven Habits of Highly Effective People," which has sold more than two million copies and has been published in over twenty countries and a dozen languages.

DiCarlo—The term "empowerment," like "quality" and "transformation" has achieved buzzword status. To some, it means pushing down authority and responsibility from the boardroom executive to the front-line employee. What's your definition of empowerment?

Covey—Well, you're right, empowerment has become a buzzword. It's kind of a bastardized term, in that, to most people, it basically means a superficial form of delegation. But it's far beyond that. It involves the four levels—the personal, the interpersonal, the managerial, and the organizational. At the personal level, the whole conviction of the value of other people and the creative potential of other people has not yet been touched. It takes an abundance mindset. People with scarcity mindset believe that if they give power away that means they have less power. If they share knowledge, that means they will have less knowledge or they will have less control. That's why there has to be some personal transformation before people will really want to empower other people.

Also, those being empowered have sometimes become so acclimated to the benevolent, paternalistic way of being managed so common in the past, that they find most of their satisfaction off the job.

And so it takes a process at the interpersonal level, at the managerial level, and at the organizational level to make sure that the systems and structures of an organization—the focus of most quality improvement programs—are aligned to reinforce empowerment. So empowerment really involves creating conditions at the personal, interpersonal, managerial and organizational levels that will enable the fullness of people's capacities to be tapped into. And not only the individual, but also the synergy between individuals because the whole is so much greater than the sum of the parts—the relationship between the parts becomes the biggest part of all.

DiCarlo—What would you say is the essence of empowerment?

Covey—The essence of empowerment is the awareness that the power is already in people. What we need to do is to create the conditions which unleash it.

DiCarlo—Are there any particular reasons why people become disempowered, both personally and organizationally?

Covey—Sure. They start blaming other people instead of taking responsibility. The moment you build your emotional life on the weaknesses of others, or on the weaknesses of institutions, you have just disempowered yourself. You have given your own unique, human endowment away to the source of that criticism.

They also disempower others by structuring the organization in such a way that people really can't use their powers. They can't use their imagination. They can't use their creativity. Their ingenuity. Their motivation.

DiCarlo—Isn't it true that some people are not ready to be empowered?

Covey—Maybe they are not ready at the level at which some people think of empowerment. But they are ready at some level. The key is to discern that level at which they are ready, and create the opportunity for people to utilize their powers. Eventually, they will reach higher and higher levels of utilizing their powers and they will show enormous accountability.

DiCarlo—It seems like it would take an awful lot of time to create an empowering organization. Given the costs involved, why do it?

Covey—Simple: we won't survive if we don't. The global marketplace has changed everything. You cannot produce quality without having people who are empowered to be, as Rosabeth Moss Kanter puts it, customer-focused, fast, friendly and flexible. You cannot compete. So your organization will not make it. This is going to happen in government, it's going to happen in hospitals, and it's going to happen in schools as well as businesses. This wouldn't be the case if we didn't have the global marketplace, because if you are in a local marketplace you are about as good as your competitor is dumb. So if your competitor is not empowering its employees, your business can fare much better in the marketplace.

Another reason to empower is to produce a responsible citizenry. If, for example, families don't empower their kids they won't be contributing members of our society. They will be consumers rather than producers. And if we have a society of consumers and not producers, there will be nothing left to consume.

DiCarlo—What are the conditions that enable empowerment to take place?

Covey—The first condition is trustworthiness, which consists of both character and competence. Character refers to a person's integrity, maturity, and what I call the abundance mentality. By competency I mean one's technical skills and conceptual skills which allows one to see the "Big Picture"—how all the pieces fit together.

They also need to develop the skills of interdependency, which means that you think ecologically and you act in terms of "complimentary teams" and synergy rather than isolated individuals and compromise.

The second condition is the trust that flows out of the first condition. When people can be trusted that means they are able to come through and deliver. They have the integrity. They are dependable. They keep their commitments. They think win-win or no deal. They apologize when they make mistakes. They always seek first to understand other people or to understand the situation before seeking to be understood. They learn how to give and receive feedback with magnanimity and appreciation and not be offended by it. They make "deposits," as I call them, into the emotional bank account that each of us has with others.

DiCarlo—And the third condition?

Covey—Well, if you have the kind of trust I've described, it enables people to develop the third condition of empowerment, which I call win-win performance agreements. This basically means that there is a mutual understanding and commitment between the people involved—for example, a supplier and a company or a customer and a company—surrounding five basic things: desired results, guidelines, resources, accountability and consequences. Purposely left off is method, the "how-to-do-it." That becomes the fourth condition. The "how" is answered by the people or the team involved so they accomplish the desired results within the guidelines in any way they want to. That taps into their creativity and resourcefulness. As long as they act within the guidelines, which include ethical principles and laws and mission statement—and any absolutely necessary but as few as possible procedures—then they are empowered.

The fifth condition is to set up structures and systems that reinforce this empowered individual or team. This is the area that is called re-engineering the corporation. This is the main area that people like

Deming, and Crosby and Juran focus upon—that is, improving the operational processes. They think the primary problem is not with the people, it's with the programs that people write. I believe that the problem always starts with the programmer. People with a scarcity mentality will always implement so-called "win-win" systems in "win-lose" ways. So while I put a lot of value upon structures and systems, for me, the deeper root is the programmer—the one who writes the programs.

The sixth condition is accountability where people can evaluate themselves using 360 degree data, meaning, financial accounting plus information from all stakeholders—customers, suppliers, employees, their families, the community and so forth. The sixth condition feeds back into the "win-win performance agreement" and nurtures it, maintains it, and gives us abundant evidence of the trust and trustworthiness that lie at the very core.

DiCarlo—But business is so "bottom-line" oriented...

Covey—Well, financial accounting is only 90 degrees. A little knowledge is a dangerous thing and financial accounting is dangerous without a full understanding of the human sources of all that data. It only tells you about the effects of the programs. It doesn't tell you anything about relationships, cultures or programmers—the individuals. Nothing, absolutely nothing. Financial accounting intoxicates the brain. It gives people a sense that they know what's going on, and they are drunk. They are drunken with this sense of concrete, precise, scientific data, unaware of how totally incomplete and inaccurate it is. So they have to add the other 90 degrees of looking at their customers and understanding the buying habits, motives and needs. To really understand them.

The other 90 degrees is to understand their own people. Their own culture. People's families.

The other 90 degrees deals with the community and with suppliers and distributors and dealers. Government. Media.

A 360 degree review basically means that you have a scientific, and a systematic and a regular approach at gathering data and putting it in front of people in ways so that it is very usable. So that they have a very good understanding of not only the acute, but the chronic sources of problems. Not only of the part but of the whole. What we call total quality management today focuses upon total customer satisfaction. That will change. The focus will shift to "total stakeholder satisfaction."

The universal mission statement is basically to increase the economic well-being and quality of life of *all* stakeholders. If one is neglected, it will have a negative, domino effect on all the rest.

DiCarlo—In your view, what would you say characterizes the times in which we live?

Covey—We are seeing the fruits of social disintegration everywhere—families torn apart, businesses failing, low trust, adversarial relationships, fighting in all sectors of society. It's across the board in hospitals, health care, schools and education. No one is trained in interdependence, in working together. Everyone is thinking independently and yet the problems we face all require high levels of cooperation. The essential message of my work has been that we need to return to the fundamental principles of the character ethic. The need is enormous.

DiCarlo—How did we deviate from these principles?

Covey—By behaving in a way that is in direct opposition to each principle. The first principle involves personal responsibility and most people don't take it. Principle two involves developing a personal vision of your life—most people don't have a vision. They don't act on purpose. Principle three involves putting first things first and keeping commitments—most people don't have integrity. Principle four involves seeking mutual benefit—most people are selfish. They think "win-lose" or if they are martyrs, think "lose-win." Principle five involves seeking to understand others first—most seek first to be understood all the time. Principle six involves synergy and looking for third alternatives—most go for compromise instead. And the seventh principle involves what I call "sharpening the saw"—most people fail to pay the price of personal renewal.

So the opposite of each of the seven habits is the deviation.

DiCarlo—Now when you say integrity, as in principle three, do you mean being honest and ethical?

Covey—No. Honesty is just one of many symptoms of integrity. Integrity means integrated. Whole. Harmonized. Unified. Sincerity means without wax, no seams. You are seamless. So integrity is the opinion you have of yourself and the concept of honesty would be one of the symptoms of a person who is integrated.

DiCarlo—How would a person go about becoming more integrated in their life?

Covey—Educate and obey their conscience. By that I mean, get deeply into the great wisdom literature of all religions and all societies that have had enduring value and study it. Study the lives of great individuals who have made tremendous contributions and who have been admired for their contributions, their service, their integrity. Identify with it until your conscience becomes extremely sensitive, strong and inside you. Then, learn to listen to it and to obey it.

That's why I believe that humility is the mother of all principles. Everything flows from the spirit of, "You are *not* in charge, you are not a law unto yourself." Your social values may have nothing to do with principles at all. In fact, most social values are not principle-centered at all. It's about accepting that, "I have to be subject to the natural law of the universe." To admit that, "I am not in control" is a humbling statement which requires a humble attitude. It makes you capable then, of having all other virtues come through you.

On the other hand, if you are a law unto yourself, that kind of pride and arrogance will preclude that level of openness and receptivity. People then gather other people around them to validate them, massage their hearts and make them feel good. But they are really very proud, arrogant and have a hard time learning. They fail to be open and teachable, and they are not growing. They begin to define all of life around their own narrow and distorted frame of reference. It's a form of self-centeredness, feeling that everything revolves around you.

DiCarlo— You mentioned that a scarcity mentality prevents individuals from establishing "win-win" relationships. What would you say is the root cause?

Covey— It comes from being compared as a child and getting your sense of security from that comparison. It is what's called "comparison-based identity." The primary six sources of scarcity come from conditional love supplies at home, competitive based grading systems at school, comparison between friends and peers, the world of work where people are up against using so-called scarce resources—they are fighting for them and they are usually up against some forced ranking systems. Also, many religions focus upon comparison so that even though they teach the religion of love they often practice exclusivity and judgements and superior attitudes. Also, a sixth one is athletics, particularly for young men—and becoming more and more for young women—where "win-lose" is deeply embedded.

DiCarlo—You've made an interesting observation, that in today's business environment there is a very close relationship between personal ethics and success in the marketplace. Why is that?

Covey—Entrance into the global marketplace humbles organizations.

It demands high quality. They have to accommodate that reality. It's external to themselves. You can't fake it. You can't produce it through a quick-fix, through chemistry, through surgery. All you can do is mess it up. The same thing is true of our own bodies. If we try to heal ourselves through chemistry or surgery we haven't fundamentally changed our life-style. You can't really produce the pragmatic fruits if you violate these principles. You can't have trust if you don't have trustworthiness. You can't talk yourself out of problems you behave yourself into. When people try this approach, it often worsens the situation even though they might temporarily get by, or deceive a few people. Ultimately, what they are comes out. Their character surfaces. Particularly in the dark, when they are alone, when they have a lot of power. When they don't have to impress people. That's when they usually manifest their true character.

DiCarlo—In your book, *Principle Centered Leadership*, you suggest that revolutionary change is now taking place in every industry and profession—a "metamorphosis" in your terms. Can you identify what lies at the heart of this profound shift in world view?

Covey—It usually involves a great deal of interior work, self-awareness, examining your past motives, examining your past scripting, and then realizing, "You are not just that." You have the power to act on the basis of a new vision. You can use more than self-awareness. It involves what I call the four human endowments: self-awareness, imagination, conscience, and willpower. And it's the combination of those four unique endowments that enable people to accommodate the new reality.

DiCarlo—I see. Well, could you explain what you mean by each?

Covey—Self-awareness is basically the fact that you can stand apart from yourself and examine your own mind, your own mood, your own feelings. This means you are not your mind, your moods or your feelings. You have an identity apart from these things.

Also, I really believe the greatest battles we ever fight are those in our own heart—finding what our own true motives are—and that comes out of periods of deep reflection. But the very fact that you can examine means that you can re-script your life.

Imagination, the second human endowment, means that you can create your future. You don't have to predict it, you create it. That's the best way to predict it. You don't have to live out of your memory. Animals have no self-awareness and no imagination. That's why they are totally a product of the past, instinct and/or training. They can't re-script themselves. They have no ability to stand apart. They can think, but they can't think about their thinking.

Third one, conscience, is I think a divine gift given to all of God's children. It is their native sense of right and wrong. It is a moral sense. The more they educate it by studying the great literature, which I think comes from God, the more their conscience becomes the source of their guidance, security, wisdom and their power.

Independent will is just the sheer grit power to swim upstream, to exercise enormous courage in the face of enormous odds and to make things happen.

Incidentally, it's a huge challenge to change world views, because people's styles, their habits, their emotional food comes from the success of the past paradigm. To move into this new paradigm—which the quality movement kind of embodies—involves a tremendous internal revolution. It's not easy, but if people don't make it, they won't accommodate the new world. It's a new day, and nothing fails like success. But people have to deal with that internally, and usually their approach is, "Other people should change" and "the problem is out there."

DiCarlo—Yes, there's a false sense of complacency in which people don't want to move out of their comfort zones.

Covey—People don't do anything until they experience pain. It's too bad the pain of conscience isn't sufficient, but it isn't. In most cases, it takes the pain of circumstance. And that humbles them, and then they become open. Then they tend to unfreeze old paradigms and look for new ways of thinking. Sometimes they don't look for new ways of thinking at all. They just look for new techniques. But you see, we're not just talking about some new techniques. We're talking about a fundamental transformation. Many individuals don't want that to happen. They just want to learn some new techniques.

Ironically, if they use their old thinking with new techniques, then the bottom-line gets worse, not better.

DiCarlo—Are there any other individuals—living or dead, who have most influenced you in your thinking?

Covey—Well, I would say that I have been influenced by Ghandi, and the way he learned "Win-Win" and law. That became the foundation for his whole philosophy and approach in liberating 400 million Indians.

I am influenced by the wisdom literature of all the religions, and all of the cultures that have had enduring value. Both suggest that principles ultimately control, not personalities. That's why we can't focus on Deming, Covey or anyone. It's the principles that ultimately control. The more people personally become centered on those principles, the greater their capacity to think abundantly, to have true integrity, to not have jealousy, to do that kind of thing that builds trust between people. Then the job is to build that into the organization so that the structures and systems are in alignment. That becomes their managerial task. But unless they work personally and build high trust with other people, the techniques just won't work.

DiCarlo—You've borrowed a quote from Teilhard de Chardin that I especially like, "We are not human beings having a spiritual experience. We are spiritual beings having a human experience." What are the implications of that recognition in the way we conduct our lives and manage our businesses?

Covey—Enormous. It means you have a sacred stewardship towards people. That they are immortal. Eternal. They are not just mortal animals.

It means that the next generation really needs to be taken care of, just like we take care of our environment. The highest and most precious stewardship we have are our children.

It would also imply that you cannot accomplish any worthy end with an unworthy mean, that the Machiavellian concept of "the end justifying the means" is totally flawed.

DiCarlo—I'm wondering how you arrived at what appears to be a deep sense of life purpose?

Covey—Well, I guess I've just grown up in the tradition that you are here to make a contribution. You are here to make a difference—not a living. That's the only thing that enables survival. Literally and physically, people cannot survive if they do not have a sense of meaning. Victor Frankl demonstrated that, Hans Seyle teaches that. I also believe that it's genetically built into us; in other words, meaning and purpose is a part of our own spiritual identity. We are intrinsically predisposed to serve and contribute. Whether you call it a sense of mission, or a sense of vision, or a purpose it wouldn't make that much of a difference. The key thing is that you are to add value—constantly.

Michael Ray

Michael Ray is the first John G. McCoy-Banc One Corporation Professor of Creativity and Innovation and of Marketing at the Stanford Business School. He has authored over 100 articles and nine books, including "The New Paradigm of Business," "The Path of the Everyday Hero," "The New Entrepreneurs," and "Visionaries for the 21st Century." Ray co-developed the Stanford University business course, "Creativity in Business," which was the inspiration for the acclaimed PBS series "The Creative Spirit."

DiCarlo—You were one of the developers of the highly acclaimed Stanford MBA course, "Personal Creativity in Business." Could you describe the origins of this innovative program?

Ray—I was teaching basic advertising back in 1961 to sophomores at Northwestern University, after spending time in the advertising industry. I developed an exercise to help students develop ads. I called this "The Great Idea Exercise" and we still use it. This exercise inspired our book *Creativity in Business*. It basically involves thinking about a time when you had a great idea, regardless of what it was. It doesn't have to be a media event, just something that you did to deal with a problem or situation. We then talked about the ideas, and began to personally understand what creativity was all about.

I emphasized creativity in my courses and it was always the most popular thing that I did, although I didn't have an entire course devoted to the subject. In the 1970s, I went through a lot of big changes in my life. I took a 13-week course called the Fisher-Hoffman process, and in that course was a woman by the name of Rochelle Myers. Rochelle had been a lead cellist for an orchestra in New York. She also developed her own style of art called nonwoven weaving. Her work is featured in art books alongside Picasso. She was operating as an art therapist at the time, and she headed an organization called The Myers Institute for Creative Studies, in San Francisco.

Before long, we began to work together, and we decided to teach a course called "Creativity in Business" at Stanford. I remember talking to her about a linear, step-by-step approach to creativity in her kitchen, and she said, "Michael, you don't expect me to listen to this, do you?" We started passing around, what some of our speakers have called "50s-creativity," kind of like a hot potato, "You do it, then I'll do it, you do it then I'll do it" and finally we decided we would develop a course that would really speak to the spirit and which was really about, as Rochelle put it, "making your life a work of art." Creativity more as a state of being that you operate out of, rather than specific things that you do.

DiCarlo—So the course was not designed to help students improve their problem solving ability?

Ray—From the beginning the course has been very different, and no, we were not interested in improving problem solving ability. We are not even interested in getting ideas, because we feel there are enough ideas. The main purpose has been to develop a way of life. We deal with challenges. Every time we teach the course we ask students to write down their personal situations so that they can use the material in the course to deal with them. We have tabulated these into what we now call "the six challenges."

DiCarlo—Could you discuss them?

Ray—For most people, the number one challenge is finding purpose and career, although we have dropped the career part of it. Other challenges are: 2) of time and stress; 3) the issue of relationship; 4) the challenge of balancing personal and professional life; and 5) the challenge of finding true prosperity. Another way of looking at prosperity is money versus self-worth, or all the external things such as money and power, recognition, appearance and health as opposed to a full, rich feeling of self-worth. We sometimes call this the "Peggy Lee Syndrome." Peggy Lee was a singer who was noted for her song, "Is that all there is?" The last challenge, number (6) is really the challenge of the whole course which is, "How do you bring your own personal creativity into the organization or into the world?" That's what the course is all about.

We structure the course around four tools. Everyone has their own way of looking at creativity. Our way of looking at it comes from the many guest speakers who have visited our classes. The four major tools are: One, "Have faith in your own creativity," two, "Abstain from judgement," the third is "Precise observation," and the last, "Ask penetrating questions." They build on each other.

We assume from the beginning that creativity is essential for health, happiness and success in business and in life. What we are talking about is not some "add on" but rather, the essential thing in life. The second assumption we hold is that creativity is in everyone. And the third assumption is that, although creativity is in everyone, it is covered over by fear, judgement and the chattering of the mind. Our students gave this chattering the acronym, "VOJ," which stands for

"The Voice of Judgement." That is the inner voice of blame and criticism that comes from our parents and those who influence us as we grow up. And this relates to that second tool of the absence of judgement. Rochelle has said that the course is the "ultimate striptease," in that you work to get rid of all this judgement, fear and mental chattering.

DiCarlo—Are there any other assumptions that serve as the underpinning of the course?

Ray—Well, our fourth assumption is kind of like that Great Idea exercise, where we say, "Although our creativity is covered over by fear, chattering of the mind, ego, false personality, judgement—whatever you want to call it—you can manifest your own personal creativity in the world by personally experiencing it. We do things in the class that force people to observe their own creativity. In the Great Idea exercise, for example, you take notice of your creative process and talk about it.

The last of our assumptions is that creativity is pretty much idiosyncratic, meaning, that everybody has their own way of doing it and bringing it out in the world. We have many different kinds of techniques and exercises that we have people do. The students even make them up themselves. For instance, we use at least a dozen different types of meditation and visualization techniques. We have all kinds of paper and pencil techniques. We use I Ching and Tarot Cards, movement and martial arts, singing and all kinds of art, from drawing mandalas to doing collages. One of the most effective approaches we use, is that each week we give students a credo for living, a guideline or rule of thumb to live by. These center around having faith in your own creativity, absence of judgement, precise observations, penetrating questions—it cycles through the class.

First we cycle through the four tools and then we cycle through the six challenges. Then, we repeat the tools. So a credo, or "live with" for developing faith in your own creativity would be, "If at first you don't succeed, surrender." But we use other ones, such as, "I don't know," or "Have no expectations." So right at the beginning of the class they exercise their ability to surrender, to give themselves up to their own inner creative resource which we tend to call Essence. We have descriptions of Essence that come from different spiritual traditions as a way of better understanding what that would all be about.

DiCarlo—Is "Essence" as you describe it the same as the soul?

Ray—Yes. I am not enough of a theologian or philosopher to know what the difference would be. We tend not to use the word "soul"; we use other terms such as "Essence," or the "Self" or the "Inner Creative Resource." "Soul" has cumbersome religious implications.

DiCarlo—Any other credos you'd like to share?

Ray—Well, for absence of judgement, we say to people, "Say hello and then good-by to your VOJ" or "Destroy judgement. Create curiosity." Or "Psyche out the Voice of Judgement."

And for precise observation we use something like, "Pay attention." But each person has to decide how they will live by the credo. Some of the people in the class will set their watch to go off at intermittent times to remind themselves to pay attention. Some people go to the beach and sit there and soak everything in as a way of paying attention. Some people will concentrate on listening, or they will make a list of all the things they have wanted to pay attention to, but for whatever reason, were never able.

We give them live-with sheets every week that guide them a little bit, but they have to figure out how they are going to do it. Each week we ask them to write a two page paper about what their experiences were.

We have a theme for each time we teach the course and the theme for the past five or six years has been to answer the questions, "Who is my Self?"—capital "S" Self—the highest aspect of myself. And the other is, "What is my Work?" Again, capital "W" in work, which is to say the purpose for your existence, not simply a job.

So this whole course involves the discovery of your whole creative process—what works for you—and who you are and what your purpose might be.

The students write weekly papers, and we tell them, "Don't argue about the "live-with" itself. Don't get into a philosophical discussion about the meaning of surrender."

When we get to the challenge of purpose, we discuss the importance of faith, and for a week they are to do only what is easy, effortless and enjoyable. Or we tell them, "Do only what you love and love everything you do." Usually that comes around the time of midterm exams, so they have difficulty doing that, but they have to.

We ask them not to get into philosophy, "Well, this is a good or bad live with," but rather to purely observe what happened to them each week— what did they do with the live-with, what effect did it have on their life? We ask them to report on at least one experience. We ask people to share their experience in a non-evaluative way. Usually, about ten percent will say, "Well, this just didn't work for me at all," but then they will write about things they did that they didn't even realize before they started writing the paper. By the end of some of the papers, I'll have tears in my eyes because of the breakthroughs these people have experienced.

I remember this one woman who, on the last day—which involves a final ceremony where the student's remaining negativities are placed into a sacrificial fire—tearfully said, "This class changed my life." And I said, "Everything in your life changes your life." I got tired of hearing people tell me how effective and great the course was. I guess what I wanted was to simply have her acknowledge that everything in life is "grist for the mill."

It's a ten week course, and the students get into this flow where they can't get away from this search for creativity. We have guest lecturers coming in, we have transcripts of past speakers, we have the stories in our books, we have the idea of the hero's journey which they are involved with by going through this personal search, and by the end of the course, this kind of shift happens to everyone.

My experience has been that people have to work really hard to bring out their own creativity. If they turn their creativity over to the organization or some leader to develop, then it isn't going to happen. I felt the service I could perform in life was to help people open up their own creativity, so that we could have organizations full of enlightened, creative people.

DiCarlo—You've mentioned that an important part of the course involved incoming guest lecturers. Some, like Stephen Jobs who started Apple Computer and *In Search of Excellence* author Tom Peters, have been quite famous.

Ray—That's right. Some of them are very well known media-type people; others are people you never hear of but who nonetheless have a very interesting story to tell. We use those people as models, so a student can say, "Well, she is just like me, with all my foibles and shortcomings, but look what she was able to do and here's how she did it." It's a constant process of discovery.

DiCarlo—Stephen DeVore of SyberVision was one of your guest lecturers. What was the main thrust of his discussion?

Ray—He is a good example. I give the students a lot of background information, so we know as much as we can possibly know before the person arrives. We even know how they got their ideas because that's usually been written about. What you really want is their personal story.

DeVore is very interesting. At the time he came to class, I remember him saying that his company, SyberVision was approaching one million dollars in sales. The class laughed at him. And he was proud of that, saying, "That's pretty good for what we're doing." He shared the story of how he contracted polio while he was young. His parents were told by the doctors that their son would live, but he'd never be able to walk again. They had to cut some tendons in his legs, and he would be confined to a wheelchair. His mother, who was very important in the beginning development of Sylva Mind Control, is a powerful person. She ended up taking her son away from the doctors and had him observe other children, playing and running. She'd say, "Now remember Stephen, really visualize the way they were walking. Soak it up."

Through that visualization work—which is kind of a model of what his company, SyberVision is all about—DeVore was able to start walking. Amazingly, when he graduated from high school he had three, full ride, baseball scholarships to colleges.

DeVore had just finished developing his program called, "The Neuropsychology of Achievement" at the time he visited our class. In the process of developing the program, he began to look at people who were high achievers and low achievers, to discover if there were any differences in their visualization characteristics and how they saw things. He worked very scientifically, and realized that successful people had real images of success. They would have images of failure too, but their images of success were three-dimensional, technicolor, with dolby sound—everything. Their images of failure, on the other hand, were sort of black and white, and two dimensional. It was just the reverse for people who weren't high achievers. They would have full color, detailed images of their failures and fears.

So he began to see an almost spiritual quality to this work. For example, Stephen talked about how, when Christ said, "faith will move mountains," that according to quantum mechanics—and Stephen works with people in that field—he wasn't just saying faith rewards a prepared mind. He was saying that with consciousness you could literally move mountains.

One definition of the new world view is that consciousness is causal. This is the shift from the current paradigm—the scientific paradigm—which suggests that everything is known outside, by objective observation, to the emerging paradigm, which involves honoring our inner resources, the essence, soul or whatever you want to call it. Consciousness, from this point of view, can literally move mountains in a physical way if we, so to speak, put our minds and hearts to it. Of course that doesn't mean this is easy to do, particularly when you are living in a culture that says, "Don't pay attention to anything that happens inside of you. It's just hallucination. Everything of value is outside, and our technology will take care of it."

So that's what Stephen DeVore talked about and it was a very vivid experience because he had this amazing story to tell. His first products were all modeling products, where Stephen's company captured perfect performances on film. His first videotape was with Al Geiburger in golf. You'd watch this program for one hour in a relaxed state, which was the equivalent of ten hours of perfect practice. He had data to prove it. He would take people who were good enough to be on the Stanford tennis team, and they would win the NCAA championship by just watching Stan Smith hit perfect tennis shots over, and over again.

It's interesting that you picked Stephen DeVore as an example because the whole creativity course is about that kind of modeling. The "Great Idea Exercise," where I ask people to think of a time when they had a great idea, is based upon what sports psychologists call "muscle memory." If you can really get into a groove and think about your own perfect performance, or recreate the experience of your own creative moments, then you will increase the probability you will be creative in the future.

DiCarlo—In listening to everything you've said so far, it seems to me that one of the objectives of the course is to help people connect with their Essence so that they may freely express their deeper nature in their everyday lives?

Ray—Yes, that's a very good summary.

DiCarlo—In your view, does business have a role to play? Can business leaders help others do this?

Ray—Yes, I think it's really critical. A few years ago, *Fortune Magazine* featured the top 100 ideas of the year. One of the top ideas had to do with spirituality in business. They interviewed me for the piece, and I talked about how business could be a spiritual discipline. The title of the article was "Can Business Save Your Soul?" In one sense, I am opposed to thinking of things that way. I think that business can have a spiritual dimension to it, but it's an individual issue. At the same time, I think that business will change in that direction.

In my view, the overall objective of new paradigm business is the enlightenment of everybody in the organization, and the corresponding service to the surrounding community. I see that as part of it. Willis

Harman and John Hormann in *Creative Work* say the same thing, that the key objective of business is not just profit, but the development, learning and expansion of everyone in the organization.

DiCarlo—Let's talk further about paradigm shifts in business, something you have been quite involved with. What are we talking about when we use the word paradigm?

Ray—When I started using the word "paradigm" in 1988 or so, people said, "Don't use that word. It will just throw other people off. They won't really know what it means. They'll mispronounce it—they'll say "para-dig-um." But it seems that not too long after that, everybody was using the word. But paradigm was being used more or less like Joel Barker, the futurist and business author has used it. He knows the larger meaning of the word, but the way he talks about it, it has to do with conceptual block busting. From that perspective, you might have "the new paradigm of telephone selling," or "the new paradigm of rest-room maintenance."

When I am talking about this, I am not using the dictionary definition. I use the word paradigm in the same sense that Thomas Kuhn used it in his book, *The Structure of Scientific Revolutions*. Kuhn observed that within any science, you have a prevailing paradigm which is composed of an individual's fundamental assumptions. In fact, these assumptions are so fundamental that people don't even know they have them. The only way you recognize them is when you start getting anomalies, when you start experimenting and things just don't go as you might have expected. At first you think your procedures are wrong and then you realize it's the result of your particular way of looking at the world. Those paradigm shifts rarely come along in science.

DiCarlo—Could you give me an example of this kind of paradigm shift that Kuhn wrote about?

Ray—If you talked to a reasonably educated and well-off person in 1601 and asked them what they believed, and then asked their equivalent counterpart in 1701, you'd find their views of the world were completely different. The person in 1601 was still living out of the medieval, Christian paradigm, and everything was moving in this hierarchy towards God. Everything was related to God.

The person in 1701 however would be speaking in terms of the scientific paradigm we have now, which is basically centered around the physics of Issac Newton and the idea that everything can be known objectively. In that paradigm, there is no need for God. Even though they may have been religious, they were seeing that there was enormous power in man. When we talk about a shift in paradigms, that was one.

Another shift occurred in the fourth century, during what was known as "The Triumph of Christianity" when Western culture moved from the classical period to the medieval period.

And we have one happening now. So when we use the word paradigm in this sense of a world view, we are talking about something that is enormous.

DiCarlo—What would you say is the essence of the emerging world view?

Ray—Attached to the new world view are ideas that consciousness is causal; systems thinking—that everything is interconnected with everything else; that inner wisdom and inner authority are more important than outside authority; and movement from hierarchy to a flatter organization; from regional or local concerns to global concerns; from competition to cooperation to co-creation; from very aggressive values to values of harmony, integrity and compassion. All seem to characterize the emerging world view.

People always get interested in these things, but I have come to realize that even those characteristics are transitory. For example, take the issue of hierarchy. We've found that if you have the spirit of cooperation within an organization, then hierarchy can be a good thing. It can become an efficiency structure rather than a power structure. Hierarchy allows everyone to know their role and responsibilities and allows people to communicate, cooperate and co-create together.

So to look at the main effect of these characteristics is not enough. It's when you begin to put them together with effective business practices that you get some very interesting results. In *The New Entrepreneurs*—an anthology of 18 entrepreneurs that I coedited—one of the authors says that these kind of "New Age" ways of doing business are great, but if the business basics are not there too, all you have is window dressing. What she doesn't say is that the combination of the two can be very powerful. We all go through this stage of thinking that we've found the answer and then a week later we find out it doesn't work. It's like systems thinking, where you get a negative feedback loop that hits you in the face. So the point is, it seems essential to consider the interaction of all characteristics from a higher point of view.

DiCarlo—If in the old world view, the central test of reality was primarily through the physical senses—"I'll believe it when I see it"—

what would you say the test of reality is in the emerging world view?

Ray—What you know inside. I quote George Gilder who said that in the latter part of the 21st century, the powers of the mind are everywhere ascended over things, that there is this inner-knowing. I think he actually uses that phrase, "the central test of reality." And he talks about the changes happening now.

It's interesting. Working at a school like Stanford, I play the game too. I am living with research based on the old world view which is still the dominant world view. But when you get below the surface, when you talk to someone about how their careers have developed and how they made their discoveries—especially in science—you find almost always, it has come from an inner-knowing that has been there all the time. Many times, this feeling can go counter to what is happening in the outside world. And that is the test.

I feel very strongly that the quality movement is tuned-in to the importance of values. Values are the inner aspect too. It's not an easy thing to deal with. It's not easy to discover what your values are. Anyone can say, "I believe in integrity, equality, respect, harmony and compassion" but there's a difference between believing that and acting upon it. It's very interesting to discover what people's values really are by observing what they are willing to act on.

Marsha Sinetar

For the past decade, prolific author and pioneering educator, Marsha Sinetar has designed model leadership and change-management programs for selected Fortune 500 type corporations. She is a foremost exponent of the practical advantages of self-actualization. Her books, which include "Do What You Love, The Money Will Follow," "Developing A 21st Century Mind," and "Ordinary People As Monks and Mystics," are now used worldwide, in university, counseling, and corporate settings.

DiCarlo—Studies reveal that there is a growing sense of dissatisfaction among American workers. As many as 85% are in jobs they do not particularly enjoy. The title of one of your books, *Do What You Love, The Money Will Follow* implies a different way of approaching the issue of work that may appeal to those who find themselves among this vast majority. Please explain...

Sinetar—My main point is, that when we do what we love—and I don't mean that in the sense of recreation or simply doing what we *feel* like doing when we feel like doing it—but rather when we activate our fascinations, our values and our talents, we tend to serve others. We certainly begin to serve ourselves. We become committed, we add value to the extent that we are fully engaged with purposes superordinate to, or beyond, ourselves. For example, the carpenter, who *loves* carpentry will begin to feel like he or she is serving the greater good through the beauty or skills that are expressed when making the work bench. If you look at American society today, you see that people are just starved for high quality craft, services, products and that those are the products and services that seem to fair pretty well. One thing I'm going to add and I state this throughout the book, is that there are no guarantees in the marketplace. There is a wonderful quote by the Clint Eastwood character in the movie, "The Rookie" when he says, "If you want a guarantee, buy a toaster."

DiCarlo—When I talk to friends and family about the concept, the feeling invariably comes up that it's being irresponsible to follow your passion. "Wake up! This is the real world," many will say. The implication, of course, is that you have responsibilities to put food on the table, to make a living and whether or not you like what you're doing is largely irrelevant. For them, work, by its very definition is not *supposed* to be enjoyable.

Sinetar—I'm not an idea "salesperson." I've simply captured an old idea, a timeless idea. The Eastern philosophers or Buddhists call it right livelihood. We Westerners call it vocation. This means that there is a practical way for us to come into ourselves as individual human beings. Now, I can't say that everybody is emotionally ready to follow that vocational summons. You know, I write primarily for self-actualizing adults. That's the starting point of viable self-sufficiency. And just because we are moving towards a self-actualizing state, doesn't mean that we fear less. It means that we're willing to take a look at something new and strive toward it if it has value. But not everybody is willing. So for the person who isn't ready, I say, "stick with what you're doing."

But, you see, the point of view with which you have posed the question echoes a kind of "either/or" mentality, and this either/or mentality is going away as we speak. This represents an old world view. As I suggest in my work, the polarized mind, the "either-I-do-this-or-that" mind is outdated. We now see an ideational merger between diverse philosophical notions and people. Former "conservatives" align themselves with selected liberal causes, and vice-versa. U.S. corporations develop odd and unexpected joint ventures with strange, foreign bedfellows. A synergy between classical, political "isms" is happening— the 'either/or' mentality is on the way out. We must all learn how to think and solve problems from a wide-open perspective that permits true synergy.

DiCarlo—You've just mentioned the fact that you write for self-actualizers, and you've done a lot of research in this area. I'm wondering what sparked your interest?

Sinetar—Certainly every interest that we have is somehow telling, autobiographically. As a teenager, even earlier, I found myself reading Maslow and thinking of his case studies as friends. I wished that my own circle of friends could have conversed with me about those ideas, so it was a very personal, maybe self-protective, self-developing, interest. Then when I became a teacher, I saw that *every* child has self-actualizing potential. If they are healthy, if their self-esteem is high, they all embody the traits Maslow spoke about. But as they got older, I noticed that fewer and fewer had that zest, that inner dynamism, that engagement with some beloved thing, hobby or activity for long periods of time, that left them more exuberant than when they started.

I observed the same thing in the teachers. You could see that some were naturally disposed to do what they were doing and doing it well and just giving such high quality energy to children, to their teaching duties. Then you could see others who were listless, mediocre and resentful for being teachers. This observation continued to spark my old early interest, which has never totally gone away and, as I mentioned, I sense that "self-actualization" is a beginning point of robust health.

DiCarlo—How would you define the term "self-actualization?"

Sinetar—You could study Erich Fromm's profile of "productive types." He calls some of us "productive" but is describing the very characteristics of self-actualizing adults that Maslow discussed. Or you could say someone is "individuated," or "fully integrated," or "whole" or, as I've done, "spiritually maturing." There are numerous paths to come at this, but "fully human," "fully integrated," and "wholeness of being" are the sorts of phrases we can use to discuss this healthy, robust functioning level of development. Let's think of it as our beginning, entry-level point of full-humanness.

DiCarlo—Some people would think that a self-actualizing person is someone who is great at everything they do. Is that necessarily true?

Sinetar—That's an excellent issue. I'm glad you brought it up because that's the myth. It's the myth borne of what I call "fast food" thinking. A self-actualizing person could be, for example, a nun in a monastic setting who prays all day. We think that the self-actualizing person is one of these super-human, beautiful people who is affluent and fit, who budgets every minute of the day, who's constantly on the go and glamorous as they're going. And, you know, they are just wonderful tennis players and then when they come home, they make a fabulous bouillabaisse and then they look gorgeous and they speak well and they're wealthy and they drive grand or racy cars. But it doesn't mean that at all. "Self-actualizing" simply means tending toward "full humanity" and there are as many ways to be fully human as there are human beings on the planet. We must also comprehend self-actualization as an amplification of our particular way of being.

DiCarlo—What do you mean by that?

Sinetar—Well, let's say you, in a self-actualizing state, are coming into your own as the best "you" you can be. You're not coming into your own as the best Clark Gable you can be, but the best "you" that you can be. That's why only some people took to the book *Do What You Love, The Money Will Follow.* Only the rare few are willing to be true to themselves. One of the characteristics of most of my readers is that they are, at least, in the incipient states of self-actualization. They have heard that little whisper that, "it is possible to be who I am and live in the world of others as a responsible contributor."

DiCarlo—So you would see self-actualization as a stage in human development?

Sinetar—Oh yes, I see it as the beginning stage. Perhaps Maslow described it as an end point. But it's a beginning point because within self-actualization there are degrees and ebbs and flows. Nothing is a straight line. It's not like an elevator we are riding up. Life is not an elevator to some top floor; it's circuitous and meandering and in a sense you could think of life instead of going up and down, as going in and in, and in and out. So, as we go in we make the inner movement, then there's the practical application in the outer, then there's a balance or integration to that. It's the inner exploration that restores and renews and regenerates and transforms us and that's new energy, new understanding.

So, then what? You don't just lay there. You just don't stay in your green-visored accountant's seat. You go out into your life, and the thrust out is now as dynamic as your movement in and so, of course, it's an eternally-open process in terms of "how far" you go.

DiCarlo—You have said that a lot of people who are engaged in self-actualization have dropped out only to drop back in to society at a greater level of capability. I like that.

Sinetar—That's right, and we've all seen this happen. We've seen young people, for example, who were not ready to go to college take a trip around the world or join the Peace Corps and in a sense that's their moratorium. It's a moratorium for adventure and service and personal reflection and growth. Then, when they come back, most of them are ready to roll up their sleeves and get involved in a community of peers and friends.

But we have a childish notion about what it means to be fully human and we interpret everything through our filter of robotic productivity, mechanistic, inhuman productivity, when in fact there are types of people like artists and certain gifted scientists, (about whom it's been said they've coined a private language). There are contemplatives for example, who serve others through a very messy, disorderly reflective process. I'm thinking of Alex Haley, the author of *Roots* who, when he was editing a manuscript or writing, would get on a steam ship and ride all over the world. He said that when he was on a ship, in the blackest sea, in the middle of the deepest night, when the waves could be heard lapping at the hull of the ship, it was during those times when he was at his best as a writer and editor. So, you see, someone who expected him to sit in an office all day with his computer and fluorescent lights and clock in and out, would have killed the very goose that lays the golden egg. We do that <u>all</u> the time and it's pathetic—well, it's not a shame it's just that we're young, spiritually speaking, and we don't understand the depths of our nature.

DiCarlo—In your book, *Developing a 21st Century Mind*, you talk about folks you've called "creative adaptives." Are these people self-actualizers or is there a fundamental difference?

Sinetar—No. It's essentially that these are individuals who are self-actualizing in a particular way. I would say that the term creative adaptive implies a utilization of higher energies and intelligence in a resourceful, problem solving mode. For example, a creative adaptive would be like an entrepreneur or perhaps a scientist in an R&D Lab or an average person just finding answers to novel questions. I think it's Dr. Robert Sternburg from Yale who calls this type of individual "non-entrenched." These are non-entrenched thinkers. It's not that they are a new breed but that I'm describing a type of functioning that we need to manifest in order to succeed in the future.

DiCarlo—What would be the more prominent characteristics of creative adaptives?

Sinetar—They are entrepreneurial (in the broadest sense of that word). Now consider an entrepreneur. Not simply someone who starts a business, but one who has the mental energy, the resourcefulness and the improvisational skills to solve problems in a practical way so that he or she serves self *and* the greater community. For me, the entrepreneur is an artist at this—a business artist. Many people call themselves entrepreneur who head up corporations, but in fact they are marching along in militaristic steps. And in terms of innovation, their problem solving leaves a lot to be desired because it's filled with old, worn out answers.

Let me give you an example, if I could. There was a story recently about a woman in San Francisco who started a secretarial service. She realized that in order for her to compete with the many secretarial services in her area, she'd have to offer a new service. She would have to be different. So she equipped a mini van with secretarial equipment, computers, fax, and mimeograph stuff—a whole office—and drove to the client's location and did the work right there instead of having *them* leave their offices to come to her. Let me give you another example: a fast food place in Seattle. I heard about this on the nightly news. The two founders examined their own experience and said, "What's missing for us when we're in a hurry for food and we want something good?" The missing ingredient for them was healthy, low fat, fast food. They eventually began a fast, healthy-food *franchise* because the first food business proved so successful.

Now, in the old way of looking at things, even people who call them-selves entrepreneurs, would be inclined to say, "Well, if we've served greasy burgers, or we've always worked at a desk in an office as a secretarial or accounting service, we're going to *have* to keep on doing that no matter what." So the entrepreneur *I'm* calling "creative adap-tive" looks beyond what's already been, sees everything through a fresh, unbiased lens, sees the world in a totally new way—like a child who sees everything is possible or asks, "Why *can't* we do this or that?"

DiCarlo—In Zen I believe that's called having "Beginner's Mind."

Sinetar—Beginner's Mind, exactly. The Buddhist call it the "Big Mind," the "Open Mind." That's what I mean by a 21st Century Mind.

DiCarlo—How would the 21st Century Mind compare to the tradi-tional mind set?

Sinetar—Well, the 21st Century Mind is really a timeless mind. As you said, it's a beginner's mind. So my prototype of that mind would rest within, say, the Zen Master. Let me suggest some traits of such a mind: there would be a high level of acuity and alertness—highly present-centered; an ability to transcend a problem as opposed to grap-pling with it (this getting deeper and deeper enmeshed with the di-lemma); it is non-dualistic thinking—what I and others have called "unitive consciousness"—and it doesn't polarize everything into good vs. bad. This gets us back to the idea you raised about people thinking they can't do what they love because, "then I couldn't make money. I wouldn't be responsible." So, *either* I do what I love and I'm irrespon-sible *or* I do what I loathe and I'm a responsible, good person. See the dilemma? They set up the conflict that way in the manner that they think. This isn't news—the great teachers of every era have pointed this out. The "news"—if there is any—is that now we're forced (by rapid change, by enormously high levels of ambiguity) to apply our best thinking to life itself.

Now the 21st Century Mind doesn't do "either/or." There is this blend or "merger" of disparities. So, for example, we often hear experts, talk about male tendencies and female tendencies. Of course, in the higher stages of awareness this is total nonsense. It's just a hoax. In our "Big Mind-Open Mind," we find an integrated use of both brain hemispheres so the logical *and* intuitive, the rational *and* the "irratio-nal" are walking hand in hand. So, it's like a dance and it's beautiful that we all have this potential.

Now, Archie Bunker would be the prototype of the traditional mind. We all laugh at him because we're all like him. We're double minded: everything is right or wrong—it's right if it is what we do and it's wrong if it's something new. You know, we have our favorite chair and that's where we want to sit and men are men and women are women. We create these very ritualized corners in which both men and women must stay and they can only come out in a highly structured way to shake hands but are not hospitable to the female inside, if male, and aren't hospitable to the male energies, if female.

Now, Edith Bunker was moving over to the creative adaptive side. She was developing a 21st Century Mind. "But Archie," she would say, "let's calm down and look at things this new way..." She was trying to see both sides. She was friendly towards novelty. That's a key—friendliness to novelty. That comes from a whole-brained perspective. It's not that some people have it and some people don't. We all have the potential. Pretty, isn't it? It's an attractive way of conceptualizing.

DiCarlo—Are there stages that a person might go through in shifting from the more traditional mind-set to the 21st Century Mind?

Sinetar—It's a matter of degrees. If you imagine a line stretching out into infinity, then Archie would sit off to one side, looking at the line wondering if it was "right" or "wrong" to travel along that path; Edith might be inching over to the middle. She certainly is not a Zen Master, but she'd be a gracious host to the Zen Master, or the stranger or someone who spoke with an accent or whatever. At least that is how I experienced Edith Bunker. The Zen Master is traveling that line, moving toward infinity with grace and ease and beauty; very present-centered, and therefore enjoying the walk.

Do you ever watch the Simpsons?

DiCarlo—Yes...Very funny show.

Sinetar—Well Homer is way, way over with Archie but his wife seems more like Edith. She sort of sees things bigger. So when you ask, "Are there stages?" There are stages, but one wouldn't rule out the sudden transformation either, because this has happened. St. Paul is our scriptural example. Here we have someone who was definitely polarized in the way he saw people and then he was struck down by the experience of God—so much so that he was blinded for several days. When he came out of his bewilderment, he began to say that there are no Greeks, no Jews, there is only Christ. Well, to me this is what we all want. We don't know it, but we all want that wholeness of mind which is, of course, love.

DiCarlo—Let's relate this to business... Would you say that in order to transform an organization's culture, that the executives at the very

top have to in some way go through a process of deep personal change—
to develop a 21st Century Mind as you call it?

Sinetar—No. You see, the transformation is going to happen whether
or not people at the top willingly accept this process. This is a little
like slipping on a banana peel. Once the person starts to slip, they are
going to go all the way. You don't get to stop in mid-slip. So, it's a
matter of physics in a way; wherever the dominant energy in the corporation is, that's what's happening. So if the critical mass in an organization begins to think along these lines, it's going to "slip" on that
banana peel and the leadership won't know what hit them. But I will
say *mostly,* that transformation does arrive through leadership. It's
just that this is not something that we will "engineer."

In organizations, it's harder to see (and it's harder and riskier to talk
about) these things but once the leadership buys in, or has the experience, it's all over because people will follow or they'll leave. And by
the way, the book *Gold Collar Worker,* written some time ago, discusses how you keep high talent, gifted people. Essentially, the author says much the same thing: you must give attention to high talent
with its creative intelligence and that the sphere of activity of that
person *is* his or her reward. It's not that money is unimportant or
that vacation time and dental plans don't matter. Without autonomy
in the area of our creative interests—our vocational interests if you
want to put it that way—no amount of money is enough to keep a
highly talented person. They are very hard to manage. That underscores what I said about transformation really needing leadership's
blessings—this is not a new management technique. That's where so
many people are mistaken. You can't fake this devotional energy.
This is almost a religious experience. It *is* a religious experience.

DiCarlo—But organizations can change, right?

Sinetar—They change when the spirit of the organization is consistent with the changes that are wanted. *Developing a 21st Century
Mind* discusses finding that kernel of spirit—of the change that you
want—and activating that from a prototype. It's like throwing a pebble
in a pond. The mark of the pebble leaves circular waves that expand-
—they get bigger and bigger. Well, this is how we could change an
organization. Unfortunately, some of the organizations that I've
worked with are too disjointed. There's no real coherency for change
to come through. We hear an edict from above, then no orchestration
of consistent standards or values which follow. So, managers leave
their meeting, scratching their heads, wondering, "How do we do this?"
There has to be an orchestration, a conductor; someone to synthesize
and fine-tune the score and direct the instruments.

DiCarlo—If, in the old paradigm of business, security was found by being loyal to your organization, where would you say security is to be found in the new paradigm of business?

Sinetar—It's obvious that in an age of rapid change, unprecedented novelty, the shrinking and revamping and emergence of new businesses, new countries, new partnerships—most of them global and multi-constituencied—our only security comes from our ability to figure out answers even when we don't know what the questions are. So, again, I'm positive that our ability to improvise and innovate and adapt creatively is essential to business. We're not just adapting to what's always been, we're launching a space ship of enterprise in a wholly new way than ever before.

It's important that I add a point that underscores my thinking: I'm *not* saying we throw away the facts or the musical score or the blueprint or the formula, but rather that we are in a position now, in our era, where we must improvise. Improvisation requires mastery of the basics. You cannot master the basics by ignoring them. You must understand them so well that you can move beyond these to new avenues of excellence. But, you're going to use the basics—your technical education, formulas, the score—as your launching pad for innovation. I don't want to come across as, excuse me, one of those "airy fairy" thinkers who suggests all achievement is intuitional and "let's just throw out schooling, rules, discipline." I do maintain that we must go one step further, and be responsible for creating the highest new standards of excellence in our own disciplines.

DiCarlo—In your view, Marsha, what is the new role of business in the emerging paradigm?

Sinetar—You know, I'm going to give you an odd reply: I don't believe there is a "new role." This is a giant misconception. The primary purpose of business is to unfold potential, to reveal possibilities, to pave the way for a kind of cosmic promise, to promote, you know, the great, eternal, undying "Yes" of the universe. In business we do that in the form of widgets and gears, so the point of business is the point of life, which is enterprise. And if we define enterprise, it means readiness to engage in a difficult undertaking. Really, when you think about it, the world of business is people who today, are all getting in on the creative art of becoming dream merchants. So business, in a sense, is a play of consciousness, just like life itself is a play of consciousness. You see what I mean? And I don't know that this is a new role. It's always been thus. Just a few more people are getting in on the act.

DiCarlo—Do you work with many companies that are starting to see things this way?

Sinetar—Oh, yes, I do. I don't ever mention names of corporate clients but I work in an "inside-out" fashion so the company would *have* to be a bit progressive to bring me in. Many, many people who think along these exact lines are searching out interpreters to help them talk to staff, to Boards, to their constituents.

My work is advisory to senior-most management. I don't do "stand-up training." I'm surrounded by people who not only *want* to think this way about their own potential but who are themselves catalytic forces for the development of others. They work on a big stage. The people that I'm involved with are travelling every month to Europe or Asia, and carrying forth ideas. One of our challenges now is how to improve and do everything that needs doing. This tidal wave of change seems to be touching everything and everyone. Those who ride it like a surfer rides, will be successful in the future.

DiCarlo—Now, Marilyn Ferguson who you eluded to earlier, has said that "The new American manager will be recognized not because they have all the right answers but because they know how to ask the right questions." I'm wondering, what are some of the questions that the more insightful managers seem to be asking today?

Sinetar—This goes back to *Do What You Love and the Money Will Follow*, and the reason that so many people have studied it is because so many are asking questions like, "What's worth doing?" How much time do I, personally, have left in life and how do I want to use that time?" Then they ask me, "How can I *invest* my time, my talents and myself in things that matter?" Or, "How can I translate what I am paid to do into meaningful, loving, nurturing work?"

So somebody who's running a business might inquire, "How can I use my enterprise to love other people or serve other people?" And somebody down in the guts of the organization might ask, "How can I earn a decent living doing what I value?" or, "How can I turn my work into meaningful activity?" or, "How can I find time to celebrate life?" So people are starting to raise the very broad philosophical issues. Ferguson is right: there are new questions and we probably are observing an emerging thrust in business where leadership will not be giving us our answers, but will expect to hear us answer questions that have been asked, and respond smartly and appropriately. It's happening already.

DiCarlo—In my conversations with employees in a wide variety of businesses, most people will talk about control as being an obstacle that stands in the way of empowerment and organizational change.

Do you feel that American managers are control addicts?

Sinetar—That's a hard question to answer. First of all, I can't speak about *all* American managers—I don't know them. My impression is that if the organization is punitive, managers find it very important to retain control over everything. Who can blame them for wanting to know how every little penny, for instance, is being handled, when they are punished in some fashion, banished to isolation or ridiculed or discounted or fired or abused if something, anything at all goes wrong. So whether managers feel the need to control ideas and processes relates to their sense of comfort. When things externally seem to be spinning around chaotically and they fear abuse for that, they're not likely to welcome change. That's the first way of viewing this.

The second thing is that even when things <u>are</u> extremely chaotic, there are people who do very well. They <u>feel</u> in control, because they are— their locus of control is within themselves. So they feel empowered, committed, centered—even when they hear they could lose their job due to corporate downsizing. Kobasa's study found that managers who seemed to do best during rapid change were the heartiest. They didn't get ill. They functioned effectively. They possessed the three "C's": they felt in "control," they felt "committed," and they felt "challenged" by the job that they were to do even though some of them lost their jobs.

So, this is worth discussion. In my work, I examine how individuals turn lights on in dark, chaotic situations, how they help each other. Our humanity lets us find control even as we surrender control. Do you see what I mean? There's a wonderful book titled *Surviving* by Bruno Bettelheim (who died recently) wherein he interviewed Holocaust survivors and found that, in the midst of their Nazi concentration camp experience, a handful of prisoners kept their dignity, sanity, and perhaps their lives, by refusing to dehumanize themselves in minor issues. They exhibited little civilities. They refused to be inhuman in inhuman circumstances. This is one way we turn the lights on in dark, dismal situations.

One other thing...You know when people get a serious illness, like cancer or heart disease, their doctor gives them a statistic relating to their chances for recovery. If the statistic is favorable, such as "98% of people who have cataract surgery do well," then they do well. But if it's a negative statistic, then they tend to get discouraged. The healers amongst the physicians will tell a patient "You're not a statistic, so don't worry about what everybody's doing. Just take a look at what the recovering patients seem to be like and follow suit." You develop those healthy responses, whatever those are, by studying health. In a sense I am saying we retain "control" by learning about centered people.

DiCarlo—What advice might you give to an individual who has just been laid-off from their job or is considering a career change?

Sinetar—One essential skill that any of us can develop to thrive in the future, is to build what I've called "figuring out" skills. Now the Buddhists may call this skillful means. Maybe some street kids would call it having "street sense." Our minds are capable of figuring out what to do even when we don't know. Dr. Paul Torrence's groundbreaking research into gifted children proved that the one significant component of effective problem solvers is that they *feel* subjectively (more than they know factually) that they'll "figure out" what to do even when they don't know at the front end. We all need to be capable of tolerating such ambiguity and novelty in this way.

We really must be able to use our mind's capacities to invent, improvise and think creatively—*especially* when we don't know what to do. That's a 21st Century mind.

Section 9

A NEW VIEW IN EDUCATION

"Knowing the capitols of all the states—that's not knowledge. I couldn't care less about such a thing."

W. Edwards Deming

Education in Western society plays a vital developmental role in the lives of children.

What children should or should not be taught has been the subject of considerable debate and heated arguments. Traditionally, the focus has been on the content. In the old world view, the purpose of education was fairly straightforward: to prepare girls and boys to be good parents as well as productive, contributing members of society by teaching them the fundamental skills they needed for success.

Additionally, education has focused on developing the intellect through analysis—picking things apart to learn more about the whole—and of sharpening memorization skills to assimilate facts and data that society believes to be important and useful.

Despite its history of success in preparing the masses for the workplace, there are many indications that the educational system as currently structured is breaking down. While Phil Gang doesn't offer a step-by-step solution to these many problems, he does offer a compelling vision. The purpose of education, he says, is not to fill young people with facts, nor is it solely to fit into the economic system; rather, it is to allow children to fulfill their greater potential, to help them understand their greater role in life and how they, as individuals, fit into the larger Universe.

Phil Gang

Phil Gang is cofounder of the Global Alliance for Transforming Education, (GATE). In 1991, he created the document, "Education 2000: The Holistic Perspective," which has been distributed around the world and translated into eight languages. Gang, who is on the adjunct faculty of the Institute for Integral Studies, is coauthor of the book "Conscious Education."

DiCarlo—It seems that every time we pick up a newspaper, we are bombarded with headlines, such as "Gifted Kids Bored By US Schools;" "Schools Asked To Make Science Meaningful"; "Many Leading Students Say They've Cheated"; or "90 Million Can Barely Read, Write."

To fix these problems, some argue that we need better parenting. Others advocate school restructuring. Additional solutions include: year-round learning, national testing, lengthening the school day— even providing financial rewards to students who pass advanced placement exams.

Phil, what's your fix on all this?

Gang—It's like moving the chairs on the Titanic.

DiCarlo—Why do you say that?

Gang—Because we're not looking at the essence of the problem, the root cause.

We're working with an industrial mind-set that tells us we can fix the machine by taking it apart. It's the whole Newtonian concept that everything can be broken down into its parts, and the individual parts can be fixed. After doing this, you put it back together and everything works fine.

DiCarlo—What would you suggest is the underlying cause of the prevailing problems in education?

Gang—Well, certainly there have been many books written about that. We could go back thousands of years or we could go back hundreds of years. If we go back thousands of years, it began when human beings first started to take ownership of things. Possessions became the measure of people, and now we have a society that prizes the accumulation of things. After all, society tells us, "whoever has the most toys wins." In that scenario you depersonalize education and make it into an objective game instead of a subjective game. It's not about drawing forth the individual's potential, it's about having the individual fit into an economic system that will create wealth for some people and poverty for others.

We could also go back to the start of the Industrial Revolution, which began several hundred years ago. The Industrial Revolution was timely, and it was needed to bring about the technology that we have, but at the same time it also gave us this feeling that human beings were the apex of evolution and we were here to control and dominate nature. If you put human beings at the apex—and not as part of the circle of life—then surely education promotes those values. As a result. people pass through the educational system who don't have any sense of ecological matters. Even if they did, they wouldn't know how to do anything about it.

DiCarlo—Well, some folks would say, "What we really need to do to salvage the educational system is to "get back to basics," the "three R's" and to model traditional values, such as hard work and "discipline."

Gang—If you look at history and you look at evolution, we never go back. Going back is not the way of progress. It's not the way of evolution and it's certainly not the answer. People aren't going to do that. Look at what's happening in our schools. Last night, there was a piece on the news regarding young children and violence. Certain people were advocating treating children who get caught doing adult crimes as adults by sending them to adult prisons. So when it comes to addressing the violence in our schools, do you think going back to basics is going to change that? Of course not.

What we have to do is find out the gift that each child has, the gift that they come into this world with and allow them to pursue that. Education should be the drawing forth of the innate spirit of each human being—not a set of imposed restrictions that squelch the spirit.

DiCarlo—What are the origins of our present educational system?

Gang—It was taken right out of the factory. What was needed to power the Industrial Revolution? Just think about it. Obedience. Punctuality. Competitive work. So we put knowledge into fixed categories. We put children into fixed categories. We give out information in an assembly-line fashion. At some point, we got the idea that human beings are just like a factory line, that all seven year olds have a certain amount of information, as do all eight year olds and nine year olds. That doesn't make any sense to me as a teacher. I have seen children who were not initially interested in reading, and when they became interested they exploded. They got "caught up" on all they had missed and had gone beyond.

We have to develop schools that touch the imagination of children, that enthuse them to their inner core so that they want to learn. This will not happen through the imposition of external demands.

The assumptions that drive education today are some of the things we've talked about: the industrial model, that learning is defined as giving students a block of information which they then spew back in an acceptable way. Nowhere will you find the premise that education is really about drawing forth the innate spirit within each human being.

It's funny, when I work with groups—and these could be business people, teachers, or superintendents of schools—I ask them two questions: "What does your ideal school look like?" and "What do you want children to know?" They come up with all of these beautiful ideas, totally in line with my comments about what I believe education should look like. I'll ask them, "If this is the way you want education to be and you are the people with the power to change it, then why is it the way it is?" And it always comes down to the assumptions that people have. And beyond the assumptions, it comes down to the fear of change. It's the thought, "Well, what if it doesn't work?"

DiCarlo—What do you suppose is the cost to American society of an educational system that is inadequate?

Gang—Well, I think we're losing our hearts! We can see the cost. The educational system is collapsing. You have fundamentalists who beat the drum that we have to go back to basics and we have people running away. I don't know the exact figures, but in 1980 there were less than 25,000 children in America being home schooled and in 1990 it was way over a million. In the beginning, it was due to religious reasons. Now, it's because people are recognizing that the educational system isn't working. In Los Angeles, the schools are recruiting because the children can go to any school in their district. If a school isn't satisfying the needs of the parents, they can send their children to a different school.

I like the idea they have in New Zealand and in some extent in Denmark. The power to control schools has been given back to the local districts and they've eliminated state departments of education. They are saying basically, any group of twenty to twenty-five parents can get together and create a school of their own. They have that choice.

DiCarlo—So the same decentralization we see happening in business and in government is taking place in educational?

Gang—Yes. But I don't know what's going to happen. There's so much fear over losing control, and some of that rests in the hands of the business community. The business community thinks that it knows what education should look like. So the message of business and government is: "You've got to give me students that can be part of the work force." Instead, they should want students who are the best they can be. These represent two different goals. So we're trying to educate a work force when instead we should be educating spirit.

DiCarlo—In listening to your earlier comments, I take it that you would assume that a person coming in to the educational system is not a tabula rosa—a blank slate?

Gang—No, absolutely not. I learn as much from the students I teach as they may learn from me. I see teaching as facilitation. I can provide an environment for children to learn, one that is attractive.

I have focused on three cosmic principles that emerge from quantum and relativity physics: Attraction; Movement; and Interdependence. I say that in the realm of education, attraction has to do with creating learning environments that build connection. Environments that draw people into relationships with themselves and with others, and with meaningful learning materials. That attraction is an expression of love.

Movement is built around action in a learning environment. And in education, this means that there needs to be experiential learning. It means getting involved by becoming an active participant rather than a passive recipient. The tabula rosa, the blank slate is the passive recipient, who relies upon the teacher to pour in all the knowledge. About fifty years ago, somebody was talking with Maria Montessori, founder of the Montessori Schools, and stated that they saw children as being similar to clay—they could be moulded into whatever adults might want. Maria said, "Children are like clay, and we have to be ever so careful with what we do so they can become who they are."

And the third aspect is interdependence and that's the idea that we're inseparable. This assumption of unity contrasts with that of the old paradigm, which is separateness, and this comes out of Newtonian physics which assumes that everything is separate. The news coming out of quantum and relativity physics is that everything is one. We know from the perspective of the microcosm—in terms of quantum physics—that within the atom, no particle is anything by itself. It's only through relationship to the whole that meaning arises. In terms of relativity physics, we have determined that the Universe is moving further and further apart from a common center, its original being is one. Each of us are articulations of that beginning fireball. We are all one. People say that, but they don't experience it.

Learners of all ages have to be aware of this unity imperative and be taught about the whole notion of a Gaian community on earth.

DiCarlo—You've mentioned Maria Montessori. What's the main thrust of the Montessori model of education?

Gang—I think Maria Montessori got it. She was like Rudolph Steiner who really understood the essence of education. Both fully understood that education has to do with the drawing forth of the spirit of each child, and that the way to do that is to create an environment in which the child can blossom. They had this notion of cosmic education to help the children understand their role, where they came from and where they might be going. The problem is, you can go to a training course and become a Waldorf teacher, or become a Montessori teacher, and not really "get it" because there's been so much watering down of the original message. Today, people tend to be preoccupied with the material aspects of the education and not the spiritual aspects.

DiCarlo—That's interesting. In the field of psychology many psychologists are coming to realize that the main thing a therapist brings to the party is not a technique per se, but their own level of beingness. *That's* what really makes the difference in therapy. There's an old Chinese proverb which alludes to this: "When the right man does the wrong thing, the result is right. When the wrong man does the right thing the result is wrong."

Gang—Exactly. Montessori really understood, but she had people who took her model and transposed it into their realm of thinking and started to codify it. This placed limits on it. In the early 1980s, there were about 5,000 Montessori schools in the United States. There are many more today, some of which are public and many of these are splendid. The rest are not really any different from ordinary and traditional schools.

DiCarlo—In listening to your comments, I get the idea that you're trying to shift the point of emphasis from the "content" of the educational process, which would be the specific courses taught, to the "context" in which the student receives the information.

Gang—Yes, you've got it. And that also comes out of my background as an engineer. It comes out of my understanding of science, of quantum physics and relativity. Energy precedes matter. Process precedes form. We've been so intent on developing the curriculum that the meaning of education has been forgotten. It's not about curriculum development, it's about human development.

There's a part of me that believes that each human being has a gift to give. I know they do, and it's up to us to draw that out. Ultimately, what we want educators to help people discover, is where their gift and the needs of the world intersect. So my gift is to talk about education, and fortunately, there's a lot of people who want to hear about it. Your gift is to do the kind of work that you're doing. Just think: how many kids, having always being given negative feedback, have no idea what's inside of them.

DiCarlo—And our present educational system...?

Gang—Just makes it worse. Exacerbates it. These children, who come from dysfunctional homes, or from a life of poverty or even the rich ones, are disadvantaged because we've lost the heart connection. Students who come from more affluent families arrive in school with a great deal of pressure to get good grades and succeed so they can take over the business or achieve superior professional success.

DiCarlo—In reading some of the research studies on employees in the work force, it seems that as many as 85% of the people don't really care for what they are doing. I sometimes wonder how our educational system contributes to this mismatch by steering people towards jobs that are valued in the marketplace rather than first of all discovering the child's true genius and passion.

Gang—No doubt. There was a survey of students done back in 1958 when I was a freshman at Georgia Tech. It was developed to determine where most of the kids came from. Most engineering students came from low, middle income families. They saw engineering as a step up from what their parents had.

DiCarlo—What would you say are some of the structural barriers that prevent beneficial changes from taking place within our educational system?

Gang—Fear. That's number one. Everything else is a further articulation of that fear. We just haven't been given a big enough picture of what life is about. We don't understand where we come from as a species, how the universe has unfolded. If we would get out of the personal dimension and see the ecological dimension, I don't think there would be as much resistance to change.

There's also this wall we have to get over, this individual fear where people say, "If I don't have this, what will I have?" It's the same thing that takes place in a bad marriage. The person feels comfortable with it because it's all they know.

DiCarlo—How would you propose that we surmount that rather huge obstacle.

Gang—When I talk to groups, I emphasize that this isn't about "us" changing "them." This is about "us" changing ourselves, and the way to a systemic change is through a personal change. My belief is that the way to change education is not to change the delivery system. That will come after educators themselves change. Here's an example...let's say we want children to understand the concept of participatory democracy. If we conduct a class in an authoritarian, teacher-centered environment, the children hear the words about participation and democracy, but what feeds their soul is the process that they've been involved in, which in this example would be an autocratic one.

There was a study that suggests that 95% of what a learner takes in is the experience and not the words. So we have to model what we believe and if we're not modeling it, who are we anyway? When I am asked to do a lecture for a group, I insist that I be given additional time for an interactive session as well. I can't model what the new teaching and learning is by getting up and talking to a group of people, where I am the person with the knowledge and they are the passive recipients of the information. I have to get them involved in an experience which is congruent with my words. And preferably, I'd like the experience to come first.

If you look at the way we are taught chemistry or physics in high school, or in college, we are given an assignment and then we go to the laboratory to prove it. The research shows that it should be the other way around. We should start in the laboratory by asking questions, and then based upon the results of our experiments make our own conclusions.

I don't know how we get from where we are now to where we want to be. Maybe it involves the total demise of what we're presently doing. Maybe it will happen as people take over the control of the schools or start their own schools. I don't know. It's such a big issue. When I look at the dimensions of the problem I want to hide. I sometimes think, "What are we doing? How is any one of us going to fix this kind of problem?"

My mission, I think, is to help people understand that we're not going to change the institution of education without changing the people within the institution. So we can't come up with a prescription—that's the important point. I continually get calls from people who say, "Well, we've seen the vision. How do you do this?" Or, "Send me a prescription." Well there is no prescription because it comes from inside each and every one of us. We can give some guidelines, but there's no prescription. Is there a prescription in business?

DiCarlo—Well, there are a lot of people who are looking for one.

Gang—Sure, and there are probably some people out there doing just that and making a lot of money in the process. There are people in education making a lot of money too, talking about redesigning and restructuring. They've got a prescription.

DiCarlo—You talk about "conscious education" in your work. What do you mean by that?

Gang—We first have to step back for a moment and talk about conscious evolution. Conscious evolution is the recognition that we are all part of the larger wholeness of life. As we become conscious of ourselves and aware of the processes of which we are involved, we'll begin to voluntarily participate in the work of evolution. So human beings are the first to realize that. Then, conscious education is a lifelong process of personal, spiritual transformation leading to self-knowledge and the ability to make a meaningful contribution to life.

DiCarlo—How would you propose reaching those objectives?

Gang—I've already stated that teacher education would be a process of personal transformation. Naropa University in Boulder, Colorado is doing this. They started a M.ED. program in which the first year of instruction has everything and yet nothing to do with teaching. It's about who the person is as an individual. It involves looking at your world view and your personal challenges. It's about personal transformation. Now I don't believe every school can do that, but I think that integral to teacher education is a process whereby people are given the opportunity to explore their inner lives, their inner dimensions. Otherwise, you just come into the classroom and no matter what you learn about holistic education, you are going to simply parrot someone else's ideas. I remember my first year teaching. I had this great education to be a teacher, and I would find myself saying things to the students that were said to me either by my parents, or by my teachers while I was in school. Boy, was that a signal to me that I had some personal work to do. The more I did the work, the more I could be in communion with the hearts of the kids instead of operating out of some predetermined notion of what I thought schooling and education should look like.

DiCarlo—It's ironic that despite our hopes to the contrary, we don't even teach children to be independent thinkers. They are as you said, merely individuals who regurgitate back information to get a good grade and the approval of their teacher.

Gang—That's not the way it's intended to be. If you look at the derivative of the word, "education" it comes from the Latin, "educare" which means to draw forth that which is already there.

DiCarlo—Russell Ackoff makes the distinction between data, information, knowledge, and wisdom. He claims that at best, our school system delivers information, sometimes knowledge and only rarely wisdom.

Gang—Sure, wisdom comes from within, and we are not asking people to be wise.

DiCarlo—What would you say would be the qualities and characteristics of the conscious educator?

Gang—First, that they have deep love, respect and admiration for the processes of life and that they convey that love to children. One of the things that I think we've lost is the ability to tell stories. For millennia, the indigenous people conveyed learning through stories; in the West we've lost that. And I think the conscious teacher is a good story teller.

DiCarlo—What is the significance of being able to tell stories?

Gang—It's such a powerful attraction. People love hearing stories and the first thing that you want to do with your children is to tap into their imagination. I am not talking about imagination as fantasy but rather the creative imagination, so that in their mind's eye they can actually picture these stories unfold. My partner has just written a story called, "I Obey." It's the story of little sea creatures who lived in the ocean hundreds of millions of years ago. They are about to die because the waters have been polluted. So they go around trying to blame everybody. First, they question the sun and the sun says, "No, I'm not to blame. Go check the wind." And the wind says, "No, I'm not to blame, maybe it's the clouds." And the clouds say, "No I'm not to blame, maybe it's the rain." And the rain says, "No, I'm not to blame, maybe it's the water. " The water says, "I'm not to blame, maybe it's the rocks," and every one of them says, "No, I'm just obeying my cosmic law." So the little sea creatures come back and decide that maybe they'll take all these pollutants from the water and make shells to protect their body. Which is what they did, and that's the story of the coral reefs.

DiCarlo—That's great. You sounded a little like Joseph Campbell...

Gang—(laughter) Well, I love that story and we're in the middle of writing five others. I'm real excited about that because although these stories have been written for children, I think the metaphor is there for all to see.

DiCarlo—You've made the statement, "Education is a matter of experience." What do you mean by that?

Gang—Well, if you go back to review how people learn, it's by doing. It's been that way since the beginning of humankind. We learn to manipulate the resources in our environment in order to provide ourselves with clothing and homes. We take action and that creates a certain result. In the past, there was with the sense that, "there were no mistakes." If you put up a crooked house it would fall. So if you then put it up a little straighter, it stood up. Same thing holds true in schools. The children have to build up their experiences in an environment in which there are no failures. There are no mistakes. Mistakes are just ways into learning. A good teacher realizes that and doesn't use a red pen.

DiCarlo—We hear a lot today about accelerated learning techniques. What are they exactly and will they provide answers to some of our educational problems?

Gang—I think they represent a really innovative step in the right direction. We are learning so much today about the brain and about how people take in information. So accelerated learning is *a* tool, but it's only one of many tools that we need to use. There are many forms of learning: we can talk about spatial learning, there's kinesthetic learning, and then there's interpersonal and intra-personal learning. So the effective teacher has to know how to present ideas in such a way that children and adults can explore them according to their particular style of learning. In accelerated learning we are really taking advantage of some of those different ways of knowing.

DiCarlo—Wouldn't you say that our standardized tests, such as IQ or SAT scores test one limited *aspect* of intelligence, but not the entire range of human intelligence.

Gang—Yes. I would burn them all. What do we need them for? What are we measuring?

DiCarlo—But these tests were developed to better serve the individual student, to find out their level of intellectual proficiency, weren't they?

Gang—I don't think so. We don't serve students by classifying them, by placing them into a labeled box that they can't get out of. They become marked through that label, instead of discovering their best mode of learning and how they learn best. It wasn't until I read Gardner's books that I realized I was a spatial learner. It was interesting because every time I read something that I found difficult, I would start to draw pictures and relate with arrows. It's the way I learn. For others, it might be through music or movement.

DiCarlo—So a more effective strategy of education would be to tailor an educational program specific to the individual's learning style?

Gang—What I think has to happen is that all learning styles should be prevalent in a learning environment, and you will see which students gravitate towards each one.

DiCarlo—George Leonard has said that if we think about how we learn and solve problems, we find that we oftentimes turn to our friends and associates, and ask, "What would you do in a situation like this?" That's how we operate in real life. Yet in school, such behavior is called cheating.

Gang—Cooperative learning is really coming into vogue. There's a whole wave of people teaching cooperative learning which is based on group work and group alignment. The only problem is that some people have taken this to its extreme and the teacher is still manipulating the group, telling each person in the group what they are supposed to do, and not letting the group, through a natural process, make that decision.

I am on the faculty of the California Institute of Integral Studies, and in our program there is the opportunity to do collaborative dissertations. It's supported. What we are creating in this doctoral process is a collaborative learning community.

DiCarlo—What might be the types of subjects you would include in a curriculum that would be in line with your vision of education?

Gang—First and foremost is the story of evolution. Out of that, all of the sciences emerge because you would talk about the biological aspects of evolution and the geological aspects of evolution. Then, when you study the coming of humanity, you would talk about the development of language—that before language was developed, people didn't even talk. They drew pictures and made sounds. Somewhere along the line we invented these little symbols to stand for these sounds. Now that we've got them we can make any word that we want. And children should be told these stories as early as six years of age. And the same thing with the story of numbers, which came out of our wanting to understand our environment. In this way, young people get turned on to mathematics. We would see education as an organic process instead of saying, "Well, the children need to learn this, this and this."

Children want to learn. Today, they are asking all the questions. I recently visited a middle school of 5-7th graders in Vermont. In the beginning of the year the students spend the first week registering their questions about everything. And they build their entire curriculum for the year around their questions. By doing that, the children are going to learn the things that are important because they are the ones posing the questions. That's powerful!

DiCarlo—That's really basic to the educational process—asking a question in order to get an answer.

Gang—Or finding out that there is no answer. That living in the question is just as important. As I get older, one of the things that I appreciate about myself is my ability to live in the question, and know that at some point there may be an answer and sometimes there may not be.

DiCarlo—What role do you think business and communities might play in the emerging paradigm of education?

Gang—I really believe that the changes that we need in order to revive our educational system have to take the form of a collaborative effort involving business, community, educators, parents and children. All need to be involved in the process. If people can sit down together and ask, "What is it that we want our children to know?" or "What do we want our school to look like?" they'll see that what they want and what they're getting are two different things. That's the starting point.

But don't forget the students. They're part of the shared vision. All too often these shared visions do not include the children.

Section 10

A NEW VIEW IN ECONOMICS

The appropriate end of the social system is development, not growth. Our society doesn't yet understand the distinction between them. You can develop without growing, and you can grow without developing. A rubber tree grows, it doesn't develop. The measure of growth is standard of living. The measure of development is quality of life. Development is what the Spaniards called, "capacitation." It's an increase in ability and confidence. Growth is an increase in resources. Robison Caruseo built a high quality of life with very little resources. We have other people who are loaded with resources who have a very poor quality of life.

Russell Aikoff

In 1776 Adam Smith inaugurated modern economic thought with his classic book "Wealth of Nations" and the "invisible hand" that regulates free-market economies.

This "invisible hand" that Smith wrote about is not some mysterious and other-than-human force—it is a relection of human behavior and day-to-day economic choices. Economies mirror our inherent values, drives and world view.

Observes Marilyn Ferguson: "A society that prizes external symbols will want showy automobiles, whatever the cost. A family that values education may make considerable sacrifices to pay tuition for a private school. One who values adventure may give up a financially secure job to sail around the world."

The traditional economic world view was built upon materialistic values and assumptions. It assumes that economic and financial considerations should be the sole basis for making decisions. It believes that we need economic growth and increasing consumption to produce jobs; that we require increased productivity and technological advance; that competition is inherently good for the economy.

These hidden assumptions are increasingly being called into question. In an economy in which there is an ever-widening chasm between the 'have's' and 'have not's,' on a resource-ravaged planet of 5.5 billion people and climbing, some at the leading-edge wonder whether it makes any sense for a whole society to be transfixed upon economic production and the consumption of goods and services. Instead, they tell us, we should perhaps center our society around issues of human growth and human development and overall quality of life.

Though we all want democracy and individual liberty, fairness and equal opportunity, and wholesome environment—some advise us that these are ironically unacheivable based upon the economic assumptions of the prevailing and dominant paradigm. "You can't get there from here," we are told.

In our next section, Hazel Henderson will discuss her ideas on the emerging economic world view. In Henderson's view of economics, GNP, as an economic scorecard, is inadequate. As a result of her efforts, a new path of economic development is being offered which centers upon human rights and the basic unmet needs of grassroots populations rather than on increased levels of human consumption. This represents a fundamental shift in focus from quantity to quality—the quality of life, quality of the environment, and welfare of future generations.

Hazel Henderson

Hazel Henderson is an internationally-published futurist, lecturer and consultant to organizations in over thirty countries. Founder of many public service groups, she has pioneered the overhauling of economics since her articles on corporate social responsibility, conflict resolution, and "greening" economics appeared in the Harvard Business Review. Her books include, "Creating Alternative Futures," "Paradigms in Progress," and "The Politics of the Solar Age."

DiCarlo—You are an individual who is highly respected around the world for your views on the emerging paradigm of economics. What, would you say, is the essence of your message?"

Henderson—My essential message is this: I believe that over the last 50 or 60 years we have been confusing means and ends. The end that most communities and most countries want is development. But of course what we really mean by that is human development, community development and the development of our society. And we also mean that this development must take place within environmentally sustainable criteria. Somehow, many countries have gotten off the track. They began to equate development with economic growth, as measured by Gross National Product, or GNP.

Almost everywhere I go there seems to be a new debate going on about development in the world. People are saying, "Hey, let's get more clarity ... what are the goals here?" And more and more, the goal is being seen as human development within an environmentally sustainable framework. The idea is arising that human development may not have very much to do with GNP measured economic growth.

DiCarlo—If GNP is inadequate, what would a more encompassing economic scorecard look like?

Henderson—We have to first of all look at what GNP does wrong and where GNP makes mistakes. There are a lot of problems with GNP that are becoming obvious to everybody. GNP is really a measure of cash transactions and production. It doesn't take into account any of the unpaid, loving, cooperative, sharing, caring work which constitutes about 50% of everything that goes on now in our society. It's completely ignored.

Of course, this is based on economic textbooks where only competitive behavior is considered rational. If you are cooperative and part of what I call the "love-economy," you are considered to be irrational. Now you can imagine what would happen if you started running a whole society based upon that kind of a recipe. Although societies rely on volunteering and cooperation, they are constantly swimming upstream against these hidden economic assumptions.

Our present measure of GNP compounds the error, by not valuing in any way, a whole range of goods and services. GNP sets at zero the value of helping human beings. It sets at zero the value of children, and even infrastructure, as well as education, health and the environment. None of these elements is even on the scorecard.

That creates another anomaly, which is this: all of the efforts to clean up and to deal with the casualties of our polluted environment, are added into the GNP. It looks as though it is extra production. So you have this perverse effect that the oil spill in Prince William Sound Alaska, actually increased the Gross Domestic Product of the state for that year because they accounted at zero the clean environment, the value of the fisheries, and the value of tourism. Therefore it looked like paying the wages of the cleanup crew was a plus.

What is beginning to happen is that there are new scorecards coming in at almost every level: community, state, national and global. At the global level, there is the United Nations Development Program and its "Human Development Index." It's still a very simple indicator but it shows you a lot of different things. It's based upon a very simple concept: "Instead of just looking at economic growth, let's also consider life expectancy and literacy." When you add those together with other measures that compensate for currency fluctuations, then the ranking of countries produce a far different result. The United States for example, dropped in global ranking from number one to number eight.

DiCarlo—How do we get more countries to adopt these kinds of alternative indices?

Henderson—Most of the alternative indices are being driven by citizen organizations and communities. They are being driven by environmental groups and people who are concerned with all aspects of quality of life. These folks are beginning to realize that we need something more precise, and something that measures results rather than just turning everything into monetary coefficients and averaging it all up into one sort of insane number that nobody understands, like GNP.

That incidentally is one of the debates going on, the use of one single number. Even the new indicators like the "Human Development Index" overaggregates and doesn't give enough useful detail.

At the community level, many communities are beginning to develop much more interdisciplinary, unbundled indicators that correspond to all the issues that the voters might be interested in, whether it be health, education, or a cleaner environment, race relations, or political participation. Voters themselves, are quite capable of making these value judgements regarding what is important to them. When these indicators are unbundled, they can see very clearly how each sector is doing. Then it becomes possible for the voters to get back into the game and keep the politicians a little more accountable.

DiCarlo—Why is it that economists have traditionally been so wrong in their economic forecasts? You say that economics is not a science, and I am wondering specifically how macroeconomic theory is flawed?

Henderson—Well, as I mentioned before, the whole idea that people will cooperate in an economy is considered irrational behavior. Most of the people in the world still don't use money. They still produce food to feed their families. They build their houses themselves and construct the schools just as we did in the early days of this society. That's not in the economic textbooks. It's an enormous error in the current economic model.

The textbooks in many cases are still assuming that the common resources that belong to everyone on the planet, like the oceans, the atmosphere, and the electromagnetic spectrum, are basically free. Economists are trying to come up with ways to measure these things, but still, there's a tremendous lag. In effect, they are still not being properly accounted for. Therefore, the problem is, if the prices of products don't include these kinds of social and environmental costs, they are being set far too low. As a result, we begin driving the economy in the wrong direction. All of the social and environmental costs get swept under the rug. These costs are "externalized" from the company balance sheets until they all start creeping up and hitting society in the face, whether it's having to clean up groundwater, which is immensely costly, or having to spend billions in cleaning up weapon sites and toxic dumps.

So basically what happens is that we end up fooling ourselves with this kind of short-term accounting system.

Another serious problem with macro-economic theory is that it is based on the whole concept that things will come back to normal. It's the idea of equilibrium. That was a nice little textbook assumption in slower moving times, but now, where the whole world is experiencing a hurricane of global change and societies and industrial sectors are restructuring themselves, you simply can't manage a country based upon the idea of equilibrium. There isn't any normal to go back to. Many of the changes that countries are undergoing right now are irreversible, whereas all of the economic textbooks still assume that everything is reversible and that the economy operates like a simple bathtub. The economy, it is thought, is like a hydraulic system. When the tub overflows, that's inflation. So you just turn off the money faucet. That is far too simple an understanding.

DiCarlo—You have mentioned that some of the more sophisticated economists are now using chaos theory to fine-tune their models.

Henderson—Yes, and as a matter of fact it's kind of sad that chaos theory is not being applied where it could really help in macroeconomic management to deal with the actual policies that governments are using. Instead, chaos theory is being used by economists as a means of developing formulas to beat the stock market. Everybody is hiring what they call "quants" or "rocket scientists" on Wall Street to come up with formulas based on chaos theory. But it's to this trivial end of trying to beat the stock market. And you can for a while, but the problem with the concept is the underlying assumption that a person or firm can act solely out of self-interest without creating systemic risks. Take the trading of financial derivatives, such as puts and calls, to hedge risk, which is growing at an alarming rate. Even bankers are quite alarmed at the way the trading of these derivatives is growing. These hedging strategies reduce the risk of the individual investor, but at the cost of increasing the systemic risk for everybody else. They increase the risk that the whole financial system may come crashing down.

This is why I am urging that we shift from this economistic view of the world, with its flawed assumptions and simplistic economic models, to systems theory, where we understand that complex systems are governed by feedback loops, and that "what goes around comes around." This is what ecology actually teaches us about the real world.

DiCarlo—In your work you talk about the "Three Zones of Transition." What are they?

Henderson— If you look across the social landscape, you do find that there is an experiential "Zone One" where things are breaking down, whether it's that ideas are breaking down or whether it's the environment because of pollution, or whether it's the destructuring of our economy or whether it's companies being downsized. All the kinds of dysfunction that people are now dealing with in their daily lives I call

"The Breakdown Zone." Zone Two is one of "transitional fibrillation" and Zone Three is that of breakthrough. Now keep in mind that these three zones are not really mapped onto flat paper. Rather, they are conceptual zones and they are effecting everybody differently. I have been giving workshops for about the last ten years on this subject, which I call, "Riding the Tiger of Change."

If you ask any average group of people, "Where are you in these three zones? Are you in the breakdown zone?" about a third of the group will raise their hand and say "Yes, our program is being downsized" or "My job is being phased-out." I always ask them if they have a "Plan B" in their pocket for what they are going to do with the rest of their life, and generally, about a third of the people say that yes, they have got a "Plan B." These people have got one foot outside of the old game. They have a sense that it may be just as safe for them to jump out of the old job rather than wait for that de-structuring and breakdown to continue.

In this scheme of things if they have a "Plan B," that means that they have moved from Zone One, to Zone Two, which I call the "Fibrillation Zone." It's a little bit like when the heart goes into an uneven sort of rhythm and is out of sync. It is in interim period. You find that about a third of any group is in that phase, and they are trying to clarify their values by asking themselves, "Well, what's really important to me? What am I going to do with the rest of my life?"

The final third of any group is comprised of the people who have reached the third, "Breakthrough Zone." That means they have taken their "Plan B" and have made an adaptation. It is almost as if they see a new landscape. If you look closely at what is breaking through rather than what is breaking down you'll find that the new companies and the new industries that are emerging are based on environmentally advanced technologies, or what I call the new caring sector. This territory would also include the new scorecard like the Human Development Index, and also basic redefinitions of the game. The people who have moved into the "Breakthrough Zone" are generally an inspiration to others. If you put these groups into small working subgroups, it is very interesting to observe. All of them are exchanging business cards furiously and the "Zone Three's" in the "Breakthrough Zone" and the group that are rethinking their careers and who are in "Zone Two," are just the inspiration that the people in "Zone One" need.

DiCarlo—Speaking of being in the breakdown zone, in your view, is the world heading for economic collapse as some economists suggest?

Henderson—It could be. At the point we are at now, most politicians have not fully faced up to the fact that they have lost control of their domestic economy. Most of the levers that were once used to control and manage economic affairs have migrated into the global fast lane. There are six processes of globalization: 1) of technology and production; 2) of work, employment and migration; 3) of finance, information, and debt; 4) of the global scope and sales of military weapons; 5) of the human impact upon the planetary biosphere; 6) of the emergence of a global culture and consumption patterns. Combined, these developments mean that countries are losing sovereignty. Politicians can no longer promise their voters that they will protect them in times of war because of the reach of weapons today, be they conventional, nuclear or biological. They can't promise to manage the economy because that has now been swamped by global financial flows. They can't deliver full employment, where almost all people have a job, because of the global rules of competitiveness which cause companies to look around the world for cheaper and cheaper work forces and more and more unprotected environments to exploit.

And so the leaders of most countries are going to have to spend over 50% of their time working at the international level. They are being forced to put together what I call a global "securities and exchange commission." It is rather like Wall Street in 1929. It's a global casino. In the early 1930s, we put together the Securities and Exchange Commission, which brought order to U.S. financial markets, saving them from their own excesses. Today, we need to do the same thing. Due to global trading, there is the equivalent of four trillion dollars sloshing around the planet each day, over 90% of which is speculation, rather than investment or trade involving real goods and services.

But to answer your question, yes indeed, that system will shake itself to pieces at some point. It may have more pockets of resilience than I can think of and frankly I amazed that it has lasted this long without some form of global securities and exchange regulation. Speaking off the record, most bankers and currency traders will tell you that the present financial system is pretty hair raising. But you see, it isn't going to be a disaster for the world. It may actually be beneficial. The breakdown of the current system will clear the path for the emergence of another system. This movement from one system to another involves the shift from money to information, where money and information are now becoming roughly equivalent. If you have the one you can get the other. I was recently having lunch with a banker and he agreed with me that if he had to choose, he'd prefer information since money is now following information. That is what you might call the "Breakthrough Zone." The old global casino based on what I call the "money cartel" is breaking up. The main insight is that information is the world's next currency.

DiCarlo—Information taking the place of money?

Henderson—Sure. People are beginning to realize that money and information can serve the same purpose, and people at the local level all over the world are reinventing money systems. This will happen any time a group of people attempt to capture or cartelize a commodity, even money, and make it too scarce. Today you have banks that are linked to money centers. These banks vacuum the wages out of communities, and put them on the electronic funds transfer system at an interest rate that prevents that community from bidding to get its money back. As a result, local communities all over the world are experiencing a monetary deficit. They don't have enough legal tender to complete all of their local trades. In reaction to this, people in the community are saying, "OK, if this game is being played by the "big-boys" and there's all this speculation and craziness going on, then we are going to reinvent a local exchange. There's a worldwide phenomenon where local communities are reinventing local currencies. Most are based upon clubs where community groups are linked together using personal computers. Each day whatever is available for trade in the community is placed on a computer bulletin board. Dentists can call up and post a 4:30 cancellation on the bulletin board. The local accountant might take notice of that and say, "OK, I'll take the appointment at 4:30. In exchange, I'll do your taxes." This is even happening in the farming community in which I live. It's all done on the radio on Saturday mornings. The farmers tune-in to what you might call a radio garage sale. One caller will say, "OK, you can borrow my tractor, and maybe in exchange you can give me some extra pepper seeds." Whatever. That's all that money systems are.

Local communities are coming to realize that money isn't scarce. It never was. Money and credit are controlled by bankers and governments, and it's bankers who make it scarce. Central bankers make it scarcer still. But now that we live in an information age, the people can say, "We're going to do it a different way." You can fund your business plan today by unloading it onto the Internet. Or imagine the new financial TV channels carrying, "The Venture Capital Show" and "The Initial Public Offering Show" complete with "1-800" phone numbers.

DiCarlo—Exciting possibilities...Could you tell me what characterizes the emerging paradigm of economics in terms of world view, values and guiding assumptions?

Henderson—Well, I think we have to talk about going beyond economics to a multi-disciplinary point of view of human evolution, progress and quality of life. In my second book, *Politics of The Solar*

Age, I tried really hard to fit all of that into an expanded economic model and then I suddenly realized, "This is ridiculous." There is no way that one discipline can be in charge of such an immense task of mapping and describing the many facets of human evolution.

When I worked at the Office of Technology Assessment during the 1970s, it became really clear to me that from now on, public policy would have to be interdisciplinary. Economics is a perfectly useful discipline as long as the prices are corrected, with all of these external costs such as cleaning up the social costs and the environment, etc... added to the costs of production. I have no objection to economics in the form of accounting, such as keeping the company's books. But the macro-economics of trying to control, manage and predict the national economy has quite simply failed. We need to shift to a multi-disciplinary policy tool, like the "Human Development Index" which continues to measure the economic factors but which also includes input from all of the other disciplines—health, the environment, education. In this way, the systemic impacts of any particular policy can be determined.

The worst part of the economic method, which should not be used for public policy-making, is cost-benefit analysis. Questions about human evolution and development, and where we want to take our society are based on goals and values, not economic numbers. These matters need to be determined in an open political debate and decided upon by votes.

Economists are hired by various interest groups who want to turn things into a technical discussion by doing a cost-benefit analysis. The flaw in the method is this: cost-benefit analysis averages out costs and benefits over the entire population. Economists, like lawyers preparing a brief, try to portray whatever their clients would like to do as being best for everyone, whether it's to build a new convention center or a road through the center of town. But when you "average-out" costs and benefits in this way, you can no longer know who are the winners and who are the losers. The economic method does not account for unequal power, information, or wealth. At the outset, the interests of the poor who live in that community are not even taken into consideration.

Another shortcoming is that economics discounts the future almost as a matter of course. You have this very short term view that says, "After ten years, this item is pretty much valueless." This leads to this compulsive "short-termism." So it's really much better not to use these pseudo-decision making tools because they actually obscure the value choices and the political choices rather than illuminating them.

DiCarlo—How would you define the terms "development" and "progress" in the multi-disciplinary paradigm you have described?

Henderson—I have been working with the Calvert Group of Washington, D. C., which manage a group of socially responsible mutual funds, to develop a group of social indicators. We have taken twelve different aspects of quality of life, which we believe is the smallest number that you can keep track of to have it meaningful and intelligible to voters.

Each month when the GNP figures come out, we will publicly release one of our quality of life dimensions, say, on education, or health care, or the environment. This can stir up a debate so that when the financial talk shows have the GNP expert in one chair talking about how the GNP went up or how much housing starts went up, we will have someone in the other chair saying, "Well, yes, but look what happened to air quality. And did the schools get better? Are the streets safer?" And all of the other things which concern people just as much.

I believe that the next decade or so is not going to be easy for Americans. The prevailing economic paradigm of global competition—which is really little more than global economic warfare—is going to make it harder and harder for Americans to maintain their current standard of living since jobs will be migrating all over the world. So if we have a more realistic scorecard of development, which takes into consideration these other quality of life measures that people are interested in, people can make their own decisions. They can say, "Well, OK, I didn't get a raise. But on the other hand, the school is better, the streets are safer and the water is cleaner and the air is more breathable." So they will have other ways of judging progress.

The debate at the international level involves these very same issues. For example, people who come to the United States from China believe that this a land of amazingly high salaries and opportunities. When they get here, they realize that their high American salary has to buy health care, it has to buy education, and that housing sometimes consumes as much as 50% of an individual's paycheck. Then they begin to say, "OK, I see. Although in China we only have one-third the purchasing power due to lower wages, we get free health care, and free education and subsidized housing."

Each country has a different menu of public and private goods and services based on what I call it's "Cultural DNA Code." All economies are "mixed." The Europeans are somewhere in the middle. Americans on the other hand, have always considered that money income was all that they needed to buy all the other things that they wanted. But we are now finding that these community goods, like safer streets and cleaner water, cannot always be provided by private enterprise or individuals. We have to work together in our communities. Markets are not created by God—they are set up (well or badly) by human policies and laws. The "invisible hand" which guides the marketplace is our own.

DiCarlo—In your view, where are we going as a society?

Henderson—Once we begin to rethink education, and keep an eye on how important it is to invest in our own people—even for a reason as crass as to become globally competitive—we'll begin to make those investments. We'll realize that they are just as important as investments in roads and harbors or the other things that we can buy individually. Economic textbooks are slowly changing to reflect that investments in people, in health, education, and training and sabbaticals are necessary, even for economic growth. If we don't have a learning society we can't really evolve at all.

We are at a stage now where we are just beginning to make the shift from a focus on "quantitative growth" to "qualitative maturation." The same thing happens to an individual, when they stop growing quantitatively. At a certain age their physical growth stops, and they start growing inwardly, toward maturity and hopefully toward wisdom and self-actualization. The quality of their being improves. I think that industrialized societies have been dependent upon and have sort of "overdosed" on mass consumption and material improvement. This kind of quantitative growth is now shifting and the focus is towards improved quality of life. Industrial societies are maturing just like individuals.

The upcoming debate is really about satisfaction and not so much about consumption. It will be about answering the question, "How do we satisfy ourselves?" It will be about self-definition and identity. That is going to mean an enormous change in marketing and advertising and television. I don't know whether the companies are really addressing it as vigorously as they should because I think there is going to be a wholesale rejection of the kind of mass consumption hyped by advertising, which cuts into people's self-esteem.

The last time I was in Mexico I learned of the many fears of the American, materialistic way of life which rests on this kind of psychological devastation, that you are "Not OK" unless you have a new car every year. You are "Not OK" unless you buy fashionable clothes. There was a great deal of sadness in the potential loss of other definitions of being a successful, happy person. So I think that those issues are going to be extremely important and I think they are going to be clarified in the years to come.

Part 4

GETTING
the
NEW VIEW

If one were to summarize the main thread, the essential realization, which ties together the work of all whom we've heard from in the preceding sections, perhaps it would be, "There's something more."

Such a realization is simple, yet it changes everything. Our science has been the simplest science, exclusively focused upon the physical dimension—there are other dimensions. Our medicine has limited its scope to the most concrete manifestation of who we are —our physical body—while psychology has ventured no further than our most earthbound sense of identity. As we've seen, similar expansions can be found in all areas of human inquiry, such as economics, business, education, etc.

If those on the leading edge are correct, if who and what we are is not confined to our physical, emotional and mental selves, if we have even greater dimensions to our nature that transcend time and space which can be expressed in this world, then it it would seem likely that what we thought of as the endpoint of our development as human beings would simply represent a point along the way towards a far greater attainment.

Infant, child, adolescent—all are transitory rungs on the ladder of human development. An individual at each level has certain broadly-based characteristics, abilities, potentials, values, qualities and world view they share with others at the same level.

The world view of the individuals in this book has been the result of attaining the more advanced stages of development, of actualizing the further reaches of human potential. And as more and more reach for this higher state, it makes it easier for others to follow.

In Section Eleven, we will consider events and experiences that call into question the prevailing world view and which have served as a trigger for the the attainment of these higher stages of human development. Finally, in Section Twelve, we will delve more deeply into this transformational process and explore its planetary implications.

Section 11

CHALLENGES TO THE
PREVAILING WORLD VIEW

"Normal science does not aim at novelties of fact or theory and, when successful, finds none. New and unsuspected phenomena are, however, repeatedly uncovered by scientific research, and radical new theories have again and again been invented by scientists....Produced inadvertently by a game played under one set of rules, (the) assimilation (of new phenomena) requires the elaboration of another set. After they have become parts of science, the enterprise, at least of those specialists in whose particular field the novelties lie, is never quite the same again."

> **Thomas Kuhn, "The Structure of**
> **Scientific Revolutions"**

No world view lasts forever, but only as long as it is able to adequately explain reality. A world view gets discarded—sometimes before another one is readily available—because problems arise which it cannot solve, or phenomenon accumulates which it cannot explain.

We might refer to these phenomena as "anomalies"—things that are abnormal, inconsistent or odd. "Abnormal, inconsistent and odd with respect to what?" you ask. With respect to the prevailing understanding of the "way things are"—our cultural world view. "Anomalies," says Marcell Truzzi, "are unexpected facts in search of an explanation." They are unexpected because they are fundamentally incompatible, like a blossoming rose in the Arctic tundra.

Examples of current anomalies in the world might include: A psychic detective who is able to identify the precise location of a murder victim's body; a healer who is able to alter someone's brainwave pattern and respiratory rate from halfway around the world; the ability, through a process of "remote viewing" to draw a picture that another human being is holding in their mind. All are examples of people knowing what they shouldn't know according to the traditional explanation of the way things are.

A little investigation reveals that experiences which call the prevailing world view into question are far from uncommon:

—A 1992 Gallup Poll shows that 25% of the American public have had telepathic experiences. One in six reports having had contact with someone who was deceased. Other studies suggest that as many as 66% of widows experience apparitions of their deceased husbands.

—Eugene Thomas and Pamela Cooper of the University of Connecticut reveal that in a national sampling of people, 34% report some form of spiritual experience. Almost five million people spoke of intense experiences, of "awesome emotions, a sense of the undescribeable, a feeling of oneness with God, nature or the Universe, changed perceptions of time and surrounding and a feeling of knowing coupled with a reordering of life priorities."

—A 1982 Gallup Poll found that roughly eight million Americans claim a Near Death Experience. The number of people reporting this experience has grown over the years, partly because more people are being snatched from death's door by improved medical technology, and partly because more people are willing to come forward to speak about their experiences.

This is extremely controversial and risky terrain. For the pioneers, promising careers have crashed into ruin, a lifetime of credibility lost. It penetrates to the very heart of our world view and our ideas regarding the nature of reality. Because it challenges our closely held beliefs, it can seem threatening. So threatening that the natural impulse is to look the other way, to pretend that such phenomena doesn't exist.

But if the world view is expanding to accomodate such odd phenomenon—and this appears so—it may be of value to give these phenomenon their proper consideration. In this way, we can better understand all of the catalyzing forces at play, assess their implications and perhaps seek new avenues for research and scientific exploration.

To that end, we will first hear from Dr. Raymond Moody, whose 1970s book, *Life After Life* has sold nearly ten million copies. It was Moody who coined the term, "Near Death Experience" and as a result of his pioneering research of over 3,000 subjects, the characteristics of the phenomenon have become widely known. According to Moody, Near Death Experiences can be transformative, profoundly affecting one's world view.

Experiencers report a more authentic sense of self. Death is no longer feared since it is seen as but a transition in which our consciousness survives. There is a change in values, characterized by greater appreciation for life, more concern, compassion and love for fellow human beings and the planet, and diminished interest in personal status and material possessions.

What are we to make of these reports? The general public seems keenly interested in learning more. Books about Near Death Experiences are frequently at the top of the bestseller list and the topic seems to be a favorite among television talk show hosts. NDE's are important—not for their ability to entertain and titillate—but because they challenge the materialistic world view that what we are is the brain and nothing more; that when the body and brain die, we cease to be. NDE's pose a fundamental challenge to the assumption that the physical is all there is.

Robert Monroe says he doesn't *believe*, he *knows* from personal experience that our consciousness is not limited to our physical bodies. Monroe is the founder of the Monroe Institute in Faber, Virginia. The Institute conducts consciousness research and offers programs to the general public intended to facilitate out-of-body experiences, a term Monroe and psychologist Charles Tart first introduced in the early 1970s. Monroe claims to have explored the non-physical dimension through his own out-of-body experiences and he offers others a "map" to navigate unfamilar territory.

Monroe suggests that our lives are far from random and meaningless, that we are here to learn about the creative process and become "generators" of love. His world view is similar to those who have had Near Death Experiences. Both NDE'rs and OBE'rs report leaving their physical bodies, but in the case of the Near Death Experience, the event is triggered by a close brush with death. The out-of-body experience, according to Monroe, is a more common phenomenon that can happen involuntarily during ordinary sleep. Furthermore he tells us, the more adventuresome among us can develop our ability to consciously have out-of-body experiences and explore non-physical dimensions at will.

Another intriguing phenomenon that poses a serious challenge (if true) to the prevailing world view is the alien abduction experience, which may have happened to as many as 1 in 50 people according to a 1991 Roper Poll. Dr. John Mack is a Harvard medical professor, clinician and Pulitzer Prize-winning author who has investigated over 90 such cases. As one might expect, Mack has been harshly criticized by some members of the scientific community who dismiss all abduction reports as being little more than fantasy, delusion or the product of irrational thinking.

Mack takes such criticism in stride. He counters by stating that this is a subtle area of investigation since we are dealing with something which may not originate in the physical world but which can enter into the physical world. There exists a great amount of evidence that cannot be accounted for he says, such as the consistency of the reports which are told with the appropriate intensity of emotion, and unexplained cuts and bruises on people's bodies.

The entire extraterrestrial debate pivots upon one's world view, and Mack questions why the most vehement members of the scientific community cannot be open-minded enough to consider the claims of other cultures throughout the ages, that there are other dimensions of reality which are non-physical, whose inhabitants can cross-over into our universe.

Alien abductions, out-of-body experiences, near-death experiences—these are outrageous phenomenon. They boggle the mind and strain our ability to take them seriously. Yet, we'd expect no less from any paradigm-busting anomalie worth its salt. It was Hiesenberg, the great physicist, who, when asked to comment on whether or not a certain phenomenon was likely to be found legitimate remarked, "It's not crazy enough to be true." History suggests that indeed, fact can prove stranger than fiction.

Yet does that mean we should mindlessly believe the claims of the NDE'rs, OBE'ers and the extraterrestrial abductees? Clearly we have no scientific, rock solid, unequivocal proof that we live after we die, nor do we have the captain's log from a fallen UFO. Yet at the same time, we have no "proof" that these phenomenon are invalid and do not exist. Lacking evidence and personal experience, Dr. Moody suggests that we adopt a position of "non-belief." A non-believer is someone who neither believes nor disbelieves. It's someone who simply doesn't know.

While the debate over the meaning and validity of these experiences is certain to continue, two points seem clear: they seriously call into question our present understanding of the universe in which we live; and secondly, all have proven themselves capable of acting as a trigger for a transformational process—a process that invariably ushers in a new world view.

Dr. Raymond Moody

Dr. Raymond Moody, M.D. is a professor of psychology at West Georgia College, and is the author of several books, including: "The Light Beyond," "Reflections on Life After Life," "Laugh After Laugh" and "Reunions." His book, "Life After Life" is considered a classic, groundbreaking investigation of the Near Death Experience, which has sold over ten million copies. Frequently featured on national television as a guest expert, Dr. Moody lectures extensively around the world.

DiCarlo—The NDE experience, which some surveys suggest has happened to as many as eight million Americans—more if you count the children—has become familiar to the general public thanks to your pioneering work. The profile of the typical NDE is as follows: the initial perception that one has been separated from their physical body, which some have reported seeing from above an operating table or at the scene of an accident; of traveling through a tunnel at incredible speeds; of arriving at the end of the tunnel and encountering a brilliant being of light that offers pure love and total acceptance. Communication with the light is instantaneous and nonverbal, and there is a sense of homecoming. This is followed by a life review of one's actions and the result they had on other people. Though most of the people would rather stay in this realm of indescribable joy, they invariably choose to return out a sense of obligation to their children or spouses who need them or because they have yet to complete their life's mission.

Tell me, what was your initial reaction to the first person who told you of their Near Death Experience?

Moody—I came from a marginally religious background. In my early years I didn't even go to church. When I was about 12 years of age my father started dragging us to church—I assume he was going through his mid-life crisis. By that time, I had already been an amateur astronomer for six years, and I had already established my basic world view. As far as I was concerned, death was simply an obliteration of consciousness. When we started going to church, I listened to all the preaching about a heaven and a life after death. I felt those people were just fooling themselves.

I went to the University of Virginia as an undergraduate, and in 1965, when I was a third-year student, I heard of a psychiatry professor, George Richie, who was known to have had a very profound experi-

George Richie, who was known to have had a very profound experience when he had been pronounced dead. And I took that opportunity to listen to Dr. Richie's account. To tell you the truth, at the time I thought that obviously this was a very sincere and fine person, and that he was relating the truth as he saw it. But I was primarily interested in it as a phenomenon of human consciousness. That was my initial response. I was surprised to learn that even beyond that point where the doctor says you are dead, consciousness is very much alive.

DiCarlo—You are familiar I'm sure with the different interpretations of the Near Death Experience. Some people feel that the experience has a biological basis and can be explained in terms of oxygen deprivation to the brain. Others believe, for example, that the sensation of moving through a tunnel can be biochemically explained in terms of phosphenes stimulating the visual cortex. Along the same lines, others state that the intense joy that NDE'rs report can be attributed to a flood of endorphins gushing throughout the body.

What would your response be to these people who promote a more biological interpretation that is perhaps more comfortable since it is in step with the traditional world view?

Moody—What I would say to those folks is, "Lighten up and relax!" The mind-body problem doesn't seem to be appreciably closer to a solution than when it was first formulated. I still respect psychologist William James' perspective that there have always been spiritual experiences as long as there have been human beings. Obviously, there is always going to be some physical and biological correlates that can be found as long as the person remains alive. For people who go through such an experience, it is self-certifying. After they go through this they have no more doubt. And for those of us who have not had the experience, the appropriate stance is one of agnosticism—of one who does not know.

Before I went to medical school, I was a professor of symbolic logic and to me, words like "evidence" and "proof" have very precise meanings. My stance has always been that there are two great mistakes that people make in connection with the systematic study of the paranormal. One is belief and the other is disbelief. What most people don't realize, is that belief and disbelief are the same thing. For example, let's let "P" represent any statement we might wish to make—belief that P is one thing. Disbelief, then, is the belief "That's not P." Those are *both* beliefs. It seems to me that in a situation where you don't have any kind of methodology available to arrive at a conclusion, then you have to stick with "non-belief." Non-belief is something that is quite distinct from either belief or disbelief.

I find it very interesting that people want to rush to judgment on this kind of thing. I've always said, "In my opinion, reports of Near Death Experiences don't furnish us with scientific proof or evidence that we live after we die." And I think that people also should realize that the opposite of that is true: We don't really have proof that we cease to exist either.

DiCarlo—One of the things that has intrigued me about the reports from NDE'rs is the common sentiment that their experiences are ultimately indescribable—ineffable is the term—which is also what people report who have, through non-ordinary states of being, directly experienced these other dimensions. I am reminded of the "Flatlands" story, where the futility of trying to describe higher dimensional reality in terms of the physical dimension is like trying to describe a 3-D sphere—like a basketball—to someone who has only experienced a two dimensional circle drawn on a piece of paper. Or the color red to someone who is color-blind. The fact that people who have had Near Death Experiences cannot relate it to anything they have ever witnessed or experienced before perhaps makes these stories even more compelling.

Moody—That's right, they are engaging in metaphor.

One of the most common things that people who have Near Death Experiences tell me, is that what they went through did not take place in time or space as you and I are experiencing it right now. And yet all of the customary language about this has to do with spacial metaphors—"The Beyond," or "The Other Side." Or temporal metaphors like "The Life After Death." I look at that and I say, "Well, I think there's something important in what people who have Near Death Experiences have to tell us." So what I grope around for is a more satisfactory metaphor. And a metaphor is always just a metaphor...

DiCarlo—Based upon your extensive research, what have been the typical after-effects for the person who has a Near Death Experience?

Moody—The first one that comes to my mind is a fundamental change in the appreciation of human relationships. Love becomes the central issue in a person's life. I don't mean a syrupy kind of love; it can be very tough love. And also I don't mean sainthood. Dr. George Richie, my professor who had a Near Death Experience, shared some words that have stuck with me all through these years in a very profound way. He said, "You know Raymond, this experience makes your humanity even more of a burden in a way." What he meant by that was, even after having this grand vision of love, it's still very difficult to put it into practice in the day-to-day world. So there's a fundamental change in the way that they look at other people.

Certainly, there's also a loss of the fear of death—fear of death in the sense of a feeling that death is the end or cessation of consciousness. They really seem to conceptualize death as a passageway into some other dimension or level of reality.

DiCarlo—Are the aftereffects of the Near Death Experience always positive in nature?

Moody—Positive and negative are troublesome terms...I would say enriching. By that I mean that before there was any publicity about Near Death Experiences, people who had the experience felt that they were alone, that nobody else had ever been through such a thing. When they would try to discuss it with their physician, nurse, minister or a friend, they would be told that they were out of their minds, or that they had been hallucinating.

Occasionally, interpersonal relationships are disrupted because of this. You can imagine the effect on the other members of the family, if someone says, "I went to this beautiful light." Yet, the person who had such an experience has committed to it. So it has sometimes brought about disruptions, even divorces. Also, I would say that there is often a longing to go back to be with that being of light.

So none of those experiences are very positive, meaning "good" in a simple sense, but they are nonetheless enriching.

DiCarlo—Would you say that everyone you have spoken with who has had a Near Death Experience has been able to successfully integrate it into their lives?

Moody—I would say that integration is a continuing process throughout their lives. A lot of people come back from this saying that one thing they learned during their voyage was that learning is a process that literally goes on forever. They come back with a renewed commitment to learning and to education. They come back with a great understanding that life is a process. Even many years later, they are still integrating the experience and hoping to understand it at a deeper level.

DiCarlo—Could you characterize the world view of the typical person who has had a Near Death Experience, in regard to the following questions: "Who am I?" and "What is the nature of the universe in which we live?"

Moody—In terms of "Who am I?" people come back with the appreciation that they are everyone. When they go through these life reviews, they say that they see the effects of their every action on the lives of everyone with whom they are interrelated. They become the person with whom they have interacted. And if they have done something unloving to someone else, they feel the sad effects, and if they've done something good they feel the good effects. That suggests that we are all very deeply interconnected.

As to, "What is the nature of the universe?" I would say that they come back with a sense of awe at the complexity of the universe. Many of them describe to me how they see not just this one physical plane of existence that we all seem to be in, but other levels of reality going on right around it. Some talk about cities of light or of a middle realm, where people seem to be shuffling around not knowing where they are; who cannot move on yet, caught up in some fixation they had while alive.

Throughout all of this, there's the sense that the universe has a spiritual nature.

DiCarlo—Would you say that this world view of the NDE'rs, is similar to the perennial philosophy as described by Aldous Huxley? That is, if you disregard the obvious differences in their "exoteric" or public form, you will discover that the much less publicized inner teachings of the various spiritual traditions are all concerned with helping people commune with the transcedent. That there's a fundamental unity of life, and that each of us is a manifestation of the divine?

Moody—Well, yes. Absolutely. Time and time again, people who come back from this, no matter what their religious background had been prior to the experience if indeed they even had one, possess an increased sense of the importance of the spiritual life and a devotion to God. And yet, they have told me that denomination absolutely doesn't count.

DiCarlo—Do you find that these people make a distinction between being spiritual and being religious?

Moody—Absolutely. Yes.

DiCarlo—How would they describe that distinction?

Moody—That religion is a set of human doctrines. There was a fundamentalist preacher who had a Near Death Experience who was a very interesting guy. He died a few years ago. He was on his way from the city he lived in to a little country church. In the latter part of his seminary training, he was required to serve little country churches that wouldn't normally be able to have a minister. While driving to this church one Sunday, he had a car wreck. Paramedics at the scene thought he was dead. In describing his Near Death Experience, he said, "I was very surprised to learn that God wasn't interested in my theology." His point being that the focus was on how he had learned to love, and whether he had been loving in his interactions with others rather than on a doctrine or an ideology.

DiCarlo—One nearly universal aspect of the Near Death Experience is the "Life Review." I am wondering, of the thousands of people you have interviewed over the years claiming to have had this experience, have any commented on a sense of being judged?

Moody—Well, judgment is an interesting word. A lot of them use the word judgment, and what they have told me is that there is definitely a judge in that situation, and it's them. The reason being is quite obvious. They see everything they've ever done and they see the effects that their actions have had on the lives and the consciousness of other people. So some people have reported being quite severe with themselves at that point.

DiCarlo—But there is no external authority rendering judgment on an individual's life and actions?

Moody—No.

DiCarlo—Now most of the experiences I am familiar with have been positive insofar as the people reported an encounter with an all-loving being of light and their feelings have been joyous and loving. In your experience, has any NDE'r, out of the 3,000 that you've interviewed, described hellish kinds of experiences?

Moody—On very rare occasions, yes. I have a somewhat larger number of people who tell me that, as part of a profound Near Death Experience, they caught a glimpse of a level of reality where one would not want to be. It was the kind of place where people were stuck-up in their own lack of love, and focused on something which they were obsessed with in physical life.

Just a couple of people felt that they themselves had slipped into hell. It's very interesting that in the Gallup survey that was published in 1980 or so, the percentage who related some kind of hellish encounter was actually quite small.

DiCarlo—It's equally fascinating that the people you've interviewed would use the phrase "level of reality." In the wisdom literature as I call it, there is mention that upon death, a person gravitates to the level of reality most in accordance with their level of consciousness in the same way vinegar rises to the top of a bottle mixed with oil.

Tell me, have you ever experienced any paranormal events?

Moody—Yes, as a matter of fact, the first one that comes to my mind—

incredible as this may seem—is the day my grandmother appeared to me. I was completely awake at the time. There she was right in front of me, full-colored, and three-dimensional. I could hear her voice as she spoke to me. I felt her presence. We talked about things that went on between us when I was a child and that seemed to heal my relationship with her.

DiCarlo—And the personal impact of the experience was...?

Moody—I'd have to say profound. Did it make me <u>believe</u> that there is a life after death? No. I would have to say that it changed my inner world view, that the metaphor I had used to describe reality was inadequate.

DiCarlo—So for you, this experience was unexpected given your prevailing world view.

Moody—Was it ever, yes! Absolutely. I now realize that I am never going to understand the nature of the universe from this physical perspective that I am in now. To me, the thrill of this lies in the search. I love the way you ask yourself a question, and then you go about trying to answer the question. What you really end up with is about a dozen more questions. So that to me, seems the nature of the world.

DiCarlo—Could you describe your present interests? What questions are you asking yourself these days?

Moody—To really put this into context I would like to explain that my work with people who have had Near Death Experiences is something I am known for, almost because of a process of natural selection. Yet logic has always been very interesting to me too, but when I try to tell other people about my interests by saying, "Well, I'm an astronomer," or, "I'm interested in logic," they will kind of walk away. But when people would ask me at parties and such, "What are you doing now?" and I remarked, "Oh, I'm studying these folks whom I've talked with who have almost died," they would then lean forward and want to learn more.

But the scope of my whole work is much larger than that. I am actually interested in human consciousness. Still, I am very interested in the Near Death Experience. And basically what I find, is that the debate on the issue has now stagnated for two interrelated reasons.

There's a controversy that's been going on since antiquity about supposedly paranormal experiences. On the one hand, you have the parapsychologically minded. They are the people who hold out the prospect that scientific inquiry, broadly construed, or systematic inquiry of some sort—rational procedure—can come up with proof or evidence that there is life after death or that paranormal things happen.

The second stream consists of people who like to call themselves the skeptical debunkers, like the Committee for the Scientific Investigation of Claims of the Paranormal, CSICOPS. They say that parapsychology is pseudoscience and this is all readily explicable as fantasy or wish fulfillment, or neuron misfirings, or hoax or fraud—any of those things.

DiCarlo—That's the organization founded by Carl Sagan, Issac Asimov, Fred Skinner and other hard core materialist scientists.

Moody—Exactly. Then the third perspective is proposed by the folks who love to call themselves Christians in our society but who really are fundamentalist in their religious approach. Fundamentalism is the same whether one is a Christian, Jew, Moslem or Marxist. It's all the same. Fundamentalists are humorless, dour people who are fixated upon anal concerns, who hold on to some abstract ideology and imagine they really believe it. But of course they really don't, which accounts for why they come across as being so insecure.

Religious fundamentalists feel that paranormal phenomenon is the work of demons. Demons are of an obsessional concern. Demons bring doubt. Demons deceive us. The kinds of things that the fundamentalists project onto demons are the same things that obsessional people report in therapy, when they have gotten themselves into some life difficulty. Demons are foul, filthy—"Doc, I wash my hands 25 times a day." "Doc, I get up in the night 15 times to see whether my clock is set." Or, "I go back in the house 20 times to see if the light switches are really off." This is just obsessional behavior.

So all three perspectives on the paranormal, terrifically run aground. I am certainly not a parapsychologist, and I can see very clearly that the scientific method as it is structured now is not going to give us answers to these things. But that doesn't make me a skeptical debunker either, because the skeptical debunkers are not really scientific either. For them, this is a social crusade. They like to say that the parapsychologists are parading their beliefs as science, yet they don't realize that they are parading their disbeliefs as science.

We have always assumed that the Near Death Experience is something that cannot be replicated under set conditions so that we can monitor the person going through it.

I have tried to break up that impasse by attempting to replicate the Near Death Experience safely.

DiCarlo—Now when you say, "replicate the Near Death Experience," it's not using the extreme measures portrayed in the movie "Flatliners," such as stopping an individual's beating heart, I take it?

Moody—No, absolutely not. Nobody in their right mind would do this using the "Flatliners" method.

Since 1962, when I had a great course in ancient Greek culture at the University of Virginia, I had been interested in the ancient Greek Oracles of the dead. About four years ago, due to a series of thoughts, I remembered that, and I went back to investigate. The ancient accounts suggested that people could actually go to these places and see apparitions of their departed loved ones. Well, we also know from the thousands of Near Death Reports that have been given, that the experience of witnessing an apparition of a deceased loved one is an integral part of the Near Death Experience. So I felt that if we could replicate that one part of it, we would indirectly shed light on the whole phenomenon.

To make a long story short, what I did was to check out the archaeology of the Oracles. One of the Oracles of the Dead was located in 1958 in Epirus, Greece, exactly where Homer and Heroditus had said it was all along. The place was excavated and it turned out to be an enormous subterranean facility with many corridors and a labyrinth opening out into a 50 foot long central apparition hallway. There, the archaeologists found the remnants of an enormous cauldron. The archaeologist concluded—as anyone might well have concluded—that the apparition seekers, gazing in the direction of the cauldron to see the apparitions, were actually seeing the Greek guides who had concealed themselves in the cauldron and who pretended to be the spirits. But I had a different thought, based upon my longtime interest in the old technique of mirror gazing, found in many cultures in the world including the ancient Hebrew culture, where Joseph had his silver cup. The idea was simple: take some sort of metal vessel, such as a bowl, cauldron, or silver cup, highly polish it on the inside and fill it with water or olive oil so as to produce a clear optical depth. This was then used as a means of bringing about visions.

I set out to reproduce that, using a special mirror that gives a clear optical depth—not a reflective mirror. Afterwards, I assembled a number of my graduate students in psychology (and later my colleagues) and took them through a preparation process.

DiCarlo—And the results of your experiment?

Moody—We found that we can recapture the experience of seeing apparitions of the deceased. To my knowledge, this is one of the first times that an allegedly paranormal experience has reliably been reproduced under set conditions of observation. We're planning to secure EEG recordings of people as they go through this experience of seeing a vivid, full colored, three-dimensional external appearing image of a departed loved one.

DiCarlo—Do all the people have a similar apparitional experience?

Moody—About 50%. We're getting a little bit better now. I figured it out, but I am not the best person to put the procedure into practice. The work has been replicated by other psychologists. There is a woman I know who has been a long time therapist and counselor at the University of Texas hospice. She has about an 80% success rate.

DiCarlo—What would you say might be some of the more practical implications of the work you are now doing?

Moody—The primary implications are the following: #1) It gives us a very plausible explanation of certain historical curiosities, like the oracles, which are well-documented in ancient literature, but which now have been ignored. #2) It opens up the prospect of making active electroencepholographic recordings of people who are undergoing the experience of seeing apparitions. #3) It opens the possibility of a new therapeutic approach to prolonged grief states. #4) It explains certain anomalies and curiosities of literature such as the Aladdin story. In the kids version that we all read, Aladdin rubs the lamp and the genie magically appears. In the actual written version of the Arabian Nights entertainment, Aladdin's mother polishes the brass lamp using sand as an abrasive and a spirit emerges from the surface into the room and audibly speaks to them. That has happened often at our facility.

Finally, as anybody who has done a lot of research in Near Death Experiences will tell you, empathic Near Death Experiences occur, where one who remains living is able to share in the death experience of another individual. Obviously they are more rare than first person Near Death Experiences, but they are not unheard of and you can definitely find them. Although I was purposefully using vague and metaphorical language, I do believe it will be possible to recapture, or to bring about empathic Near Death Experiences. We will actually be able to go "part way over," to use that metaphorical language, with people who are in the dying process. My evidence for this is the very fact that in many cultures, this was actually done.

What I like to say is that I have rediscovered an ancient technique of bringing about an interesting altered state of human consciousness. One that has had profound effects upon our culture, upon our literature, and upon our folk beliefs. Everything.

Robert Monroe

Robert Monroe enjoys a background as a radio executive who directed, wrote and composed music for more than 400 radio programs in the forties. In 1958, he unexpectedly found himself consciously out of his body. The experiences led him to author the groundbreaking book "Journeys Out of the Body." Monroe is founder of the Monroe Institute of Applied Sciences, which conducts research into human consciousness. Its six-day Gateways Voyage program has attracted thousands interested in pain control, healing, and exploration of the psyche.

DiCarlo—You've been an explorer in the true sense of the word—a real Christopher Columbus. But instead of charting outer unknown worlds, you claim to be an explorer of inner unknown worlds. I'm wondering, what prompted this exploration. Was it curiosity?

Monroe—Well, I can give you a very simple answer. It began out of vital necessity. After encountering phenomenon that I didn't know anything about, I consulted with various so-called authorities—psychiatrists and very well-read psychologists—in hopes that they might give me a reasonable explanation. They could not. So I began to investigate it on my own, to find out, first of all, how to control this phenomenon. I was quite fearful at first because I thought I might be dying. But after I found out it wasn't going to kill me, I then began to investigate it out of a sense of curiosity. I established a company and a research team that could begin investigating these "out-of-body" incidents. It took about a year of cause and effect experimentation on my part before I moved from a position of *believing* these OBE's were real, to *knowing* them to be real.

DiCarlo—Is the out-of-body experience different for you now as compared to many years ago when you first started experiencing this phenomenon?

Monroe—Oh, very much so. You accumulate experience. Experience creates information which converts itself into what I call "knowns" instead of "unknowns." That makes a great difference in the way you perceive things.

DiCarlo—So, what's an OBE experience like for you now?

Monroe—It's simply as if this normal, everyday consciousness—and its limitations—suddenly shuts off and I'm not in this physical reality because the other reality is so alluring.

I do it every night when I go into deep sleep, as does everyone else, I might add. The difference, say, between my out-of-body experience and any other person's is that I am able to direct my activities while in this state. Mine are workable. Also, I can recall my experiences when I awake. The average person doesn't remember their out-of-body states. We have done enough research over the years to show that everyone has these out-of-body states, so you can think about that when you go to sleep tonight.

DiCarlo—Do you feel that you are really entering another body as is commonly believed, or is it a shift in focus to another level of consciousness that's always there, even now as we speak for example?

Monroe—No, not another body. You can organize—and I don't use the word materialize—another body in another energy system, but actually you're more like an energy vortex. You are like an intelligent energy vortex filled with the experience of this lifetime—plus a lot more than that. People are often overwhelmed to find out how much more they are than just this simple here-and-now consciousness.

DiCarlo—But we're always in this other state; it's just that we are not consciously aware of it while we go about our everyday lives?

Monroe—Yes, that's very true.

DiCarlo— So the Monroe Institute trains people how to consciously have these out-of-body experiences?

Monroe—We set up a means whereby a person can do what we call "phasing." In other words, let's say you're listening to me now as I am talking to you and all of a sudden your attention drifts as you think the thought, "Well, did I turn the coffee pot off before I left the house?" For a moment, you're out of phase. A part of you is out of phase with the here-and-now moment and the words I am speaking. And then you flip back so that you are. We teach people to deliberately move into phases where a certain percentile of your consciousness, your mind, is not in this time/space. This is what meditators do. They call it something else but basically it's the same thing. So we help people to develop conscious awareness of these other states and then use them in a constructive way.

DiCarlo—What would be some of the benefits to the individual of being able to consciously control these out-of-body experiences?

Monroe—First of all, a person realizes that they truly are more than their physical body. That's the first step. Once realizing that, they get to a point where they not only believe that they survive physical death, but they know it as a fact based upon personal experience. This creates a great and magnificent change in the individual that effects their entire life. It doesn't make you any less cautious in what you do, but fear of death, that great governor of so much of what we do, is no longer present.

DiCarlo—Now, I've had my own out-of-body experiences so I am an easy sell. Also, 25% of Americans have had OBE's that they remember. But there is this very real tendency to discount these experiences that you speak of as fantasy productions of the mind. I'm curious, how do you respond to the skeptics?

Monroe—Well, my response has been that there are ways to test this out for yourself. We have a lot of skeptics that come to the Institute just to find out. I'd say two-thirds of the people visiting the Monroe Institute are over 40 years old and half of them are professionals of one kind or another, such as professors at Universities. It's interesting, the skeptics sit there with folded arms the first night and three nights later, their hands are flopping and waving!

We have the means to help people have these experiences.

DiCarlo—Over the 30 or so years you have been having these out-of-body experiences, could you please elaborate on how your world view has changed? For example, what is the nature of the Universe in which we live?

Monroe—As I've reported, I know that I am more than my physical body. I know—I don't believe—that I will survive physical death, that I have an existence beyond physical death. It's interesting because as I look outside and I see a leaf on a tree or consider all of nature, including animals and humans, this tremendously brilliant creation and creative process reveals itself to me. I don't see how one can think of it in any other terms. This indicates to me that there was or is a creative mind that has established some basic rules that we have to abide by. I don't want to call it intellect because it's far more than that, and I don't like to use the word "God" either, but our religions call it that. Man didn't put this whole creative pattern together. I have reached the point now of having gone—through my out-of-body experiences—to the Creative Source of all of this. I found that I couldn't go through the aperture of this particular reality system so as to shake the hands of the Creator and say, "You did a wonderful and magnificent job," because I was "incomplete," as it was put to me. I needed to go back.

DiCarlo—Through what process would you eventually become "complete?"

Monroe—It's a bonding with others through "super love," founded upon life experiences together on the planet. It may be millions at one time who are bonded together with us and who "wink out" with us through the aperture to directly experience the Creative Source.

DiCarlo—Super love—that's an interesting term. What do you mean by that?

Monroe—Well, the main problem is that we as humans equate sexual drive and attraction to love and that's one of the ways that love can be expressed, but from my perspective, it is not in itself love.

Super love is a whole concept separate and apart from the rules under which we live in this earth/life system. In other words, it's an application of the law of survive. Survive, in this earth/life system means, "Keep yourself alive and reproduce so that the species will be maintained." Well, the whole point is that there is something very much beyond that and super love doesn't have any of those limitations. It may use all of these things to in turn, generate new life, but it's a form of consciousness that we don't understand as such. That's basically it. And we share that consciousness with other people who we love and who love us. It's an energy form—that's my impression.

DiCarlo—So to say that super love is simply unconditional love would be too limiting in your view?

Monroe—Yes, it would be in the sense that I don't know of any limits to super love. It's a super-empathetic understanding of other people and even other animals, I might add. And it goes so far beyond. It's hard to really express exactly; I suspect that Creator is the epitome of super love. That's my opinion.

DiCarlo—Would you agree with many of the people who have had Near Death Experiences who tell us that one of the reasons why we have come to experience life on the Earth is to learn how to generate this "super love?"

Monroe—Yes, that's my opinion.

DiCarlo—Does this bonding through love result in any loss of individuality for a person?

Monroe—No, not at all. It just adds to your totality. You then discover the enormity of who you really are.

Since becoming aware of all of this, I must add that my perspective toward people that I meet and know has changed. It's very interesting. You begin to feel common bonds with certain people and it's a feeling which comes up of its own accord.

DiCarlo—So in some way, we are bonded to the people that we feel strongly about?

Monroe—Yes, very much so. Before she died, my wife Nancy and I discovered that we had at least eighteen previous lives together. And there were more, but those are the ones that we explored and knew about. She was as astounded as I was.

DiCarlo—What is the key to recognizing others with whom we may be bonded with?

Monroe—It's the intensity. Because of our cultural norms, we put up shields against recognizing these bonds. But we are bonded with a lot of people. It's very fascinating.

DiCarlo—Well, aside from superlove, and based upon your experiences to date, what would some of the characteristics of the Creative Source be?

Monroe—That's a hard one since it's beyond our concepts of mind, consciousness and energy. It's just beyond our ability to know. I do know that there is indeed, a part of this creative process that has been inserted in every living carbon mechanism on the planet. There is a Creator behind life on the planet—I know it does exist—but to understand it is beyond my capability.

DiCarlo—But your view isn't that of the cosmic "Big Daddy" who judges us after death?

Monroe—No, not at all.

DiCarlo—Are we basically and distinctly separate from this Creator or are we part of this Creator as some people have suggested?

Monroe—This is an interesting point. It took me a while to find this out, but in our core self there is that same energy, minuscule though it may be, of that Creator. Human beings have it, and so do animals, I might add, though it is of a lesser degree. So do plants. You would say that's the soul of you, but as I interpret it, it's a clone or a part, or a replica of that original Creator-energy. It's the best way I can describe it.

DiCarlo—Would you say that in our own growth and development that part of our nature—some would call it "divine"—is enhanced, that it becomes more prominent?

Monroe—That greatly depends upon the person. The greatest teacher of all is experience. If you don't learn from your experience, you've got to keep doing the same thing over and over again until you do.

DiCarlo—As I said earlier, you have been a true explorer. One thing explorers sometimes do is draw maps for other people to help them explore unfamiliar terrain. I'm wondering if you could sketch a verbal map of the nonphysical reality as you have come to know it?

Monroe—Yes, this is relatively easy. We have a system so people can experience this directly for themselves. What are they? Well, we have set up guideposts—artificial labels that help us identify these different states of being. For example, there's a state of consciousness that we call "Focus 10," which simply means the mind is awake and the body is asleep. During that state, your attention is focused in a nonphysical reality. In Focus 15, you're out of time—time does not exist. Focus 21 is on the edge of space.

Focus 22 is what we call the "H Band" which is disorganized human thought—sort of like random street noise. The sooner you get through it the better. Focus 23 is a state beyond time and space, and it is where people go who have just died physically. Focus 24, 25, and 26 are what we call "belief-system territories." This is where people who have strong religious convictions go shortly after physical death. So there's a Catholic heaven, and there are "areas" for Islam and Hindu believers too—they're all there. If you have been deeply ingrained in a particular religious belief system during this life, these are the areas where you go.

It's fascinating that if you do not have these deeply ingrained beliefs, these dimensions appear as vague shadows. You can't go there because you can't perceive them that well. For example, I can observe "nirvana" in flickers and flashes, but it isn't a place where I can go since I am not a Buddhist who deeply believes in nirvana, you see.

DiCarlo—So, the nature of one's belief system at the time of death effects one's afterlife experience?

Monroe—Very much so. Now, Focus 27 is an area I first encountered in 1963. It's a place where people who don't know what they want to do can go and be until they get over the trauma of physical death. Doctors, psychologists, businessmen—those who are very intellectual and strongly willed—have come to our institute to learn the process of rescuing and retrieving the confused people from Focus 23. They then take them to Focus 27 where they can rest and recuperate before deciding where they're going to go and what they're going to be. Focus 27 is a nice place to be, and at the entrance way there's a park with flowers and trees and grass. There's also a running stream and a bunch of benches along the walk. But that's just an entry point. It's amazing how quickly people get acclimated and decide what they're going to do. Two months later, they're off playing around somewhere.

Now, you might say to me, "Why end at 27?" Well, if you take up residence in Focus 28 or beyond (we've met people who have done so) you can no longer inhabit a physical body. You can come back visiting but you can't take up another life in a physical body.

DiCarlo—After we die, are we eventually reunited with those we love, in your view?

Monroe—We can be, yes. There are some peculiar things that can happen though. I can give you an illustration. A lot of people who have just died and find themselves in Focus 23 might be projecting their expectations so that they perceive you as their father or their mother. I have had this happen to me many times while trying to retrieve people from this level. In order to keep them quiet, you don't say no and you don't yes; you just say "Come on with me," or something to that effect.

Most people soon lose interest in this physical life experience soon after they die. It's only the person who has a lot of guilt or is caught up in some type of attraction that wants to stay. They become a "ghost" as it were. I've met a couple of these people and found out why, but the vast number will stay attracted to the physical earth for a little while, but then gradually their interest wanes. They get involved in other things which begin to captivate their whole consciousness more and more. To my knowledge, the longest time a person has been "earthbound" and has maintained an interest in the physical world (and I mean an active interest, don't misunderstand) was about 6 months. After this period of time they usually make up their minds as to what they're going to do. They just go and do or be something else. We have our fun when we say these kinds of things, but for those who move on, this life becomes the latest story to tell at the cosmic cocktail party.

DiCarlo—Well, if everybody's playing around in areas of personal interest, are we ever reunited with people that are close to us?

Monroe—In a way which is hard to accept. One of the things that we have found out—it's a "known" for us—is that the life that each of us is living now is but a finger of a hand. We have had many, many previous human life experiences. Each of those personalities is a part of us. It's astounding to discover this and I had missed that obvious point early on. Some of the tendencies in my life are attributable to previous lives.

DiCarlo—Would you like to share any examples?

Monroe—Sure. As a six or seven year old kid, I was building two and three storied wooden shacks. I had a whole childhood full of keen interest in construction, especially large buildings. After I had grown, I got into the construction business in Virginia and built a modular home. In about 1986, while visiting London, I couldn't help but notice that certain buildings made me feel very sad. The same thing happened in Paris. When I got back to the States I had somebody I knew in London and Paris check out the construction dates on the buildings that had evoked such feelings of sadness.

In the meantime, I discovered that I had been a builder/architect in the 12th century in London and then in Paris in a previous life. Suddenly, all the pieces came together. I had a very special tower designed and built which formed the east wing of the Monroe Center building, here in the states. Well, my brother, who is a doctor, was vacationing in Europe, where he stayed at the Lawyer's Castle in Monroe Fields. When he got back, he didn't think I'd be interested, so he didn't tell me about it, nor did he send me any of the pictures he had taken.

However, sometime afterwards, he got a flyer from the Monroe Center in Virginia with a picture of this new east wing that he had not seen. He was shocked, and he's a very conventional individual. He immediately sent me copies of the photographs he had taken of the Lawyer's Castle in Europe. To my shock and amazement, it was identical in dimensions and appearance to the tower that I had put on the east wing of our building.

Soon afterwards, we had somebody dig into the history of the Monroe family, and do you know what came back in the clan records? The tower on Lawyer's Castle in Monroe Fields was constructed in 1151 by a Donald Monroe and his son whose name was, did you guess, Robert Monroe. Isn't that interesting documentation?

Up until about 1990, I didn't have any particular interest in the fact that I was part of a being that had had all these multiple lives, or previous life experiences. I didn't even give it a thought.

Let me add, 50 people including myself, took lie detector tests to prove that we knew nothing about any of this when the tower was built at the institute.

DiCarlo—You've already mentioned that one of the reasons we might decide to experience the earth plane is to learn how to generate what you call superlove. In closing, are there any other reasons?

Monroe—To learn to manipulate physical matter energy. We don't look at it this way and it doesn't seem that way to us at the time, but that's exactly what we are doing. I'm sitting here talking to you and I'm manipulating energy. We learn these things so automatically but beyond time and space, these abilities are incredibly valuable because you can then manipulate other energies just as easily.

DiCarlo—Wouldn't we know how to do that coming in?

Monroe—Not to the degree that you learn here; this is a very intensive school.

And I have a deep suspicion that it goes as far as the knowing and understanding, eventually, of the whole creative way of being and thinking so that you could be a creator yourself—if that's what you so desire. There's plenty of room down the energy spectrum. That much I can tell you.

Dr. John Mack

Dr. John Mack, M.D. is the Pulitzer-Prize winning author of the book, "A Prince of Our Disorder," (a biography of T. E. Lawrence) and professor of psychology at The Cambridge Hospital of Harvard Medical School, where he is the founding director of the Center for Psychology and Social Change. Mack has also authored the book, "Abduction," which features thirteen in-depth case studies of extraterrestrial abductions out of the nearly one hundred he has investigated.

DiCarlo—You've been involved in some pretty unusual, if not extremely controversial work with individuals who claim to have been abducted by extraterrestrial intelligences. To start off John, could you describe what it is that you do?

Mack—Basically, I am a clinician who works with people who have had experiences which, according to the prevailing world view, are not supposed to happen.

As I talked to people, I simply began to describe what I found both with face-to-face interviews and then with a kind of modified hypnotic approach which is little more than a relaxation exercise. There is a range of phenomena that appear in individuals who claim to have had these experiences. You get reports of quite literal, physical occurrences. For example, an individual might be in their home or in their car and suddenly a beam of blue light is projected towards them and they are floated through the window. As they are lifted up, they may see a spaceship, which they then enter. Inside, there are these little guys with big black eyes who do various things to them. They may come back with cuts, scoop marks, scars and other lesions—very physical evidence of their experiences.

I didn't take this abduction phenomenon seriously when I first heard about it. I certainly didn't suppose that some strange beings could enter our world and abduct people. I thought that was preposterous.

DiCarlo—How would you characterize these individuals who have purportedly been abducted?

Mack—These are people who are not particularly New Age. They range from the very center of the culture—just ordinary folks—to quite sophisticated business professional people. Many were doubting it themselves. These are not people who are seeking publicity of any kind nor have they had anything to gain; in fact they are usually quite shy because they have been so ridiculed and cut down.

DiCarlo—You realize I'm sure, that the usual, knee-jerk response to tales of extraterrestrial encounters is, "Ah yes, this person must be crazy." It's traditionally been fodder for the TV and newspaper tabloid industry and not something one would ever take seriously.

Mack—A number of these individuals have been psychologically tested. There's not one shred of evidence that the critics have put on the table to suggest that this is anything other than what these people say it is. James Glieck of *The New Republic* gives it the back of his hand by describing it as fantasy and hallucination. It is not that. He has not studied the phenomenon clinically. It doesn't behave like fantasy or hallucination.

Carl Sagan becomes a psychologist and calls this phenomenon "hallucinations" in *Parade* magazine. He hasn't examined these people or worked with them clinically either. The reason he says that is because in his world view, this can't be. So it has got to be hallucination by deductive reasoning, not by empirical research.

I've approached this as a clinician, looking at this every way I could. That's what I do—I make discriminations about mental states. That's what a clinician is supposed to do. I can validate it because in every way it acts like a real experience—I could not find any reason to discount the experiences these people reported. From my point of view, I've established that the abductees were largely of sound mind. It doesn't mean that they were not experiencing post-traumatic stresses from the abduction experiences or that they had no problems in dealing with what had happened to them. But there was no material from the first thousand or so hours I spent with these people that would account for their abduction experiences as originating from anything in their psyches. By that I mean psyche in the conventional, psychodynamic sense.

DiCarlo—Please explain.

Mack—Usually, when psychiatrists or mainstream mental health professionals refer to the psyche, they define it as a bundle of thoughts, feelings, drives and identity fragments that somehow cohere into a self that's separate from the physical world. I found nothing from that view of the psyche which would account for the experiences.

Now, if you want to extend your definition of psyche to that of the Jungian notion of resonances, of vast synchronicities between the inner and the outer, then we are able to perceive UFO's differently. In this view, psyche would be seen as everything manifested from consciousness, mind and matter, but that is not the standard Western mind.

DiCarlo—What have been some of the criticisms of your work?

Mack—The subtlest criticism I face is that I'm a "believer," that this is a matter of faith and religion and not science and empiricism. I deeply question and challenge that. I arrived at my present understanding using every bit of clinical and psychological skill I had at my disposal in 40 years plus in this field, and then came to the conclusion that this phenomenon is in some way real. I did not make leaps of faith. This was not about beliefs. It was about the evolution of my thinking through my clinical work. Now did I use my whole psyche? My intuition? Yes. I think that's what a good mental health professional is supposed to do. But it was not a matter of a belief. Belief means that I have made a leap of faith through a kind of epiphany or religious conversion of my own. That's not been the case.

DiCarlo—So you were playing the part of the ideal scientist, following the facts wherever they might lead, even if you didn't like what you found?

Mack—Maybe not scientist, but hopefully knowledge seeker. I think that science is really about understanding through the physical senses and reason, whereas intuition is less understood in science. Actually, it shouldn't be. But I think we generally think of science as studying the physical world and in using reason to make sense of it. But we're really talking about gaining new knowledge, which is a broader notion than traditional science embraces.

DiCarlo—What would you say, John, is the purpose of these purported abductions?

Mack—I don't know. You would have to know the alien intention to give an adequate answer to that question. However, I can say what the abduction pattern is and its effects. We know them by their deeds, by the effect of the abductions. What seems to be occurring has three interrelated elements, all connected to human evolution and the Universe. You might look at it as a kind of desperate effort on the part of the Universe's intelligence to set limits upon an aberrant element, namely us.

If there is some intelligence at work, if evolution and creation possess some kind of intelligence that's not purely random, and if the earth matters in some larger universal pattern, then surely that intelligence, that creative principle, would be engaged in some kind of effort to set limits upon the destruction of the earth. It's an attempt—in some ways feeble and in some ways brilliant; in some ways awkward and in some ways distressing—to intervene in our evolutionary development on the part of the cosmic intelligence.

That's what it looks like and it has three elements. One is this hybrid program, which is very awkward. We can think of it as some other, less densely embodied species than we are—set at a much higher vibratory energy intensity—which has exerted some effort to modify us. The work with the abductees suggests that other intelligences are being mated with us to create some sort of less-embodied species that can operate in this dimension but also potentially in another dimension in a way which is less destructive.

One of the most important things about this phenomena I might add, is that it acts as a kind of psychological Rorschak Test for our egoism. If we are aggressively colonizing our earth, if we operate out of an aggressive mentality, then we say "Oh, they must be colonizing us." I don't think this is anything like what we do. Say you could talk to a caribou who has been tagged by naturalists. We're trying to protect them, but from the caribou's point of view, this treatment is mean, cruel and not nice. But a caribou can't really figure out what's going on in the situation.

DiCarlo—I see...And the second element?

Mack—Another dimension might be called "ecological learning." The abduction phenomenon includes a huge amount of material and information that is given telepathically—mind to mind—or via scenes shown on a television monitor portraying earth changes, such as vast scenes of pollution. The experience affects the way the abductees feel about themselves in relation to the earth. They feel profoundly concerned about what's happened to the earth. They become deeply involved in teaching about environmental matters in schools or in trying to convince people to live more lightly in nature. These people are not environmentalists. It's not an intellectual experience. They feel it in the depth of their souls and that's an almost universal phenomenon.

DiCarlo—And the last element which seems to point to the purpose behind these abductions?

Mack—The third element is harder to define but seems to be related to a transformation of consciousness. A shift in identity occurs, from the individual thinking of him or herself as a limited, earthbound, creature who lives in a family or clan, to, as one female abductee described herself, "a child of the cosmos." Personal identity grows to encompass the whole cosmic landscape. It expands the individual's sense of who he or she is. It's an ego-destroying phenomenon in the sense of an exclusive focus on ourselves, our personal positions and property. There is a change in the direction of opening to the whole grand flow of consciousness through time. This leads to a deep connection with the soul level of the earth and with others. It's not just ecological. It's a change of consciousness. It's as hard to define as is any other transformation process.

In considering all three elements—and again, I have to say that I really don't know what the aliens are up to—the effect of this suggests some kind of "bio-spiritual-evolutionary process" that is consistent with other transformative experiences such as shamanic journeys and near death experiences. I don't think this abduction phenomenon should be seen in isolation from all other paradigm-shifting phenomenon.

DiCarlo—Do you feel that for some people, this experience of being abducted represents a "Right of Passage" into higher states of consciousness?

Mack—If you took a survey of people across socioeconomic and religious lines, the ones that would seek an initiation—say, by going on a vision quest for a week in the mountains—would be the most sophisticated, avant garde, adventurous, probably relatively wealthy minority, of our culture. The fact is, most people would not initiate their own initiation.

You can think of the abduction phenomenon as being a sort of involuntary initiation, like the person who has a heart attack and experiences a movement in consciousness that causes them to realign their values. Something happened to them from some other source. The initiative is "out there" in so far as we can make a distinction between out there and in here—which is admittedly dualistic thinking. I sometimes refer to this phenomenon as an "outreach" program of the cosmos to the consciously and spiritually impaired.

DiCarlo— Could you describe the typical abductee's subjective experience as they go through this transformational process?

Mack—I'll give you an example. One of the abductee's I've worked with is Peter, a hotel manager who lived with his wife on a Caribbean island in the late 1980s. As it turns out, he returned to the United States and changed careers. He decided to become an acupuncturist in the Boston area.

A conversation he had with another student in the acupuncture school triggered memories of nights in the Caribbean which involved some really strange happenings—intense lights, UFO's. During several hypnosis sessions with him, he began to question intensely the reality of his experiences. It's not as some people suppose. There is intense resistance. It's not like some sort of religious belief system.

The first two or three sessions were horrifyingly distressing as this quite handsome, quite masculine, aggressive male is overpowered by these little beings and subjected to the typical intrusive procedures. But gradually what happens—which isn't simply post-traumatic—is this: because he acknowledges that this is a real experience and that the beings exist, that they have a purpose, that the Universe contains intelligences other than ours, his ego breaks down. His sense of masculine omnipotence breaks down. He engages in a kind of tissue learning. He has to acknowledge in every cell in his body (he said during the regression session, "every cell in my body is vibrating") that there are these little beings and they can do these things and he's not all powerful. There is, in that kind of death of arrogance, an ego death as he realizes he is not so powerful and that the Universe—whether it's through these little beings or through some other means—has a way of reducing us to the powerless creatures that in a certain sense we always were.

DiCarlo—And what happens as a result of this ego-death?

Mack—Through this acknowledgment of powerlessness, he begins to grow. He begins to realize that he is not all powerful and that we are connected beyond the earth. He realizes that he is part of something larger. But the story doesn't end there. He begins to feel that he's a part of some kind of life creating process. He's not just being used (though he is, in a sense being used) for his sperm as part of a hybrid breeding project. Peter then discovers in subsequent abductions that not only is he part of this project, but he's committed to it. He's involved in it. He's gone from resisting hints that there are some aliens and UFO's around, to being part of some cosmic evolutionary transcending process. Not everyone has gone that route, but that would not be an untypical process.

DiCarlo—I find it interesting that in the transformational process that is triggered, one of the initial experiences is the individual's perception that they've lost control, that they are helpless. This would seem to parallel the experience of people addicted to alcohol, drugs or whatever, who must admit their powerlessness and surrender to a higher power if they are to successfully cope with their problem. What is the significance of this sense of loss of control?

Mack—Well, you have to back up a little bit. To understand the fix we're in, you need to go back to the original scientific impulse, which can be viewed as a legitimate effort to gain some mastery over the physical world. Look at what was going on in Europe, say in the 14th Century. The Black Death was wiping out a third of Europe's population, and there was a sense of helplessness that people felt due to war, famine and disease. As a result, there would have been an impulse, particularly a masculine impulse as Richard Tarnas has written about, to gain some mastery of the physical world. That's been the Western civilization's male enterprise—to dominate, to control and to be master of nature. We carry this impulse to its extreme.

DiCarlo—And the ultimate consequence of this need to control?

Mack—Taking this impulse to its logical conclusion, we have arrogated to ourselves the control of the Universe. We feel we have the freedom to desecrate the ecology of the entire planet. There's a book called *The Control of Nature,* by John McPhee, in which he gives three examples of this: trying to control the mudslides that are destroying houses in the canyons of California; trying to control the icebergs in Iceland; and trying to reroute portions of the Mississippi Delta. Here we have an effort to completely engineer the earth in a sense, with wildly destructive side effects. I would refer to this manifestation of *extreme* control as "the astrodome mentality." It's where you cut yourself totally off from nature to play sports on astroturf (you control the temperature and other elements) so that you never have to deal with nature at all. You have completely controlled everything. We are beginning to see the breakdown of the ecosystems as a result of that effort to achieve total control.

This extreme desire to control may be leading to this backlash of nature. That's one way to think of it. And you have all the new disciplines which are training us to let go of control. "Est" was the big one in the 1970s. There's also learning from the Native American traditions which entail a more harmonious, less controlling, respectful relationship with nature. The vision quests and initiations which you mentioned earlier are intended to cultivate harmony in our relationship with nature, a respectful mutuality with no urge to control. The books by Castenada pivot around this same theme.

So the abduction phenomenon, when seen from the point of view I've just described, is perfect. If I were God, and I wanted to design a phenomenon to subvert the dominant world view, to demonstrate the futility of our efforts to control, you couldn't find a better one than UFO's that can run circles around any of our proudest aircraft, that can enter our radar scopes and just flick off the radar screen at will and make a mockery of our technologies. Aliens that can seemingly float us through walls, paralyzing the people they select.

But it's not just loss of control as an experience per se—which I call "trauma one"—it's loss of control in the process of what I call "ontological shock," reality shock. The individual's whole world view has been shattered. Reality is shattered. Our notion that we are the pre-eminent intelligence in the cosmos is also destroyed, along with the idea that intelligence itself is not simply a property of scientists and smart people's brains, but that intelligence is apparently inherent in the universe. It's terrible in some ways, and yet it is magnificently designed to shatter our arrogant sense of control. When that sense of control has been shattered, the person is then able to open up to the possibility of learning, to the possibility of growth.

Say a two year old is wrecking the house. In comes mom who says, "No, stop." And the child cries. From the two year old's point of view, mother is a cruel terrible person, particularly if she's had a bad day. Yet the alternative is that the child might set fire to the curtains, slam the door on the dog, dump alcohol onto the stove and generally wreck the house.

I don't recommend this experience, but that's not the point. Does it enable the Universe to evolve in more transcendent, ecstatic ways that we can participate in? Will it enable us to know ourselves better, to expand our identity and live in greater harmony with nature? These might be the real questions. But is it going to help our marketing efforts so we can sell more goods in Asia? I don't think so.

DiCarlo—Does this phenomenon of alien abduction suggest that indeed we reside in a multidimensional reality?

Mack—Yes. The effect of abduction experiences upon the psyche is to open us to an expanded possibility of reality for several reasons: Number one is that aliens exist as life, or as beings, or as energy, which simply does not reside within our material universe, so by definition there is another dimension. If they are in the Newtonian, three-dimensional universe, or a four-dimensional universe which adds time, they sure are an element that Einstein hadn't found.

I've been talking to physicists like Ron Bryan at Texas A&M who says that from a purely mathmetical point of view you need to posit at least eight or nine dimensions to account for the behavior of certain subatomic particles. Their behavior simply doesn't work in a three or four-dimensional universe. I don't understand the mathematics of it.

Now multiple dimensions and multiple realities, this is all language. The way we perceive reality is constructed through language. After all, the word reality is simply a word which points to, "What is." We have language for the laws of physics. Does this phenomenon fit into that universe as described by Newton and Einstein? Yes and no. Many physicists argue that UFO's cannot exist because there is no known propulsion system that would allow them to get to this galaxy from another galaxy. But that presumes that the laws of physics cover everything we know. There may be all kinds of potential energy-like transfers from one dimension to another that we don't know anything about.

There are objective elements of the UFO phenomenon that seem to violate the known laws of physics. Just a simple example: UFO's witnessed as a streak of light on video or radar screen with a velocity of 5,000 miles per hour, which suddenly makes a right angle turn and goes even faster with no skid. According to the laws of physics, nothing in the universe that has mass can do that. So what's involved here? Is this high tech or an advance into a whole new realm of being that is seemingly outside physics as we understand it? I am not a sophisticated philosopher, so I don't know how to think rigorously enough about these matters. To me there is a kind of blurring between where technologies we can't grasp in the universe end, and other realities or other dimensions begin. I don't know where the margin is.

DiCarlo—Well, in what ways does this alien phenomena help to tear down the infrastructure of the prevailing world view?

Mack—I have a concept called "The politics of ontology," which has to do with decision-making among the elite of our culture, the people who decide "What is." The elite in this culture have decided that at least officially—although the situation is changing—the things I am talking about do not exist. But that's a political conclusion. It's not a scientific one.

Ken Wilber talks about the "eye of the flesh"—the senses—as being the best way to study the physical world. But there are other ways of getting information. There's the "Eye of Reason" and the "Eye of Contemplation" and I would add intuition. With these eyes we can learn vastly more about reality.

This very small but dominant group of hard scientists who comprise perhaps less than 1% of the population are, in a sense, physical literalists. They claim that there is no intelligence in the universe, that the universe is simply a mindless mechanism, that consciousness is equal to the physical brain and nothing more. When the body dies, they would say one's consciousness is forever extinguished. That 1% minority has a disproportionate impact upon what reality is officially thought to be, even though the majority of the population doesn't believe it anymore. The great majority of people seem to grasp intuitively that the universe is filled with intelligence and spirit.

What really drives the dominant, physicalist world view crazy—and this is why I think the alien phenomenon is so powerful—are phenomena that cross over; phenomena which belong in the spirit world and enter into the physical world. Why? Because then the adherents of the dominant paradigm do not have any choice. Either they say, "It doesn't exist," and has not entered the physical world or they say, "It's only in the physical world." A purely physicalist world view, or even a view that radically separates the physical and spiritual planes, can't come to terms with such phenomenon, which gets us right where we live..

We don't want to deny the physical world—it's part of reality. It should be respected, and we should credit its achievements. I have a sign up on my office wall that says, "Subvert the Dominant Paradigm," but it's really not about subverting it. It's about subsuming it into a larger, spiritual context. The *exclusive* focus on a purely physicalist world view is leading to the death of the planet.

Rick Tarnas has studied this more than I have, but if you look at the evolution of the Western intellectual enterprise, you get this split in the 17th century between science and religion, which went their separate ways. They were established as very separate realms. Religion was to take care of the subjective world, the spirit world. Medicine and science would take care of the physical world—disease, weapons, communications. And we all sort of came to believe that. But as Theologian Ted Peters said, "The deal never really worked." It was a kind of gentleman's agreement.

I believe that in a way myself. The hardest thing for me to accept is the idea that something, which is supposed to belong to the unseen, spiritual realm, can show up in the physical world and be photographed, or cause a cut or mark on the skin. That's really scary because that means the universe is really different than we thought, that we are truly helpless—which we always were anyway—and it destroys the illusion of control. This abduction phenomenon refuses to respect that artificial divide, and this is where, I think, its power and opportunity to bring about change reside.

Section 12

ACHIEVING PERSONAL AND
GLOBAL TRANSFORMATION

"Every life crisis of significance is something that Man has been facing forever. One great crisis—the transition from the dependency of childhood to the responsibility of maturity—is represented by the death of the infantile ego. It's a death and rebirth...Similarly, to move from any constellation of your life into another one involves a death and rebirth."

Joseph Campbell
Mythologist

"Synergy is the process by which the parts contribute to the whole, by which individual humans interacting with open hearts and commitment to serve each other's needs create a collective reality greater than the sum of their individual actions....High synergy means more than cooperation. Each part is called on to do his or her best, to fully offer their own unique contribution to the whole, making it greater than and different than the sum of its parts."

Barbara Marx Hubbard
Futurist

The individuals at the cutting-edge with whom I spoke varied greatly in terms of their background and life experiences, areas of interest, temperment and personal characteristics. Yet they were nearly unanimous in their belief that the very survival of humanity and the planet wrests upon the ability to in some way enlarge our world view and get out of our limited and distorted egocentric way of perceiving life. It is this, they tell us, which lies at the heart of all the social and institutional problems reported on the nightly news. "The crisis of our time," says Peter Russell whom we'll hear from in this section, "is not so much an environmental crisis, an economic crisis, a population crisis, or a political crisis. It is, in essence, a consciousness crisis—a mismatch between our psychological development and our technological development."

Yet if a new world view is needed, by what means might this happen? For example, could a person's world view change simply from reading a book, absorbing new information, and thus altering one's beliefs and assumptions about the way things? Or is more involved?

As it turns out, getting the new world view involves going through a process of personal transformation, which as psychologist Frances Vaughan explains, is not the same as change:

> "Transformation has certainly been used a lot and it seems to mean different things to different people, but I think it is essentially a more profound change than what we think of when we try to change and operate at the same level as before. We tend to confuse transformation with change. Ken Wilber's distinction is important. He says that change is like moving the furniture around on a certain floor in a high rise building. Transformation on the other hand, would take us up to a different floor. When we talk about transformation, we are talking about emotional development, mental development and essentially, a different view of reality."

The process culminates in a new state of being, in which the person is as fundamentally different as a butterfly is from a caterpillar. As one NDE'r put it, "I am physically the same, but there is a new me inside."

Those on the cutting-edge in medicine and psychology are telling us that the primary constitution of the human being is unified, yet two-fold in nature. What we are consists of both a personality (which is itself comprised of a plethora of subpersonalities), that part of us which we have become most identified with—the part that lives in time, moves in the physical world and dies—and an immortal soul or transpersonal self, which exists outside of time on a higher (not 'better-than,' but simply 'more-than') dimension of reality.

Some have drawn upon insights derived from quantum physics—where light has been found to paradoxically behave at times like a particle and at other times like a wave—for purposes of characterizing the difference between the two. The particle aspect of our nature has been compared to our personalities, localized in time and space; the wave to our spiritual nature—the circle whose circumference is both everywhere and nowhere.

The moments in which we touch upon our higher, spiritual nature is intense—Abraham Maslow referred to them as "peak experiences." At these times we feel in our depths that we are a creative force, not at all helpless or powerless. Maslow referred to individuals who were able to express their spiritual selves in this way as being self-actualizing—they were "actualizing," making actual or real in physical reality, their most essential nature. To do this consistently, on a moment-to-moment basis requires that an individual undergo this process of transformation.

Few people are as knowledgeable about the transformation process as Jacquelyn Small, who shares her insight with us in the following section. This is the hero's journey of courageously exploring both the depths and the heights of one's being.

It is the process of finding the deeper impulses of our own individuality, and learning to express oneself in the world in an easy and natural way without hesitating, without deliberating, without judging and second-guessing. It's simply about being who you are at core, doing what you do—effortlessly. Simply stated, but as it turns out, not so easy to accomplish since it represents a 180-degree shift in the way most people live their lives. It requires that a person function primarily from their knowing—their inner truth and light within—rather than from cues given by external figures of authority or from habit or memory.

As Maslow had barely glimpsed, there are those on the leading-edge who tell us that the challenge of earthly living is to become perfectly physical by "bringing down" as much of our spiritual nature as we can. In this way, all of who we are can reflect itself totally, perfectly and without distortion in the physical world.

Gary Zukav is the prize-winning author of *The Dancing Wu Li Masters*. Zukav suggests that true empowerment is not being granted authority to make decisions or about learning to manipulate the physical world, but is rather the result of coming into alignment with our very souls. As Zukav sees it, present social problems are but a harbinger of an unprecedented evolutionary transition, a fundamental, perceptual reorientation of humanity. We are, he says, in the midst of a change in interior capabilities, of being able to access a *higher* order of reason and logic based not in the mind or through data received through the five senses, but in the heart. This process is changing the very fabric of our society and all its institutions.

Finally, Peter Russell will further elaborate upon the social implications of this evolutionary process. Russell states that humanity is in the very early stages of functioning in an integrated and synergistic way. Global information systems allow for a level of interconnectiveness and sharing which is giving rise to a "global brain," a planetary consciousness. The question of our times, he suggests, is whether or not this global brain is going to be one that is sane or insane.

The world he says, is now at a crossroads, with "breakdown" or "breakthrough" as our two fundamental choices. Humanity can move on to its next evolutionary stage of development, which involves a higher degree of interconnection and capability or backslide into disintegration, polarization, fear and chaos.

This higher connectivity and synergy says Russell, does not work against one's individuality, but instead nurtures it. Our problems stem from the fact that we are neither fully ourselves, nor are we meaningfully connected with our families, communities, and the whole of creation. To live life in this way is to find peace, fulfill our highest potentials, and create a world undreamed of by the most compelling of science fiction writers.

Gary Zukav

Gary Zukav is the author of the book, "The Dancing Wu Li Masters," which won the 1979 American Book Award in Science, and helped to establish him as one of the foremost interpreters of the new physics. A graduate of Harvard University, he has also authored the book, "The Seat of The Soul," which describes the evolutionary journey of humanity from external power based upon the perceptions of the five senses, to authentic power based upon the perceptions and values of the soul.

DiCarlo—It seems that there are more than a few people today who, after observing the many breakdowns that are happening—in government, in education, in health care, in the family, in business—feel that a collapse of Western civilization is immanent. Surprisingly, you have a rather different assessment.

Zukav—Yes. In the larger, evolutionary context in which these changes are taking place, the disintegration of our social structures is a profoundly positive phenomenon. Without understanding the larger context, it is easy to mistake these breakdowns as pathologies.

The evolutionary transition that humanity is now in has no precedent. There is nothing in our past from which we can extrapolate our future. It is not only unprecedented—it is as significant as the genesis of the human species. This evolutionary transition is one from a five sensory species that is evolving through the exploration of physical reality with the five senses to a species that is evolving through the alignment of the personality with the soul and that is not limited to the five senses. The before and after circumstances are very clear. In our before picture, humanity, for the most part, was limited to the five senses. I say "for the most part" because there have always been multi-sensory humans among us. They have been the founders of our religions. But for the most part, humankind was limited in its perceptions to the five senses. As it evolved through the exploration of physical reality, the human species developed the ability to manipulate and control those things that the five senses can detect, those things which appears to be external.

In other words, our former evolutionary modality was the pursuit of external power—the ability to manipulate and control what appear to be external. Our present is much different. Humankind—all five and one-half billion of us—are beginning to move beyond the limitations of the five senses. Becoming multi-sensory means being able to obtain data that the five senses cannot provide.

DiCarlo—Sounds like your referring to intuition?

Zukav—Exactly. Five sensory humans are not much interested in intuition, but multi-sensory humans are very interested in it because intuition is central to the multi-sensory human. Intuition is the voice of the nonphysical world. As we become multi-sensory, we become able to distinguish between personality and soul.

DiCarlo—What do you mean by personality?

Zukav—Personality is that part of an individual that was born into time, matures in time and dies in time.

DiCarlo—And the soul?

Zukav—The soul is that part of the individual that is immortal, that evolves in eternity.

DiCarlo—Recently, there has been much more emphasis on the reality and substance of the soul, and I am thinking of the work that is being done in transpersonal psychology and medicine. Why the sudden interest?

Zukav—Because we are becoming multi-sensory.

DiCarlo—Wouldn't you say that in the past the soul has been taken for granted, "Well, yes we all have a soul," or so our religions have told us, but it's never been described in great detail, nor has the relationship between the soul and the physical self that we normally identify ourselves to be, been adequately explained. It has not been a real factor in one's daily life.

Zukav—Yes, there are people in religious orders who take the soul quite seriously, but for the most part, we do not, and by "we" I mean most humans. We talk about the soul in Sunday school but we don't give it much thought afterwards. We believe, no matter how much we talk about the soul in church, that consciousness and responsibility end with biological death. If we really believed that we were responsible after we leave the Earth for everything that we create while we are on the Earth, we would create very differently.

DiCarlo—Do you think there is a lot of conflict between what we want as personalities and what we want as souls?

Zukav—Yes. The degree of that conflict is the degree of pain that exists in your life. The match, or mismatch, between the wants of your personality and the needs of your soul also determines the degree of meaning, or lack of it, that you experience.

DiCarlo—Is it possible to align the interests of the personality and soul?

Zukav—Yes. That is now our evolutionary path. When a personality is authentically empowered, its interests are aligned with the interests of its soul. The personality usually wants an attractive mate, money, a comfortable place to live, a healthy body—but the Universe gives us what the soul needs, in every case, in every instance, at every moment. Understanding this will help you to find the meaning in your experience no matter how difficult it is.

There is a difference between pain and suffering. Pain is merely pain, but suffering is pain with meaning. There is a reason for your suffering that is worthy of your suffering. Because it has meaning, your suffering is acceptable and it is endurable.

DiCarlo—How might this alignment be accomplished?

Zukav—Aligning personality with soul is done through responsible choice with the assistance and guidance of nonphysical guides and Teachers. To a five sensory personality, talk about nonphysical reality and nonphysical guides and Teachers is, literally, nonsensical. Five sensory personalities are still living their lives solely based upon the data that they receive from the five senses.

More and more people are now leaving behind the limitations of the five senses. Eventually, within the span of several human generations, all of humankind will be multi-sensory. That is how significant our evolutionary transition is. It is the transition from a five-sensory humanity that is evolving through the pursuit of external power—exploration of physical reality through the five senses—to a multi-sensory humanity that is evolving through the pursuit of authentic power—the alignment of the personality with the soul through responsible choice with the assistance and guidance of nonphysical guides and Teachers. This is transforming everything.

DiCarlo—What exactly do you mean by responsible choice?

Zukav—Responsible choice means making choices that create consequences for which you are willing to assume responsibility. Whenever you make a decision, and act upon that decision, you create consequences. The consequences that you create reflect the intention that you hold when you perform the action. Responsible choice requires that you become aware of your intentions. That requires that you become aware of all of the different parts of yourself. Many of these parts operate outside your field of awareness. In turn, that means that you must become conscious of everything that you are feeling. This is difficult because there is so much pain and fear in our world, but all of this is necessary in order to become authentically empowered.

You create consequences no matter what you choose. If you do not choose consciously, you do not create consciously. It's as simple as that. You create, but you create unconsciously. What you create unconsciously is what you have created in the past. If you do not choose to create consciously, you will continue to create the same painful experiences that you have created previously. You will continue to do that until, in this lifetime or another, you understand the origin of the pain that you are experiencing. Then you will change. The change will be thorough, complete, and permanent.

That could take a long time. It could take a lifetime. It could take more lifetimes than one. As we become multi-sensory, we enable accelerated spiritual growth. That is what consciousness provides—accelerated spiritual growth. You can look ahead at what you are going to produce if you create again in anger; if you create again in fear; if you create again in jealousy. You can decide that you want to create differently, and then set the intention to do that.

You have the ability, for example, to set the intention to create harmony—or at least not create further discord. You can *choose* to cooperate instead of to compete. You can *choose* to share instead of hoard. You can *choose* to revere Life instead of exploit Life. You can *choose* to be interested in and support the growth of others instead of exploiting others. All of these choices produce different consequences than the choices that you've been making in the past.

DiCarlo—So what do you mean when you use the word intention?

Zukav—Intention is the quality of consciousness that you bring to an action.

DiCarlo—You have commented that if you have a healthy personality, then you really don't know where the personality ends and the soul begins....Would you view this process of becoming multi-sensory as representing an expansion of our being so that as we live our life *as* our soul, that this becomes our primary identity?

Zukav—Yes! Yes!

DiCarlo—So the experience would not be one in which the person would feel as though he or she is submitting or surrendering to a higher, outside authority?

Zukav—It's becoming all that you are. There is no higher authority when it comes to your decisions. Only you can make them. As you become aligned with your soul, you become who you are. You fulfill yourself and those around you. You do not harm—it's not a part of your consciousness. You are a torch that has been ignited. You are a beacon that shines. You have no fear. You care for Life. You care for those around you. You care for the Earth. You revere Life. You value it simply because it is.

DiCarlo—I find it remarkable that what you would characterize as an authentically empowered human being, others have referred to as "a soul-infused human being."

Zukav—How beautiful. But is it really remarkable? These truths belong to the Universe. As we become multi-sensory, we will understand them more fully. We are in the process of creating a world that is based upon these understandings. These other people didn't make them up and I didn't make them up, either. They come from the Universe.

DiCarlo—How might this transition from external power to authentic power affect, let's say, our economic system?

Zukav—The transformation in the human species is changing all of its social structures, including economics. The economics in which current commercial activities are embedded is based on the assumption of scarcity and the orientation of exploitation. Economic theory assumes that it is natural for a significant portion of the human family to be in need, to be lacking the basic necessities of life, in addition to many things that are necessary for physical comfort.

This perception is contrary to the reality of the Universe in which we are living and growing. As we become multi-sensory, this becomes more and more evident. The Universe is compassionate and abundant. It is alive, wise and eternal. It provides what each soul needs at each moment.

To a five-sensory human all of that is nonsense. It doesn't relate to the five senses. To a multi-sensory human, it is apparent. Whatever economics we develop in our future, it will reflect the perceptions of the soul. The soul understands that this is an abundant Universe— the grass grows again every spring. We are always given opportunities to grow and to learn. If we don't make use of them, we are given others. Ask yourself, for example, how many times you have been given the opportunity to love and to be loved, and how many times you have squandered those opportunities. They will come again. That is the nature of the compassionate Universe of which we are a part.

There is no scarcity in this new perception, so whatever economics we will develop, it will be based upon the assumption of abundance.

Our current economics is oriented to exploit, to obtain the maximum and give the minimum. This is how investments are made. An investor is someone who invests as little as possible and hopes to obtain as much as possible.

The soul strives to give. It has special gifts, and in giving them an individual finds meaning. If you have no meaning in your life, if you do not know why you are alive, you are not on the path that your soul wants to walk. As you begin to move in the direction that your soul wants you to move, you begin to get a sense of meaning. When your life is alive with meaning, when you are excited every day about what you are doing, when you want to get up, when you want to be with people, when you have no fear, when you have forgotten to worry, when you are fully engaged with your life, you are moving in alignment with your soul. That is authentic power.

Souls have agreements with the Universe. We incarnate with sacred contracts. As we develop authentic power, we develop the ability to fulfill them—to give our gifts. Each of these ways of speaking is a different way of saying the same thing: we are now evolving through the pursuit of authentic power, the alignment of the personality with the soul—which means living meaningful, engaged, responsible, joyful lives. I am not speaking of work-a-holism. Beneath work-a-holism is fear, deep insecurity. Every attempt to build an empire is a reaching outward to fill a sense of powerlessness inside. That is our former evolutionary modality. Our new evolutionary modality is to become inwardly whole and healthy and secure.

The old economics which is based upon the assumption of scarcity and the orientation of exploitation will be replaced with a new economics that is based upon abundance and oriented toward contribution. This new economics is so different from our current economics that it is evident that we are in for a big change. That change is underway.

DiCarlo—As we shift from a five sensory species to a multi-sensory species, and as we recognize ourselves to be immortal souls first and physical beings secondly, and also as power shifts from being external to being authentic and inwardly derived, what effect will that have in business?

Zukav—The soul is that part of an individual which strives for harmony, cooperation, sharing and reverence for Life. As individuals begin the process of aligning their personalities with their souls they move towards these values. So every aspect of business would be effected.

DiCarlo—Well, let's consider leadership. How might leadership change as a result of the shifting perceptions and values you've mentioned?

Zukav—Leadership today is based upon the perception of power as external. A leader has more external power—more ability to manipulate and control—than others. A business leader can say, "Do this" and you must do it. If you don't, you'll lose your job, or your life will become miserable—or at least unpleasant. Maybe you'll lose a promotion, or a stock option. Leaders assume responsibility, and for this they are given the authority to direct the activities of others. When I went through infantry officer candidate school, I wore a patch on my shoulder that had a sword over the words, "Follow Me." That concept of leadership is not what individuals who are growing in authentic power gravitate toward or desire.

Leadership is a state of mind. If you have a need to build an empire or to dominate a market, you are driven by fear. But if you have an inspiration that excites you and fulfills you, one in which there is no fear, then you will move into your activities with joy, and you will attract other people who are similarly oriented. As you step forward, others of like interest will constellate around you. You will be the pole star that magnetizes their interests. They will align the parts of themselves that are interested in the same thing with you. Then, as a leader, you will support, coordinate, and nurture them. The people with whom you are working will be more important to you than the activity that has brought you together. Your activity is the means by which you have attracted one another.

This means that, as a leader, you will spend a lot of your time interacting, heart to heart, with fellow souls. In business now, all of this is excluded by intention. If too much concern is given to an individual, someone within the organization who is impatient for results—usually a leader—will say, "Let's get to the bottom line. This doesn't really have to do with why we're together." As you become authentically empowered, you become interested in Life. That means other people. So business will no longer be the arena in which primarily you strive to accumulate profit at any emotional cost. And, as we can see by looking at our global ecology, at great physical cost, too. It will become an arena in which you interact consciously with fellow souls for the purpose of mutual spiritual growth.

DiCarlo—How might decision-making change in business?

Zukav—Decision-making today is primarily an intellectual function. We use logic and understanding that originates in the mind. This logic and understanding is linear and exclusionary. That is, you cannot think of one thing without excluding others. You cannot understand something one way and understand it in other ways simultaneously. We are now developing a higher order of logic and understanding that originates in the heart. The heart is inclusive. It accepts. The intellect judges. The higher order of logic and understanding that originates in the heart comprehends nonlinear realities and simultaneous realms of truth.

All of this effects decision-making in all aspects of life, including business. It means that intuitive processes will replace intellectual processes as the main decision-making faculty in business, as in all other human activities.

DiCarlo—What will happen to the intellect?

Zukav—The intellect will not be discarded. A business executive may have a hunch about which area of activity to move into. Once she decides that, she can use her intellect. For example, she may have a hunch to produce a certain product, and then use market analyses to confirm that there is a receptivity for the product, and then use statistical quality control to produce it well. But the mind will no longer be the boss, the "leader" in the old sense. Decision-making will be intuitive. The logic and understanding utilized will be the higher order of logic and understanding of the heart.

Collective decisions will be made by consensus. This is inconceivable to the business community now. We cannot imagine an efficient organization that's run by consensus. That is because there is so much dissension and pain—which are the same things—in business today. So the ability to make decisions by consensus will require that an organization's environment be transformed into one of safety for all involved.

DiCarlo—Would all decisions be made collectively, or would there be some decisions that would be deferred to particular individuals within the organization, who have been given proper authority.

Zukav—Whether that happens or not would be a consensual decision. Every time someone writes a letter it does not have to be approved by other people. If you trust your colleagues, and you know in your heart that their intentions are to contribute to your good and to the good of the whole, then it will be easy for you to say, "Do what you know needs to be done." Later, if it doesn't work out, the appropriate part of the community can come together to understand what went wrong, or why it didn't feel good to everyone involved. This is quite different from a manager executing external power because he has seniority or political skills that have elevated him or her in the hierarchy of external power. In that case, there is no trust in either direction. There is simply the necessity to do what must be done in order to survive physically—to keep your job.

Imagine a work environment in which you *like* the people that you are working with. You are interested in who they are. You are interested in their children. You are interested in their spiritual partnerships. You like being with them. You like growing with them. It's not always easy but you know that the friction between you is what allows you to grow, and to recognize patterns of behavior within yourself that need to be released in order for you to grow spiritually, to become more whole.

In that context, imagine what a delight it is to work with and to accomplish projects with your colleagues. That is our future.

DiCarlo—Are there any other implications regarding the consequences of moving from being a five sensory human to a multi-sensory human? For example, how might the judicial system, government, and personal relationships be impacted.

Zukav—All of them are changing dramatically. The changes that are now underway in the business world and the changes that are underway in health, education, the military, science, art, law and every other human endeavor are parts of the same change. The changes that are underway inside millions of individuals now are also the same change. There is one change occurring, and all of these are different expressions of that change.

Changes in the way that you relate to your brothers and sisters, your spiritual partner, yourself as a male and to other males, or yourself as a female and to other females, are all parts of the same change.

DiCarlo—In talking with a number of individuals whom I've interviewed, there has been quite a variance in opinion as to when this shift from a five sensory species to a multi-sensory species might take place. Ken Wilber for example says he doesn't feel these changes will effect most people for another couple hundred years. Peter Russell on the other hand suggests that these changes are immanent.

Zukav—They are immanent from an evolutionary point of view. A hundred years is less than an eye-blink in terms of our evolution, but I think that they will happen faster than that. Look inside yourself, and you will see how fast change is occurring. Now try to understand what humans three generations from now will be like if this change continues or accelerates. Also, the change that is now occurring is nonlinear. As you open to your heart, you open to multiple realities in which nonlinear change is occurring.

DiCarlo—If someone were to come to you and say, "Why should I choose to develop into a multi-sensory human being?" what would you tell them?

Zukav—You are in the process of becoming multi-sensory, as are all humans. Humanity is becoming multi-sensory.

This transition is not yet complete, but within several generations, the human species will be very different than it is today. One of those differences will be that every human will be multi-sensory.

Being multi-sensory and being authentically empowered are not the same. To become authentically empowered requires that you align your personality with your soul. This is where the rubber meets the road. This is where intention and courage are often required. To align your personality with your soul means that you consciously strive for harmony, cooperation, sharing and reverence for Life. This can be difficult.

So to someone who says, "Why should I become a multi-sensory and authentically empowered human being?" I would say, "Humanity is becoming multi-sensory. It is not a matter of choice." To the question of why you should become authentically empowered, I would say, "To heal the pain in your life." This is not something that you have to do. You have free will. But you are a creative being and if you don't, you will continue to create unconsciously, and to experience the pain that you are experiencing now.

DiCarlo—How would you characterize the experience of authentic power?

Zukav—Joyful. Complete. Engaged. Fulfilling. The first time I experienced this was writing *The Dancing Wu Li Masters: An Overview of the New Physics*. I had never been interested in physics before, and I was not interested in it when I got invited to a weekly meeting at the Lawrence-Berkley Laboratory in Berkley, California, by a physicist friend of mine. I went because I wanted to see what scientists looked like.

I got so excited by what I heard there that I could scarcely contain myself, but I didn't understand what I heard so I returned the next week and the next. I started to read about physics, then I decided to share these things that were exciting me so much in the form of a book.

I asked some physicists if they would help me. They agreed, and I began to write. I was delighted in this activity. I was stimulated and fulfilled by it. At that time, I didn't have an income, so when I wasn't writing I was worrying about the rent. When I was writing, I entered a new domain of experience that I had not encountered before. I was gratified, fulfilled, and excited about what I was doing. It was fun.

DiCarlo—Did you find that your study of quantum mechanics has helped you to further understand a multidimensional Universe. Ken Wilber, in speaking about a quantum reality, says that quantum physics cannot tell us anything about the higher dimensions—you cannot extrapolate from the lower to the higher at all. Is there anything of value in quantum physics that helps when it comes to trying to intellectually grasp these higher realities?

Zukav—Yes, but they can't be grasped intellectually. That is why science has gone as far as it can go as it is currently structured. It is an empirical endeavor, which means that all that can be accepted as valid by science is that which can be consensually verified with the five senses. This has been the strength of science since its origin, but that is what now blocks its growth. Quantum physics is the pinnacle development of science. It leads us to the intellectual realization that consciousness is an aspect of physical reality, that the two can't be separated.

There are five major interpretations—and others that are not so prominent—of the quantum formalism. Some, such as the statistical interpretation, deny that consciousness is involved in subatomic phenomena. Some, like Wigner's interpretation, are based on the opposite point of view. Others fall between these two, or maybe they just fall elsewhere. But the point is, no one can discuss the quantum formalism without addressing the relationship of consciousness, or the lack of it, to the fundamental structures of quantum physics, namely, complimentarity and the uncertainty principle.

The answer to your question is, my study of quantum physics didn't directly lead to anything in *The Seat of The Soul*, but it was stimulating and it was fun. It was an exciting adventure to the limits of the intellect. Those limits, in my view, are represented by the quantum theory.

DiCarlo—Did something happen to you between *The Dancing Wu Li Masters* and *The Seat of the Soul* which allowed you to write so profoundly about higher realities of which we are a part?

Zukav—Yes, I discovered nonphysical reality.

DiCarlo—Was that the result of any intentional activity on your part?

Zukav—I didn't know at the time that there was such a thing as non-physical reality. But intentions of the soul operate at very deep places within us. You do your part by setting intentions consciously, to the best of your ability. That brings you into alignment with your soul, with your deepest sense of meaning, but not necessarily into alignment with what your rabbi, priest or President tells you.

DiCarlo—You have stated, "I am not a speculator. I know that we are immortal, and that we are wearing what our Native American brothers and sisters call an 'Earth suit.'" What has allowed you to possess such a strong conviction that we are more than our physical bodies?

Zukav—There's a difference between conviction and experience. Conviction is something that you need to have if you don't have experience. Having conviction can create an experience which will then let you know if your conviction is correct or not. I do not have a conviction that nonphysical reality exists and that we are part of nonphysical reality. I do not have a conviction that we are immortal souls and that we are part of a living Universe of physical and nonphysical beings. I do not have to be convinced of these things any more than you have to be convinced that oak leaves are green in the summer. Do you see? If you were blind, if you had no physical eyesight, and enough people told you that in the summer oak leaves are green, you would develop the conviction that this is so. But if you see it for yourself, you do not have to be convinced.

DiCarlo—So you are speaking about your own personal experience?

Zukav—Yes.

DiCarlo—Well could you elaborate upon what that experience has been like for you?

Zukav—I have these experiences because humanity is becoming multi-sensory and I am part of humanity. But the deeper answer is that these experiences and everything else come by grace. Life is a miracle at each moment. It is miraculous and I have no explanation for that.

DiCarlo—Frequently, you hear people remark that if we lived in a just world, then we wouldn't have illness, we wouldn't have atrocities against our fellow human beings. We wouldn't have war. How do you view these things from a multi-sensory perspective?

Zukav—The underlying question is, "Why is there pain in the world?" There is pain in the world because we create it. We have not yet learned to create otherwise; that is what we are learning. There is pain in the world in our relationships with each other, and these, by the way, are the vehicles through which we grow. There is no other way to grow except through your relationships to others. You cannot grow only through a relationship to a business or a career. Your growth depends upon your ability to interact with your fellow souls. You will not grow until you have the courage to enter into relationships with them.

This question is important because there is so much pain in the world. This has been our history until now. Human history has been the sequential recording of one brutality after another. You will know in yourself that you are striving for authentic empowerment when a part of you decides that it will not participate any longer in this brutality, that your life will contribute something else to the human experience, and you find a way to do that in your day-to-day interactions. These will cumulatively form the course of your life.

DiCarlo—Do you feel that we as souls have made the decision to come to this Earth plane intentionally?

Zukav—Yes.

DiCarlo—Well, why might we choose to experience a physical reality limited by our five senses?

Zukav—There are two reasons. First, we choose as souls to experience what we have created in the past but have not yet experienced. Whenever you act in the Earth school you create consequences that effect others. You will also experience these consequences, in this lifetime or another.

In the East this is called karma. In the West this is called the Golden Rule. This is a compassionate dynamic through which each soul learns, in the intimacy of its own experience and therefore learns how to create wisely. If you create something in the life of another person, and do not experience that yourself by the time you return home—leave the Earth school and return to the fullness of your soul—your soul will create another personality with another body and another intuitional structure and it will voluntarily enter the Earth school again in order to experience what it has created but has not yet experienced. This is not a punishment—there is no such thing. It happens because the soul, in its full wisdom, strives for ever-increasing wholeness and perfection.

An incarnation is planned with the loving assistance of nonphysical Teachers. Arrangements are made with other souls to create interactions within the Earth school. The outcome of those interactions is not known in advance because the soul does not know how its personality will respond to the opportunities that it has arranged for it.

That is where your free will comes into play. When you encounter difficult circumstances in this Earth school, you have the option to take things personally, to become angry and blame others. You also have the option to understand that every one of your interactions in the Earth school is meaningful, offers you potential for spiritual growth, and there is a karmic factor at work in all that you encounter. Therefore, when someone offends you, or does something that you do not agree with, you do not have to react with anger, judgement and vengeance. You can take a step back and understand that there is a lesson in this for you. This does not mean that you become a doormat to the world. It means that you choose your responses consciously and responsibly create what you desire to experience in your future.

The second reason that souls incarnate is to give *gifts*. When you are doing what your soul wants you to do, when you are giving your soul's gifts—your life fills with meaning, excitement and satisfaction.

So the two reasons that souls incarnate is to experience what they desire to experience within the Earth school and to give their gifts—to fulfill their sacred contracts with the Universe.

As we become multi-sensory we begin to understand this. We begin to appreciate how extraordinary the Earth school is and what a privilege it is to be in it. When you see this, you will walk the Earth with awe and gratitude.

Jacquelyn Small

Jacquelyn Small, MSS is the author of "Becoming Naturally Therapeutic" and "Awakening in Time." Another of her books, the "Transformers" has become a classic. Small is the former Director of Training for the Texas Commission on Alcoholism and Drug Abuse; and she served on the external degree faculty of the Institute of Transpersonal Psychology in Menlo Park, California, for four years. She currently sits on the Advisory Board for the National Council on Codependence. Her company, Eupsychia, Inc., is a healing and training center dedicated to bridging traditional and transformational psychologies.

DiCarlo—In your work you take a transpersonal view of psychology which means you recognize, accept and study the terrain of the human spirit and soul. How did you get started in this field and who are some of the pioneering psychologists who influenced you?

Small—I opened to transpersonal psychology before I knew the term even existed through the work of Roberto Assagioli.

DiCarlo—Who was he?

Small—Assagioli was the founder of a psychological school of thought called "psychosynthesis" which had as one of its objectives the harmonization and integration of all aspects of the psyche. He was a student of Freud who was born in Venice, Italy in 1888. He died in 1975.

There is an often told story about Roberto. At one point, Sigmund Freud asked him to bring psychoanalysis to Italy. Roberto replied, "Well Dr. Freud I would be deeply honored. However, you need to know that there would be things about psychoanalysis that I would have to change. Where your mansion has only a first floor and a basement, mine has a basement, a first floor, second floor, third floor, sunroof and an elevator."

I read that in an article written about Roberto in 1974. When I came upon that one statement it just struck me because I knew what he was talking about. I knew that we are both a spiritual essence, a Higher Self and a lower self or earthly ego—that when we are operating in life from pure "ego" we bring a lot of unhappiness upon ourselves because we get confused. But when we operate from the real truth and wholeness of our being, we tend to be magnificent creatures.

DiCarlo—In Western psychology there is virtually no mention of the soul? A rather incredible omission, wouldn't you say?

Small—Western psychology is based upon ego psychology. Unfortunately, even though the word psychology comes from the word, "psyche," which means "soul," Western psychologists really have not been very knowledgeable of the fact. They have focused their attention upon the ego, which is like studying the shell of an egg and not looking inside to discover the essence of the chick.

If you bring in a little Eastern thought about the energy centers called "chakras," you will realize each of us has seven different levels of consciousness that we are capable of experiencing while we, as consciousness, are in human form. Historically, ego psychology in the United States has studied the first three levels of consciousness—the physical body, emotions, and workings of the mind, which has been narrowed unfortunately to the intellect. What many psychologists don't realize is that beyond body, emotions and mind we have yet another level of consciousness which you might think of as the heart. When anything in your life upsets you, or you suffer a loss or go into a rage or have what is called psychological, "unfinished business," your heart activates and you go through deep, deep processes. When people block or deny these feelings, they get stuck in the heart. Their heart closes down. They can't feel and they can't process their material. They can't grow. Personally, I feel this is what causes so many cases of heart attack in our country. So many people have blocked emotions accumulated in their hearts.

Beyond these four levels are three additional ones, but you have to believe in an inner life before these higher, more expansive levels of consciousness are even recognized.

The fifth level of consciousness gives you the ability to use your imagination creatively, to decipher abstract concepts and bring them down into concretized thoughtforms.

The sixth level of consciousness involves a sense of compassion for all of life, for the whole. You stop being so egotistical and always concerned with yourself. I think of it is a shift from passion to compassion, from taking things personally to seeing the broader view.

The seventh level of consciousness is where you begin to live your deepest truth and embrace your spiritual will. When people come into that stage of consciousness, they become "transformers." If they walk into a room full of other people, their very presence begins to cause energy shifts to occur.

DiCarlo—A transformer? Could you explain what you mean by that?

Small—Transformers are people who are working on themselves and are beginning to develop profound insight from having consciously traveled the path of direct experience. They are not intellectuals. They are individuals who know about life through the wisdom of their own death and rebirth processes. They become excellent guides for others who are in trouble because they understand that through the continuous process of dying to some aspects of oneself and getting born to other aspects, we grow and evolve.

DiCarlo—What's the difference between reformation and transformation?

Small—The transformer is flowing through life, allowing you to be, and they don't ever view you through judgmental eyes, as needing to be changed. The reformer is always trying to change you because they have already got a preconceived notion of what's right. If you don't live up to their ideal, they have a way of either punishing you, making you feel wrong, or pulling away from you.

A transformer just doesn't view you that way at all. They simply meet you in the moment and because they see you from the "Bigger Picture," they know that you are a spirit in human form and that you've gotten caught in a condition, trapped in something that is scaring you, beating you up, or taking your energy. They will have a lot of compassion and complete acceptance for you because they have a great deal of understanding.

DiCarlo—It sounds like this might create sort of a "sacred space," a nourishing environment where something new can be born.

Small—Yes, that's exactly right. They create sacred space. Transformation just spontaneously happens to those whom you are with even though you aren't doing anything but being yourself. Some people are really afraid to be with me because they know if they come into my life things are going to move very swiftly. There's not going to be a lot of opportunity for resting on laurels. People have given me this feedback a lot over the past ten years.

DiCarlo—Can anyone be a transformer?

Small—Absolutely. But, *will* every one be a transformer? No. The reason for that is because to become a transformer you have to become deadly honest with yourself. You have to let go of playing ego games. You have to just stop all artificial behavior, like people-pleasing and doing things just because society says you should. You have to start thinking for yourself, willing to *be* yourself. You must be willing to recognize and own your own shadow, knowing that you are not always going to be positive and you are not always going to be perfect.

And a lot of people are not willing to let down their barriers. They won't come into the heart enough to do the work that a transformer has to do.

DiCarlo—So I guess you could say that the process of becoming a transformer is about being brave enough, courageous enough, to take what some would refer to as"The Hero's Journey?"

Small—Yes. It's like becoming a true philosopher. Plato said once that true philosophers make dying their profession. When I first read that I was very put off. I thought, "I don't want to be dying all the time." But I realize now what that means. We are always saying good-by to the parts of ourselves that we've finished. Unfortunately, a lot of people mistakenly think they are failing when they no longer have an interest in a thing. That's actually an indication that it's time to let go of something which has been completed. It's time to open to a place of vulnerability for awhile, to allow some new aspect of ourself to enter into our consciousness. We are always in that process of dying to "the lesser" to make room for the "greater."

DiCarlo—I suppose another part of this process involves healing our addictions and obsessions?

Small—You'll notice that when somebody first starts using something habitually, it never occurs to them that they are going to become addicted. They just start it because they enjoy it. It feels good. It's very innocent, really. I've never known anybody in my life that ever set out to become an addict. But to me, the underlying cause of all addiction is blocked creative expression.

DiCarlo—Really?

Small—Don't you agree? Addicts are usually people who possess a lot of passion and desire. They are all excited and turned on. They want to do something with their energy but because a way hasn't opened for them, or they haven't realized what their creative self is wanting to express, they do what the rest of society is doing. So some people reach for a bottle of wine. Others find somebody to fall in love with over and over again or chase people sexually. Others eat too much food, or get hooked on melodrama and crisis. Or they begin to unconsciously chase after fame and fortune, which builds stress and demands the instant relief chemicals can often bring. These are all ways that the ego acts when it is not aligned, when it is not able to express its own inner truth, its own inner wisdom.

I see addiction as a way of being stuck in the past through repetitive, self-destructive behavior. Going out to a bar every night and getting drunk. Hanging out with the guys and smoking cigarettes. Same old, same old. Robotism.

I also feel that there is a spiritual aspect to most addictions. And this especially applies to those individuals who use the consciousness drugs, like LSD and MDMA which is called "Ecstasy." These drugs tend to open the psyche and facilitate the experience of high, non-ordinary states. Many of these people are simply inwardly focused by nature. They're more at home in nonphysical reality and they look for drugs to take them "up and out." They don't quite trust that they can achieve these natural states through meditation or dedicating their life to service, or communing with nature or falling in love with an artistic expression. There are so many ways to do it naturally without having to use drugs. As Ram Dass used to say, "drugs will take you there but only for a visit. They won't let you stay."

I think most people who get addicted to certain aspects of life are really just searching for God. They are searching for mystical awareness. I think *everyone* is an addict, quite frankly.

DiCarlo—Why is that?

Small—Everybody I know is addicted to something. Starting with the skin we're all inhabiting. Try to take my identity away from me and I'll get real mad at you. There are so many addictions—some are just more subtle than others. The chemical addictions are the easiest ones to spot. People even get addicted to their ideas and beliefs and become extremely unwilling to change their rigid and dysfunctional points of view. Sometimes I think those are the worst addictions of all because they block growth.

DiCarlo—It almost seems as though in these cases the person resists because their very identity becomes enmeshed and intertwined with whatever it is they are addicted to—even a belief or concept.

Small—That's a beautiful way to say it. I hadn't thought of it that way but you're absolutely right. It's like you merge with something and it becomes the entire focus of your attention. Then you are all caught up with it and you don't know how to dis-identify. You're hooked.

DiCarlo—Do you feel human nature is intrinsically flawed as some theologians might have us believe?

Small—No, not at all. I am so sorry that religion has done that to us. Our intrinsic nature is spiritual. We are made of light particles. We have the ability, just as physics is showing us now, to manifest as both the particle, localized in time and space as the personality that we know so well, and also as the wave function, which is our spiritual nature. The law of complimentarity rules us. I am an ego in concretized, physical form, but I also can evaporate and be spirit. But spirit is not a belief or dogma. It's not religion. Spirit is an internal force that moves you towards the realization of your ideal. When we relax our ego-driven controls, we flow naturally toward what inspires us.

I go back and forth between being really "ego-ed out" and very much "Jacquie Sue"—being a plain ordinary human being just wanting what she wants when she wants it—and into a state in which I am much wiser, much more compassionate and expanded. I can't always do that at will, but I know that we are all made up of both spirit and matter. We are a "hybrid" species.

DiCarlo—Hybrid species?

Small—To be healthy individuals we must learn to honor our human nature and also honor the fact that we are spiritual beings and not try to be either/or. If I fall down in my consciousness and think I am just an ego, I get stuck in the muck. Every condition that I butt up against will start defining me—"I am a neurotic. I am a divorced woman. I am a basket case. I can't get it right." All those things we say and do when we are in a lower state of consciousness.

On the other hand, if I try to rise up out of my body and play like I am this exalted, enlightened woman who is really spiritual and not physical at all, then I move into a state which John Welwood defined as "spiritual by-pass"—I become so heavenly that "I ain't no earthly good." I am sure you've met people like that. They are always pretending to be positive. Everything is just so full of love and light all the time, but you don't feel as though you have touched a real person. And you have a little secret knowledge that if you ever did punch one of their buttons an overheated "shadow self" would come out. And in fact, you can bet it does behind closed doors.

DiCarlo—You've already alluded to the "lower self." What exactly is the lower self in terms of its nature and characteristics?

Small—The lower self is the ego, the self that's evolving on the earth. It has come through the mineral kingdom, the plant kingdom and now we're human. We're very earthy, and very animalistic. We have appetites. We have feelings. We have physical bodies that get wounded very easily. We are actually quite fragile as human egos. We feel separate, competitive, and often inadequate or lost.

Most of us are from dysfunctional families which means we've got some very core issues to deal with—with mom, with dad, with life, with self-image. So our little earthy self is made up of an ego nature that takes on a "persona" which means "mask" in Greek. It tries to live according to society's standards so that it won't get in trouble. It is a very basic structure called "personality." When I call it "lower self," I don't really mean that it is "less than" the Higher Self. It's just closer to the earth, very susceptible to destruction. It's concrete.

DiCarlo—Is the "ego"—which is a confusing term I realize since different people, both inside the field of psychology and outside the field, define it very differently—the same as the lower self?

Small—The ego is the lower self, yes. It is an instrument, form or vehicle inhabited by spirit, which is formless.

DiCarlo—In a lot of Eastern psychologies we get the impression that the ego is to be done away with. Is that your view?

Small—Not at all. In fact, I think that's a very dangerous philosophy. There is a lot of Eastern philosophy that I love, but that particular thought doesn't interest me. We have seen what people are like who have no egos. They are in back wards of state hospitals. They can't function in the world. The ego is living the earth life and it knows the ways of the outer world. It was born of a mothers flesh, it came through kindergarten and society's school system. It has taken on the masks that society has told it to wear according to the cultural and societal conditions it is born into. It is our consciousness turned outwardly.

And it's a very wise self. It's really our spirit in concretized form. However, we're living on a planet that is operating through the law of free will, which means, no higher consciousness, no higher energy, is allowed to come in and impact our consciousness unless we invite it in—whether it's an extraterrestrial from Venus or whether it's God Himself or Herself. So the bad news is we can be just an ego with no alignment or recognition of anything higher. We can cut ourselves off from our source. We can operate in the world through the laws of materialism, of limitation, of separatism, of sensation and of survival. We can live our lives locked into a sense of separateness and isolation, of only looking out for ourselves. We have that power. Unfortunately, some people do that without even knowing it. Some people even die saying to themselves, "Is that all there is?"

DiCarlo—Why should a person decide to evolve the ego, this lower, more earthbound aspect of their being?

Small—You have to build up an ego and it has to become integrated before you can die to it. You can't become "selfless" if you have never developed a sense of self. In terms of human development, we have to start out in life looking out for ourselves. We have to attend to and meet our own needs for a long, long time—for food, for shelter, for belongingness and for self-esteem. We have to learn to do that and it's a pretty egotistical way of living. You especially see this in teenagers. Not to put them down, because they're wonderful, but they are very, very "ego-centered" and usually this is because they are busy developing their sense of a personal self.

Once you have developed a strong ego and personality structure and have become identified with it, then you've got a foundation and the strength to go through the transformational process and experience more of your spiritual nature. And that transformational process is going to be chaotic at times because it's a "death/rebirth" process. If you don't have a strong ego, you will not be able to make it. People can shatter into fragments and become mentally ill.

DiCarlo—In *The Transformers* you make an intriguing statement, "The body knows, the soul knows, and only our intellects can lie." What do you mean by that?

Small—My body seems to be connected directly to spirit. For example, when you feel in love with somebody, your body just naturally responds, but if you try to make yourself be in love with someone, your body doesn't cooperate at all. It is something that we have no control over whatsoever. The intellect can do nothing about that and you can verify this by reflecting upon your own experiences.

The same with other things that repulse us or which draw us magnetically. The body does this on its own because it has a wisdom. And the body is always going to tell you the exact truth about how you really, really feel about something. You will have a "gut reaction."

The soul is the same way. The soul is your deepest, wisest Self. It's your essence, your core. And the soul just is. There's not one ounce of ego in the soul consciousness. The soul can be innocent and it can spontaneously dive into things that can get it into trouble. But it has no ulterior motive. It's light, it's love, it's joy. The soul wants to play, to dance, to experience life. It just is what it is. The soul lives totally in the moment. When it picks up a piece of paper, it starts to feel the texture of the paper and begins to get really into it. It gazes into a sunset, captivated by its beauty. It is totally caught up in whatever it is doing at the moment. And if you think about it, that's the way we love to be in life more than anything else—totally and intensely involved. And when we are in that state of consciousness there is no sense of time. You might think you have been sitting somewhere ten minutes and it's really been an hour. You think you've just started the book and you've finished it. These are the moments when we have gone into our soul consciousness. These are the times which are intensely gratifying.

The intellect is in between, and it serves as a bridge between our conscious and unconscious mind. It serves as a gatekeeper. The intellect will only let in so much soul power at once because the soul is light and it's terrifying to an ego that's not able to handle it. So our intellect serves as a filter and it will restrict our awareness to as much of reality as we can handle at any one time. The intellect is like a computer, very mechanical and always being programmed with information from what is already the past.

DiCarlo—With the soul being the one doing the programming?

Small—No, the lower self programs the intellect. The soul kind of bypasses the intellect and comes into the heart, where it primarily expresses itself through our true feeling nature.

The intellect is always drawing its knowledge from the past. It's like a little researcher and it makes a lot of mistakes because it is using the person's perception which is going to be distorted if there is a lot of unfinished psychological business going on all the time. Let me give you an example. Let's say I walk into the room and there is a woman sitting on my husband's lap. Immediately, I go into reaction and have a jealousy fit. My heart starts pounding. I feel angry, frightened and possessive. I later find out that this is my husband's sister, whom I have never met because she had been living abroad ever since I've known my husband. Of course, after learning this everything changes instantly. Well, that's how the intellect creates data. It's just looking around in the world, putting one and one together and sometimes getting five. It trucks along in life with this programmed information. And this is where we get our complexes. It's the basis of all dogma and rigid thinking. It's also where we get our false ideas about things.

Right now this world is so full of false ideas about how materialism is supposed to make us happy and frankly, it's all currently crashing and burning. The world is falling apart from allowing materialism to be our God. That's the way the intellect puts things together—"Oh, he makes $500,000 a year so he's happy." Well that's not necessarily the truth. Society's rewards are often earned just as we're losing interest. They don't fulfill us in the long run.

DiCarlo—Would you say that an attribute of the intellect is judgement, and how does that differ from discernment?

Small—The intellect bases its reality on the idea that we are just individual egos, which of course modern physics has disproven. Because the intellect sees each of us as disconnected, unrelated and separate, it thinks its job is to look out for our one ego. And it thinks in separatist ways—it analyzes, compares, judges, and it wants to be better than. It wants to be right. It wants to feel good about itself. And so it's constantly looking for ways to be the winner or to at least be "OK."

On the other hand the Higher Self mind, which operates from a very expanded state of consciousness, sees whole patterns. It thinks in terms of the whole, not the part. It might move in and dissect something for a minute, but it won't get lost in it. It can pull back out and see the whole picture, putting all things in their proper perspective. In Eastern thought, it's called "Big Mind."

Let me give you an example of these two different kinds of mind: the lower self intellect might be a scientist who is studying anxiety by measuring blinks of the eye—a very specific means of collecting data. On the other hand, a philosopher who is thinking about the nature or meaning of one's anxiety and, coming from Higher Self consciousness, would know that no matter how many times your eyes blink per minute, that information is not going to be very helpful. It's going to see that little research study as a fragment of a much bigger picture. So we are constantly shifting I think, from third to fifth level consciousness, from lower self to soul in our minds. As we grow and evolve and learn from our experiences, we begin to take on more and more aspects of our higher mind. It's so beautiful because when we live from higher mind, we don't get so caught up in all the little ups and downs of day-to-day life. We are not so reactive.

DiCarlo—You have spoken of our "core issues" and I am wondering if you can define what a core issue is?

Small—There are so many levels to that question. I think that we only have three or four core issues in our entire lives, and we keep enacting them over and over again. They are usually referred to as "complexes" in psychology. I have two core issues, two patterns that are very strong in me. And I can see that they are interconnected. One deals with relationships. The other involves a disbelief in rebirth. I have had two miscarriages, a stillborn and I have a chronically ill son, who was born with sugar diabetes. I almost died at birth and my mother miscarried twins when I was six years old, and I thought it was somehow my fault.

There's a thought pattern behind this core issue which I think relates to my own near death as a newborn. I was a 7-month, four-pound, premature baby. I barely made it. I think the thought I encoded into my belief system from the very beginning was: "babies die," "people don't make it," "relationships die," "death wins out in the long run."

I have gone through a whole process of dealing with death so that I can learn that there is something beyond death. When I was twenty-nine I had a clinical near-death experience. I was out of my body for a while, looking down upon it from above the hospital bed saying calmly to myself, "You don't want to go back into that body do you? That body has had it." But when my thoughts turned to my son who was eight years old at the time, I felt compelled to return. He didn't know how to take care of himself. It was my compassion for my son that brought me back.

Through this experience I had a wonderful opportunity to know that there is no such thing as the death of the individual. There are only shifts of consciousness to other states of being. In that next state beyond where I am now, my body dissipates and I just become space. Using the language of the new physics, I am dissolving my particle nature and I am moving into a wave function. But I am still consciousness and I am still the same consciousness. I can dialogue with myself and with others, even when I am out of my body.

I know from my own experience that when I was up there speaking from the ceiling of the hospital room, I was speaking as my Self—the capital "S" Self—the soul. And I was seeing that Jacquie was lying there on the bed hemorrhaging to death. She had already lost two babies; she was losing another one. She wanted to die. She was still very young. She was obviously not very happy because she was trying to leave all the time. She had not yet found her Self.

After that experience I internally received information that told me to stay in my body. That I was here for a reason and I would be guided. I had a mission and a purpose that manifested as a vision. This mystical experience changed my life.

So one of my core issues has been this idea of death. I always wanted to be right at death's door and I think that was because on a deep level I was wanting to learn about life.

DiCarlo—Ken Wilber talks about thanatos, the death, dissolution and transcendence urge and eros, the urge of life and self-perpetuation....

Small—I believe it now because I experienced it. We have to continuously be stepping out of our old skin, "making dying our profession," if we are to grow. And right now, as one Humanity we're stepping out of one big, huge, "human soul skin" and we are moving into a new dimension of consciousness.

The other core issue involves, as I have said, relationships. I have a pattern of co-dependence, of always looking for the perfect man to "do my life for me." I was going to be more like the sidekick. When I look at all my relationships, they have all been absolutely perfect for me and for my partner. But what happened every time is that we just grew to the end of it, and grew away from each other. I now have the insight that I've never really believed relationships can make it, either. So hopefully, this pattern is healing.

If you allow the law of attraction to draw you, if you allow yourself to be pulled by your bliss rather than deciding from the intellect whom you should mate with, you will find that you are exactly with the partner you need to be with at the time. It may not need to be a marriage. It may just be a love affair. Or it may be a real close friendship or a business partnership. Sometimes we have to go through the trials of a relationship to find out what is our right-relationship. Sometimes the role or label we put on a relationship mis-identifies it.

DiCarlo—Let's talk for a moment about desire because I think it's an area of confusion for many people. Eastern philosophies would seem to suggest that our desires cause suffering and should be extinguished. On the other hand, we hear people such as yourself and Joseph Campbell saying, "Follow your bliss." What's the proper role of desire in your view?

Small—First of all, I think the terminology has caused some confusion. When Easterners talk about desires, they are really referring to addictions and obsessions, the cravings of our lower self. The inherent desire of the soul, which is expressed through our lower nature, is ultimately a yearning for wholeness. It is a yearning that is called "pothos" in greek. It's a yearning for the beloved, a longing for your true partner. It's the yearning for knowing you are completely settled into your life's work and true purpose for being.

Your desire nature is always moving you towards fulfillment of your ideals. It leads you to God. So I say it is very important to stay in touch with your desires. But if your desires are distorted and begin moving you towards self-destructive, addictive and self-defeating behaviors and activities, then you're going to mess up your energy for awhile which will really slow you down in your growth. Sometimes I think we deliberately choose something dysfunctional to slow us down or send us off course because we start moving too fast. Or because, for some reason, we need the lesson this dysfunction will provide.

DiCarlo—So you don't think it's wrong to desire material things in life, such as a nice car and home?

Small—Not at all. In fact, I have an Infinity J30 which I absolutely adore! I buy cars about every five years and I like them to stay in perfect condition so I don't have to worry about them. I am not mechanically oriented and I do a lot of traveling by myself. So I think material objects like that should be in your life to help support you by providing convenience and comfort. That way you won't have to be constantly focused on fixing a leaky radiator, or having to worry about an air-conditioning system that doesn't work when the temperature is 110 outside. It's wonderful to have a material life that will support your spiritual goals and the intention that you are really here to serve.

What's "wrong" would be if you *had* to have it. You have to be willing to throw away your material life in a heartbeat if it's in the way of something more essential. And I've done that before. I was married to a man who was a multimillionaire, so I know how to live with a lot of money. But I have also lived on $400 per month with a sick child and no automobile to drive and that was one of the happiest periods of my life. I think I have resolved the dichotomy between affluence and lack of wealth.

DiCarlo—So in your view, what makes the difference is whether or not an individual is "attached" to material things, to borrow an Eastern philosophical concept.

Small—Yes, the real issue is the extent of your attachment to the material life. If you make decisions based on greed, or want too much luxury, or put yourself into debt financially just so you can have a lot of goodies, then you are letting the lords of materialism become your god and rule you. That kind of life always leads to misery.

DiCarlo—Isn't there a misconception that being "unattached" in life means that you don't care?

Small—Yes. There's a huge misconception around that issue. But actually, I think that misconception comes from something we've seen modeled by people who hold themselves out as spiritual authorities. People who get on spiritual paths prematurely, before they have worked on some of their ego issues, get into the state of "spiritual by-pass" that I mentioned earlier. They walk around as though they are really aloof and removed—kind of "above" it all. I think a lot of that type of energy has given us a basic misunderstanding of how spirit moves through this reality. People tend to equate the spiritual life with becoming uninvested in the ordinary. Some who claim to be "on the path" even abhor any focus on the ego life, viewing it as "bad" or "sickening," while claiming a higher life of "oneness" as their station in consciousness. This is dualism—not oneness.

I think because we are living in a dualistic universe, where everything has become concretized, there is a sense of "otherness" here. I can reach out and touch a chair. This chair seems very different from me. And this is the reality we are living in. Consequently, I think it is very important to be in our bodies, and to be fully involved with life. To really be willing to commit to being here. The wonders of planet earth are just truly amazing. This is an incredibly gorgeous place to be! It's unbelievable. I am really sad that people think the spiritual life means that you rise above it all and you no longer see the beauty here or even care.

Attachment involves getting hooked on outcomes and expectations. It's an ego thing. It is not a Higher Self state. If I have become attached—let's say to my mate—in a jealous, possessive way and I feel as though I own him, look how I am going to behave. I am going to act in a way that is going to make me less than proud of my reactions. So attachment is the exact opposite of love. It's paradoxical because we tend to think of attachment as meaning you are really close and intimate with someone. But attachment blocks intimacy. It blocks *true* intimacy.

DiCarlo—Let's talk at greater length about the Higher Self. Based upon your experience, what would you say is the nature of this aspect of ourselves?

Small—To use an analogy, the Higher Self is really more an artist than a scientist. It really doesn't care if it is validated empirically. It just wants to express. It is full of life, full of creativity, full of joy. It is loving whatever is happening in the moment. Even if it is something "negative" it can honor the fact that both positive and negative are part of life.

I am quite Jungian in my approach to the Higher Self. I think of the Higher Self as being the Self, with a capital "S." I think of it as the archetype of the human being, meaning it's our highest and truest design that we are growing into and it's also the origin of our species. The Self is both the Alpha and Omega of humanity.

DiCarlo—Wait a minute... does that mean that your Higher Self is identical to my Higher Self?

Small—Yes, at the highest levels. But we each have an individualized soul, or higher nature which is fundamentally united to all of humanity, and even beyond. Remember, it is "both/and." We are both individual and "the field," or group soul.

We experience our Higher Self when are able to express our natural wholeness. These are the times when we are not fragmented and acting out of some subpersonality with a selfish need that it has to resolve in the world.

The Higher Self, coming from our pattern of wholeness, tends to live from the "bigger picture." It possesses a creative imagination—meaning that its thoughts are creative—and it knows it. It takes responsibility for how it thinks. It is full of inspiration, so it is a very passionate, "in-love" kind of nature. It falls in love with everything since it sees the beauty of all of God's creation and beyond. It also has the ability to have incredible spiritual insight, meaning that it can receive through direct knowledge the actual will of God. It can walk around in the world as a representation of the will of God. Now that would be someone who is totally aligned with their Higher Self.

The Higher Self, if you want to think of it this way, is our bridge into our spiritual nature, which you cannot even define as a "self" because the minute you say self you have already given it some sort of limitation. So the Higher Self is like a mediator between spirit and matter. That's how I think of it. The Higher Self to me, is the one Soul of Humanity.

DiCarlo—Does the "Higher Self" refer to the "observer self" that psychologists sometimes refer to?

Small—The "observer" is a function of the Higher Self. From its standpoint, it can observe the bigger picture. You can think of it as being "above," or "bigger than," or "more expanded than." Again, if you want to use an analogy from modern physics, it would be more like the wave function than the particle. It is pure, undifferentiated Light, Love, Intelligence.

It's light, it's energy, it's vibration. It's experienced through sound, color, music, movement, flow—those are all words that pertain to the Higher Self. The Higher Self is not "in-formed," meaning it's not in form. It's energy. It is an energy matrix, or scaffold, that formulates matter into an individual. It is an archetype.

Another apt metaphor to use here would be to think of the cross. The ego lives on the horizontal arm of the cross and the Higher Self lives on the vertical dimension. The horizontal is the outer world, and the vertical is the inner life. It's interesting because our consciousness is constantly moving up and down on the vertical dimension. It doesn't go out ahead of us or lag behind us because it's not in time. It's beyond time. So consciousness is always <u>now</u>.

We need to always be conscious of what we are saying "I" to because, I don't know about you, but my identity moves up and down on the vertical arm. There are times when I'm just very stuck in my lower self and ego. I'm trying to get some fragment of myself glorified, you know, almost to the exclusion of anyone else's happiness. I've gotten hooked on something. But there will be times when I can rise above it and see the bigger picture. I can clearly see what it is that I am doing. My emotions or moods sometimes go up and down.

Right now, I might be speaking to you from my Higher Self, but you could say something that threatens me and I might drop down into an ego stance. If we had a little Geiger counter you and I could measure how we relate to each other as we engage in dialogue. We are probably going up and down in various dimensions, but I would say we are basically staying between three, four or five in our consciousness because we are coming from the heart. There is no past history between us so we don't have any anger and we don't have any issues. We don't have any unmet needs driving us to try to get something from each other. We have a very clear relationship because it's a new relationship. So we can stay pretty much in the heart and then we might drop into our concrete mind and think a little bit, and then we might move up into a higher dimension and come up with an abstract principle.

DiCarlo—What you're saying is significant I think, since there's a tendency to think of the Higher Self as being foreign and distant—separate from us—when in fact you express that Higher Self consciousness on a daily basis, even if only for moments at a time.

Small—Yes, because above and beyond the Higher Self would be what those in the addictions field would call the Higher Power. And that's just like a socket you plug into. You can't really give it a form. It's very much like ancient Judaism which says you can't name God. You get to a place where it's way too abstract and the minute you start trying to name it or put a label on it you limit it. I think of that as more of a Higher Power.

The Higher Self allows me to personify my spiritual nature in a way in which I can idealize it, think about it in my mind and start making it real. If I am really willing to focus on it and invoke its qualities, I can literally start becoming a living representative of that Higher Power in my life. Then people start calling you teacher, or they say, "you are representing an archetype." You have to be careful. As you begin to attract people to you, which happens when you begin to express your Higher Self a lot, you have to know the responsibility that's involved. You are more influential than you perhaps realize, so you have to be careful about the words you use and the things you do and be willing to take complete responsibility.

DiCarlo—It sounds as though the lower self and the Higher Self are motivated by different things. Can both of these aspects of our nature be aligned?

Small—Yes, the two can be aligned. In fact that's happening to a lot of people right now. People are awakening to their soul consciousness. The soul comes into this reality through a mental process we call "recognition."

DiCarlo—What do you mean by that?

Small—Actually it means "re-cognition." So it means memory. The minute that I start realizing that I am a soul in human form, everything changes and my soul consciousness comes alive in me. It always has been, but I just didn't notice it before. Now I have noticed it; it is a conscious aspect of my experience. I begin to learn about the soul's qualities—the soul just *is* quality actually. That's the definition of the soul, it's qualities such as inspiration, imagination, joy, celebration, light, play, spontaneity, deep compassion, hope, and faith. The soul is really not a thing, it is our essence, our "flavor."

The soul desires to manifest here on the earth through our physical forms. Our souls are wanting to spiritualize matter. What that means in ordinary language, is that we are learning how to bring the good, the true and the beautiful through in all our relations and in all our activities.

DiCarlo—Learning to bring through the "good," the "true" and the "beautiful"—I like that. Would you say that large numbers of people are going to be able to do just that during this period of our collective history?

Small—Yes, I think we are shifting away from fear consciousness to a consciousness of love and compassion. We are shifting from separatism to more of a unified wholeness. I think we are realizing now that we are not individual countries, that we are all living on one globe. Television and the media have helped us to realize that we just can't separate off from each other as we've done in the past.

And yet because we are both an ego and a soul, we also have a right to have a personal life. We have a right to our privacy. We have a right to make our own decisions and choices and to honor each others individual nature while at the same time recognizing our right relationships with each other as soul brothers and sisters. Ultimately, we're all here for one reason and that is to bring spirit into the material world. And the only way we can bring spirit into the material world is by becoming it. It's so exciting I don't know why anybody would be interested in anything else!

DiCarlo—Someone else has described this project as bringing a fifth-dimensional reality which theosophists would say is the reality in which our souls reside, into the third dimension, the physical reality we know so well.

Small—It is! That's exactly right, that's exactly what it is. It's moving into a totally new dimension of consciousness which has a whole different set of rules. You know, it's not all the same gameboard.

The material world on its own has no meaning until we put meaning into it. We are the meaning makers. And we can walk around blind and unconscious and not give anything meaning. We can say there is no God and we can say there is no meaning or purpose to anything here, that this all is just one big giant mistake. And that can be our reality. And I think that's what happens to some people who commit suicide. They decide, "There's no meaning in life—I'm outta here." I can see how people might arrive at that state if they are solely looking outward.

DiCarlo—How does the Higher Self relate to the lower self?

Small—The Higher Self will move in and overshadow the ego when the ego starts running to the edge of its own demise. That is happening now by the way. Our materialistic world which is based on third level, lower self consciousness is no longer working. Yes, there are parts of it that are working and there are parts of it that should be honored, but there are other parts of the man-made world that just aren't working. Our technology is running too far ahead of human consciousness. We have gotten so good at making machines, and yet our consciousness has not caught up with our abilities as technicians.

So the way I see it, and the way I experience it in my life, is that we as a human species may go along for quite a while, just doing what the ego needs. We are building machines and we are making better houses and we are learning how to till the soil better. But then all of a sudden this machine called materialism just starts outrunning everything. I think that just as we get to the place where we are just about to die, we come to the end of the cycle, the Higher Self moves in and begins to send us dreams and visions. We feel it as a calling. Don't you meet people all the time who tell you they are hearing an inner call?

DiCarlo—Sure.

Small—Where does that come from? Isn't that a thrill to know that there is someone inside of us that does all of that? I just love it. So I think the Higher Self watches.

In my work I use the myth of "psyche" and "eros"—or the Adam and Eve story— to explain this. We start out as abstract spirit and there's no way to define us. We're just "The All." As we start having lifetimes in the physical world, we take on a soul, and the soul splits itself into two aspects, two lovers, Psyche and Eros. Eros is the masculine principle who stays spirit and refuses to come down into the world because he says it's too dangerous. So Psyche does come down to experience life in the physical world. Psyche is the feminine aspect of the soul, and she just moves right on in to the earth. She takes on the whole thing. She marries death. She accepts the pain and suffering of childbirth, which practically destroys her body. She just absorbs experiences which she willingly does for her lover, Eros. And at some point she seeks to unite with Eros again. And Eros will swoop down and take her back into Mt. Olympus, which is the collective unconscious mind. It's a beautiful story.

And so I think the soul is dual, both masculine and feminine.

DiCarlo—Some people I have spoken with have espoused the idea that the soul communicates through the conscience and I often wonder if they are not actually receiving the messages from their own internalized parent.

Small—When I think of conscience, I immediately think of something like, "Uh, oh, I am feeling guilty about something" or I am feeling ashamed. If you switch to the word consciousness, then that removes some of the misconceptions. Conscience is more what Freud would call the superego. When we are listening to our "conscience" we get hooked through 'should's'—"I should do this because my father said so" or "I should do this because the church says so" or whatever. That's not what I think of as the true, inner Self. What you are listening to is coming from the ego.

DiCarlo—Why would the soul choose to have a human experience in your view?

Small—Here is my way of seeing it: The soul is God's agent. God decided he was bored and lonely being the "All" because there was no other to play with. So God made a creation planet so he could perform the play of consciousness. I say "He," because to me, the "Feminine" God is down here in the world, and the "Masculine" God is up there in the ethers. Feminists get mad at me when I say "He" but it's the masculine principle that's in all of us I'm speaking of.

I picked up this idea from psychologist Carl Jung: God is antinomous. The Law of Antinomy is two complimentary opposites living harmoniously within the whole. God is both masculine/feminine; God is both the darkness and the light; God is both the created and the uncreated. So God, as whole, contains a dualism. But interestingly, the dual nature of God doesn't struggle against itself. These aspects don't war with one another. They accept each others nature as being contrary, and they love their contrariness because contrariness is the friction that creates matter. You can't have a creation if you don't have a masculine and a feminine, or some kind of "two-ness." So why did the soul come to earth? Because God decided to spread out his whole creation and make it something "other" so he could interact with it.

So the soul is down here experiencing the play of consciousness. It's waking us up—as us—so we can interact as spiritual beings in human form. What a world this is going to be when we all realize that we *are* spiritual beings in human form.

DiCarlo—Could you explain what the essence of the transformation process is as we fundamentally shift from a lower level of consciousness to one that is higher, with its more expansive world view?

Small—It involves the death and rebirth sequence.

DiCarlo—And what's dying?

Small—The old ways of being that you have outgrown and which, for whatever reasons, no longer work. They are no longer operational. They're either too limited, too outmoded, or no longer necessary. Complete. It could have been something dysfunctional that never worked which you've decided to drop. You just lose interest. Or it's something you've been cycling in that you have finished.

DiCarlo—Through your experience in working with many others, have you been able to identify any stages in the process?

Small—Yes. The first stage of the transformational process is the taking on of something that's later going to be transformed. You are unconscious of this in the first stage. You just embrace it. Let's take a new relationship as an example. You're madly in love with your partner and everything about them is wonderful. You don't see any shadow in them at all and it seems that you've found the perfect person. It's the perfect love and you're going to get married and live happily ever after. Carl Jung called this being involved in a "participation mystique." It's what Ken Wilber would call the "pre-conscious state"—it's the state of innocence. You are completely absorbed in the experience, with no part of you separating off to observe or critique it.

After awhile, you begin to see that there are a few problems: "Uh-oh, this person isn't perfect after all. They have a temper; they don't know how to make money; they're too dependent." And then you begin to get a little bit worried that things are not going to be as idealistic as you previously thought. You've opened up your eyes. Many times this second stage of transformation gets blocked because there is the tendency to avoid dealing with the imperfections. You don't want to make waves, you don't want to cause any trouble, you want to try to put it back to that original state of bliss. You want to stay in a state of denial. According to our work, you go into a pattern that we call "second birth matrix," based on Stan Grof's model of the psyche. It's the stage of the birth process (in our analogy the transformation is like being born into another state of being) where the mother's body has gone into labor but the baby doesn't know what to do yet and the birthing process hasn't really begun. There's just constriction, pain and confusion and the baby's vital forces are being cut off every time the mother's body has a contraction. It's a time when your path is blocked and anger and rage is just starting to build which will help propel you through the obstacles. It's the stage of transformation everybody hates and people call it "getting stuck." They just say, "I'm stuck. I don't know what's coming. I don't know where I'm at. I feel hopeless." It's a 'no exit' feeling.

DiCarlo—Would you say that that's the point of maximum tension between the higher and lower self. We want to bring forth the best in ourselves but we also want to play the game by the rules of our lower nature and that's a no-win situation. This creates excruciating tension and conflict since we're sort of at war within ourselves.

Small—Yes. Absolutely. And interestingly, this is the stage where a lot of people get depressed. Many people think that depression means that you have no energy and that is not true. Depression means that you're "re-pressing" your energy—you're like a pressure cooker. Depression is extremely hard on us because it is not a passive and neutral state. You've got the new coming towards you and you've got the old still trying to hold on and the two forces start mulching each other, which seems like a state of no energy but in truth, you're sitting right in the middle of the tension of these opposites. At some point the birth process is going to take over and catapult you through the birth canal and on into the third stage of transformation where you are actually changed from an underwater creature to one who breathes air.

DiCarlo—Now, would the point between the second and the third stage, the point of feeling blocked and depressed and the beginning of the transformation to a new state of being, involve surrendering to one's Higher nature after bottoming out, as frequently happens in the addictions field?

Small—It can be. It can also involve a lot of struggle and resistance. People eventually have to surrender because if a person keeps struggling and resisting the changes, some horrible thing will eventually happen. I hate to say that, but it's true. A person will get fired, somebody will get killed, they'll develop a bad disease, or they'll suffer a public humiliation. This is the sacred purpose of the human shadow and that's a very important point. When we try to deny and deny and deny something that's trying to change in us because our soul has determined it, and when our ego resists, many times the shadow will create an event and act out through us in a way that forces us to change. We hit bottom and this humbles us and opens us up. We surrender to the changes which are occurring naturally.

An example: you might be in a very important business meeting with people you are wanting to impress. You're sitting there in the meeting and all of a sudden you burst into a temper tantrum. You show your 'true colors,' the part of you that you wanted to hide.

I was an adoption worker for awhile, interviewing possible adoptive mothers. They would try so hard to prove to you that they were mentally and emotionally stable but sometimes, halfway through the interview a woman would burst into tears or scream at her child in an abusive manner. And later, they go, "Oops, how did that happen?"

I think the shadow will take us all the way to the end of something to allow us to complete it and move on. You might continue to remain in a relationship that's dead and you're trying to play like it's not dead. You're trying to appease your partner when really it's a lie and all of a sudden the shadow will pop right out and you hear yourself telling your partner, "I'm in love with another woman" or "I don't love you anymore" or "I want to leave." At the same time you're thinking, "God, who's saying this—I didn't even mean to bring this up this morning."

DiCarlo—So, the shadow would contain all the feelings and thoughts you have repressed and chosen not to express?

Small—Yes, the repressed self is loaded with all those stuffed feelings and comes right out and exposes the denied part. It just tells it like it is, and in a way it's a blessing because it gets it all right out on the table and you're no longer dealing with an unconscious process. An unconscious process is the most dangerous thing we could have going.

DiCarlo—What's the third stage of the transformation process?

Small—The third stage of the birth process always involves a lot of chaos and confusion. That's the stage when you really do leave your job—you really do leave the old life. You've lost your money supply or you've lost a relationship and for awhile you don't know what's going to happen. You really don't know how things are going to turn out. The new way hasn't opened yet so you are in the chaos of a whole lot of change and yet you don't feel much reward. You feel very small, and completely vulnerable and raw.

DiCarlo—And the final stage?

Small—In the fourth stage, the new life just sort of lands in your lap. Suddenly it's here—you get that new job or you meet that new person. The next right step for you has opened up. You have a dream, you have a vision, you discover a passion. Something happens and suddenly you look around and say to yourself, "Wow! It's here." You've stepped out onto the new life. It seemed to happen while you were looking the other way. Yet you can look back and see that you participated in setting it up behind your own back.

When we walk into the new life—which is the rebirth stage of transformation—we are in a state of bliss and we absolutely *know* that we are the Self. We know that we are a spiritual being in human form. At this stage we often have a peak experience.

DiCarlo—Would that be the point where the person would realize, "I have a body but I am not my body. I have emotions but I am not my emotions. I have a mind but I am not my mind."?

Small—Yes, you can see that you are in the world and you are not of it.

DiCarlo—And what happens to our earthbound personality, the lower self, during this process?

Small—The lower self is gradually integrating into the bigger self and it's bringing the wisdom of its past and its birth experience with it. It's bringing the wisdom and knowledge of the senses too. We're going to carry the essential quality of the ego nature into the 5th-dimension, so we can actually *experience* Being.

DiCarlo—So our individuality would, in fact, be maintained?

Small—Yes, but it's also permeable by the whole, but we don't care. We just all love each other so much and we're so harmonious that if I pass through your whole body or you pass through my whole body, it just feels like bliss. We are not competitive or protective—there's nothing to protect because we all know that we are aspects of the One. It's a delightful play of particles and waves. It's just an incredible consciousness. I've experienced it in altered states. It's hard to maintain when you are in your conscious, ego aware state.

DiCarlo—Would you say that in the transformation process, then, a person learns to stabilize their life around their divine and eternal spiritual essence rather than transitory and external forms of the physical world they may have unknowingly identified with as part of who they are?

Small—Yes, I think that they learn to "stand in the light of their own being." The way that I experience that, which is so beyond words, is that I'm just operating in the moment spontaneously, not having to think about what I'm doing or being because I just *am*. One moment passes into the next moment into the next moment and nothing feels like an interruption.

DiCarlo—Kind of a "flow state" that has been described by researchers?

Small—I guess that's what I am describing. I'm not really aware that I'm me. I can stop anytime and notice if I want to, but I'm just not choosing to. I'm experiencing myself more as an energy flow.

And time is irrelevant during those periods because that particular consciousness state is beyond time.

DiCarlo—Would you say that in those states you're actually manifesting as your Higher Self?

Small—Yes. Or you might want to say "whole" Self rather than "higher" Self. Whole self because I'm still in an ego body and if you meet me on the sidewalk you're going to see me and recognize me and I'm going to have the personality traits of Jacquelyn Small with certain characteristics, certain behavior patterns that are recognizable and that make me unique. So, I'm not just a lower self, I'm a whole self. But this consciousness level is beyond egoistic.

DiCarlo—Meaning, perhaps, a preoccupation with the personal self?

Small—A narcissistic urge to have my needs take precedence over someone else's.

DiCarlo—Well, what would you say then is the "price of admission?" What must we be willing to pay if we are to go through this process of transformation and realize these higher states of being?

Small—You have to be willing to die to all places where you are still trying to be separatist, competitive, better than. Let me tell you, the shift from ego dominance to essence dominance is quite a rough one. We don't even know all the ego attachments we have until we're confronted with the possibility of loss. Suddenly, we're grabbing onto something that we didn't even think mattered. As a result we have a process to go through. People don't like to hear this, but if you're wanting to undergo a transformation as opposed to incremental growth—meaning that you're willing to really move at an accelerated

pace into a whole new state of consciousness—you've got to be w
to go through an upheaval in "fast-forward" speed. In Christ's words,
you must "lose your life so you will find it." For the Buddha, it was
letting go of all attachment.

There's chaos connected with transformation because it's operating
through the three laws of creativity which are "thesis," "antithesis,"
and "synthesis." You're going to spin through those stages and the
antithesis side hurts. It's saying good-bye to what cannot be contained
within "the new." It's letting go. It's dying to. Most of us have a huge
number of control issues. We've been very well trained by mainstream
society to try to be in control of everything and to have to let go of
control is not such an easy thing to do. Essentially it's about making
the shift from thinking "you" were living life to suddenly realizing life
is living *you*! It's a dedication to service.

DiCarlo—What would you say is the ultimate goal of the transformational process? Is it some sort of perfection, of moral sensibility and
uprightness?

Small—Through this process we're growing into our completed archetype. There's a design for the perfect human being and "perfect" just
means completed. The completed human being is going to operate
through the law of antinomy, of complimentary masculine and feminine energy, just like creator God in whose image we are made. When
we are completed as a human being, we're not going to look like an
angel floating ten feet above the earth. We're still going to be a human being. We are going to be fully human, with an open heart.

I feel that for a lot of us, our time of completion has come and we're
being called to stand tall in the archetypal Self. I think that Jesus
modeled that for us. I think the Buddha did too. And Shiva/Shakti—
and all the World Teachers. There have been quite a few on the planet
who have demonstrated for us what it means to be a fully enlightened
human being. As a result of doing this, at some point they pass on into
higher dimensions of reality. We don't experience them in the flesh
anymore but we experience their wisdom and energy.

DiCarlo—Would you have any advice for people who want to make
the shift more smoothly from a lower level of awareness to one that is
higher?

Small—I think a really good piece of advice would be to have people
start affirming every day, "I'm a spiritual being in human form." Put
another way: "We're not human beings trying to become spiritual.
We're spiritual beings learning how to be human." That recognition
changes everything. If people would just start reflecting on that state-

...ld become known because we really *are* spiritual
...orm and we really do already know everything. So,
...of having to gather a lot of new information, it's just
...ing up. It's not cognition, it's recognition. Isn't that

Di... ...rough your associations with so many of the great minds
who hav... ...rophetically described this paradigm shift, you have been
in a rather unique position to get a glimpse of "The Big Picture." In
your view what characterizes the times we live in?

Small—One of the most exciting things happening right now is that
we have come to the end of a millennium. We've come to the end of a
360,000 year cycle and several smaller cycles are completing as well.

We're moving from what astrologers would call the Piscean Age to the
Aquarian Age. The Piscean Age was ruled by the law of devotion and
involved the worship of gurus and the God transcendent. We were
taught during that Age, during the last 2,000 year millennium, that
the wisdom was outside of us. Now, the shift is away from the law of
devotion—because we've learned what we needed to learn about that—
to the law of self-empowerment. Realizing the "God-within," the "God-
imminent," as opposed to the "God-transcendent." We're supposed to
be it rather than look for it outside ourself. The old way of viewing
"guru-dom" is dying and there are people reverting to cultish or fa-
natical positions. They're looking for some absolute to hold onto because this transformation process from one age to another and from
one state of being to another is so scary.

I don't really know how to talk about this in a way that everyone will
be able to understand, but I know it's true—There is a great big dimensional shift happening right now.

DiCarlo—Would you say that there is going to be increased commerce
between dimensions as a result?

Small—Yes, yes it's already happening. There are so many openings
happening it's unbelievable. I'm even having UFO experiences and
that's never been an area of personal interest. To me, these extraterrestrial experiences are internal *psychic* events—like dreams—ways
our unconscious mind expands us through modern-day metaphor and
new mythologies.

There are a lot of different words people are using to explain this shift,
but the simplest way to know that it is true is to notice that a lot of
people's lives are simply falling apart or their usual ways of being in
the world are no longer of interest. There seems to be a new life open-

ing up for many, either through their professions or through their love lives or through whatever philosophy they seem to be shifting to. People are experiencing changes in their religion. They are becoming more spiritual, which is one of the biggest characterizations of the times we live in. We are leaving a male dominated, patriarchal society that has been ruled by science for the last couple hundred years and we are returning again to an honoring of the intuition and to what Joseph Campbell called, "following your bliss."

The shift in consciousness that we are experiencing right now represents the completion of an entire way of life which was ruled by what I call "the lords of materialism." They are no longer going to determine our choices. The heart is now expressing itself. We're wanting to go back to the basics. To honor abundance instead of scarcity. To honor love instead of fear. To let go of competition and realize that we are all one. To develop more compassion for each other by dropping judgement. Letting go of the past and honoring the present. There is so much going on right now, it's so very exciting. It's also very scary because a lot of our familiar institutions are dying.

This planet has its own path and purpose and it's always going to be doing what planet earth does. In the decades to come, some of us will be moving on and some are going to remain in the old ways. It's very much like what they talk about in scripture—it's "the parting of the ways." We've all got free will, so everybody gets exactly what they want and I see that some people are going to create another materialistic life where they can struggle to see how many Joneses they can keep up with. Others of us will move into another dimension of consciousness where we may live and operate in a world that is different from the world that is ruled by materialism. In this way we can move in and out of the materialistic world as we choose. In fact, I think that's what many are already doing.

DiCarlo—So you are saying that the change underway involves a shift in focus—from outer form and appearances to indwelling essence?

Small—Yes. Another way of saying that would be to say a shift from the outer life to the inner life. And it doesn't mean either the outer or the inner. I think we get confused sometimes in our "either/or" thinking. It doesn't mean I have to stop being effective in the outer world, nor does it mean I have to stop having relationships in the outer world and become a recluse who denies life's pleasures.

What I am realizing is that it's our inner life which is determining our outer conditions and *not* the other way around. So when we talk about the inner life, I have come to think about it as the unfolding of my soul and my soul has a much longer and greater story than my little ego life.

So in my inner life I can go into the dream state, which is a non-ordinary state of consciousness. I experience it in the breathwork that I do and in meditation. There are other ways too. I know how to do that and I know how to teach other people how to do that.

When I go internal, I am able to live from "The Bigger Picture." In other words, I can see that my soul is here for a purpose and that I have taken on the form of an ego for awhile, living in the human condition. This gives my life a sacred meaning, and a deep sense of belonging.

I also realize I am a self that is much bigger than this human condition. I might swoop in and choose to experience a certain facet of the human condition simply in order to acquire a trait or a skill. I might take on that condition to help humanity. I feel that every time any one of us takes on a disease process, we learn it from the inside out. We are then able to help clean it out of the mass consciousness.

The inner life is the life of the psyche, which is the soul. Here, we get our instructions from our own Source, which is the higher power within us—the "God-within" as Carl Jung called it. If we learn to go in and listen to our true hearts desire, to our real fears, to the honest truth of ourselves, we develop an expanded consciousness and we rise above our human condition. Not that we walk off and leave anything unintegrated. That never works. It's simply that we are able to live here more in the way that Jesus taught, which is to be in the world but not of it.

When you step onto the path of the inner unfolding life, you realize that there is no place to ever stop. *You* become the journey and *you* become the bridge. And you realize the journey is your home.

Peter Russell

Peter Russell graduated with first class honors in theoretical physics and experimental psychology at the University of Cambridge (England). He has been a business consultant for fifteen years to international corporations such as Apple Computers, Shell, BASF, American Express and BP. He produced a series on meditation for BBC Radio 4, and is the author of seven books, Including "The Global Brain," which explores the psychological dimensions of the global crisis and "The White Hole In Time."

DiCarlo—First things first. In your work, you talk quite a bit about the evolution of consciousness and I'm wondering if we shouldn't define our terms. What is consciousness? It's a rather slippery concept, isn't it?

Russell—Yes. Consciousness is used in very many different ways. You can talk about consciousness in the context of whether you're awake or asleep, or in terms of a social consciousness, which involves one's value system. I discuss consciousness in the sense of the faculty of being aware, but to me, that awareness goes on even in sleep as well. We have dreams and we are aware of those dreams, so we are still conscious. What we are conscious of in the dream state may be very different from what we are conscious of in the waking state. All sentient beings are conscious in that sense; all beings that experience the world are conscious. When I talk of the evolution of consciousness, I'm really talking about the evolution of what we are conscious of—the contents of consciousness if you like. Strictly speaking, consciousness doesn't evolve. What does evolve are the forms that consciousness takes. It's a bit like talking about the evolution of living creatures. There are many different sorts of living creatures and the creatures themselves evolve but life does not. In the same way, it is what we are conscious of that is evolving. This is true for both the human species and other forms of life on the planet.

DiCarlo—What would you say is the essential thrust of your work?

Russell—I tend to look at the current times from a different perspective. As human beings, we are experiencing the most significant era of change in this planet's history—not just in human history but probably in the history of this planet. Never before has a species arisen which has so much creativity and so much intelligence but also so much destructive capability, which has shown itself through such things as the environmental crisis. In my view, we are really being pushed to work inwardly and to go through an evolutionary process. If we don't, I doubt we'll survive much longer. We've come to this point in history where we have to learn how to use our powers of creativity and our intelligence in ways that do not threaten our own future, nor the future of the rest of this planet. I think many people are looking at the ecological crisis as signaling the need for people to change their thinking and to change their values.

In my work I have attempted to place this present period in history into a much larger context. To accomplish this, I look at things from an evolutionary perspective. This point in time was probably inevitable in the history of life on this planet. That is, sooner or later a species would emerge with the creativity and intelligence of humanity, and once that species emerged, then sooner or later it would have reached a point at which it was met with a challenge—an inner psychological or "spiritual" challenge—of moving beyond limited modes of perception to a different way of perceiving itself. By taking an evolutionary perspective, one is able to paint a larger picture. To paint that picture, I include many other elements, such as cosmology and physics. I try to bring things together, to make sense of things. The reason for doing that is both to give people an expanded sense of just where we are in historical time—and the significance of these times— and also to inspire people to actually do something about it in their own lives.

DiCarlo—Would you be able to paint an evolutionary backdrop so that we could better grasp where the human species is right now?

Russell—Well, yes. If we look at it in terms of the evolution of consciousness, all creatures are conscious. Even a simple bacterium is conscious. It's not conscious of very much, maybe just sensing heat or light. As life has evolved, sensory systems have evolved. Living creatures have become conscious of their world. Nervous systems have evolved to process all that sensory information. In mammals, we have probably the most conscious species—speaking in terms of their consciousness of the environment. If we look at mammals, we find that we are not any more conscious than a dog is, at least in terms of sensory experience. In fact, from this perspective, we're less conscious. A dog is aware of sounds and smells that we are not aware of. Similarly, a dolphin has senses which we don't have, such as sonar. So, in terms of our sensory awareness, we are very similar to other mammals.

Two things have made a difference in human consciousness. One is language. Through verbal language we are able to share our experiences with each other. Whereas a dog learns primarily from its own experiences in life, we learn from each other's experiences. The deliberate attempt to learn from each other's experience is basically what we call education. But even non-deliberate learning happens all the time. We're learning as children from our parents, we learn from our siblings, from our peers. So, as soon as we developed language, we moved into the realm of collective learning. That marks us as unique among other species of life on the planet.

The second thing that happened was the evolution of the human hand, which is probably one of the most flexible, manipulative organs that nature has ever evolved. It's more flexible than the hand of a chimpanzee, for example. It can rotate about its base, which a chimpanzee's thumb is not able to do. That has given us remarkable ability to manipulate the world.

If you pull those two things together, language—which has given us the ability to share ideas, develop science, and understand the world, and understand how the Universe works—with an organ that's able to manipulate the world, you have this incredible creativity. Human beings can almost materialize anything we can dream of. We can imagine something in our minds, and then go out and through our technology, make it real in the external world.

That has given us remarkable powers, but at the same time, it's conditioned our consciousness in a way that's not proving very helpful in this day and age. It has given us a belief system that's very, very deeply embedded in our society which says that if we're not happy, if we're not at peace, then there is something wrong with the external world—we need to manipulate the world in some way. We need to change our physical environment or change how people relate to us or change our job or clothing. That has come out of the very real success of our past history and past development.

Up until the Industrial Revolution, people's basic needs were material needs; how to feed ourselves, clothe ourselves, keep ourselves warm in winter—how basically to survive physically. Since the Industrial Revolution, we've dealt with those things pretty well. In the developed world, most people, though certainly not all, have their physical needs met. We can go and buy the food and clothes we need from the store and we have central heating in the winter to keep us warm. We have satisfied our physical needs, and if we still find ourselves dissatisfied, it's probably because some inner need is not being fulfilled. We may feel emotionally insecure or in need of greater self-esteem. We don't really satisfy those needs by going and getting more things or by changing the world, but we are indoctrinated and subtly hypnotized into a belief system that says, if you're not happy, you must go out and do something. That it is the belief system which is, to put it mildly, driving the world crazy at the moment. That's why we in the West are consuming so much more than we need. That's why we're abusing other people and abusing other creatures. That's why we love money so much. We love it because we think it will buy the things that will make us happy. So we keep on with this incessant search for something external when we really are at the stage in our social evolution of having to look for something internal. We've successfully dealt with the external issues and we are now being driven to look at the internal issues, but we haven't yet woken up to that as a society. Well, we are beginning to, and it's interesting that the people who are beginning to wake up to it are the people who are the richest in Western society. They have their VCR's and their two automobiles and they have come to realize that having "more," doesn't work.

There's a growing realization that what we are looking for is inside of us. That's why at this stage in history, there is a movement towards looking back to spiritual traditions, to personal development, to therapy, to the whole area of personal development. The challenge that humanity is facing is—"Can we accelerate this inner growth?" "Can we wake up to who we really are and what we really want before this old set of attitudes and values wipes us out?" It's really a question of breaking through or breaking down.

DiCarlo—Do you see a polarization taking place right now? There are those who feel that some of the problems that we in America have are due to the deviation from some of the founding principles this country was based on—such as free enterprise, rugged individualism, patriotism, the American work ethic and traditional family values. Others feel that looking back isn't the answer at all. That we have to move forward in a creative, bold way. What are your thoughts on that?

Russell—I can see there is an apparent polarization in American society, but I don't think what we're facing is really a polarization. A lot of what the founding fathers of America were talking about are exactly the same values that the more liberal side of society is talking about. In that sense, we need to return to some of the wisdom of the past, but using the language and metaphors of the present time. You can take it back further, before the founding fathers, to Christianity. If we go back and look at what Jesus was saying, we find it is very similar to what I think all the great spiritual teachers have been saying all through the ages—before Jesus and after Jesus. I think there's a common thread through all spiritual teachings and I think the founding fathers were part of that thread.

Over time, unfortunately, we've lost the sense of what they were talking about. Partly because things have been handed down from one person to another, translated from one language to another, or made to fit different societies over time. The truth has, in a sense, decayed. It's what I sometimes call "truth decay." It's decayed over time and I think there may be a conflict between our current understanding and what was meant originally. What we need to do is apply this wisdom in the current time. That doesn't mean going back and reviving ancient teachings. It does mean discovering that truth within ourselves and finding out how can we live that and put it into action in our own lives.

DiCarlo—Do you feel, as do others, that we're in a period of rapid expansion of consciousness.

Russell—Yes.

DiCarlo—How would you respond to authors like Ken Wilber, for example, who feels that this metamorphosis is going to be playing itself out over a longer period of time, perhaps many hundreds of years?

Russell—One of the patterns that is apparent throughout the evolutionary process is that things move faster and faster and I see that as very natural. The reason for this is that each new development stands on the shoulders of previous developments. For example, the information revolution which we are now in, is standing on the shoulders of the industrial revolution, so we don't have to go back and reinvent factories and global distribution systems and all of that. In the same way, the advances which are happening in terms of telecommunications these days, like Internet, are built on the advances which have been made in information processing. Each stage builds on previous levels.

The same happens throughout biological evolution as well. That's why the first half of life on this planet, which spanned two billion years, was just an evolution of very simple bacteria. Then more complex living systems came along and evolution speeded up with sexual reproduction. This has been going on, getting faster and faster. Human beings have only been around for a million or so years on this planet, which is a fraction of its history. And our Western society is just a tiny fraction of the history of human civilization. So when we talk about everything that's happening in the current time, we have to realize it's just a tiny fraction of human history. Even in terms of our consciousness, it's evolving faster and faster and I don't think there's anything that's going to keep it from evolving faster still.

If we look back at the degree to which consciousness has expanded over the last 5,000 years—say from the beginning of the awakening that's represented in things like the Vedas of Ancient India right through to the present day—I think we will have a similar expansion of consciousness taking place within the next fifty years. And there may be an expansion of similar magnitude collapsed into the following ten years. So things are going to keep moving faster. There is this tendency to think that it's going to take thousands of years to happen, since if we look back, that's how long it previously took. But I don't think we have hundreds of years to evolve. We have to do it very rapidly.

DiCarlo—How might this rapid expansion of consciousness come about?

Russell—If you look at what's happening in the world, you will find that now, we're all becoming interconnected. The linking together of humanity, which began when the emergence of language allowed us to share information with each other, has now reached a global level. We are sharing information through television, through print, through video, through computer networks. We are beginning to function as a single information system.

As we move on to the next stage, which is characterized by the movement from simply sharing information to waking up—the expansion of consciousness on a global level—we will see that same acceleration happen. In fact, we can already begin to see it. You may write a book that pulls together different people's experiences. The experiences of those people are themselves a result of their learning from many people around the world. Now your book goes out into the world, and as people read it certain insights are triggered which they, in turn, may share with people in their local community. All the time, we're learning from each other, and whenever that occurs you have an exponentially expanding situation.

The population is exponentially expanding and so is compound interest, but so also is human awakening. The more that we awaken, the more we learn, the more we can get other people to awaken. Of course this is providing we don't destroy ourselves in the near term. If we can put sufficient emphasis on the shifting of consciousness and the changing of values, then I think we are going to see an acceleration beyond anything we could have dreamt of. Science fiction writers of thirty or fourty years ago had no idea of what was going to happen to computers and information processing. Most science fiction writers were talking about huge computers. They didn't see the advent of the small, portable personal computer, the lap-top computer which could be networked with other computers. In the same way, very few people can foresee the incredible speed of change and awakening that is possible on the level of consciousness, once things start taking off.

PETER RUSSELL

DiCarlo—To what degree have the findings of the new sciences, such as morphonogenic fields, dissipative structures, chaos theory and quantum physics, influenced you in your thinking?

Russell—Some of them quite a bit. They've been, if you like, support for things that I have felt intuitively. Dissipative systems and the work of people like Prigogine have shown that out of ordinary, natural evolution, more complex forms can appear. For me, it's made the evolution of life more understandable. If a system is sent into a chaotic, disordered state, it can—though not every time—reorganize itself into a higher state of organization and capability.

On the global level we are going through chaos. We are seeing breakdowns of economic systems, and the turning around of some of the political systems in Eastern Europe. It appears to be the breaking down, but it's also a field in which new levels of organization could emerge. They haven't emerged yet, but the time is ripe for something new to happen.

DiCarlo—Seems like Chaos Theory might apply here as well.

Russell—There are two things about chaos theory that interest me: firstly, we are not talking about chaos as we normally understand it. When we normally use the word chaos, we mean disorder. Chaos theory is about highly ordered systems; very, very precisely ordered, but highly unpredictable. The chaos means you cannot predict what is going to happen in the future. I'm fascinated by the fact that history itself appears to be chaotic in this sense—the more we accelerate, the faster things go, the harder it is to predict what is coming next.

One thousand years ago, you could probably predict the next hundred years. One hundred years ago, we could probably predict the following twenty to thirty years. Today, we really can't predict more than a few months ahead in many areas. What I call the "prediction horizon" is getting closer and closer and closer, so we are certainly moving into a much more unpredictable world. But within that unpredictability, there is so much potential for change. I think we're in the most exciting time in human history. In our own lifetimes we are going to see as much development, and as much evolution, as perhaps the whole of humanity has witnessed over the last 5,000 years.

DiCarlo—You've stated that you believe society is evolving towards a higher level of integration and synergy. What you mean by that?

Russell—Two things: the higher level of integration has been happening for the last 3,000 years, and it's really been brought to a head at the end of this Century through global communications. We can fly

Page 365

anywhere we want to in the world these days, but we can also tune into our television sets and see what is happening all over the world. Through computers we can exchange data very rapidly indeed. We are interconnecting in much the same way a brain seems to wire itself up, which is why I coined the term "global brain." If you look at the way a brain evolves during the time the fetus is in the womb, it goes through an initial period in which the number of nerve cells rapidly explodes. After that, the number of nerve cells stabilizes and the cells begin to connect and link together. Growth of the brain through the rest of the pregnancy and throughout the rest of life after birth is really the growth of connectivity in the brain.

I see parallel things happening on the planet. We've been through this massive population explosion of human beings. We now have—interestingly enough—about the same number of people living on the planet as there are nerve cells in the human brain. We are now entering this process of connectivity. We aren't yet as interconnected as the nerve cells in a brain and we only communicate with one or two people at a time, but I think the way our technology is going, over the next ten, twenty or thirty years, that connectivity will probably rival that of the human brain. When that happens, I think we are in for a major transformation on a global level. But what it will be like is very hard to conceptualize or characterize. It's a bit like the unborn human brain wondering what it's going to be like to be born and wake up and be conscious.

The synergy, the second part of that, has to do with the way we function together. If you take an individual brain, that brain can behave in ways that are sane or insane and the difference has nothing to do with the connectivity. The same brain with the same degree of connectivity could behave in ways which are totally mad or in ways which are very healthy. That's the second challenge facing humanity. Greater levels of connectivity are happening across the planet and there's noth-. ing we can do to stop it. The question is, "Is this going to become an insane global brain or sane one?" The answer has very much to do with our values and how we see ourselves in relationship to each other and the rest of the planet. This is where synergy comes in.

DiCarlo—Could you define synergy?

Russell—The word "synergy" comes from the Greek—"syn" and "ergos"—literally meaning to "act together." In a high synergy system, the individual units—whether they be people in a society or nerve cells in a brain—while acting in their own interest, are also acting for the good of the whole system. It's an alignment between individual interests and group interests.

Anthropologists have found societies in which there is this kind of alignment. Often, they are very simple tribal societies, and they also tend to be very healthy societies. Today, part of the problem in Western society is that we have lost this alignment. We have a big focus on self interest, accentuated by the Industrial Revolution and by contemporary economic theories that place a big focus on individual interests. Because of this we find it very hard to fit into the collective interest. There isn't a natural alignment and this is a recipe for disaster.

DiCarlo—Why is this so?

Russell—Because if everybody continues looking after their own individual interests, if they continue in their own self-centered ways without at the same time finding a way to tune into the collective interests, then the collective will break down. We will have chaos at the social level and we will see the breaking down, the falling apart, of Western civilization.

If we are going to survive, we have to find ways to align our individual interests with the collective global interests. That, again, comes back to an inner shift of values—a shift in consciousness. I think, at the moment, we are stuck in a very egocentric mode of consciousness. But I think that mode of consciousness need only be transitory. As a child grows up and moves into adolescence, it moves through an egocentric phase, and eventually, moves out of it. I say "eventually" because for many people it takes another twenty, thirty years to actually grow out of adolescence into what we call maturity. Some people only reach maturity in their old age.

As a society, we should be focusing our attention on helping people reach that level of maturity at a much, much earlier age. My ideal would be that when children leave school, they should have already been encouraged to fully move through that phase of ego-centeredness, so that as adults they are naturally able to act as mature people. Their individual consciousness would be in line with the needs of the collective; they would no longer be concerned about the material things that so many of us are caught up in.

This would be a movement towards what we would call "wisdom." And with wisdom comes love. Love not just for one's partner—romantic love—but love for other people, a love for the rest of the world, for all living creatures. That's the goal that we must move towards. If we do that, if we can develop the unconditional love that all the great religions have spoken of, that universal compassion for all creatures, then I think we have the basis for a high synergy society. If we can love all creatures as we love ourselves, then our needs are aligned with those of the group. Only then, I think, will the global brain, this great inter-connectivity which is manifesting at this time, become sane and healthy. If we don't develop that inner awakening and love, then I think there's very little hope for us.

DiCarlo—When you mention that we are heading into a time of higher connectivity with others, does that in any way compromise our own sense of individuality?

Russell—Not at all. I think it's the opposite. Many of us compromise our individuality. We don't really express ourselves. We don't live our own truths. We tend to live the truths that the media tells us. We live the truths that the fashion houses tell us. So we wear the latest fashions, do the right things, go to the "in" places. Not because, "that's who I am" but because we want to belong to the right group. We want to be seen to be part of the system.

As we begin to wake up, we also become more open to other people—more compassionate, more loving towards other people, more able to interconnect with other people. At the same time that's happening, we also gain a greater inner strength to actually be ourselves, to ex-press our own truths. To live what we know is right even though that may not be what everybody else thinks or feels. So I see a greater individuality, along with a greater inter-connectivity. I don't see the two as being in opposition at all. Part of the synergy is, that as we become true individuals, we become more a part of the collective.

Part of the problem today is that we are neither truly an intercon-nected part of the collective, nor are we truly individual. We are in this half-asleep, robotic mode in which we suppress our individuality far too much.

DiCarlo—Would you say that this development or this movement to more advanced levels of human development entails a shift in world view?

Russell—Yes, it does. It's a question of how we see the world and how we relate to the world. This comes back to the more fundamental question, "What is it that we consider important?" And that is basi-cally a discussion about values. Every human being is looking to avoid pain, avoid suffering, and to find a greater peace and inner fulfillment within themselves. We do that in many, many different ways.

A spiritual world view is one which sees the inner work as a means of freeing ourselves from a lot of our resistances, a lot of our fears, a lot of our anxieties. It is the way to find peace. On the other hand, a materialistic world view places great emphasis on what you achieve in the world, what you have, what you possess, and what you do. That more materialistic world view is now out of date. It was perhaps very appropriate a few hundred years ago, maybe even one hundred years ago, but is now a source of continuing self-destruction and planetary destruction. That world view has to be transcended so that we come to a more encompassing world view which is large enough to embrace ourselves as spiritual beings.

DiCarlo—Would you say that this shift in world view can be attained by simply reading a book on quantum physics?

Russell—I don't think it can be helped by reading a book on quantum physics because I don't think quantum physics affects our experience of the world. It may affect our intellectual understanding. In fact, we haven't even changed our consciousness since Galileo. Copernicus showed that the sun is the center of our solar system, not the earth. But when we look at the sky, we still see the sun going around. Our perceptual world view hasn't changed at all, and that's with a very, very simple world view. So reading a book on quantum physics is not going to change the way you and I actually experience the world.

The change in world views that I think needs to come, is a shift in values of what we consider to be important. That comes back to a fundamental belief about how we find the peace that we're looking for in the world. It could come from reading books, but I think they would be books of a more spiritual nature. If one goes back and reads some of the old classic spiritual teachings, one finds the same basic message about letting go of attachments, letting go of our beliefs about how to find happiness and beginning to recognize that whether or not we're at peace is not a question of what we have or do, but is a question of how we see things.

One example I often use when I'm working with business people to get this across to them is the example of a traffic jam. Most people stuck in a traffic jam feel upset, angry, and frustrated. They actually think it's the traffic jam that's doing this to them. In fact, a traffic jam isn't that powerful. A traffic jam simply stops cars from moving. If they're feeling upset or angry, it's because the voice in their head is telling them, "I'm going to be late and if I'm late, all these awful things are going to happen to me." Or, "I shouldn't have chosen this route." The voice in the head is creating the stress, not the external situation. Somebody else, sitting in exactly the same traffic jam, might be saying "Hey, this is wonderful, I've got five minutes off. I can sit back. I've got no phones ringing, no problems to solve. I've got no computers to stare at. I can relax, put on some music, adjust the air conditioning. What a wonderful opportunity."

Now the difference is not in the external situation. The difference is in the way the person is perceiving the situation—their whole world view—and how they are reacting to that perceived situation. One person sees a dangerous situation, something to be gotten rid of. The other person sees an opportunity. The critical decision rests upon how we perceive the world. In each of our lives, in every single moment, and regardless of whatever is happening to us, we have the opportunity to either see this as a threat or as an opportunity: an opportunity to learn more about ourself, an opportunity to develop our consciousness in some way or other, an opportunity to grow. Part of the shift entails putting this into practice in our own lives so that at every moment of the day we begin to make that choice. Instead of seeing things through the eyes of fear, the eyes of anxiety, the eyes of separation, we begin to see that we are actually in control of our lives. We are in control of how we see things and we begin to exercise that control and learn to use what is happening in the world for our own inner growth and development.

DiCarlo—Two perceptual questions that cut right to the heart of the new world view might be "Who are we?" and "What kind of universe do we live in?" What are your thoughts on those two very important questions?

Russell—In answer to the question, "Who are we?" the short answer is that we are conscious, biological and social beings. The much deeper question is "What does it mean?" The way to rephrase that is "What does it mean to be a conscious entity? What is consciousness?"

Consciousness is something completely nonmaterial and totally undefinable by modern science and yet it is something common to us all. We all use the world "I"—it's the simplest word in the English language and with one stroke of the pen, the simplest word to write Yet none of us really know what we mean by the word. We tend to define "I" in terms of what we do, what we look like, what we're interested in—our past history, all these sorts of things. None of those is "I". These are things that "I" have, that "I" do, that "I" look like. The "I" itself is something which is absolutely undefinable but common to us all. What so many of the great mystical teachings throughout the ages and a lot of the wise philosophers have said is that, in essence, that "I" ness, that indefinable sense of "I"-ness is what religions mean by "God." If God is in everything and everything is created from the essence of God, then God as it appears within is that sense of "I"-ness. Not the individual "I"-ness, but that universal "I"-ness.

The most profound answer to the question "Who are we?" is that beyond all our different layers of individuality, beyond all the things we think we are, beyond all the ideas we have, beyond all the different elements of personality and all our hopes and fears, beyond every-thing, at core, each of us is a droplet of divinity—a manifestation of God. The phrase, "I am God," is something which many mystics have uttered. Many have been persecuted because it seems to be blasphemy. It seems to imply that if I am God, then I am something special—above everybody else in the Universe. But what it really means is that "I am God and every other human being is God and every other single living creature on this planet and anywhere else in the Universe is God." That the essence of consciousness is God.

That, I think, is the realization we are beginning to wake up to at this time in history.

DiCarlo—And the nature of the Universe in which we live....?

Russell—....is friendly.

DiCarlo—Thomas Kuhn observed that world views shift when phe-nomena that is left inexplicable by the prevailing world view piles up until it can no longer be ignored. In your own life, what experiences have you had that suggested the traditional paradigm is inadequate.

Russell—First, we have to identify the paradigm that's inadequate. Beyond the current scientific paradigm, there is a deeper one that is inadequate. I'm not so much interested in the paradigms in science, biology, physics and chemistry. I am more interested in our current, psycho-social paradigm, how we interact with other people. How we see ourselves. How we see what is important for us. This I sometimes call a meta-paradigm. This meta-paradigm underlies all the other paradigms. The meta-paradigm of Western society suggests that the material world is real, and that consciousness and mind are somehow offshoots of material reality. That is the paradigm which basically underlies all of science and within that, you have ordinary paradigms like the Newtonian paradigm and the Einsteinein paradigm. But they are all based on this larger paradigm that the material world is real and consciousness is somehow arising out of the material world.

I think the new meta-paradigm that is beginning to emerge is saying that consciousness is primary to the universe. In some sense, matter is created in our consciousness, we are the creators of our experience of reality. For me, the changes that led me to this world view were the result of experiencing levels to my own consciousness which I had never dreamt existed.

DiCarlo—Please elaborate.

Russell—About twenty-five or thirty years ago, I got very interested

n and Eastern teachings. I lived in India for awhile, stud-
ion and participated in some long meditation retreats.
t time, I realized that there is much more power in our
onsciousness than we ever realized. I realized, "I'm not a
victim of the world. In a very real sense, I am creating the world I live
in."

For example, consider the experience I am having right now. I am
sitting down looking out into the trees as I am talking to you. I don't
experience that tree directly. Scientifically speaking, what is happening is that there are photons coming into my eyes from that tree, which
are being turned into electrical impulses by the brain. Those impulses
are moving around and interacting with past experiences in the brain,
and out of that I create, in my mind, the experience of looking at this
tree. And anything else I look at or anything else I might hear, anything else I might feel, in any moment of the day, is an experience I
have created in my mind. So in that sense, I am creating the whole of
the world I know. It is in that sense that consciousness is primary. If
I were not conscious, I would not know anything at all about the world.
The world would not exist for me.

It was my meditation experience in India that made me realize that
consciousness is primary, and matter is something we create in our
awareness. That's not to say matter doesn't exist out there somewhere, but every time I experience it I am re-creating a version of it
for me in my mind.

The second part of that is the realization that I have much more influence in how I create the world, which comes back to what I was saying
about how we perceive things. I can actually choose how I perceive
something. I can choose whether I view something as a threat or an
opportunity. I can choose how I react to something. Again this implies there is much, much more power in our consciousness than we
have ever thought. So that's how the shift happened for me.

I think on a more global level, the shift is going happen as the anomalies build up, as we begin to realize that consciousness cannot be excluded from our understanding of the world as has been suggested by
modern physics. As we begin to realize the world doesn't work without including consciousness, that consciousness is primary. Then I
think the shift in world views will happen. But as Kuhn pointed out,
the shift is often brought about by a whole new generation who are
uninvested in the old ways of seeing and doing.

DiCarlo—Why should the average person—educator, business person,
whatever—care about all that we've discussed?

Russell—Two reasons. If we don't take this seriously, there's no future for any of us. We all care about the future, our own and that of our children, the future of other people, the future of the planet.

The second reason: it's basically the pathway towards what each of us wants whether we're a business person, a parent, or a politician. Each of us is seeking ways to reduce the pain and suffering in our lives, and move towards greater inner peace and an inner sense of well being. We all ultimately want peace of mind. This is our true bottom line. We have just become caught, in the moment, in ways of trying to find peace of mind that don't actually work. The real exploration that is going on now, that I've been talking about and many others are talking about, asks, "What does it really take to find peace in our lives?" And it may not be through becoming a more powerful person or becoming a richer person. It may be by doing inner work.

A person should care about this, because it's vitally important that we discover how we can be more at peace with ourselves. If I am coming from a place of composure in myself, I am not going to start attacking other people unnecessarily out of my resentments or grievances. I am not going to start responding to people out of fear or anxiety. I am going to be much more loving towards them. I am going to be able to look after other people's needs, because I am not going to be so needy. As a result, my life is going to be more fulfilling and healthier. It's absolutely clear that people who are much more settled, composed, and at peace with themselves, live much healthier lives. They are more useful members of society. So for ourselves, for others and for the future of the planet, it's extremely important.

Index

INDEX

Institute for Transformational Leadership

Leading-Edge Programs
for Personal,
Organizational and
Community Transformation.

ITL

- ❖ Training Videos
- ❖ Conferences
- ❖ Workshops
- ❖ Books
- ❖ Journal/Newsletter
- ❖ Resource Guides
- ❖ Electronic Networking

For a free catalog of available programs, send stamped, SAE to:

I.T.L.
PO Box 427
Erie, PA 16512